Exploring Everyday Landscapes

Exploring Everyday Landscapes

PERSPECTIVES IN

VERNACULAR ARCHITECTURE, VII

Edited by
Annmarie Adams
and Sally McMurry

THE UNIVERSITY OF TENNESSEE PRESS / KNOXVILLE

Copyright © 1997 by The University of Tennessee Press / Knoxville.
All Rights Reserved. Manufactured in the United States of America.
First Edition.

The paper in this book meets the minimum requirements of the American National Standard for Permanence of Paper for Printed Library Materials.

∞ The binding materials have been chosen for strength and durability.

Printed on recycled paper.

ISBN 0-87049-983-1 (pbk.: alk. paper)

to Charlie
—*A. A.*

to the memory of my father
—*S. M.*

Contents

Acknowledgments   xv
Exploring Everyday Landscapes: An Introduction   xvii
    Annmarie Adams and Sally McMurry

PART I. EMERGING VERNACULAR FORMS: THE EIGHTEENTH CENTURY

1. Wealth and Houses in Post-Revolutionary Virginia   3
    Edward A. Chappell and Julie Richter

2. Dissenting Faith and Domestic Landscape in Eighteenth-Century Virginia   23
    Clifton Ellis

3. The Embedded Landscapes of the Charleston Single House, 1780–1820   41
    Bernard L. Herman

4. The Dynamics of Architectural Design in Eighteenth-Century Charleston and the Lowcountry   58
    Carl Lounsbury

Part II. Varieties of Urban Forms

5. A Factory without a Roof: The Company Town in the Redwood Lumber Industry 75
   James Michael Buckley

6. The Miracle Mile Revisited: Recycling, Renovation, and Simulation along the Commercial Strip 93
   Timothy Davis

7. Architecture for the Future at the Charleston Exposition, 1901–1902 115
   Bruce Harvey

8. The Urban Cemetery and the Urban Community: The Origin of the New Orleans Cemetery 131
   Dell Upton

Part III. Redefining Work Space

9. The House and Garden: Housing Agricultural Laborers in Central Delaware, 1780–1930 149
   Rebecca J. Siders and Anna V. Andrzejewski

10. Story, Storage, and Symbol: Functional Cache Architecture, Cache Narratives, and Roadside Attractions 167
    Susan W. Fair

11. The Spatial Order of Work 183
    Carolyn Torma

Part IV. Beyond Religious Institutions

12. East Slav Identity and Church Architecture in Minneapolis, Minnesota 199
    Geoffrey M. Gyrisco

13. Housing the Grey Nuns: Power, Religion, and Women in fin-de-siècle Montréal 212
    Tania Martin

14. "To Hold Communion with Nature and the Spirit-World": New England's Spiritualist Camp Meetings, 1865–1910 230
    William D. Moore

Part V. House and Home

15. Reading Sanborns for the Spoor of the Owner-Builder, 1890s–1950s 251
    Richard Harris

16. The Other Side of the Tracks: The Middle-Class Neighborhoods
    That Jim Crow Built in Early-Twentieth-Century North Carolina 268
    M. Ruth Little

17. Linoleum and Lincrusta: The Democratic Coverings for Floors and Walls 281
    Pamela H. Simpson

Select Bibliography 293
Contributors 299
Index 303

Illustrations

Figures

1.1.	Pear Valley, Northampton County, Va.	5
1.2.	Eagle's Nest, Charles City County, Va.	7
1.3.	Carter Croxton House and Outbuildings, Essex County, Va.	9
1.4.	Comparative Size of Four Southampton County Properties	10
1.5.	Dixon Ferguson House and Martha Channell House, Southampton County, Va.	11
1.6.	Amos Council Kitchen or House, Southampton County, Va.	12
1.7.	Sally Jordan House, Isle of Wight County, Va.	14
1.8.	Building Evaluations for Four Tidewater Virginia Counties	16
2.1.	James Hunt's Plan for Gilbert Hunt's House, 1782	24
2.2.	Francis Roberts's House, Halifax County, Va., 1750–75	25
2.3.	Moses Terry's House, Halifax County, Va., 1771	27
2.4.	Belle Isle, Lancaster County, Va., 1761–78	28
2.5.	Alexander Shaw's House, Halifax County, Va., c. 1780	29
2.6.	Woodford, Richmond County, Va., 1750–75	30
2.7.	Jarrod McCarty's House, Halifax County, Va., 1785	35
3.1.	Street Elevations of Charleston Single Houses, Hassel Street, Built c. 1840	42
3.2.	First Floor and Lot Plans, Charleston Single Houses, Hassel Street	43
3.3.	Charleston Single House Lot Plan, 176 Meeting Street	44
3.4.	Charleston Single House Lot Plan, Elijah Hall Bay House, c. 1780	44
3.5.	Church Street Elevations of Peter Leger House, Alexander Christie House, and Cooper-Bee House	46
3.6.	Reconstructed c. 1760 Plan of 90 Church Street	47
3.7.	First-floor Front "Office" at 90 Church Street	47

3.8.	Peter Bocquet House, 95 Broad Street	48
3.9.	Blaydes House, High Street, Hull, England	49
3.10.	View from the Single House Yard toward Street	53
3.11.	Backbuildings, Aiken-Rhett House, Elizabeth Street, Charleston	53
4.1.	Charleston County Courthouse, 1883 View	59
4.2.	St. James Church, Goose Creek, S.C., c. 1800 View	61
4.3.	Courthouse, Warwick, Warwickshire, England, 1725	64
4.4.	Bishop Roberts, *Prospect of Charles Town,* c. 1739	65
4.5.	Pompion Hill Chapel, Berkeley County, South Carolina, 1763	67
4.6.	Plan of Pompion Hill Chapel	68
4.7.	Plan of St. Mary's Church, Avington, Hampshire, England	68
5.1.	Jolly Giant Mill near Arcata in the Late 1870s	77
5.2.	Interior of a Lumber Company Bunkhouse in Washington	78
5.3.	Aerial View of Scotia, 1970	80
5.4.	Plan of Scotia, c. 1960	81
5.5.	Scotia, 1902	82
5.6.	Winema Theater, 1920	84
5.7.	Scotia Savings Bank, 1921	86
5.8.	Scotia's Main Street, c. 1920	87
6.1.	Delwood Plaza, Austin, Tex.	94
6.2.	Strip Mall Church and Thrift Store, Lexington Park, Md.	96
6.3.	Strip Mall Succession, Ballston, Va.	98
6.4.	Original Ben and Jerry's in Former Gas Station, Burlington, Vt.	100
6.5.	Eden Shopping Center, Arlington, Va.	102
6.6.	Multicultural Strip Mall, Arlington, Va.	103
6.7.	Majestic Diner, Austin, Tex.	105
6.8.	Shopping Center, Silver Spring, Md.	107
6.9.	Strip Mall, Lexington Park, Md.	109
6.10.	Vendor in Abandoned Gas Station, Austin, Tex.	110
7.1.	Agricultural Building, Atlanta, 1895	120
7.2.	Minerals and Forestry Building, Nashville, 1897	121
7.3.	Sunken Gardens and Auditorium, Charleston, 1901	123
7.4.	South Carolina Building, Charleston, 1901	124
7.5.	Palace of Commerce, Charleston, 1901	124
7.6.	Cotton Palace, Charleston, 1901	125
8.1.	Lafayette Cemetery No. 1, New Orleans	132
8.2.	The French Cemetery, New Orleans	136
8.3.	St. Louis Cemetery No. 1, New Orleans	137
8.4.	John H. B. Latrobe, *St. Louis Cemetery No. 1,* 1834	138
8.5.	Mid-Nineteenth-Century *Fours,* Lafayette Cemetery No. 1	139

8.6. Irad Ferry Monument, 1840	140
8.7. Sketch Plan of Cypress Grove Cemetery, New Orleans	140
8.8. Live Oak Avenue, Cypress Grove Cemetery	142
9.1. Ridgely Tenant House, Little Creek Hundred, Kent County, Del.	150
9.2. Moody–Clayton House, St. Georges Hundred, New Castle County, Del.	151
9.3. Kent County Orphans Court Plot, 1823	153
9.4. J. B. Bordley's Plan of a Cottage and Garden, 1801	155
9.5. Wharton Tenant House, Murderkill Hundred, Kent County, Del.	156
9.6. Front Elevation of Wharton Tenant House, Murderkill Hundred, Kent County, Del.	157
9.7. Barker's Landing Tenant House, Murderkill Hundred, Kent County, Del.	158
10.1. A Bering Sea Eskimo Man Hangs His Nets, c. 1900	168
10.2. The Kenneth Condit Cache, Moose Pass, Alaska	169
10.3. Goodpaster–Big Delta Athabaskan Plank Cache, c. 1898	170
10.4. Ivory Pipe, 1870–1900	172
10.5. Non-natives often Built Their Caches Opportunistically	173
10.6. "The Great Alaskan Cliche," by Byron Birdsall	175
10.7. "The Mail Cache," Anchorage	176
10.8. Yard-art Cache	176
11.1. 1313 East 60th St., Chicago, Ill., 1938	185
11.2. 1313 East 60th St., Large Meeting Room	186
11.3. 1313 East 60th St., Sketch of Second-Floor Plan	189
11.4. Morning Coffee Line, 1313 East 60th St.	192
11.5. Office Bulletin Board, 1313 East 60th St.	193
12.1. St. Mary's Church, Minneapolis, 1887	201
12.2. Iconostas, St. Mary's Church, Minneapolis, 1892	203
12.3. St. Mary's Church, Minneapolis, 1904	204
12.4. Iconostas, St. Mary's Church, Minneapolis, c. 1907	205
12.5. St. Constantine's Church, Minneapolis, 1913	206
12.6. St. Constantine's Church, Minneapolis, 1970	208
13.1. Drawing of Mother House of the Grey Nuns, Montréal, c. 1900	213
13.2. Engraving of Mother House of the Grey Nuns, 1875	214
13.3. Diagram of Mother House of the Grey Nuns	215
13.4. Five Floor Plans Showing Distribution of Occupant Groups	217
13.5. Corridor Saint-Joseph, Mother House of the Grey Nuns, 1910	220
13.6. "Imprimerie," Mother House of the Grey Nuns	221
13.7. "Cuisine," Mother House of the Grey Nuns	222
14.1. Hoosac Tunnel Route, Lake Pleasant, Mass.	233
14.2. Founders of the Spiritualist Camp at Lake Pleasant	234
14.3. Annual Gathering of Spiritualists at Lake Pleasant	235
14.4. Onset Bay Grove, Wareham, Mass.	236

14.5. First House Built at Onset Bay Grove, Onset, Mass.	237
14.6. Plan of Ocean Grove, Monmouth County, N.J.	240
14.7. Mt. Auburn Cemetery, Cambridge, Mass., 1831	242
14.8. The Wig-Wam, Onset Bay Grove	243
15.1. Earlscourt, 1916	253
15.2. Milwaukee, 1899	256
15.3. Polish Flats, Milwaukee, 1894–1910	257
15.4. Polish Flats, Milwaukee, 1910–51	258
15.5. No. 2845 North Weil, Milwaukee	259
15.6. Flint, Mich., 1937	260
15.7. Vicinity of Thornton, Flint, 1931–50	261
15.8. No. 2540 Thornton Avenue, Flint	263
16.1. 600 Block of New Street, New Bern, N.C., c. 1912	270
16.2. Hayti Neighborhood, Durham, N.C., c. 1920	271
16.3. Map of North Carolina	272
16.4. J. T. Barber House, New Bern, N.C., 1920s	274
16.5. Sunrise Breakfast Gathering in Raleigh's "Culture Town," c. 1920	275
16.6. Hilliard Yellerday House, Raleigh, in 1995	275
16.7. African American Residences in Hayti Neighborhood, Durham, in 1995	277
16.8. African American Residences in College View Neighborhood, Durham, in 1995	278
17.1. Frederick Walton	282
17.2. Linoleum Assembly Line	283
17.3. Walton's Giant Rotary Press	284
17.4. Armstrong Advertisement	284
17.5. Walton's Showroom, 1900	286
17.6. Armstrong Advertisement	287
17.7. Straight-line Inlaid Linoleum	288

Tables

1.1. Comparative Size of Four Southampton County Properties	10
2.1. Wealth in Halifax County, 1785, and the Northern Neck, 1782	26

Acknowledgments

We are grateful to the University of Tennessee Press for its support and especially to our editor, Meredith Morris-Babb, for her interest and encouragement. Hal Barron, Catherine Bishir, James Borchert, Elizabeth Collins Cromley, Alan Derickson, Howard Davis, Peter Gossage, Greg Hise, Kim Hoagland, Carter L. Hudgins, Donna Hudgins, Linda Johnson, Myron Stachiw, Bruce Thomas, Paul Touart, David Vanderburgh, Gene Waddell, Camille Wells, Melissa Westrate, Michael Ann Williams, and Gwendolyn Wright contributed generously of their time and expertise. Penn State University and McGill University provided valuable assistance. Sally McMurry extends special thanks to Karen Ebeling and Linda Nihart of the Pennsylvania State University history department staff.

We thank the Vernacular Architecture Forum and its directors for the opportunity to work with them on this series, and, finally, we are grateful to the nineteen authors whose research appears in this volume. Their work has advanced the cause of vernacular architecture studies.

Exploring Everyday Landscapes: An Introduction

Background

Vernacular architecture studies bring together a host of scholars in related disciplines to explore the relationship of people and their everyday landscapes. Students of vernacular architecture typically come from the diverse fields of architecture, architectural history, geography, folklore, anthropology, material culture, history, archaeology, urban studies, art history, women's studies, and many other disciplines. Perhaps because the field is such an interdisciplinary endeavor, the term "vernacular" has remained somewhat ambiguous, referring to a broad range of environments and methods of analysis.[1] What students of vernacular architecture share, however, is the conviction that architecture itself is a primary source in research and that fieldwork and artifact analysis are fundamental to the interpretation of place.

The essays included in each volume of *Perspectives in Vernacular Architecture* consist of refereed papers selected from a larger number presented at the annual meetings of the Vernacular Architecture Forum (VAF). This volume is the most recent in a series which began in 1982, following the establishment of the VAF in 1980. It includes papers presented at the 1994 VAF meeting in Charleston, South Carolina, and the conference in Ottawa, Ontario, in 1995. These two meetings represent especially important events in the history of the organization: the Charleston meeting was a landmark in terms of sheer scale (thirty-two papers were delivered and an unprecedented number of people attended); the Ottawa meeting represented the first VAF conference held outside the United States.

Perhaps most significantly, both Charleston and Ottawa are cities ordinarily characterized as "official" or "elite" landscapes. Charleston, of course, is well known for its grand public monuments (the courthouse, city hall, churches, etc.), the single house with its distinctive piazzas, and the surrounding low-country plantations. As Carl Lounsbury remarks in his contribution to this volume, eighteenth-century Euro-American Charlestonians were four times wealthier than their

Chesapeake counterparts and six times richer than New Yorkers or Philadelphians. This concentration of wealth is reflected in the city's unique architectural heritage. We are pleased that three papers in *Perspectives, VII* address the architectural traditions of Charleston, from three different perspectives.

Similarly, as the capital city of Canada since 1857 (it was selected as such by Queen Victoria), Ottawa boasts some of Canada's finest public edifices: the parliament buildings, many foreign embassies, national museums, and distinctive hotels. As the capital, it has been home to many powerful and wealthy people. A host of well-known architects, including Ernest Cormier, Cass Gilbert, and Moshe Safdie, have had the opportunity to exhibit their skills in an array of stunning public buildings, many of which subsequently have become icons of Canadian nationalism. The original Canadian parliament buildings are considered some of the best examples in the world of the so-called "Ruskinian Gothic Revival."

Of course, monumental buildings have never been totally neglected by the VAF, but in recent years the organization and the discipline have been moving beyond a simple definition of the vernacular as common or typical buildings to embrace *both* the ordinary and extraordinary and to consider them in relationship to one another, which is, after all, how they existed in past time. Charleston and Ottawa offer opportunities to explore the social context of building in environments uniquely suited to confronting the relationship between the rich and powerful, on the one hand, and the poor and subordinated, on the other. Such places represent a vivid architectural record of these various layers of society. They forced observers to come to terms with the relationship between buildings designed by and for a powerful elite and the "other" sides of such cities.

Thus the conferences from which these essays are drawn are evidence that the association has outgrown a single vision of vernacular architecture that consisted only of "old, rural, handmade structures built in traditional forms and materials for domestic and agricultural use."[2] In 1986, in her introduction to *Perspectives, II,* editor Camille Wells suggested that "pretentious buildings" could be equally worthy of attention—that vernacular architecture might offer new questions to scholars of the elite landscape—but pointed out that this notion had not been widely accepted among students of vernacular architecture. Eight years later, the Charleston meeting was the first step.

The same lesson was offered the following year in Ottawa, at a conference appropriately entitled "Capital Vernacular." There were fewer participants, but an unprecedented number of papers on Canadian topics, reflecting the association's growing international following. As had been the case in Charleston, the conference tours considered the city of Ottawa and its surrounding region through an extremely wide lens. Rather than ignoring the omnipresent power of the federal government in the capital region, VAF conference organizers emphasized power in its many manifestations on the landscape. The conference theme was the relationship between people and power, wood, and water, which implicitly referred to industrial, agricultural, residential, and government spaces constructed and controlled by a range of social classes in the National Capital Region. Participants followed construction of the Rideau Canal system, completed in 1832 to provide a connection for trade between Upper and Lower Canada. Tours also focused on the impact of industrialization on the area, including a trip to workers' housing in Hull, Quebec, the Chaudière Falls industrial and hydropower area, and Ottawa's Lowertown neighborhood.

Ottawa also marked a growing trend toward understanding architecture in a truly North American context, as recent cultural and political events (the North American Free Trade Agreement, for example) underscore. The transnational collaboration of a Canadian editor and a U.S. editor on this volume is another indication of movement in this direction, as is the inclusion of essays by Canadian scholars Richard Harris and Tania Martin. Moreover, several other essays—for example, those by Susan Fair and Geoffrey Gyrisco—acknowledge the indeterminacy of national borders for the particular building types they study. With this volume we see a move away from regionally based studies. These nineteen authors, instead, are more concerned with broad questions of class, race, and gender than with regional identities. This is particularly evident in comparison to *Perspectives, IV,* which included no fewer than ten regional case studies.

Issues

Many of the issues brought up at these two conferences are reflected in this collection of conference papers, selected, refereed, and revised from the original presentations. The relationship of vernacular forms to the socially constructed categories of class, ethnicity, gender, and race have been major preoccupations of the authors. In this particular group of essays, several scholars also explore the intertwining of religious culture with built form.

Form and Class

Taken together, the contributions in this collection contain highly suggestive implications for our understanding of the relationship between vernacular form and social class, and hence for the dynamics of social power as well. Bernard Herman shows how in colonial Charleston, the single house became an arena for status display within the context of a global mercantile economy. Within the single house, members of the mercantile elite acted out rituals of competition which reflected the culture of exchange. In a broader context, the single house also spatially expressed the salient underpinning to the region's social hierarchy: African American slavery. High walls were meant to confine slaves; rough finishes in the service areas they inhabited unmistakably communicated their low status. By setting the single house in its proper context, Herman has gone well beyond previous treatments of this type, which focused not upon social dynamics but on style and form.

For Charleston's surrounding low-country region, Carl Lounsbury shows that Anglo-Charlestonians, more than perhaps any North American urbanites of the era, blended prevailing English fashions with local idioms. In this partial "Anglicization," they embraced not only English stylistic conventions but also English patterns of social hierarchy. Lounsbury (and Herman as well) bring to bear recent approaches to historical scholarship which emphasize the Atlantic world. Rather than treat Europe or North America in themselves, historians are recognizing that the colonial period may best be characterized as an era when peoples from Europe, Africa, the Caribbean, and both Atlantic shores mingled in complex patterns.[3] Surely the architecture of Charleston and the low country bears eloquent testimony to this transoceanic dynamic.

The correlation between social power and vernacular forms in Charleston was fairly transparent, even if sometimes resisted or contested. But in other regions, the correlation between elite status and architectural expression was much less pronounced. In tidewater Virginia, for example, Edward Chappell and Julie Richter suggest a much weaker connection during the late eighteenth and early nineteenth centuries. The local gentry controlled wealth and held political and religious office disproportionate to their numbers. Yet, they seem to have shared building traditions with their less well-to-do neighbors; their houses were small and finished in comparatively modest fashion. Chappell and Richter have further advanced along a path first blazed by Henry Glassie in his landmark study *Folk Housing in Middle Virginia.*[4] In that work, Glassie had suggested that folk builders drew from a complex set of spatial templates passed on from generation to generation. Based around a common module of consistent dimensions, these templates expressed shared proxemic values. That is, they generated spaces in which people felt most comfortable given their cultural preferences (for example, preferences regarding social or private space). Chappell and Richter add depth and nuance to our understanding of the culture of building in eighteenth-century Virginia, putting these simple buildings into a socioeconomic setting. Their findings significantly challenge our conventional association of social elites with the famous mansions constructed by the Carter and Byrd families. The paper also raises intriguing questions as to what prompted later, more emphatic connections between display and power.

Clifton Ellis's article on the architecture of religious dissent in eighteenth-century Piedmont Virginia presses this point further. In this case, "the Anglican gentry of Halifax County were not interested in differentiating space according to a social hierarchy. Although some of these houses made substantial claims on the resources of their owners, plans show that their claims to status did not extend to creating social barriers, processional spaces, or genteel rooms for entertainment." The reason, Ellis argues, was that architectural expression in Halifax County was "dictated not by the Anglican elite, but by a dissenting sect of Evangelicals." The emerging cultural dominance of the Evangelicals reflected the rise of a class of middling planters whose "social status did not match their economic status." The Anglican elite did not share religious beliefs with the Evangelicals, but found it politic to adopt the Baptists' proxemic language.

In these two Virginia cases we have a fascinating counterpoint to Charleston. The Piedmont elite eschewed the very "social barriers" and "genteel spaces" developed by Charlestonians with such passion. Certainly, we learn about social power from the homes of the Piedmont, but we also realize that it did not take predictable forms. The contrasts between Charleston and Virginia should remind scholars not to make quick assumptions that elite status will inevitably be expressed in opulence and spatial hierarchy. It is also interesting to speculate on why these contrasts emerged. Was it because Charlestonians operated in much closer proximity to the global mercantile world and because their black-majority slave economy required oppressive social controls, buttressed by overt demonstrations of power? These factors might predispose Charlestonians to attach greater value both to the artifacts of trade and to the emphatic architectural display of power. To be sure, Piedmont residents owned slaves, and they participated in the global market economy too. But their dependence on trade and slaves never reached the same extent as it did in South Carolina. Trade involvement was carried on through middlemen rather than directly; moreover, as a more diversified economy developed in the eighteenth century, Tidewater and inland dwellers did not depend on transatlantic trade to the same degree as did their South Carolina counterparts. And since a more diversified agriculture challenged a staple crop economy, neither did they depend upon slavery to the same extent.

These analyses of Charleston and the Virginia Piedmont contribute to our more general understanding of vernacular architecture in the colonial period. Several scholars, for example, have argued for a trend toward "Anglicization" in colonial culture. Some argue that this may have extended to architecture. Archaeologist James Deetz contends that the emergence of the formal Georgian style is evidence for a "re-Anglicized popular culture of America on the eve of the Revolution."[5] He cites the external symmetry and internal, formal social spaces of New England houses such as the Mott House in Rhode Island and suggests that the pattern was part of a larger movement which occurred, in different guises, from South Carolina to New England in a variety of structures, ranging from plantation houses to merchants' dwellings. Kevin Sweeney's analysis of the buildings erected by the Connecticut Valley "River Gods" and their successors convincingly sets out a local variation on this pattern. Sweeney's findings, however, focus not on a "popular" culture but on local elites.

But this notion of Anglicization has been debated; indeed, the colonies' Anglo-American population was a minority by about 1750. In areas dominated by non-English immigrants, different patterns may have prevailed. For example, Henry Glassie advances a caution about the impact of the Georgian revolution; hidden behind formal, Georgian facades of Pennsylvania's Delaware Valley were traditional social spaces. William Woys Weaver has analyzed some of these spaces in an article entitled "The Pennsylvania German House." The *stube,* or stove room, was preeminent among the rooms Weaver examined, and it persisted as a characteristically Pennsylvania German space.[6]

In *Architecture and Rural Life in Central Delaware, 1700–1900,* Bernard L. Herman found a still more complex set of transformations. External asymmetry and undifferentiated internal space gave way, by the late eighteenth century, to a new spatial order which included Georgian symmetry, separate entryway and stair passages, and separate kitchens, together communicating a new class order. Yet, inventories show that the functions of these spaces were not as precise as their arrangement suggested, thus Herman infers that people still *used* space in traditional ways. Like the people of the Virginia Piedmont, then, Delaware residents used space to assimilate change, in very complex and occasionally inconsistent ways.

In future work, scholars thus will want to follow the suggestive path these works have laid out. How extensive was the transformation of space in colonial America? How did the nature and extent of the changes wrought relate to the specific regional or local context? Certainly by the time of the Revolution, it would seem that elite Americans had developed a shared visual language. Yet, they clung to sharply variable proxemic values and interior interpretations. Did these lines of sharing and division have parallels in other realms? Most obviously, it would seem as if the tension between locality and nation in the Early Republic and antebellum period was manifested not only politically but culturally. Vernacular architecture may thus serve as a means of linking up the dynamics of political culture.

As a capitalist economy emerged in the nineteenth century and later, the relationship between vernacular forms and power assumed yet more new shapes. Employers in different regions and times sought to control their work force in various ways. Laborers responded with a variety of strategies, ranging from outright rebellion (which was relatively uncommon) to subtle resistance or accommodation. Analyzing the struggles over building and space can offer revealing insights into these ever-changing social relationships. In nineteenth-century Delaware, for example, the emergence of a "free labor" system brought with it a new housing form: the house and garden. Rebecca Siders and Anna Andrzejewski explore the emergence and implications of this new form. Farm laborers, some recently released from chattel slavery, now had to contend with the vagaries of wage labor and tenant status, but a separate house and garden, provided by the landlords who employed them, also afforded them some autonomy and means for subsistence. "Both parties possessed something the other needed very badly, giving them each some power and authority in the relationship." Landlord/tenant relationships were flexible, but the limits of tenant influence were always implicitly understood; the "authority of the landowner" prevailed.

These Delaware agrarian patterns can be

profitably compared with others in different regions of the country. In the Northeast and Midwest, the relevant comparison is not so much with other forms of tenancy (in which farm tenants usually rented land which they farmed) as with the changed relationship between farmers and their hired laborers. All over the North, a shift occurred from shared work (in which laborers were often neighbors or kin, and often worked as part of local in-kind exchange systems) to wage labor (in which laborers, mainly immigrants, worked for cash wages). Class differences became more pronounced, and with this social stratification came spatial segregation; workers were increasingly isolated within the farmhouse proper (for example, in separate attic bedrooms with independent access). More often, they were excluded altogether and were required to find their own room and board. Though their class status was perhaps deteriorating, farm laborers also found a measure of autonomy in these new arrangements; no longer were they directly under the eye of an employer throughout the day and night.

In the Cotton South, the system which evolved in the post-emancipation struggle also differed substantially from the Delaware "house and garden." As the staple-crop economy slid into overproduction, poverty, and repression, sharecropping tenants received shelter, but little more; in fact, contracts often explicitly forbade tenants from having gardens. Landlords forbade gardens partly to consolidate their control over tenants (black and white) by depriving them of a key element toward self-sufficiency. Landowners felt they had little choice but to allocate every spare acre to cash-crop production because they, in turn, were being squeezed by northern creditors.[7]

Set within this context, the "house and garden" approach appears as an unusually formal and measured response to the new realities of agrarian labor. Tenants had less freedom than their counterparts among Northern farm laborers to organize their own domestic and garden space, but they had far more autonomy than sharecropping tenants farther South. It is tempting to speculate that this form was especially appropriate to the peculiar "middle ground" of the Upper South, where slavery and freedom had intertwined in such complex ways during the antebellum years.[8] More research, however, is needed before we can thoroughly understand the changing architecture of agricultural work and workers.

By the twentieth century, lumber magnates in the Pacific Northwest experimented with the built environment in their quest to secure a stable, cooperative labor force. Company towns such as Scotia, California, represent ideas of "welfare capitalism" (in which corporations provided various benefits to employees such as health services, educational programs, and housing) realized in physical form. While some elements represented control, even coercion (for example, the elimination of company saloons), others (for instance, hospitals) catered to workers' real needs and perhaps even deflected worker resistance. James Buckley concludes that "[i]f we measure redwood workers' contentment by the subsequent record of labor unrest, then mill owners' extra investment in company towns seems to have paid a significant dividend."

Scotia was just one of hundreds of company towns scattered throughout the country. Some experienced a quiescence similar to Scotia's; the Endicott-Johnson company towns in southern New York State come to mind. Others, however—such as Pullman, Illinois, or mining towns in the Appalachian region—were torn by constant labor strife. Future comparative study will investigate how corporations' urban planning efforts contributed to these very different outcomes. Investigation is needed of how industry-wide conditions, market competition, labor law, and individual corporate policies influenced building programs.

The examples of both agrarian Delaware and

the northwestern lumbering industry reveal employers making some concessions to workers, but always catering to a strong element of self-interest and ultimately holding the upper hand. Other cases, however, illustrate how middle- and working-class people took the initiative to shape environments that suited their own needs, in the process stating implicit alternatives to the dominant modes of social and cultural power. In late-twentieth-century America, older commercial strips have been superseded by huge malls, and the abandoned strips have been refashioned by immigrants and working-class people. The new uses to which these strips have been put are evidence of creativity and resourcefulness. They also can be read, as Tim Davis points out, as challenges to elitist notions of preservation and as emblems of "relative freedom from authority."

But even middle-class suburbia harbored more variety than is commonly assumed. Richard Harris has found that in many American and Canadian suburbs of the early to mid twentieth century, a significant proportion of homes—as many as 25 percent—were owner-built, not mass-produced. This suggests a degree of resistance to the standardized consumer culture. It also suggests questions for further study. For example, were as many homes owner-built in other suburbs? If so, what are the implications for our interpretation of suburbia? Have suburbs been less homogeneous than previously thought, at least in terms of class? To what extent (if at all) did this suburban experience modify prescriptive norms for bourgeois "domesticity"? The very term "middle-class domesticity" is coming increasingly into question among historians, as we learn more about "real" domestic lives as opposed to prescription.[9] Like this accumulating body of conventional historical evidence, the emerging vernacular architecture record suggests that "domesticity" has taken a wide variety of forms.

If Harris's findings suggest alternatives to consumer culture, Pamela Simpson's analysis of what she calls the "democratic" floor coverings—linoleum and Lincrusta—reveals users' enthusiastic participation; the widespread popularity of these floor coverings was at least partly due to the classic tactics of advertising and marketing. But, at the same time, implicit in the popularity of "faux" floor coverings was a hearty rejection of elite aesthetic standards. Again, issues of cultural power and social class come to the fore.

Thus, by organizing space, style, and ornament, people have communicated both power and resistance. Since colonial times, a continual contest has taken place, and social groupings formed and re-formed in different ways. The built environment offers clues as to how this process has played out in specific contexts. The essays collected here possess rich implications for future directions of research into the connections between building forms and power structures. For example, in the colonial period, did architecture in other regions show the same variety of configurations between form and power as existed in Charleston and Virginia? Did differences in economy and society assert themselves spatially? How? As the economy and the architecture produced within it modernized, did conflict over building form assume similar contours regardless of region?

Form and Ethnicity
Our understanding of the connection between building and ethnicity has undergone significant revision over the years, but many scholars still hold that ethnicity can be a useful category for analysis—recognizing, however, that it is socially constructed as much as is gender or race.[10] The essays in this volume suggest a variety of associations between ethnic identity (however constructed) and building form. Susan Fair, for example, analyzes the storage caches of Alaska. These structures—consisting of small huts elevated on posts—figure prominently in both the

Native American landscape and in Native American legend as symbols of cultural identity, security, generosity, and achievement. Euro-American immigrants to Alaska, however, also appropriated the cache motif as a symbol of their own identity as Alaskans. The Euro-American interpretation of the cache often took a highly commercialized form, as the cache motif was used in advertising, and actually commodified through souvenirs, paintings, and the like.

Geoffrey Gyrisco shows how the architecture of East Slavs in America was even more malleable, yet still functioned as a distinctive ethnic "marker" in the landscape. Such buildings as St. Mary's Church in Minneapolis represented a syncretistic combination of Russian and American architectural conventions; the American flag, for example, was suspended with traditional icon church banners. Many Eastern European immigrants, moreover, fashioned ethnic identities not necessarily congruent with those of ethnic groups in their geographic region of origin; thus, in America people who called themselves "Russians" would not have been recognized as such by Russians in the Old World. Gyrisco's work contributes to a growing body of scholarship which examines the ways in which ethnicity was fabricated—in this case, quite literally.

By contrast, according to author Ruth Little, the African American middle class did not make such overt attempts to express ethnicity in building form. She points out the dangers of searching for Africanisms in African American architecture. "Many African-Americans," she suggests, "would be surprised to learn that their architecture is sometimes considered ethnic." Was architecture, in this case, part of a conscious strategy to assimilate, at least outwardly? How did architecture figure in the debates within the African American community about accommodation versus resistance to the oppressive social order of segregation and discrimination? How did African-American architecture fit within the context of patterns in food, music, and other forms of popular culture? What might Little's model offer for continuing research on other subcultures such as those in Chinatown, the Lower East Side, or (for that matter) Pennsylvania German Lancaster County? Perhaps this is the time for scholars of vernacular architecture to reconsider the search for ethnic distinctiveness and to probe more carefully the relationship between ethnicity and spatial form.

Form and Gender

Issues of gender are a more recent concern of vernacular architecture scholars than class and ethnicity. In fact, it was not until the publication of *Perspectives, IV* in 1991 that a number of papers addressed the role of gender in our understanding of ordinary buildings and landscapes. Four years later, the editors and authors of *Perspectives, V* embraced gender as a major category of analysis; this was reflected in the volume's subtitle, *Gender, Class, and Shelter.*

Like the development of gender studies in the field of architectural history, the feminist critique of vernacular architecture studies has evolved from an early search for the roles of women as designers of buildings and places to a more complex questioning of the ways that men and women may perceive space differently. This recent line of inquiry has proven difficult for scholars of ordinary environments. As Carolyn Torma and her co-author in volume IV, Rebecca Sample Bernstein, explained, "when one turns to primary source material, a major stumbling block is encountered." Women are seldom acknowledged in the traditional sources of vernacular architecture studies: maps, tax records, diaries, local histories, etc. As a result of this absence of women in the conventional historical record, many scholars interested in gender have turned to alternative sources, such as photographs and oral histories, to illuminate women's experience of the built environment. Vernacular architecture scholars concerned with gender have thus absorbed the lessons of work on other hitherto invisible people, while at the same time exploring new methodological approaches for this ever-growing category of architectural analysis.

For example, gender studies published in previous volumes of *Perspectives* relied heavily upon prescriptive literature as a key to women's spatial experiences. Popular magazines and other forms of advice literature written for women offered scholars of the built environment tantalizing glimpses of how real spaces may have affected the everyday lives of ordinary women. Leland Roth, for example, in volume IV, showed how the *Ladies' Home Journal* popularized the private house and foreshadowed the huge success of the mail-order house industry before and after World War I.

Using similar evidence, Janet Hutchison in *Perspectives, II* looked at the campaign in the 1920s and 1930s to reform housing, Better Homes in America, which was intended to improve the lot of women in the home through better design. Both these essays were typical of this early work in their use of popular printed sources to interpret popular house types.

In *Perspectives, V,* gender issues converged with vernacular architecture studies in a major way. The volume included pointed discussions of methodological issues and also repeated reminders that "gender" is not synonymous with "women," but rather refers to the ways in which cultures construct the biological realities of sexual difference. First, pioneering work on the spaces of masculinity were included in *Perspectives, V,* such as Deryck Holdsworth's and William Moore's essays on distinctly masculine environments. Indeed, the real mark of maturity in the authors' analyses of gender issues was that most of the essays in the volume included gender in the context of other concerns (though not necessarily the central issue) in their investigation.

Perhaps as a further development of this contextual way of thinking, *Perspectives, VII* includes fewer papers on gender per se. Several essays, however, build on the pioneering work in previous issues and suggest new avenues for understanding how gender affects ordinary buildings. Tania Martin, for instance, casts a new light on the ubiquitous Quebec convent; her work also serves to underline how "vernacular" is as much an approach to the material as a building type. The convent is a monument, but by looking at the drawings of a resident nun (rather than at those of the architect), Martin shows how this superficially patriarchal institution actually functioned as a type of cooperative housing. Martin concludes: "Clearly the nuns did not fit into the neat construction of the 'separate spheres' theory, as their own work and physical environment breached the clear divisions of male and female, public and private, active and passive." In this case, incorporating gender into the analysis has meant a complete inversion of our former understanding of the building type.

Other authors have incorporated gender into more general studies of a particular material, building, or community type, confirming Kwolek-Folland's suggestion that making gender a standard avenue of inquiry can only enrich our interpretations of every landscapes. William Moore, for example, in his study of New England's spiritualist camp meetings, points out how such places permitted the expansion of the "boundaries of behavior prescribed by American society." Spiritualist organizations, like the Montreal convents, offered women new leadership roles unavailable to them in other realms. In the spiritualist camps, this meant that certain days were set aside for the discussion of the political advancement of women, clearly blurring the limits of religious and political activity. In the case of both the convent and the spiritualist camp, then, spaces seemingly designed for religious purposes may have led to more choices in the secular lives of women.

The use of spaces, too, often operate quite differently according to gender. Susan Fair shows how caches in Alaska, for example, were used variously by women and men. While men typically stored tools or supported vehicles in caches, women used them to store fish or furs. Gendered patterns of work and identity show up vividly in Fair's case study, as when Athabaskan people prohibited others from even touching caches belonging to members of the opposite sex.

Form and Race

Similarly, recent scholarship has emphasized the degree to which race is a socially constructed category rather than having any biological basis. Several essays in this volume provide insights into how racial lines were literally constructed into the fabric of the American built environment. In colonial Charleston, of course, the prevailing racial order was clear in the spatial organization of walled compounds, slave quarters, and back-alley gathering places. In central Delaware, emancipation brought a different racial order, one in which African American wage laborers achieved a measure of autonomy but were pointedly placed on the margins of landowners' property; this pattern can be compared with post-emancipation spatial organization of sharecropping farther South, in which the concentrated slave "quarter" gave way to dispersed sharecroppers' cabins.[11] As middle-class African Americans experienced disfranchisement and segregation in the late-nineteenth and early-twentieth-century South, they constructed housing that was visually indistinguishable from middle-class neighborhoods anywhere in the United States, pointing to the complex intersection of class and race in American society. The ironies are further reinforced by Richard Harris's suggestion that American suburbs were less homogenous than previously thought with respect to class, because suburbs continued to be racially exclusive.

Form and Religious Culture

Just as vernacular forms can aid in the understanding of class, gender, and racial structures, they can help us interpret the expression of religious values. In antebellum New Orleans, for example, Dell Upton shows how the profound ceremonies of death as enacted within the urban cemetery—the "city of the dead"—reflected the urban community of the living. The Grey Nuns of Montréal used their ability to organize space to express a strong religious identity and community. Tania Martin argues that within this community, women achieved a measure of autonomy impossible in the discriminatory secular society. By contrast, William Moore finds that Yankee spiritualists' attempts to create spaces congruent with their beliefs foundered under the weight of ambiguity.

Perhaps it is a coincidence, but it is worth noting that the more successful of these attempts to merge environment with religious culture came from within Catholicism. Perhaps Catholics exploited their rich institutional and ritual history to fashion vernacular spaces. The spiritualists, on the other hand, lacked any such history and, moreover, were likely handicapped by the anti-authoritarian nature of their beliefs.

These patterns recall those analyzed by Dolores Hayden in *Seven American Utopias*.[12] Builders in these American communitarian experiments used a variety of means to express corporate beliefs. The Shakers, for example, successfully balanced discipline with release by making a mix of highly organized spaces and more flexible ones. Their shared beliefs and carefully organized (if unconventional) gender system contributed to a coherent building plan. The Fourierists, on the other hand, failed to combine conventional sociability with a fundamental challenge to the dominant social order, and their experiment failed both spatially and socially. These experiences all remind us that enduring vernacular forms generally result from a complex mix which grows from both cultural expression and original design.

Design Versus Use

Cutting across social categories and institutions, yet another theme in contemporary vernacular architecture studies stresses how people who use buildings appropriate space in ways quite different from those intended by designers. When Charleston's slave owners erected walls and quarters, slaves found breathing room in the back alleys. Standardized forms of commercial strips were appropriated for uses quite different from those of the original occupants. Office workers modified the open, architect-designed spaces by creating partitions and other barriers. All of these essays are richly suggestive for showing the way to analyzing how space is continually negotiated.

While these contests are often waged along class, ethnic, gender, or racial lines, the lines between designer and user are also worth considering. Architects, landlords, and corporations often set the original shape of a given building type; but ordinary users just as often modify or challenge these spatial prescriptions. They do this through various devices, such as Carolyn Torma's "informal codes" or through an outright reorganization of space. Thus, an expanding field for students of the vernacular is in asking how people respond to buildings designed by professionals or generated by standardized, corporate planning.

And still beyond this model of design and response, there is room to investigate the continual interactions between designers and their audience. As scholars continue to chip away at the conceptual lines between "vernacular" and "high style," new avenues of inquiry open up. Just as elements of "high style" design have been incorporated into everyday buildings, professional architects and planners have drawn from shared culture and values as well.

Whatever the specific subject, the body of work contained in this volume also points to an even more intensified interdisciplinary approach in vernacular architecture studies. The implications for history scholarship, for instance, are many. Roman Catholic nuns' ability to shape their own spaces, for instance, offers insights for the debate in women's history over the relevance of the "separate spheres" model. The urban cemetery becomes a vehicle for a new understanding of American urbanization in general. Tracing the actual pattern of owner-built housing in North American suburbs puts to the test assumptions about standardization and homogeneity and, in the process, forces historians to reformulate their approach to postwar culture. Gender studies, historical geography, anthropology, and women's history also will intersect with vernacular architecture studies to a greater and greater extent in the future. These essays also abundantly confirm that "vernacular" building cannot and should not be regarded as a hermetically separated category of building, studied apart from "high style," "popular," or "folk" architecture. Previous PVA editors and authors have pointed this out, but it comes across here with more force than ever.

Landscape

We hope that this collection of essays will communicate the vibrancy of vernacular architecture studies today. Along with this vigor, however, comes the potential for confusion and fragmentation, as subject matter grows ever more disparate. One conceptual idea which most vernacular architecture scholars do share, however, is the notion of landscape. This is of course not a new idea; some of the most revered pioneers of vernacular architecture studied landscapes. But it is worth making this point because rich insights may be derived from setting an individual structure into its wider building context.

Developing methodologies and approaches to

vernacular landscape, however, is a daunting task; not only because the term "landscape" is so all-encompassing, but also because landscape studies is in tremendous intellectual flux. At one time, the study of American landscapes was compartmentalized into various disciplinary pigeonholes. Art historians analyzed landscape paintings according to widely received aesthetic canons; geographers variously attempted painstakingly detailed reconstructions of past landscapes or ventured grand interpretations underpinned by the assumption of a monolithic American culture; literary scholars analyzed the landscape imagery and metaphor embodied in the classical literary canon; vernacular architecture scholars turned their attention to "common" landscapes.

In the past decades, the study of landscape has grown much more interdisciplinary and much more theoretically and methodologically contentious. While the very nature of the subject always made cross-disciplinary forays necessary, increasingly the boundary lines are not simply being crossed but are being challenged, even obliterated. Now the scholar who is interested in landscape is likely to find work which addresses literary and artistic representations together or which probes the symbolic import of built structures, interpreting buildings as texts. Aesthetically based evaluation has given way to locating the cultural roots of the aesthetic itself and to placing landscape painting in its cultural and ideological context. From this approach, important insights have emerged about many hitherto unstudied aspects of landscape; for example, scholars have advanced provocative arguments about the cultural and political significance of Anglo-American landscape painting.

In addition to dealing with the increased fluidity of disciplinary boundaries, all students of the historical landscape have been vigorously challenged to rethink their methods and theoretical assumptions. The assault on long-held conventions was inspired principally by more general intellectual and social currents, themselves potentially in tension with one another. Among the forces driving these massive re-evaluations was the social ferment of the 1960s and 1970s, in which dominant class, gender, and racial structures were questioned. Scholars became aware that landscapes are manipulated to enforce or contest power and authority. At the same time, another challenge to scholarly methods and theoretical frameworks came from postmodern thought, which challenged the modern paradigm of knowledge, positing the Western ideal of "objectivity" itself as a subjective, ideological construct.

Influenced by postmodern thought, many scholars of landscape have turned their attention to the visual and verbal languages of landscape representation. Some would hold that *all* landscapes (whether material, visual, or literary) are representations, and thus that analysis need concern itself *only* with representation. Others see landscape representation as inflexibly dictated by socioeconomic context, especially power relationships, and so conclude that interpretation must reach to the social background as the ultimate "reality."[13] Regardless of their specific ideological stances, most stress the transitory, deceptive, subjective nature of representations.

These swirling currents of thought pose a vigorous challenge to vernacular architecture studies, which is, after all, irrevocably committed to documenting and interpreting the built environment. Clearly, vernacular architecture studies will continue to be grounded in materialist assumptions. As such, perhaps vernacular architecture scholarship may serve as a corrective to the tendency in some interpretations of landscape representation to ignore (or even deny) actual geologic features, biota, buildings, and field patterns. Careful documentation of the material record can offer important insights for inquiry into the cultural dimensions of landscape, for without knowing what was on the land it is difficult, even misleading, to make conclusions about how it was represented.

Of course the ultimate goal of vernacular architecture studies is not to reconstruct a physical landscape but to interpret it. If it has been hesitant fully to embrace postmodern epistemology, the discipline has been centrally involved in the movement away from monolithic interpretations of American thought and culture—and thus of landscape also. Because vernacular architecture scholars approach the built environment as a cultural product, they inescapably confront how built landscapes are shaped by the social, political, economic, and cultural structures of the people who produce them. And historians of the last few generations have demonstrated abundantly that American society has not been monolithic but fragmentary and often conflicted, its landscapes a scene for ever-shifting contests and negotiations among different groups. Future studies can make a significant contribution to understanding the complex dynamic between the physical makeup of landscapes and the cultural processes of representation.

Several of the essays in this volume point to such explorations. Bruce Harvey has analyzed the architecture of Charleston's 1901-2 exposition. Charleston's business leaders attempted to create a landscape which symbolized a thriving industrial future for the city and region. But their attempt failed: the exposition landscape was egregiously anomalous in the context of the city's culture and the region's political economy. Northern California lumber magnates, on the other hand, seem to have achieved more success in their quest to reproduce in the company town a "factory without a roof." Perhaps it is significant that the company town landscape (unlike the largely imaginary Exposition landscape) grew out of pre-existing industrial conditions in the forest economy of the Northwest.

We hope that, taken together, the essays in *Perspectives, VII* will help scholars to move forward with the study of vernacular buildings in their physical, intellectual, and cultural contexts. We invite readers now to join in exploring a diverse, dynamic collection of everyday landscapes.

Notes

1. The development of the field has been outlined in the introductions of earlier volumes in this series; see also Dell Upton, "Ordinary Buildings: A Bibliographical Essay on American Vernacular Architecture," *American Studies International* 19 (Winter 1981): 57–75, and "The Power of Things: Recent Studies in American Vernacular Architecture," *American Quarterly* 35 (1983): 262–79.
2. See Camille Wells, "Old Claims and New Demands: Vernacular Architecture Studies Today," in *Perspectives in Vernacular Architecture, II*, ed. Camille Wells (Columbia: Univ. of Missouri Press, 1986), 1.
3. See, for example, the new series published by Johns Hopkins University Press on Atlantic history and culture.
4. Henry Glassie, *Folk Housing in Middle Virginia: A Structural Analysis of Historic Artifacts* (Knoxville: Univ. of Tennessee Press, 1975).
5. James Deetz, *In Small Things Forgotten* (Garden City, N.Y.: Anchor Books, 1977), 112; see also David Grayson Allen, *In English Ways: The Movement of Societies and the Transferral of English Local Law and Custom to Massachusetts Bay in the 17th Century* (Chapel Hill: Univ. of North Carolina Press, 1991); Rhys Isaac, *The Transfor-*

mation of *Virginia* (Chapel Hill: Univ. of North Carolina Press, 1982); and Patricia Bonomi, *Under the Cope of Heaven: Religion, Society, and Politics in Colonial America* (New York: Oxford Univ. Press, 1986).

6. Henry Glassie, "Eighteenth-Century Cultural Process in Delaware Valley Folk Building," *Winterthur Portfolio* 7 (1972): 29–59; William Woys Weaver, "The Pennsylvania German House," *Winterthur Portfolio* 21 (1986): 243–64; Bernard L. Herman, *Architecture and Rural Life in Central Delaware, 1700–1900* (Knoxville: Univ. of Tennessee Press, 1987).

7. See, for example, Theodore Rosengarten, ed. *All God's Dangers: The Life of Nate Shaw* (New York: Knopf, 1974).

8. Barbara Fields, *Slavery and Freedom on the Middle Ground* (New Haven: Yale Univ. Press, 1985).

9. See Linda Kerber, "Separate Spheres, Female Worlds, Women's Place: The Rhetoric of Women's History." *Journal of American History* 75 (June 1988): 9–39; Jeanne Boydston, *Home and Work* (New York: Oxford Univ. Press, 1990).

10. See Bernard Bailyn and Philip Morgan, eds., *Strangers within the Realm: Cultural Margins of the First British Empire* (Chapel Hill: Univ. of North Carolina Press, 1991).

11. Herbert Gutman, *The Black Family in Slavery and Freedom 1750–1925* (New York: Random House, 1976).

12. Dolores Hayden, *Seven American Utopias: The Architecture of Communitarian Socialism, 1790–1975* (Cambridge, Mass.: MIT Press, 1976).

13. See Angela Miller's helpful essay, "Magisterial Visions: Recent Anglo-American Scholarship on the Represented Landscape," *American Quarterly* 47 (Mar. 1995): 140–51. Miller calls for a "fusion" of approaches which would "resolve the dichotomy between internal and external, text and context, form and history."

PART I

EMERGING VERNACULAR FORMS: THE EIGHTEENTH CENTURY

CHAPTER 1

Edward A. Chappell and Julie Richter

Wealth and Houses in Post-Revolutionary Virginia

For nearly two decades, the rural landscape of the early Chesapeake has been perceived in terms of dichotomies, with sharp distinctions drawn between the costly and permanent houses of rich landowners and the relatively poor and impermanent houses of virtually everyone else. We have assumed that the rough-and-tumble nature of housing for most people who lived in the seventeenth-century Chesapeake continued to characterize all but gentry housing in the following century. As a result, the story goes, most of it has disappeared. This perspective seemingly contradicts Henry Glassie's assertion that vernacular houses are the principal means of understanding ordinary people; an examination of surviving dwellings, however small, appears to offer a glimpse of housing only for wealthy Virginians and some of the poor people, black and white, who worked for them. But does it?[1]

While the distribution of wealth and goods in the eighteenth-century Chesapeake was overwhelmingly weighted in favor of the rich, the population did not form an entirely bipolar configuration of haves and have-nots. Recent fieldwork and historical research suggest that the rural landscape of eighteenth- and nineteenth-century Tidewater and Piedmont Virginia included a considerable range of permanent and well-finished houses, some built by successful middling planters. A lengthy project pursued by the architectural research staff at Colonial Williamsburg has provided an opportunity to examine, record, and analyze buildings and complexes spread over seventeen counties in the Old Dominion.[2] Surviving domestic and work buildings represent a category of structures superior to the crudely built houses and outbuildings used by the region's poor majority, yet less refined than some of the center-stage edifices put up by colonial grandees. More significantly, successful middling planters participated in a housing revolution that accelerated dramatically with the dawning of the early national era. These individuals either built or remodeled existing structures to create dwellings that reflected their position between the gentry and the poor. Houses existed at points along a continuum that cannot be adequately described by rigid categories. Yet, slicing people and their possessions into distinct groups—like rich, middling, and poor—can be analytically as well as politically useful. Most people continued to live materially simple lives in the years after the American Revolution, but housing standards began to shift toward a clearer tripartite social model.

For the purposes of this essay, "middling" is used to refer to the group of free people located between landless tenants and wealthy plantation owners on the economic ladder. The concept of "middling" developed during the 1700s. At the beginning of the eighteenth century, one's status was primarily dependent upon rank at birth, leaving a person limited opportunity to improve upon his or her place in the social order. Over the course of the eighteenth century, status became increasingly defined by one's social and economic position, which could improve or decline. In addition, there was recognition of a group of people who were between the rich and the poor. The desire of these individuals to acquire fashionable goods and to live in more comfortable houses both set them off from those below and fueled the consumer revolution.[3]

Though oriented toward the upper end of society, middling people ranged from those who planted slightly less than a hundred acres to those who owned a thousand, from individuals who did not own slaves to those who possessed as many as twenty slaves.[4] The new homebuilders and remodelers of older structures tended to be acquisitive people who increased their acreage and labor force throughout their adult lives, until they began to transfer property to their children. Only a handful of the families studied did not own slaves, and, while free blacks owned land in the subject counties, none owned the specific properties studied here until the mid-nineteenth century.[5] It is important to understand that the tax assessments and most surviving buildings reflect landownership by only a fraction of the residents in Tidewater Virginia. Between two-thirds and three-quarters of white heads of households owned or rented land at a time when whites constituted roughly half of the population of this region in the Old Dominion. Our subjects were middling in their position between rich and poor, but they did not stand at the center of the total population.[6]

The historical research for this project provides information about the identity of individuals who built, remodeled, and lived in surviving houses. Research on deeds and wills has yielded a conventional chain of title for each of the sites.[7] Land and personal property tax lists, first compiled in 1782, were employed to chart the real and personal wealth of all propertied inhabitants in each of the seventeen counties, much as Dell Upton has done for the owners of an Isle of Wight County house.[8] Analysis of the annual assessments has made it possible to place owners of buildings within the economic context of their counties and to define their status.[9]

Fieldwork reveals that few rural houses of any kind survive in the Chesapeake from the century before 1725. The impermanent construction of many and the inability of most to fulfill the domestic expectations of subsequent generations brought about the disappearance of almost all of these structures. The next fifty years saw the construction of three- and four-room-plan gentry houses with multiple stories, brick or well-crafted wooden walls, and refined interior finishes. Smaller houses of comparable quality survive from the second and third quarters of the eighteenth century in relatively small numbers beyond Williamsburg and are scattered throughout the Tidewater.[10]

The traditional image of entire colonial communities housed in such dwellings, a picture reinforced by most American history museums, is obviously far too rosy. The impression that everyone—merchant, wigmaker, and laundress—occupied a trim house in a well-kept landscape owes more to twentieth-century hopes and expectations than to preindustrial reality. It is clear that surviving early houses in Williamsburg, Yorktown, and the few similar Chesapeake towns were occupied by affluent families; yet, these were often successful tradespeople and retailers rather than rich landowners. The survival rate in the countryside argues for fewer well-housed subgentry sorts there. But such buildings did exist, and they appear relatively well-represented in the site histories of existing rural houses.

A sampling of extant buildings and their colonial owners reveals that one- and two-room-plan houses with plastered walls and brick foundations and chimneys were sometimes the homes of household heads who held county offices and served on petit or grand juries as well as those who were ruling-class gentry. Several examples illustrate the range of middling and gentry households involved. Pear Valley in the Eastern Shore's Northampton County is a well-constructed single-room house with 346 square feet on the first floor (fig. 1.1).[11] It was built with an impressive brick end and frame walls plastered inside between chamfered posts, though the attic bedchamber was, like many of this scale, left unfinished. The oversized fireplace suggests that the main room was the scene of cooking as well as of eating, visiting, and sleeping, just as the principal room was used in other Eastern Shore houses of this period. Robert Nottingham, a man who held the county-level office of tobacco inspector, built Pear Valley for his family home about 1740, when he owned 150 acres. In spite of the title of his office, it is likely that Nottingham produced corn as his cash crop, not tobacco, after he moved into Pear Valley.[12]

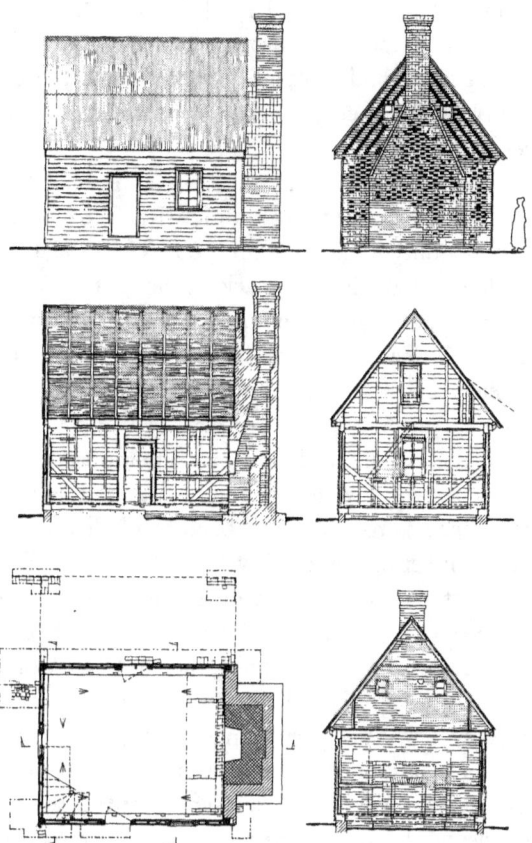

Fig. 1.1. Pear Valley, Northampton County, Virginia. Additions were apparently carried out by Maria Widgeon after 1837. Jeffrey Bostetter. Courtesy of Colonial Williamsburg Foundation.

The Rochester House on the Northern Neck is a similar single-room-plan house built about two decades later by John Rochester. Its accommodation was slightly better—the walls were insulated and attic bedchamber plastered and heated, for example—but the first floor still contained only 320 square feet, its ceiling remained unplastered, and cooking may have taken place there. Rochester was a more lofty character than Nottingham, illustrated by his service as a parish vestryman and sheriff for Westmoreland County. Unlike Nottingham, Rochester probably gained a portion of the capital for his house from tobacco. The rest would have been from wheat, the product that had replaced tobacco as the Northern Neck's cash crop by the end of the eighteenth century.[13]

A house built in the same era as Pear Valley, Eagle's Nest on the Chickahominy River in Charles City County (fig. 1.2) and the 1729 William Andrews House in Accomack on the Eastern Shore offered better accommodation than Rochester's house. Both are story-and-a-half brick houses with a central passage separating two rooms on each floor.[14] All the spaces were plastered and well-lit from the beginning. Based on contemporary Virginia probate inventories for houses of this size, these spaces probably functioned as a hall and best bedchamber on the first level and lesser chambers above stairs. Cooking and other rough work took place outside the house. The first floor at Eagle's Nest encloses 756 square feet, the Andrews House 800. Eagle's Nest stood on a 340-acre tract by mid-century, and its owner, Francis Tyree, served only as a petit juror, not as a major county officeholder. Tyree was a modestly successful planter, never a gentleman.[15] Though the houses were comparable in size and finish, William Andrews *was* a "Gent."—identified as such when he purchased 800 acres near Guilford Creek in 1722. His family had been near the top of Accomack society since his grandfather served as a Burgess in the seventeenth century. Perhaps Andrews switched to corn production soon after he moved to Guilford Creek, near the border between Virginia and Maryland.[16]

The Rochester and Andrews families notwithstanding, some of the smaller well-built houses were home to successful middling folk like the Nottinghams as early as mid-century. They are a segment of the population absent in Rhys Isaac's portrait of Virginia society. While the evidence is spotty and the ranks of Nottinghams may have been thin, the role of such people forms a background for the larger developments in the years following the American Revolution.

The post-Revolutionary period represents a watershed in American building. Though the technology of construction changed only modestly, the extent of new building and the nature of people occupying the spaces were dramatically transformed. Evidence of a housing revolution beginning at the end of the eighteenth century can be seen in all parts of the new country.[17] The number of surviving buildings rises significantly when one looks for relatively small houses built in the decades following the Revolution.[18] While grand houses with eight or more rooms and highly decorated trim remained rare (fewer than their pre-Revolutionary counterparts in some counties), the number of small but well-built houses in the Tidewater section of Virginia increased. This proliferation was a product of two related factors, one involving a growing sense of group identity and the other changing economic conditions. First, men and women were caught up in a consumer revolution that began in England at the end of the seventeenth century. People increasingly sought dwellings that were more refined and permanent, structures that provided an unmistakable indication of an owner's status as one of the middling residents in his or her community as well as material comfort. Second, a greater number of Tidewater residents were able to build or remodel their houses once their local economy become more diversified. By 1800 the majority of Tidewater planters had made the decision not to depend on tobacco as their main cash crop. They shifted to grains (corn and wheat), forest products, and livestock.

Cary Carson and others have plausibly argued that Maryland and Virginia planters who relied on tobacco as their cash crop were unable to improve upon their poorly constructed dwellings.[19] Grain production did not require planters to invest in land and labor to the same degree that tobacco did. While crop diversification provided an enabling condition for the Chesapeake building boom in the early republic, it did not create the

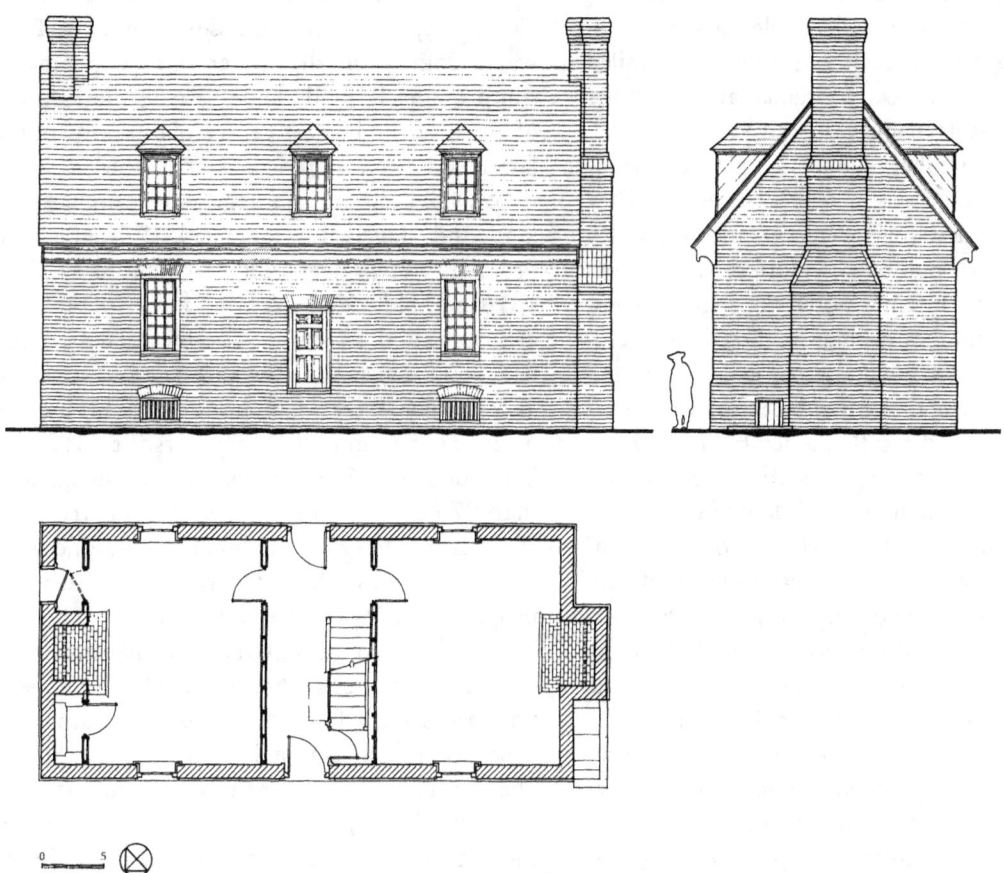

Fig. 1.2. Eagle's Nest, Charles City County, Virginia. Jeffrey Bostetter. Courtesy of Colonial Williamsburg Foundation.

sole impetus for the housing revolution. The change in housing standards was far more widespread than the region affected by the gradual shift from tobacco to grain production. Related architectural developments took place throughout the new nation and beyond its boundaries. It became equally evident in the housing stock of Bermuda, for example, in an era when the island had little to do with the Chesapeake and the Bermudian economy was ostensibly on the skids.[20]

Surviving post-Revolutionary Virginia houses with one to three rooms on each floor are arranged in a variety of configurations, some with central or side passages, but many with none at all. These buildings contain as little as three hundred or as much as twelve hundred square feet on the principal floor. What they share is a concern for permanence and refinement expressed in well-rendered frame or brick walls, with level wooden floors raised above masonry foundations. The principal spaces are commonly plastered and even wainscoted, though ceiling framing and floorboards overhead are often left exposed; they were built this way almost a century after plastered ceilings had become standard in high gentry houses. Even when plaster is omitted on the walls, leaving unfinished framing exposed, openings are trimmed with planed boards or cased with simple classical moldings. Baseboards and chairboards (generally called bases and surbases in early Virginia) are sometimes used to trim walls that never received plaster.

Successful middling planters employed various strategies for acquiring a refined dwelling. They could build a new house, enlarge and remodel a standing one, or pull two or more separate structures together. Specific motivations are evident throughout, and they distinguish these homebuilders as a group representing a particular place and time. Unlike the mid-eighteenth-century occupants of Pear Valley and the Rochester House, for example, owners of these newly composed houses, whether with six rooms or one, desired to separate cooking from living space. Most also lacked English people's willingness to leave oversized fireplaces and archaic woodwork in place. They perceived both the activity of cooking and those doing the work—often slaves—as best relegated to the cellar or, most often, to a separate building.

During the years following the American Revolution, there were in landowners' careers some predictable points at which they felt it possible to build a well-finished, permanent house. These points were generally after they had begun to work an amount of arable land that met their relative expectation for profit, and most often after a person or couple was roughly thirty years old. In the case of widows, adult sons in residence seem to have provided some of the labor security that made quality housebuilding likely.

A few well-chosen examples help chart the contours of this now-vanishing landscape. The first is a man who rose from the middling rank toward the upper crust. Although he remained below the level of the richest local landowners, he lived in a house similar to the dwellings of the country's wealthiest residents. These individuals often invested in housing of the same general quality rather than in the Georgian mansions built in the eighteenth century.

An entrepreneurial farmer named Carter Croxton spent his life in Essex County, a Tidewater county on the upper middle peninsula south of the Rappahannock River, the location of some of the biggest gentry plantations in the late colonial era. Croxton was a deacon in the Baptist Church and an aggressive purchaser of land and slaves. He inherited 177 acres and probably a few slaves from his father in 1775. In 1810 he held 599.5 acres of land, including a grist mill, and 13 slaves. The fact that Croxton had a mill suggests that he had switched to wheat as his principal crop, and he added to his income by grinding grain for his neighbors.[21] By 1821 his land totaled 1259.65 acres, an amount greater than 97 percent of Essex County property owners. His buildings on the home tract alone were assessed at $2,000, higher than 90 percent of property-owning county residents.

In addition to the mill, the 1821 assessment included a brick house that provided all the essential spaces for a family of Croxton's status in a compact and painstakingly resolved form. Raised above a high service cellar were two rooms separated by a passage. The best room was a parlor; the smaller one seems to have been a dining space, served by a pantry in a porch just outside its exterior door, and a diminutive, unheated room added to the rear soon after initial construction. The first-floor contains a total of 890 square feet. Croxton's builders used a gambrel roof to create generous space for two heated bedchambers and a small unheated one upstairs. All the rooms were given plaster walls and ceilings and basic trim around their openings. Above the main attic story was a low, unheated room of the variety thought suitable for workers and storage. As orderly as the house was Croxton's complement of two dairies, a smokehouse, and a privy ranged along the back of his rear yard (fig. 1.3).[22] Each of the ancillary buildings was carefully framed, covered with beaded siding and shingles, and (except for the smokehouse) plastered inside. Attention to the quality of support buildings was a mark of success on many post-Revolutionary farmsteads of such status, far more common in 1820 than before the war. On farms of this scale, the very existence of work buildings that survive today is a phenomenon of the nineteenth century.[23]

A useful contrast to Croxton is found in the Ferguson family living in the southern Tidewater's Southampton County, the scene of Nat Turner's slave revolt. By 1802 Dixon Ferguson had inherited a hundred-acre plantation on which he grew peas and sweet potatoes and raised swine. For the next twenty years, he acquired no new land and maintained ownership of three slaves—more slaves than 70 percent of the county's personal property holders. In 1820 Ferguson's hundred acres placed him in the bottom third of Southampton's landowners (fig. 1.4). Ferguson increased his landholdings between 1820 and 1825, about the time he built a new single-room-plan house for his family. He died in 1825, and five years later his widow, Rebecca, lived on 320 acres—a plantation that ranked the estate in the seventy-fourth percentile of landowners. The widow Ferguson also had six enslaved laborers—a total that placed her in the top 10 percent of the county's slaveholders. The family continued to occupy the same small house until they sold the property in 1848.[24]

The Fergusons' house lacked the embellish-

Fig. 1.3. Carter Croxton House and Outbuildings, Essex County, Virginia. Edward Chappell. Courtesy of Colonial Williamsburg Foundation.

ments that Croxton created, but its first-floor room was respectably finished (fig. 1.5). There were generously proportioned glazed windows downstairs, plastered walls, exposed ceiling framing, chairboards, and double architraves around the openings. The attic room was largely unfinished, much like the interior of the nearby kitchen. The Fergusons' house had 324 square feet on the first floor, and the kitchen had 328.

More representative of Southampton housing is the home of Martha Channell. She was a widow in 1810 when the tax lists indicate that she owned 77 acres and two horses. The county's median landholding was 150 acres, and the typical personal property holder had a single steed (fig. 1.4, table 1.1). At 7 shillings and 8 pence an acre, her land was also valued below the median county rate of 9 shillings and 8 pence. By 1820 Channell's landholding had not changed, but the value of her house and other structures had risen to $200, the median value of buildings in Southampton.[25]

It was in the decade 1810–20 that Martha Channell apparently built her permanent house (fig. 1.5). This too had a single room on the first floor, slightly larger than the Fergusons' with 360

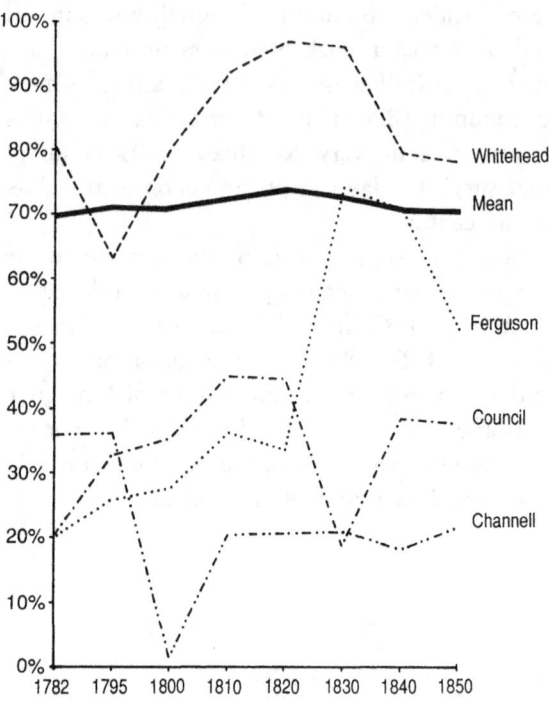

Fig. 1.4. Comparative Size of Four Southampton County Properties. The chart includes property histories beyond the date of ownerships described in this chapter. Jeffrey Bostetter and Mark R. Wenger. Courtesy of Colonial Williamsburg Foundation.

Table 1.1
Comparative Size of Four Southampton County Properties

	1782	1795	1800	1810	1820	1830	1840	1850
Whitehead	451.00	260.00	385.00	727.62	1244.62	1245.12	461.00	461.00
Mean	335.23	305.82	301.71	273.06	291.24	307.68	352.12	370.35
Ferguson	100.00	100.00	100.00	100.00	100.00	320.50	320.50	211.50
Median	217.00	198.00	192.00	150.00	159.50	161.00	193.00	202.50
Council	100.00	130.00	130.00	129.50	143.50	55.00	143.50	143.50
Channell	165.00	149.00	9.00	67.00	67.00	63.00	63.00	68.00

Wealth and Houses in Post-Revolutionary Virginia 11

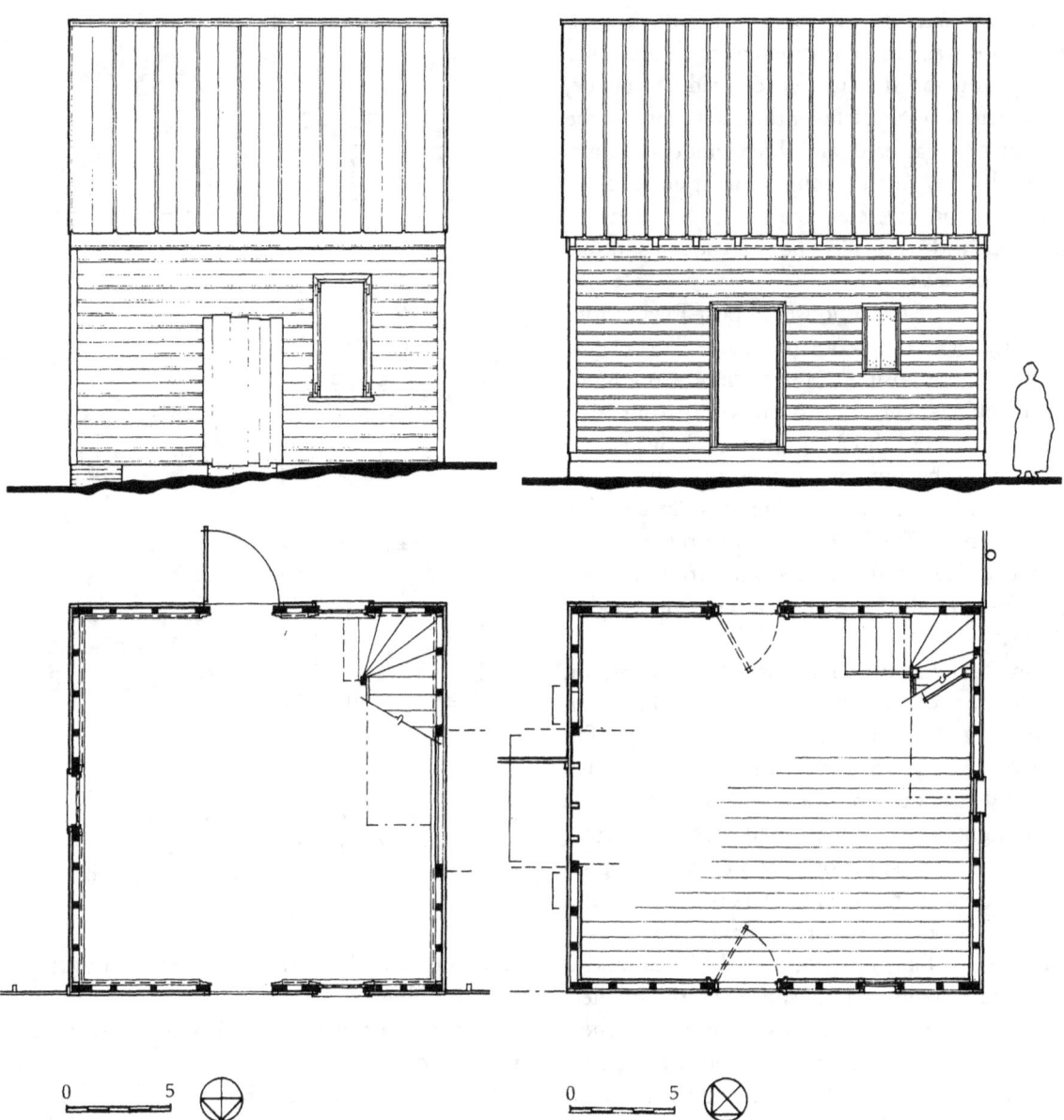

Fig. 1.5. Dixon Ferguson House (left), Martha Channell House (right), Southampton County, Virginia. Jeffrey Bostetter. Courtesy of Colonial Williamsburg Foundation.

square feet, and a second room in the attic. Again, the house was well-constructed, with a proper sawn and tenoned frame, beaded siding outside, and carefully planed trim within. Yet, none of the interior was plastered, and three windows admitted a relatively small amount of light downstairs. These apertures were as small as 1 foot, 8 inches by 3 feet, with vertically sliding wooden shutters rather than sash.

Many landowners' houses in post-Revolutionary Virginia were inferior to Channell's, but few survive. A composite picture of these more modest dwellings can be constructed from two sources: details about surviving kitchens and other more cheaply built ancillary buildings that were examined and analyzed in the course of this project and evidence for the continued use of wooden chimneys and frames with earthfast posts, ground-laid sills, or sills raised on wooden blocks.[26]

One tantalizing remnant is a little round-log building constructed by the small Southampton landowner Amos Council about 1810–25 (fig. 1.6). Measuring 18 feet by 14 feet, it may have been either a kitchen or a house. The low walls sit on light brick footings, and there is a brick-lined root cellar superior to those archaeologists have excavated in large numbers of quarters and kitchens around the Chesapeake. There is a single short door, hung on wood hinges, and 2 very mean windows, both shuttered, the smallest measuring only 5 inches by 1 foot, 8 inches. Rather than a brick or framed wooden chimney, the building previously had a smoke bay at one end, with a clapboard and plaster hood directing smoke out through the roof, much like a later example at Road View Farm in New Kent County recorded by the Historic American Buildings Survey in the 1930s. While the building lacks all the self-conscious refinements of the Fergusons' house and Martha Channell's house, it was carefully crafted with skinned logs and planed boards, not thrown together in a few days like

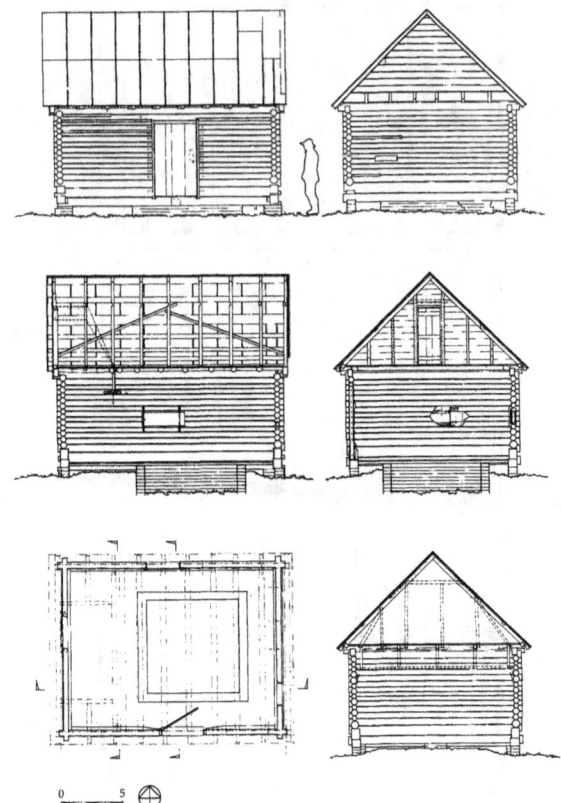

Fig. 1.6. Amos Council Kitchen or House, Southampton County, Virginia. Jeffrey Bostetter. Courtesy of Colonial Williamsburg Foundation.

some eighteenth-century quarters and agricultural buildings.[27]

Amos Council had 141.5 acres of relatively poor land when he put up his log structure (fig. 1.4, table 1.1). In 1820 the total value of buildings on his property was assessed at $150. The median value of structures in Southampton at this time was $200, and the average was $351.08. We assume that this was the Councils' kitchen, and that roughly $100 would buy a better dwelling. But the possibility of the round-log building being the family's house remains.[28]

The annual tax rolls also indicate that women made building choices to a remarkable degree.

About a third of the middling houses studied were built or transformed by women following the deaths of their more parsimonious husbands.[29] Maria Widgeon was born at Pear Valley about 1800, and spent most of her life there. Yet, it was only after the death of her husband in 1837 that she remodeled the house. She removed the cooking space to a separate building, added a small wing, and reworked the attic to create two bedchambers where there had previously been one—all at about the same time she built a new granary (fig. 1.1). The improvements reflected the rising standards of a farm family that had maintained essentially static upper-middling status since the second quarter of the eighteenth century. Until Widgeon remodeled this structure, her family lived in a house that was functionally more modest than the early-nineteenth-century dwellings which less successful residents of Southampton County, such as Martha Channell and the Ferguson family, called home. Like most of these women, she took advantage of her new independence. Widgeon chose to live out her life in the remodeled Pear Valley and did not remarry.[30]

Sally Jordan's house in Isle of Wight County was more pretentious in its elaboration. Jordan inherited a single-room plan, story-and-a-half house when her husband died in 1804. William Jordan had owned a 393-acre tract in 1800, sufficient to place him in the top 13 percent of the county's landowners. Three years later his slave force totaled thirty-one individuals, including a cooper. During his lifetime, Jordan probably depended on Isle of Wight's staple forest products—tar, pitch, turpentine, and lumber—as well as field crops to provide for his family. Individuals who produced naval stores needed labor and large landholdings in order to make a profit.[31]

It is difficult to know if the 352-square-foot house functioned as the Jordan home or as a tenement before the husband's death. It seems extremely small for a slave-owning family with nine children, but other families of this size crowded into the same amount of space. With a paneled fireplace wall, too, it would have been exceptionally well-finished for an ordinary tenement. No one has yet presented evidence to demonstrate that size of families rather than their wealth significantly affected the scale of houses in early America.

The widow Jordan made the house her own and expanded it dramatically, adding a new two-story front block with a single room and passage on the first floor and two rooms above. Jordan then had perhaps four bedchambers and a parlor, conceivably with a dining room in the cellar or in a separate building.[32]

The first-floor space was not particularly large: 929 square feet. However, Jordan's attention to interior details turned it into a model dwelling for a middling family. The house had many of the genteel conceits of a great eighteenth-century house: dentil or modillion cornices inside and out, a wooden arch over the stairway, decorated overmantels in the parlor and best bedchamber, pilasters on the lower fireplace projection, and proper paneled doors (fig. 1.7). She did not have a buffet for display of tablewares, but there was a pair of closets, one intended for hanging clothes on pegs, the other for storage of housewares on shelves.

Sally Jordan seems to have created her miniature mansion between 1810 and 1820. In the same decade her acreage increased from 81 acres to 168 acres (due to the death of several of her husband's heirs). The widow Jordan reduced her slaveholding from 18 people to 9, probably by transferring possession of 9 workers to her sons. Jordan was among the top 15 percent of Isle of Wight's personal property holders, based on the number of slaves and horses, and the top 45 percent on acres of land. Her land was of higher quality than most, and in 1830 the buildings on her property were valued at $1,500, far above the median of $200 among Isle of Wight's real property holders.[33]

A final Southampton County example permits comparison of a more successful widow's career

Fig. 1.7. Sally Jordan House, Isle of Wight County, Virginia. Willie Graham. Courtesy of Colonial Williamsburg Foundation.

with land and buildings comparable to Carter Croxton's in Essex. John Whitehead paid £200 for a 260-acre farm with an existing house and moved there with his new wife, Catherine, in 1795. That year his acreage placed him ahead of 60 percent of Southampton's landholders (fig. 1.4, table 1.1), but he had no slaves when the typical property holder had two. By 1800 Whitehead had 4 enslaved workers and 385 acres, raising his relative position within the upper half of the county's planters in both categories. Whitehead prospered and bought more land and slaves until he owned 727.62 acres and 12 people in 1810. This planter died in 1814, leaving his wife with control of the entire estate.[34]

Catherine Whitehead continued to turn a profit and to purchase more land—she paid $1,200 for two tracts in 1816, and by 1820 she owned 1244.62 acres, placing her in the top 4 percent of Southampton's landowners. The same year, 1820, she paid taxes on 10 slaves when half of Southampton's taxpayers owned a maximum of 3 slaves. In the 1820s she acquired more workers rather than investing in additional land. She owned 29 people in 1830, a year before she, 5 of her children, and a grandchild were killed on their farm by Nat Turner's followers.[35]

County assessors placed the value of Catherine Whitehead's buildings at $800 in both 1820 and 1830, in the top 12 percent of the structures in the county. The figure was high because of the sizable number of outbuildings and the substantial nature of her house. Sometime between 1815 and 1820, she had carried out a wholesale transformation of the home she had occupied with John Whitehead and their children. The old house had had two rooms on the first floor—a hall and rear chamber—and a second chamber in the attic. She nearly doubled the size (from 486 square feet to 828 on the first floor) by adding a side wing with two rooms on the first floor and another in the attic.

Clearly she desired to increase significantly the spaces occupied by herself and her children, and to create a more refined environment in general. The two new first-floor rooms had higher ceilings, and the old spaces as well as the additions were newly finished with woodwork and plaster. Neighbors who inventoried her possessions after her death called the old front room the "hall," and they listed a "dining room" with a carpet, apparently the old rear bedchamber. The larger of the new rooms, provided with a fireplace and fitted out much like the hall, appears to have been her bedchamber, while the three other bedchambers, for use by her eleven children, were more plainly finished and left unheated. Whitehead resheathed the outside of the house with beaded weatherboards, boxed the old exposed eaves, and covered the once-visible ceiling framing with plaster. Yet, both the house and outbuildings lacked the extreme sense of order seen at Croxton's farmstead and failed to provide any system for enforcing seclusion. The new house had a single stair and no passage, so family members had to pass through one another's bedchambers to reach theirs, or have others pass through en route to their own.

While some differences in the size and quality of houses reflected the personal preferences of builders, other variations were a product of the economic distinctions within the region. Analysis of land and personal property tax lists demonstrates that housing standards within Tidewater Virginia were tied to varying degrees of economic opportunity in the early nineteenth century. The combination of tax lists and United States Federal Census returns provides some insight into wealth distribution. Slaveholding became more concentrated in the hands of Charles City County's richest planters—the top 10 percent of taxpayers in this county held 48.4 percent (1,398 out of 2,890) of the enslaved laborers in 1782, and 73 percent (2,199 out of 3,012) in 1820. The perceived lack of opportunity for economic improvement led some white Tidewater residents to migrate to western areas of the Old Dominion and outside its borders. This movement provided a chance for some of the individuals who stayed behind to become landowners or to add to their real property holdings. Southampton County experienced a 16 percent population decrease between 1830 and 1850. During the same period of time, the median landholding increased from 161 acres to 202.50 acres.[36] Residents of Piedmont, Goochland, and Chesterfield Counties used capital from tobacco and wheat production and mining to invest in transportation projects (such as the Upper Appomattox Company, the James River and Kanawha Canal, and the railroad) and the Bank of Richmond.[37]

Land tax lists began to specify building valuations in 1820, and a sizable percentage of the assessed buildings in Essex, Northampton, Southampton, and Westmoreland Counties were between $101 and $500 (fig. 1.8). This range, which included reasonably substantial single-room and proper hall-and-chamber houses, was consistently greater than *assessed* buildings under $101 or over $500, though building assemblages below $101 are probably underreported. In general, the middle tier increased slightly from those at the bottom rung. Interestingly, the lowest percentages of the middle category were in Essex County, where the survival rate is quite good for such buildings, and the highest were in Northampton on the Eastern Shore. It is likely that the surviving buildings were well-constructed and met the housing needs of the people who later occupied them. Between 1821 and 1830, $101 to $500 building valuations in Essex rose modestly from 41.3 percent to 43.6 percent, while valuations below $101 declined from 33.2 percent to 24.1 percent. Other groups of reported valuations remained relatively static in these four counties between 1820 and 1830, with the largest proportions of poor buildings remaining around 37 percent to 38 percent in Southampton. The increased valuations represented both new construction—usually indicated by a note on the tax list—and improvements to existing structures. A decreased value usually reflected the fact that fire destroyed a portion of a dwelling house or an outbuilding.[38]

A synthesis of architectural and documentary evidence demonstrates that the transformation of housing standards had varying complexions within the Chesapeake region, but it was sufficiently broad to be properly called a revolution. A wide range of people from the middling rank participated. Some rich Virginians in the new re-

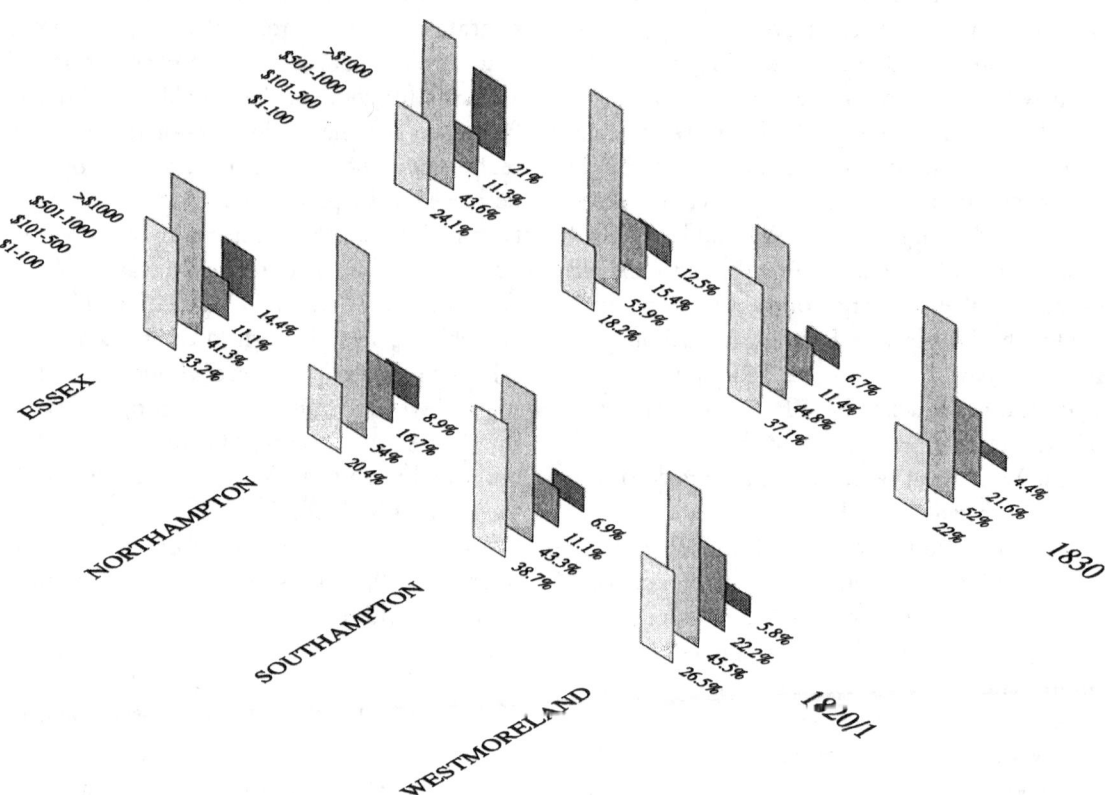

Fig. 1.8. Building Evaluations for Four Tidewater Virginia Counties in 1820–21 and 1830. Mark R. Wenger. Courtesy of Colonial Williamsburg Foundation.

public still lived in small houses with a handful of rooms which would not meet middle-class expectations by the time of the Civil War. On the other hand, far more men and women occupying ranks around the middle of Virginia's landholders—such as Carter Croxton, Sally Jordan, and Catherine Whitehead—began to use available funds to build or remodel existing small houses nearly as well-crafted as those of their gentry neighbors.

Stewart Blumin and other historians argue that the American middle class was a self-conscious urban creation of mid-nineteenth-century professionals.[39] The housing revolution that swept most of the new American nation earlier in the nineteenth century was, by this definition, not middle class. Perhaps this is underscored by the fact that much of the material transformation in Tidewater Virginia had to do with building houses that were permanent and refined in quality, yet much smaller than those which Blumin's urban professionals sought to occupy. The chief change was in the quality of buildings rather than in their size. And most of the Virginians who made the move were farmers largely dependent upon slave labor, not urban professionals.

Yet, the rise of "vernacular gentility" that Richard Bushman proposes (but never really defines) is expressed in the new houses of these materially assertive men and women.[40] Martha Channell and Dixon Ferguson were two of the many residents of the Tidewater region who strove to redefine themselves as respectable and to distance their families from the materially deprived who constituted more of the population than the tax lists overtly suggest.

"Blumin's Law" posits that all historians find the action at the center of their own era of study, preceded and followed by calm. Perhaps it would be more useful to recognize the continuity of change in material life, extending from the scattered and slower developments of the eighteenth century through the creation of model middle-class housing in the following century. The broader change evident in the new republic and the samples in Tidewater Virginia are a fundamental chapter in this story.

The years after the American Revolution saw rising expectations among property owners, manifest in the creation of refined and permanent houses and often accompanied by simpler but equally durable work buildings. The growing ability and desire of more people to house their families in such secure and self-conscious settings represents a quickening in the pace of social change in early America. Ultimately, the development of this expectation may be as important in class formation as the particular time and manner in which people acquired the means to build their dreams.

Notes

The authors wish to thank Barbara and Cary Carson, Willie Graham, Orlando Ridout V, Lorena S. Walsh, and Mark R. Wenger for assistance with this essay. Vanessa Patrick and Donna Hole conducted early stages of documentary research. The project has been supported by grants from the National Endowment for the Humanities and the Graham Foundation for Advanced Studies in the Fine Arts, as well as by budgeted funds from the Colonial Williamsburg Foundation.

1. Rhys Isaac, *The Transformation of Virginia, 1740–1790* (Chapel Hill: Univ. of North Carolina Press, 1982); Dell Upton, *Holy Things and Profane: Anglican Parish Churches in Colonial Virginia* (Cambridge, Mass.: MIT Press for the Architectural History Foundation, 1986); Camille Wells, "The Planter's Prospect: Houses, Outbuildings, and Rural Landscapes in Eighteenth-Century Virginia," *Winterthur Portfolio* 28 (Spring 1993): 1–31; Edward A. Chappell, "Housing a Nation,"

in *Of Consuming Interests: The Style of Life in the Eighteenth Century,* ed. Cary Carson, Ronald Hoffman, and Peter J. Albert (Charlottesville and London: Univ. Press of Virginia for the United States Capitol Historical Society, 1994), 167–232; Henry Glassie, *Folk Housing in Middle Virginia: A Structural Analysis of Historic Artifacts* (Knoxville: Univ. of Tennessee Press, 1975).

2. The counties are Accomack, Amherst, Campbell, Charles City, Chesterfield, Essex, Goochland, Hanover, Isle of Wight, King and Queen, Mecklenburg, Nansemond (present-day Suffolk), Northampton, Prince George, Southampton, Warwick (present-Newport News), and Westmoreland. Fifty-eight sites have been studied in detail, drawn from a larger group selected for their relative completeness, often endangered quality, and geographic distribution. Additional sites studied in Maryland are omitted from the present analysis. Reports including analysis of physical evidence and documentary research are available for all the sites studied.

3. P. J. Corfield, "Class by Name and Number in Eighteenth-Century Britain," *History* 22 (234) (Feb. 1987): 38–61; Gordon S. Wood, *The Radicalism of the American Revolution* (New York: Alfred A. Knopf, 1992), 21, 23, 136, 347–69; Richard L. Bushman, *The Refinement of America: Persons, Houses, Cities* (New York: Alfred A. Knopf, 1992); Kevin P. Kelly, "Was There an American Common Man? The Case in Colonial Virginia," in *Common People and Their Material World: Free Men and Women in the Chesapeake, 1700–1830,* ed. David Harvey and Gregory Brown (Williamsburg: Colonial Williamsburg Foundation, 1995), 107–13.

4. For a similar definition of middling people, see Daniel W. Crofts, *Old Southampton: Politics and Society in a Virginia County, 1834–1869* (Charlottesville and London: Univ. Press of Virginia, 1992), 11–14. Joan E. Cashin uses the ownership of at least twenty slaves as the definition of the planter class in her book, *A Family Venture: Men and Women on the Southern Frontier* (New York and Oxford: Oxford Univ. Press, 1991), 7. See also Allan Kulikoff, *Tobacco and Slaves: The Development of Southern Cultures in the Chesapeake, 1680–1800* (Chapel Hill: Univ. of North Carolina Press for the Institute of Early American History and Culture, 1986), 128, for a definition of a "middling planter" as the owner of a few hundred acres and a few slaves.

5. For an English perspective on the middle ranks of a largely nonslaveholding society, see Jonathan Barry and Christopher Brooks, eds., *The Middling Sort of People: Culture, Society and Politics in England, 1550–1800* (Houndmills: MacMillan, 1994). For extensive analysis of landownership by free blacks in one Tidewater parish, see Caroline Julia Richter, "A Community and its Neighborhoods: Charles Parish, York County, Virginia, 1630–1740," (Ph.D. diss., College of William and Mary, 1992), chap. 8 (which carries the subject past 1740).

6. Kulikoff, *Tobacco and Slaves,* and Lorena S. Walsh, *"To Labour for Profit": Plantation Management in the Chesapeake, 1620–1820* (Charlottesville and London: Univ. Press of Virginia, forthcoming). The number of heads of households with land is based on a comparison of the number of landholders (from the various land tax lists) and the number of families (from several Federal Census population schedules). Julie Richter, "The Economic Prospects of Residents of Tidewater Virginia, 1782 to 1850," paper presented at the Southern Historical Association annual conference, New Orleans, November 1995.

7. Sometimes wills and inventories contain details about outbuildings which do not survive today and about the ways in which occupants furnished and used the rooms in their houses and their ancillary structures. For example, the 1832 inventory of Catherine Whitehead's estate noted that the house had a hall and a carpet in the dining room. She might have had different buildings for cooking and washing clothes, since the kitchen equipment and

the laundry equipment were separate entries in the inventory. See Southampton County Wills (11) 40–41, ordered Dec. 22, 1831, dated Jan. 3, 1832 and recorded Jan. 21, 1832, Southampton County Courthouse, Courtland, Va. (unless noted otherwise, all county court records are located at the courthouse in the respective county). See below for a discussion of Catherine Whitehead's house and outbuildings.

8. Dell Upton, "The Virginia Parlor, National Museum of American History, Smithsonian Institution: A Report on the Henry Saunders House and Its Occupants," July 1, 1981.

9. The land and personal property tax lists that historian Jackson T. Main used to identify the one hundred wealthiest Virginians in the 1780s also can be used to learn about the real and personal holdings of other inhabitants of the Old Dominion. See Jackson T. Main, "The One Hundred," *William and Mary Quarterly,* 3d ser., 11 (1954): 354–84.

10. While the number of buildings popularly identified as "colonial" seems infinite, only rarely do counties well-populated in the seventeenth and eighteenth centuries have more than half a dozen credible pre-Revolutionary houses still standing.

11. The square feet of this and other buildings discussed here are measured as interior space, rather than exterior shape.

12. Northampton County Deeds, Wills, Etc. No. 21 (1718–25) 125–26, dated Dec. 16, 1720, and recorded June 14, 1721, Northampton County Courthouse, Eastville, Va.; H. R. McIlwaine et al., eds., *Executive Journals of the Council of Colonial Virginia,* 6 vols., (Richmond: Virginia State Library, 1927–66), 4: 238, 286, 335; Herman J. Heikkenen, "The Last Year of Tree Growth for Selected Timbers Within Pear Valley as Derived by Key-Year Dendrochronology," (unpublished report, Dendrochronology, Inc., 1993). Planters on the Eastern Shore of Virginia began to plant corn instead of tobacco in the early eighteenth century. Walsh, *To Labour for Profit*; Cary Carson, Norman F. Barka, William M. Kelso, Garry Wheeler Stone, and Dell Upton, "Impermanent Architecture in the Southern American Colonies," *Winterthur Portfolio* 16 (Summer/Autumn 1981): 171, 173–75.

13. William Meade, *Old Churches, Ministers, and Families of Virginia* (Philadelphia, 1857), 2: 153; Sherwin McRae and Raleigh Colston, eds., *Calendar of Virginia State Papers and Other Manuscripts, from Jan. 1, 1794 to May 16, 1795, Preserved in the Capitol at Richmond* (Richmond: Superintendent of Public Printing, 1888), 7; 377–78; Peter J. Albert, "The Protean Institution: The Geography, Economy, and Ideology of Slavery in Post-Revolutionary Virginia," (Ph.D. diss., Univ. of Maryland, 1976), 29, 31, 93; Walsh, *To Labour for Profit.*

14. Herman J. Heikkenen, "The Last Year of Tree Growth for Selected Timbers Within the Mason House as Derived by Key-Year Denrochronology," (unpublished report, Dendrochronology Inc., 1990); Rind, ed., *Virginia Gazette,* Sept. 1, 1774; Dixon, ed., *Virginia Gazette,* Apr. 18, 1777.

15. Charles City County Orders (1737–51) Apr. 1740, p. 121, Library of Virginia, Richmond, Va. Tyree probably relied on tobacco as his main crop because he owned land along a river, the location of the best acreage in the Tidewater.

16. Accomack County Deeds, Wills, Etc. (1715–1729), 410–11, dated Jan. 22, 1721/22 and recorded Apr. 16, 1722, Accomack County Courthouse, Accomack, Va.; *William and Mary Quarterly,* 2d ser., 8 (1928): 36–38; Paul G. E. Clemens, *The Atlantic Economy and Colonial Maryland's Eastern Shore: From Tobacco to Grain* (Ithaca, N.Y.: Cornell Univ. Press, 1980).

17. See, for example, Orlando Ridout V, "Re-editing the Architectural Past: A Comparison of Surviving Physical and Documentary Evidence on Maryland's Eastern Shore," in *'A Singular List of Buildings': American Architecture and Landscape at the End of the Eighteenth Century,* ed. Bernard L. Herman and Michael Steinitz (Knoxville: Univ.

18. Present-day survival is not a direct reflection of the durability of buildings constructed two hundred or three hundred years ago. We are beginning to recognize that seventeenth-century Virginia houses could indeed be substantially built; some were doomed by their perceived social shortcomings rather than by the flimsiness of their walls. The relatively large numbers of apparently pre-1750 houses on Virginia's Eastern Shore and Princess Anne County (part of present-day Virginia Beach) at the mouth of the James River may have more to do with the economy of those areas in the nineteenth century than with more vigorous building impulses. The most extensive groups of surviving post-Revolutionary rural houses are in Tidewater counties like Southampton, Isle of Wight, and Sussex, south of the James River. While such areas did see extensive development of farms in the late eighteenth and early nineteenth centuries, the extent of the sample may reflect the survival of middling farms into the twentieth century more than the relative strength of the area's building boom in the new republic. The appearance of late-eighteenth- and early-nineteenth-century buildings—glazed windows and plastered walls, for example—also suggests that the builders put up houses which fulfilled the material expectations of their nineteenth- and twentieth-century occupants.

19. A number of scholars have examined the shift of tobacco production from Tidewater Virginia to the Piedmont section of the Old Dominion. See, for example, Carson et al., "Impermanent Architecture," 171, 173–75; Richard R. Beeman, *The Evolution of the Southern Backcountry: A Case Study of Lunenburg County, Virginia, 1746–1832* (Philadelphia: Univ. of Pennsylvania Press, 1984); Alison Goodyear Freehling, *Drift Toward Dissolution: The Virginia Slavery Debate of 1831–1832* (Baton Rouge and London: Louisiana State Univ. Press, 1982), chap. 2; Lynda J. Morgan, *Emancipation in Virginia's Tobacco Belt, 1850–1870* (Athens and London: Univ. of Georgia Press, 1992), chap. 1.

20. Edward A. Chappell, "Interpreting Bermuda's Architecture," *Bermuda Journal of Archaeology and Maritime History* 6 (1994): 148.

21. John Croxton left his real property to his eldest son, Carter, in 1775. The inventory of his estate included eight slaves, and it is likely that Carter gained possession of some of these people. Essex County Wills (13), dated July 31, 1775, and recorded Dec. 18, 1775, pp. 32–33; ibid., pp. 81–83, ordered Dec. 1775, dated Dec. 18, 1775, and recorded Dec. 20, 1775, Essex County Courthouse, Tappahannock, Va. For a discussion of agriculture in Essex, see James B. Slaughter, *Settlers, Southerners, Americans: The History of Essex County, Virginia 1608–1984* (Salem, W.Va.: Don Mills, 1985), 114–16. Walsh notes that most planters in the Rappahannock Basin shifted to grains in the early 1790s and that the soil in this area was particularly good for grains. Walsh, *To Labour for Profit*.

22. Presumably there was a kitchen there as well, but the present kitchen was newly built in the third quarter of the nineteenth century.

23. Archaeological excavations have shown that eighteenth-century ancillary buildings, even in the mansion yards of large landowners like James Bray II (at his plantation in James City County) and Peyton Randolph (at his Williamsburg home), could have earthfast frames or frames partially supported by earthfast stumps. William M. Kelso, *Kingsmill Plantations, 1619–1800: Archaeology of Country Life in Colonial Virginia* (Orlando: Academic Press, 1984), 104–6; Randolph excavations by Colonial Williamsburg Foundation, 1982–85 and 1995.

24. Southampton County Land Tax Lists, 1802, 1810, 1820, 1822, and 1830; Southampton County Personal Property Tax Lists, 1802, 1810, 1820, and 1830, Library of Va. (all land and personal property tax lists consulted are at the Library of Va.); Southampton County Deeds (18) dated Aug.

22, 1820, and recorded Nov. 19, 1820, pp. 253–54; Southampton County Deeds (19) dated and recorded Feb. 17, 1823, pp. 77–78; Southampton County Wills (9) dated Oct. 18, 1825, and recorded Nov. 21, 1825, pp. 289–90. Only a small number of Southampton's planters grew tobacco or wheat. Crofts, *Old Southampton,* 78, 81–90.

25. Southampton County Land Tax and Personal Property Lists, 1810 and 1820.

26. Houses with wooden chimneys remained occupied by poor people in numerous rural Chesapeake communities around 1900, though they were diminishing with sufficient speed to make them a popular subject to photographers with an eye for picturesque poverty. Most have now disappeared, along with houses on earthfast wooden footings, though the archaeological record of all these archaic constructions remains strong. Architect Benjamin Henry Latrobe sketched a number of cheaply built Virginia houses, like "Wm. Robertson's house near his quarry on Acquia Creek" in 1806. See *Latrobe's View of America, 1795–1820: Selections from the Watercolors and Sketches,* ed. Edward C. Carter, et al. (New Haven: Yale Univ. Press, 1985), 270–71.

27. Chesapeake documents seldom provide direct evidence for the amount of time employed in the construction of modest late-eighteenth-century buildings. Read together, however, certain records left by rich planters suggest the brief time invested in constructing quarters and agricultural buildings. See, for example, *The Diary of Colonel Landon Carter of Sabine Hall, 1752–1778,* ed. Jack P. Greene, 2 vols. (Richmond: Virginia Historical Society, 1987), II: 855–56, entry dated Sept. 3, 1774, concerning enslaved men and women to "knock up a set of log houses"; Daybook, Jan. 13, 1787–Feb. 20, 1788, Robert Carter Papers, Library of Congress (Oct.–Nov. 1787 entries concerning construction of corn and meat houses on a tenanted property); agreement between Robert Carter and carpenter Robert Hall for a corn house, June 28, 1789, Carter Papers, Virginia Historical Society; Robert Carter Letter Books, vol. 9 (July 1789–July 1792), Duke Univ. Library (concerning repairs and addition to a tenement and construction of smokehouse and corn house, 1791).

28. Southampton County Land Tax Lists, 1810, 1820, and 1830.

29. We recognize that this figure is unlikely to be broadly representative, but it suggests much more active involvement by women in Chesapeake building than has been previously assumed.

30. Northampton County Wills, Etc. No. 38 (1829–53), dated June 28, 1837, and recorded Dec. 11, 1837, pp. 72–73; Northampton County Deeds No. 37 (1867–71) dated July 8, 1867, and recorded Aug. 12, 1867, pp. 83–84; Northampton County Land Tax Lists, 1839 and 1840. Many of Petersburg's widows, especially the wealthier ones, also chose not to remarry. Poorer widows' lives were more precarious, and they were more likely to remarry. Maria Widgeon and the other female builders studied in the course of this project were widows when they began to construct a new house or to make improvements to their dwellings. They remained widows for the rest of their lives. The sex ratio was almost equal in the counties of Northampton and Southampton (home of Martha Channell and Catherine Whitehead—see below). Isle of Wight's Sally Jordan faced slightly higher odds because females outnumbered males by a few hundred in the early nineteenth century. Suzanne Lebsock, *The Free Women of Petersburg: Status and Culture in a Southern Town, 1784–1860* (New York: W. W. Norton, 1984), 25–27, 39; Julie Richter, "Women and the Housing Revolution in Eastern Virginia, 1782–1850," paper presented at the Berkshire Conference on the History of Women, Chapel Hill, N.C., June 1996. For information on the sex ratio see the Population Schedule of the Third Census of the United States, 1810; Population Schedule of the Fourth Census of the United States, 1820; Population Schedule of the Fifth Census of the United States, 1830; Population Schedule of the Sixth Census of the United

31. Albert, "The Protean Institution," 43, 93. The Jordan family probably did not fall into Isle of Wight's upper tier of residents because of the size of the house and the fact that William Jordan was not referred to as "Mr." or as "Esquire." It is likely that Jordan's widow sold some of his slaves to raise funds to cover the £345..18..10 and three farthings that she owed to the estate. The widow Jordan paid taxes on 18 slaves in 1810. Isle of Wight County Wills (12) dated Apr. 13, 1804, and recorded Aug. 1, 1808, pp. 494–97; and Isle of Wight County Wills (12) dated Feb. 27, 1807, and recorded Jan. 4, 1808, pp. 422–23; Isle of Wight County Courthouse, Isle of Wight, Va.; Isle of Wight County Personal Property Tax List, 1810.

32. Lucian E. M. Wills lived in the house prior to his death in 1868, and his inventory lists the "dining and cooking room" and a "piazza" as well as rooms on the second floor above the parlor and over the passage. The ell room, the parlor, and a passage were on the first floor. Isle of Wight County Wills (29), dated Sept. 22, 1868, and recorded Dec. 7, 1868, p. 395; Isle of Wight County Wills (30) dated Oct. 20, 1868, and recorded Jan. 2, 1871, pp. 44–46.

33. Isle of Wight County Land and Personal Property Tax Lists, 1810 and 1820.

34. Southampton County Deeds (8) dated Jan. 7, 1795, and recorded Jan. 8, 1795, pp. 155–56; Southampton County Wills (7) dated May 22, 1814, and recorded Mar. 20, 1815, pp. 438–39; Southampton County Land and Personal Property Tax Lists, 1795, 1800, and 1810.

35. Southampton County Deeds (15) dated Feb. 5, 1816, and recorded Mar. 18, 1816, pp. 23–24; Southampton County Deeds (15), dated Feb. 5, 1816, and recorded Apr. 15, 1816, pp. 24–26; Southampton County Land and Personal Property Tax Lists, 1820 and 1830; Stephen B. Oates, *The Fires of Jubilee: Nat Turner's Fierce Rebellion* (New York: Harper and Row, 1975), 83–86, 88, 89, 135.

36. Population Schedule of the Fifth Census of the United States, 1830; Population Schedule of the Seventh Census of the United States, 1850, Library of Va.; Southampton County Land Tax Lists, 1830 and 1850.

37. Goochland County Land and Personal Property Tax Lists, 1820–50; Chesterfield County Land and Personal Property Tax Lists, 1820–50.

38. The assessment rates for real property remained the same during the 1820s and the 1830s. The next change took place in 1840. Essex County Land Tax Lists, 1821 and 1830; Northampton County Land Tax Lists, 1820 and 1830; Southampton County Land Tax Lists, 1820 and 1830; Westmoreland County Land Tax Lists, 1820 and 1830.

39. Stuart M. Blumin, *The Emergence of the Middle Class: Social Experience in the American City, 1760–1900* (Cambridge: Cambridge Univ. Press, 1989).

40. Bushman, *The Refinement of America*.

CHAPTER 2

Clifton Ellis

Dissenting Faith and Domestic Landscape in Eighteenth-Century Virginia

When Gilbert Hunt, a well-to-do Anglican, decided in the fall of 1782 to build a house on his land in Halifax County, Virginia, he went to see his cousin James Hunt, a local carpenter and Baptist minister who lived nearby. Gilbert Hunt knew what he wanted, and he knew his cousin's building experience. At some point in their conversation, James Hunt opened his account book and sketched a plan of the house he and Gilbert Hunt were discussing (fig. 2.1).

He drew a trim, well-constructed wood-frame house built to one full story with a loft above the joists, a gable roof, and one masonry chimney. The house had one principal room—a hall—that measured eighteen by twenty feet with a fireplace and a closet at one end and a stair to the loft at the other. On the opposite side of the chimney was a chamber which measured eighteen by ten feet, half the size of the hall. Both rooms had two windows and at least one door to the exterior.

When Gilbert and James Hunt had determined matters to their satisfaction, Hunt wrote above the sketch in his most florid hand "Plan of Gilbert Hunts House." He worked on the house through the winter and apparently completed it in the spring of 1783.

The way in which Gilbert Hunt arranged his domestic space is significant. The traditional two-room plan is at odds with what architectural historians of eighteenth-century Virginia expect from a prosperous Anglican planter. Scholars of the period have argued convincingly that the wealthy Tidewater planters adopted the forms and motifs of the Renaissance as ideological statements for their status and power in colonial Virginia. Furthermore, the development in Virginia houses of the central passage as a social channel and barrier and the dining room as a setting for the newly popular rituals of display and hospitality represent the gentry's attempt to dis-

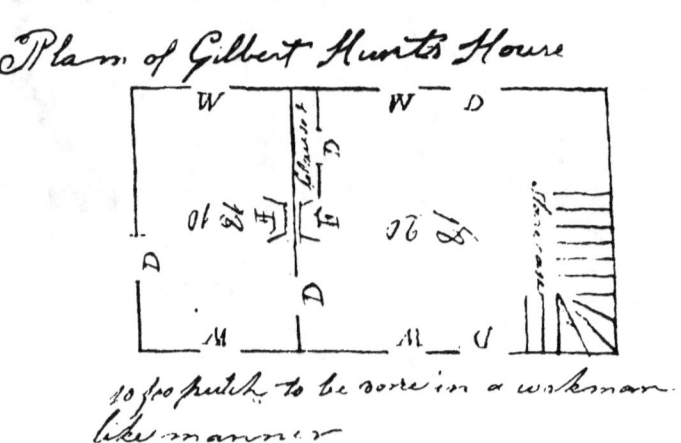

Fig. 2.1. James Hunt's Plan for Gilbert Hunt's House, 1782. Courtesy of the Library of Congress.

tance themselves from middling and lower planters. Thus, the architecture of the Tidewater gentry expressed the ideology of the Anglican ruling class. But Gilbert Hunt was expressing no such ideology when he built his house. Rather, Hunt and other members of Halifax County's Anglican elite found themselves deferring to a very different ideology. By the last quarter of the eighteenth century, the Baptists had made significant gains in Virginia society, and it was the Baptist faith that determined the architectural expression of Halifax County's elite.[1]

Not long ago architectural historians would have characterized the informal, collaborative design process that Gilbert and James Hunt engaged in as being drawn entirely from a local, ostensibly unpretentious architectural tradition termed "vernacular." But recent studies of surviving eighteenth-century Virginia documents and comprehensive surveys of existing eighteenth-century Virginia houses show that a well-built, two-room, and wood-framed house such as Gilbert and James Hunt contemplated was larger and better finished than the houses of most Halifax County residents.

A tax list from the late eighteenth century provides convincing evidence for this conclusion. In 1785, two years after Gilbert Hunt moved into his house, James Bates and twelve other Halifax County justices began enumerating the county's inhabitants and buildings pursuant to an order of the Virginia General Assembly. The purpose of the enumeration was to determine how much money Virginia could raise toward its share of the federal budget. Unlike his fellow justices, who simply tallied heads and counted buildings in their districts, Bates systematically described over one thousand buildings on the farms and plantations in his district, noting the dimensions and construction materials for each structure. Bates's list is a remarkable record of the architectural landscape of Virginia's Piedmont Southside at the close of the eighteenth century, and it provides a context in which to place Gilbert Hunt's house.[2]

Bates recorded no brick houses, and he counted only 5 framed houses in his district. The rest of the houses were built of hewn logs, what Bates called "logwalled" houses. The most common dimension among these houses was 16 by 20 feet, but 77 percent of the houses were smaller. Most dwellings in Bates's district were comparable to Francis Roberts's one-room frame house, which measures 16 feet square and dates from the third quarter of the eighteenth century (fig. 2.2). Of the

141 houses that Bates recorded, Gilbert Hunt's house was larger than 133 of them. To put it another way, Gilbert Hunt's house was larger than 95 percent of the houses in Bates's district.

The unpretentious character of the building stock that Bates described might lead to the conclusion that this was a Piedmont terrain of predominantly small planters. Certainly, Piedmont Virginia was more recently settled than the Tidewater region, and travelers noted the rough conditions of early settlements. While William Byrd II was surveying his land in the Piedmont region during the summer of 1733, he stopped for the night in what he called "a castle containing one dirty room where we were obliged to lodge very sociable in the same apartment with the family. Reckoning women and children, we mustered in all no less than nine persons, who all pigged lovingly together."[3]

With 564 acres, however, Gilbert Hunt was no small landholder. Indeed, 20 percent of Halifax County's landholders owned between four hundred and one thousand acres (table 2.1). In the Tidewater, only 6 percent of the landholders owned the same amount of acreage. Thus, more planters in Halifax County were ranked in terms of wealth than planters in Tidewater, but the houses of the Halifax planters were strikingly unpretentious.

Yet, the landscape that James Bates recorded in 1785 was not that of William Byrd's frontier experience fifty years earlier. In fact, most Virginia planters lived in unpretentious structures like Gilbert Hunt's house. An analysis of houses advertised for sale in the *Virginia Gazette* over the course of the eighteenth century shows that 45 percent of Virginia's landowning planters lived in houses with fewer than the 540 square feet which Gilbert and James Hunt contemplated. Thus, the landscape of Halifax County, like the rest of Virginia, was dominated by one- and two-room houses of one-story pitch built of wood framing or hewn logs and clad with clapboards or weatherboards. Even so, comparisons between planters of comparable means in Piedmont and

Fig. 2.2. Francis Roberts's House, Halifax County, Virginia, 1750–75. Courtesy of Camille Wells.

Tidewater Virginia reveal a significant difference between the landscapes of the two regions.[4]

In Halifax County, for example, Moses Terry owned 500 acres and ranked in the top 12 percent in terms of wealth. He was a member of the Anglican Church and served on the vestry of Antrim Parish for more than 20 years. In 1771 Terry built a one-story frame house near the banks of the Banister River (fig. 2.3). It measures 18 by 32 feet enclosing a hall and chamber with a loft above stairs. Like Gilbert Hunt's house, it was larger than 95 percent of the houses that Bates recorded on his list. William Towles, a Tidewater planter of the same economic means as Terry, built Belle Isle sometime shortly before 1778. It measured 18 by 39 feet—only 7 feet longer than Terry's house (fig. 2.4). Towles, however, built his house to two full stories using brick laid up in the fashionable Flemish bond and he divided the principal rooms of the first floor with a central passage.

Moses Terry was not exceptionally modest in his architectural aspirations. Alexander Shaw, another member of Halifax County's Anglican gentry, who ranked in the top 2 percent in terms of wealth, built a one-story frame house identical to one that James Hunt drew in his account book. It measures 18 by 32 feet and has stone chimneys on each gable end that heated the hall and the chamber as well as the loft above stairs. Later, Shaw added an 8-foot shed bringing the total ground dimensions to 18 by 40 feet (fig. 2.5). In Tidewater, Daniel McCarty, a planter of comparable wealth as Shaw, built Woodford, a central-passage house which measures 21 by 41 feet (fig. 2.6).

Table 2.1

Wealth Structure of Halifax County in 1785 and the Northern Neck of Virginia in 1782

	Landowners Ranked by Acreage					
Acres Owned	No. of Landowners		% of Total		Cumulative %	
	Halifax	Northern Neck	Halifax	Northern Neck	Halifax	Northern Neck
0	403	1,141	26.6	42.3	26.6	42.3
1–99	76	459	5.0	17.0	31.5	59.3
100–199	301	521	19.8	19.3	51.3	78.6
200–399	376	336	24.7	12.5	76.0	91.1
400–599	190	70	12.5	2.6	88.6	93.7
600–999	105	95	6.9	3.5	95.5	97.2
1,000–2,000	46	57	3.0	2.1	98.5	99.3
2,000+	23	20	1.5	.7	100.0	100.0
	1,117	2,699	100.0	100.0		

NOTE: Northern Neck statistics are from Wells, "Planter's Prospect." The Northern Neck of Virginia is a peninsula consisting of Lancaster, Northumberland, Richmond, and Westmoreland Counties. Land Tax Records, Lancaster, Northumberland, Richmond, and Westmoreland Counties, 1782, Virginia State Library and Archives, Richmond. Statistics for Halifax County were compiled by the author from the tax lists from 1782 to 1785.

These comparisons should not lead to the simple assumption that the domestic landscape of Halifax County was smaller than that of Tidewater Virginia. After all, only the wealthiest could afford to divert labor from the tobacco fields and devote it to building a large house. No one would expect to see a house like Westover or Mount Airy in Piedmont Virginia during the eighteenth century. Rather, the comparisons point to a significant difference between the architectural expressions of the Tidewater and Piedmont gentry: there were planters wealthy enough in the Piedmont to build houses like Belle Isle and Woodford, but they chose not to do so. The gentry of Halifax County either did not possess or did not accept the genteel notions of domestic space as did the gentry of Tidewater.[5]

The rearrangement of domestic space to accommodate the gentry's pursuit of a genteel style of life took place in Tidewater after about 1725, when prosperous planters began to abandon the hall-and-chamber plan. The wealthiest planters built houses with symmetrical facades and classical details that reinforced the symmetrical and

Fig. 2.3. Moses Terry's House, Halifax County, Virginia, 1771. Courtesy of Camille Wells.

Fig. 2.4. Belle Isle, Lancaster County, Virginia, 1761–78. Courtesy of the Library of Congress.

hierarchical arrangement of their plantation outbuildings. Gentlemen like John Tayloe of Mt. Airy built their houses with pediments, central passages, and dining rooms that imparted a sense of procession, progression, and restricted access to their lives. Visitors destined for John Tayloe's dining room, the center of gentry social ritual, passed through a series of physical and social barriers. The drive through the park showed the house from a number of angles set upon two terraces. Having gained the first terrace, the visitor climbed another terrace to a flight of stairs leading to a recessed loggia. The front door opened onto a large central passage off which several public rooms, including the dining room, opened.

In all, seven barriers confronted a visitor, and passage through each one signified an increase in his status. This arrangement reinforced the notion that the owner of such a house was at the center of a carefully arranged and deliberately controlled order.[6]

The gentry's houses were the hubs of an economic system that ordered the lives of all Virginians and, as such, were the foci of gentry power. Wealthy planters affirmed their centrality in the landscape and their dominion over it by deliberately arranging their houses, barns, and outbuildings in a hierarchical fashion and by carefully and proudly tending their orchards, crops, and meadows. As early as the 1680s, European trav-

Fig. 2.5. Alexander Shaw's House, Halifax County, Virginia, c. 1780.

elers in Virginia described the plantations they saw as large villages, remarking on the prominence of the planter's houses at the center. This manner of arranging the landscape persisted through the eighteenth century. In 1780 the Marquis de Chastellux wrote that William Byrd's plantation, Westover on the James River, "with its different annexes, has the appearance of a small town and forms a most delightful prospect."[7]

The early Virginia gentry were perhaps at their most persuasive when shaping the landscape in which they and the rest of Virginia society lived, acted, and moved. The most prominent buildings in this landscape were the church, the courthouse, and the houses of the gentry themselves. Members of the gentry made the landscape into a series of ceremonial processionals that emphasized their connections to the institutions of power in the colony. They linked their buildings together by a network of roads, and if they built in an area where public roads already existed, they often altered these roads to suit their own designs. Prominent planters often made a road directly from

Fig. 2.6. Woodford, Richmond County, Virginia, 1750–75. Courtesy of Camille Wells.

their estate to the church. Robert "King" Carter of Lancaster County built such a tree-lined road between his country seat, Corotoman, and the parish church. This deliberately planned landscape expressed the gentry's ideology in which the social and political order was arranged hierarchically—a small elite determined the movement of the majority through both society and the landscape.[8]

When the Rev. Devereux Jarratt wrote his memoirs in 1806, he left a vivid description of the colonial society the Virginia gentry created. The son of a small planter and artisan, Jarratt knew that he ranked well below the elite of the colony. As a youth, he did not question his station in life; indeed, he regarded with awe those who by their dress and manners demonstrated themselves his betters. "We were accustomed to look upon, what were called *gentle folks,* as being of a superior order," wrote Jarratt. "For my part, I was quite shy of *them,* and kept off at a humble distance. A *periwig,* in those days was a distinguishing badge of *gentle folk*—and when I saw a man riding the road near our house, with a wig on, it would so alarm my fears, and give me such a disagreeable feeling, that, I dare say, I would run off, as for my life. Such ideas of the difference between *gentle* and *simple,* were I believe, universal among all of my rank and age."[9]

In Halifax County, the young Jarratt might have been impressed by the substantial houses that well-to-do planters like Gilbert Hunt and Moses Terry built, but it is unlikely that he would have been intimidated by either the room arrangements or the owners. The gentry of Halifax County retained the hall-and-chamber plan. Gilbert Hunt, for instance, planned his staircase right by an outside door. Traffic could pass straight through the hall, making the room part of a thoroughfare. Although the chamber was less public—as it was protected by a door from the hall—this room too had a door to the outside. Both houses are very open to visitors, as well as to the yard surrounding the house. The gentry of Halifax County were decidedly uninterested in differentiating their living space.[10]

When Gilbert Hunt sought out his cousin James Hunt for advice on building a house, there was more than kinship at work. Gilbert Hunt, a member of the Anglican gentry, was consulting a Baptist minister about how to construe the living space in his new house. This encounter is suggestive of what was in fact the case in Halifax County in the late eighteenth century: the Anglican gentry held the institutional power in the county, but the Baptists held social and ideological control.[11]

Gilbert Hunt, Moses Terry, and Alexander Shaw were among the wealthiest men in Halifax County who constituted the Anglican gentry. Unlike their Tidewater counterparts, however, the Halifax County gentry could not lay claim to social or economic status by arranging their domestic space to accommodate the genteel notions of living. Gilbert Hunt acknowledged this, however tacitly, when he consulted his Baptist cousin about building a house. Evangelical religion is thus the key to understanding the differing architectural statements of the Tidewater and Halifax County gentry.

Evangelicalism made its way into Virginia during the 1760s, transforming many Virginians by a profound religious experience. Daniel Marshall and his brother-in-law Elder Shubal Stearns had established a Baptist stronghold in the northern section of North Carolina during the First Great Awakening of the 1740s. From there, they preached and taught the beliefs of the "New Light" Separate Baptists and converted many to their faith. These two Baptist ministers trained a zealous lot of young preachers and in 1758 brought their message to Virginia, the bastion of Anglican culture.[12]

The Separate Baptists had their origins in a blend of pietism and Puritanism preached by George Whitefield and Jonathan Edwards in New England. Pietism emphasizes a Pauline conversion experience, one in which God forces the believer to confront his sinful nature, renounce worldly pleasures, and accept in his heart a personal relationship with Jesus. This notion of salvation was combined with the Puritan doctrine of assurance, which holds that those who are saved must make a witness of themselves to the world. The believer assured himself and his community of his salvation by adhering consistently to an exacting moral code.[13]

Formal theologies such as Calvinism or Arminianism were irrelevant to a faith grounded in pietism. John Leland, a Virginia Baptist preacher of the period, said that among Baptists "some held to predestination, others to universal provision some adhered to confession of faith, others would have none but the Bible some practiced laying on of hands, others did not." A religious experience and moral conduct were the only requirements for membership in the Baptist church. An entry in the minutes of the Roanoke District Association in Virginia's Southside reads: "We believe that Christ's church in her militant state, is not national, but congregational, and that no person young or old, has a right to church membership till regenerated by the power and grace of God—as such alone are they Abraham's spiritual seed, theirs according to the promise."[14]

The regeneration that was so important to the Roanoke Baptists most often occurred at revival meetings. Although preaching was usually a man's prerogative, men and women alike converted to the new faith in a ritual that made no distinction between class or gender. The conversion ritual had three stages. First, the person was "called out" of a sin-filled world by God himself. The individual who was called out usually felt a profound ecstasy when God's Holy Spirit entered a contrite heart. Next, the person made a "profession of faith" and came under the sovereignty of God. Finally, the convert was "filled with grace," a state of new self-awareness, a consciousness of joining the elect of God's kingdom. Possession by the Holy Spirit usually included a highly emotional display in which converts had physical convulsions and uttered incoherently. Contemporary Baptists called the experience an ecstasy, and when the converts regained their senses, they were pronounced "born again." The proof of this salvation experience lay in the converts' conduct thereafter.[15]

The overall theme of Baptist preaching was new birth based on such New Testament texts as Matthew 16:26: "For whosoever will save his life shall not lose it; and whosoever will lose his life for my sake shall find it." Richard Dozier of Westmoreland County noted in his journal in 1771 that "At this time there was scarce a person heard to talk about the new birth in the place." Six years later, however, Dozier judged ministers by their teaching of the new birth experience: "Mr. Brooks showed how people in reproaching religion hated Christ, but he did not preach the Christian experience." The new-birth experience, in Dozier's view, was becoming a standard by which to judge a preacher. Conduct was equally stressed using such New Testament texts as Luke 13:24: "Strive to enter in at the narrow gate, for many I say unto you, will seek to enter in, and shall not be able."[16]

Only those who were truly saved would be welcomed into the church. The Baptist ministers, then, preached for a decision. Unlike the Anglican ministers who moralized in their sermons but asked little of their congregations beyond the responses in the Prayer Book, the Baptist preachers forced each individual in the congregation to make a choice between this world and the one to come. Implicit in this choice was a rejection of the values and lifestyle of the Anglican culture. In effect, these preachers took the question of social differentiation within Virginia and cast it in terms of a moral dilemma. The question for a Baptist was not "Are you a gentleman or a common planter?" The questions were "Are you saved or lost?" and "How do you measure in the eyes of a morally demanding God?"[17]

To be born again and to strive for moral conduct in daily life represented a new way for the self to stand in relation to society. The Baptists forged a new criteria for social bonding that eventually challenged the traditional terms of social differentiation organized and controlled by the gentry. A new status consciousness took hold of the Baptists, and possession by the Holy Spirit replaced wealth and birthright as the social marker in eighteenth-century Piedmont Southside Virginia.[18]

This message found fertile ground in the imaginations of those middling planters whose social status did not match their economic status. The institutions of tobacco and slavery expanded simultaneously in Halifax County and in the Southside generally, and middling planters were quick to exploit the relationship between the two. The average planter owned 397 acres and 6 slaves. William Oliver, for example, worked 389 acres with 9 slaves, and he operated a mill. He lived in a log house and cured his tobacco in a log barn.[19]

The tax district of Halifax County justice James Bates yields more detailed information, and a curious but telling picture of Halifax society emerges. Middling planters dominated Bates's district, 47 percent of whom owned between 100 and 600 acres and 39 percent owned between 1 and 9 slaves. Bates counted 107 heads of households, or 45 percent, who owned no land. Yet, these tenants owned 22 percent of the slaves in the district. Elisha Cox and Francis Petty both rented the land they cultivated, but each owned 3 slaves. Cox and Petty each had 4 cabins, which their white families shared with their slaves. Clearly the economic development of the Southside did bring a wider distribution of slaves among planters. Moreover, the landless planters realized that investing first in slave labor was more prudent than investing in land without the hands to work it.

Before the rise of these middling planters and aspiring landless slave owners, the traditional order, in which society was divided between the active ceremonial world of the gentry and the acquiescent, observing world of those in the lesser ranks, seemed inevitable. Nothing in the gentry's carefully ordered scheme allowed for the recognition of the successful middling planter. The gentry still controlled the means of socialization and the terms of social interaction. The Baptist ideology, with its promise of sanctification through personal experience and conduct, bestowed a recognition on the middling planter that the gentry denied him by creating new criteria for judging the worth of a person based on personal experience and moral behavior.

Like the rituals of the gentry, the Baptist conversion experience had a social context. It took place before a congregation and a minister who acknowledged and encouraged the convert's new relationship with God. The social confirmation enjoyed by the convert was a significant, empowering phenomenon which appealed not only to the lesser sorts, but especially to the middling planters, whose growing economic standing conflicted with their dependence upon gentry culture for a sense of identity. The Baptist culture offered an alternative to the gentry culture, one that promised a rapturous, transcendent experience of the Heavenly world to come. The conflict, then, arose not over political power or economic wealth, but over ideology—over how individual worth and standing should be measured.[20]

Inevitably, friction arose between the middling Baptists and the Anglican gentry. These new evangelicals challenged the gentry who were accustomed to their public rituals of churchgoing, court day, horse racing, and cockfighting. The Baptists condemned all the important venues for gentry display and bearing as godless and decadent, while Anglicans looked upon the Baptists with contempt, especially the Baptist inclination toward intense and public emotional religious experiences. Always reserved in manner, the Anglicans saved their most derisive epithets to describe the Baptists' religious experience. The result of this antagonism between the two groups was a cultural war.[21]

The Rev. John Williams described a clash between leaders of the established church and a Baptist preacher in 1771:

> Brother Waller Informed us . . . (that) about 2 Weeks ago on the Sabbath day Down in Caroline County he Introduced the Worship of God by Singing. . . . While he was Singing the Parson of the Parish (who had ridden up with his clerk, the sheriff, and some others) would Keep Running the End of his Horsewhip in (Waller's) Mouth, Laying his Whip across the Hum Book, &c. When done Singing (Waller) proceeded to Prayer. In it he was Violently Jerked off the Stage, (they) Caught him by the Back part of his Neck, Beat his head against the ground, some Times Up, Sometimes down, they Carried him through a Gate that stood some Considerable Distance, where a Gentleman (the sheriff) Give him . . . Twenty Lashes with his Horse Whip . . . Then Brother Waller was Released, Went Back Singing praise to God, Mounted the Stage and preached with a Great Deal of Liberty.

By "liberty" Williams meant the spiritual freedom Waller gained by his convictions—convictions only made stronger by persecution. Waller did not waiver when his faith was tested. Indeed, he reported that "the Lord stood by him . . . & pour'd his Love into his Soul without measure, & the Brethren & Sisters Round him Singing praises . . . so that he Could Scarcely feel the stripes. . . . Rejoicing that he was Worthy to Suffer for his Dear Lord & Master." The fact that Waller's humiliation took place in front of his congregation only heightened the differences between the gentry and evangelicals, making the cause of the Baptists stronger in the eyes of many Virginians. Where Anglicans gained status with their fashionable dress and public rituals, the Baptists gained prestige by being humiliated in front of their peers.[22]

Baptists were mocked, beaten, and imprisoned, but their determination never abated, and it was this zeal that accounted for the phenomenal growth of the Baptists in the Southside. Baptist activity in Halifax County soon eclipsed that of the Antrim Parish vestry and congregation. In April of 1770 Antrim Parish approved the purchase of two acres near a spring and the construction of a church 40 feet by 24 feet. The next entry in the vestry book is dated 1787, seventeen years later. This inattention to record keeping suggests faltering activity on the part of the vestry and congregation. Furthermore, there is no indication that the church was ever built.[23]

In contrast, by 1771 the Baptists had formed an association consisting of 14 churches and 1,335 adult members living in 4 Southside counties. By 1789 this association had divided for administrative purposes, and the Roanoke Baptist Association was formed from Halifax and Pittsylvania counties with 2,140 members. In May 1789 the representatives of church in the Roanoke Association met at Grassy Creek Meeting House in Pittsylvania County to discuss business and voted to send this circular letter to be read to each congregation:

Dear brethren suffer a word of exhortation—we live in an extraordinary day. No nation of people since government was first introduced into the world, ever enjoyed equal privileges with in. Not merely a tolerance from civil laws . . . but without any kind of check from the hand of oppression. How ought we to be engaged in asking God in prayer for grace equal to the day that we might not wax fat and grow wanton and abuse the glorious privileges! The major part of our neighbors and families, perhaps careless in sin and unconcerned in iniquity, many reveling in vice and Luxury.[24]

Two important themes dominate this letter. First, a grateful people rejoice that two years after the Disestablishment they no longer are subject to persecution at the hands of the state. Second, the Baptists are wary lest they "wax fat, grow wanton and abuse their glorious privileges," the very sort of complacency they condemned in the Anglican gentry. Such exhortations from a tightly knit but prominent religious group speaking with authority and in unison claiming a substantial percentage of the population's allegiance suggest that such sentiment was widespread. A fear of falling into the decadent ways of the Anglican gentry pervaded the circular letters of the day.

The message of the Baptists was clear and their personal testimonies of a life transformed by a rejection of this world inspired their listeners.[25] By the 1780s James Hunt, the Halifax carpenter and aspiring Baptist minister, expressed the Baptists' disdain for the things of this world when he penned these lines in his account book:

When I can read my title clear,
To mansions in the skies,
I bid farewell to every fear,
And wipe my weeping eyes.[26]

By the last quarter of the eighteenth century, the Baptists had succeeded in their bid for cultural dominance in the Southside's Piedmont. They did so by redefining the notion of what gave status to an individual in Virginia society. The Baptists believed that the basis of self-worth lay not in a birthright, but in a "new birth" experience. This "new birth" experience sanctified the Baptists and appealed to the middling planters, who had been denied a position in society commensurate with their economic status. Their conduct according to a strict moral code was an outward sign of inward grace and took expression in the way they ordered their lives, their households, and their landscapes.

The material advantages of Halifax County's wealthy citizens were seldom expressed in the way they arranged their living space or in the size of their houses. The houses that Gilbert Hunt, Moses Terry, Alexander Shaw, and Jarrod McCarty built indicate that the Anglican gentry of Halifax County were not interested in differentiating space according to a social hierarchy. Although some of these houses made substantial claims on the resources of their owners, plans show that their claims to status did not extend to creating social barriers, processional spaces, or genteel rooms for entertainment.

When Jarrod McCarty built his logwalled house in 1785, he covered it with weatherboards, set it on a Flemish-bond brick foundation and built a substantial brick chimney on the east end of the house with two fireplaces with which to heat the hall and the loft above stairs (fig. 2.7). It measures 18 by 32 feet and was larger than 95 percent of the houses in James Bates's district. McCarty could well afford such a fine house. He owned more slaves than 98 percent of his fellow slaveholders and more land than 88 percent of the people in Halifax County. McCarty's house was an impressive sight in the landscape, and he proudly marked his initials and the date of the house's construction in a chimney brick. The inventory taken a year after his death in 1794 is an impressive record of McCarty's prosperity and acquisitiveness. McCarty furnished his house

Fig. 2.7. Jarrod McCarty's House, Halifax County, Virginia, 1785.

with four commodious bedsteads with feather bedding, one pine table and one of walnut, twelve chairs, two chests, a desk and bookcase, two candle stands with pewter snuffers, and two flax wheels.

McCarty was a member of the Anglican church and stood in the top 12 percent of the wealthiest men in Halifax County. Yet, the plan of McCarty's house indicates that, while he might have been eager to build a relatively fine, obviously expensive house, his intention was not to create living spaces different from the traditional one- or two-room Virginia houses so familiar to his neighbors. McCarty's house had no central passage. Any caller who stood in one of the three thresholds would have found himself looking into the heart of McCarty's domestic space. No architectural or spatial buffers existed to protect the family's privacy from the activity of the yard.

Houses, as the gentry of the Tidewater so clearly proved, were actions and intentions in built form. For a people like the Baptists, whose form of church governance required consensus, building a passage in a house or devoting a room to the rituals of dining and toasting would have been a contradiction. Since the Baptist ideology changed the way the people of Halifax County perceived themselves in relation to the old Anglican order, there was no constituency who sought access beyond a set of social barriers. Nor did anyone in Halifax County aspire to inhabit—or to be invited into—domestic spaces designed for refined social rituals. Moreover, the Baptists of Halifax County were not passive or aspiring observers of the gentry's world. They were a scrutinizing social force. Thus, in Halifax County, architectural expression was dictated not by the Anglican elite, but by a dissenting sect of evangelicals. The old gentry model of deference was inverted.

For a people of faith whose actions were an outward sign of inward grace, buildings too became signs of grace. At home, the Baptists required a domestic setting in which their earnest, personal, experiential ideology could be lived. The traditional Virginia house met their requirements. One- or two-room plans, easily and readily accessible to all who called, predominated in Halifax County. And even the gentry had to acknowledge the efficacy of this arrangement.

For Jarrod McCarty and other members of Halifax County's Anglican gentry, there was little to gain from building a central passage or by furnishing a room with the accoutrements of fine dining. Such spaces where the Tidewater gentry proposed and confirmed their dominion were useless in Halifax County. McCarty's Baptist neighbors would not have been impressed. Possibly, they would not notice—certainly they would not care—for they did not consult this world for instruction.

Notes

1. Dell Upton, "White and Black Landscapes in Eighteenth-Century Virginia," in *Material Life in America 1600–1860*, ed. Robert Blair St. George (Boston: Northeastern Univ. Press, 1988), 357–69. Dell Upton and Camille Wells have discussed architecture as a proposition: Dell Upton, "New Directions in the Study of Virginia's Material Culture," a paper presented at the Virginia Historical Society conference "New Directions in Virginia History," Richmond, Oct. 12, 1990; and Camille Wells, "Contested Ground: Domestic Space and Enslaved Labor in the Houses of Ante-bellum Virginia," a paper presented at the Society of Architectural Historians Annual Conference, Philadelphia, Apr. 28, 1994. The method of inquiry used in this chapter is based on Marxist thought as it has been modified and expanded by other scholars. While the Anglican gentry was an elite group that shared common economic and social interests, the Baptists defy such convenient descriptions. In his Ph.D. dissertation, "In Search of Status Power: The Baptist Revival in Colonial Virginia, 1760–1776," (Ph.D. diss., Univ. of Pennsylvania, 1982), J. Stephen Kroll-Smith argues that Max Weber's term "status group" is more applicable to the Baptists of eighteenth-century Virginia. Weber accepts Marx's proposition that economic power devolves from control over the means to produce and distribute property, but he recognizes forms of social power as well. Weber defines "status groups," as distinct from economically determined "class," as communities whose members are bound together by a common "style of life." This style of life can only be maintained or propagated if members of a status group are able to control the means of socialization and social intercourse. Thus, in eighteenth-century Virginia, the Anglican gentry was a status group. The Baptists formed another status group that successfully challenged the Anglican gentry. In his *Symbolic Crusade,* Joseph Gusfield interprets a status movement in terms of symbols that deal with noneconomic aspects of power. Gusfield argues that status movement is a power struggle between competing status groups using symbols rather than "fists." See Joseph Gusfield, *Symbolic Crusade: Status Politics and the Temperance Movement* (Urbana: Univ. of Illinois Press, 1986), 184. Thus, the houses of early Virginia Anglicans and Baptists correspond to Gusfield's symbols, but there is a distinction. These buildings were not mere symbols; they were embodiments of the world—or competing propositions by the Anglicans and Baptists concerning how the world worked. Kroll-Smith's contribution to this analysis of power is his assertion that status movements can be subversive to a dominant culture, eventually gaining control of the means to produce and legitimize a lifestyle. Kroll-Smith argues that the Baptists represented an economic group that seized upon an opposing ideology as a means of gaining status. He does not, however, overlook the powerful message the Baptists brought to early Virginia. The Baptists did not reject the economic system that supported Anglican rule. In fact many Baptists embraced the tobacco economy but sought to purge it of some resulting social inequalities and material excesses. The Baptist culture changed the way Anglicans viewed their role in society, the way they shaped their houses, and the way they arranged their landscape.

2. James Bates Tax List, "A List of White Persons and Houses taken in the County of Halifax 1785," MSS in "Lists and Buildings, 1782–1785," Box 2, Virginia State Library and Archives, Richmond; Michael Nichols, "Building the Virginia Southside: A Note on Architecture and Society in Eighteenth-Century Virginia," unpublished manuscript; Halifax County Pleas 11, 152. William Waller Hening, ed. *The Statutes at Large: Being a Collection of all the Laws of Virginia . . .* XI (Richmond, 1823), 415–17. The law ordered each justice to "take a list from each person with the [district] of the number of white per-

sons in each family therein, and the number of buildings, distinguishing dwelling-houses from other buildings." No record exists telling the boundaries of each district. Further research, however, will determine the boundaries of Bates's district and lead to a complete survey of buildings surviving from his list.

3. Richard Beeman, *The Evolution of the Southern Backcountry: A Case Study of Lunenburg County, Virginia: 1746–1832* (Philadelphia: Univ. of Pennsylvania Press, 1984), 14–15. Byrd's accounts are from William Byrd, "A Journey to the Land of Eden, Anno 1733," in *The Prose Works of William Byrd of Westover: Narratives of a Colonial Virginian,* ed. Louis B. Wright (Cambridge, Mass.: Belknap Press of Harvard Univ. Press, 1966), 381–412.

4. Camille Wells, "The Planter's Prospect: Houses, Outbuildings, and Rural Landscapes in Eighteenth-Century Virginia," *Winterthur Portfolio* 39 (Summer/Autumn 1993): 1–31. Historians measure wealth in eighteenth-century Virginia by landholdings and slaves. Robert and Katherine B. Brown first used acreage as a measure of wealth in 1964 to compare different regions in Virginia. Later historians used this method in analyzing the development of economic and social trends in colonial Virginia. Comparative analysis of land and slave holdings is the basis for all these studies, and this essay continues the dialogue opened by the Browns and others by using the same methodology. See Robert E. and Katherine B. Brown, *Virginia, 1705–1786: Democracy or Aristocracy* (East Lansing: Michigan State Univ. Press, 1964); Beeman, *Evolution of the Southern Backcountry*; Allan Kulikoff, *Tobacco and Slaves: The Development of Southern Cultures in the Chesapeake, 1680–1800* (Chapel Hill: Univ. of North Carolina Press for the Institute of Early American History and Culture, 1986).

5. It is important to remember that the basis for comparison between Halifax County and the Northern Neck region is land and slaves, not the buildings themselves. Buildings do not factor into a wealth analysis because they are not an index of productivity. Buildings are an index of consumer intentions and aspirations. The Page family of Gloucester County, for example, greatly diminished its fortune by constructing Rosewell (c. 1725). The debt incurred by Mann Page accrued to his children and grandchildren, who never gained the economic security the large and imposing Rosewell implied. As Thomas Jefferson's heirs discovered, a large house did not necessarily represent the wealth of the builder. Jefferson's debts totaled more than $100,000 at his death, and his heirs eventually lost the estate. Thus, the size of the house and the quality of materials are not indicators of the builder's economic standing. The question of how to determine the value of land remains. By the last quarter of the eighteenth century, however, planters in Tidewater Virginia looked to the hinterland for more fertile land. Northern Neck planters, whose land no longer produced as much as it did for previous generations, would have recognized that even an unimproved acre in Halifax County was more valuable than a cleared acre in Northumberland County. Moreover, the inventories analyzed thus far show that while the Anglican gentry of Halifax County chose to present a modest architectural face to their community, they lavished their interiors with fine furnishings.

6. Upton, "White and Black Landscapes," 363–64. The importance of the dining room, its accouterments, and accompanying rituals is explained by Mark R. Wenger in "The Dining Room in Early Virginia," in *Perspectives in Vernacular Architecture, III,* ed. Thomas Carter and Bernard L. Herman (Columbia: Univ. of Missouri Press, 1989), 149–59.

7. Rhys Isaac, *The Transformation of Virginia 1740–1790* (New York: Norton, 1988), 35. The quote is from Howard C. Rice, trans., *Travels in North America in the Years 1780, 1781, and 1782 by the Marquis de Chastellux* (Chapel Hill:

Univ. of North Carolina Press, 1963). Camille Wells, "The Planter's Prospect," 28–31. Wells's analysis of real estate advertisements in the Virginia Gazette suggests that, by the second quarter of the eighteenth-century, middling planters as well as the gentry were "[e]nsconced in houses that they perceived to be at the very top or center of their fixed and orderly rural landscapes" and that "planters thought of themselves as unquestionably in control."

8. Dell Upton, "White and Black Landscapes," 357–69.

9. Isaac, *The Transformation of Virginia,* 43. The quote is from Devereux Jarratt, *The Life of the Reverend Devereux Jarratt, Rector of Bath Parish, Dinwiddie County, Virginia, Written by Himself in a series of letters Addressed to the Rev. John Coleman* . . . (Baltimore, 1806; facsimile reprint, New York 1969).

10. It is not possible to determine the house type favored by the Anglican gentry in Halifax County before 1770. No studies have been done comparing the various counties of the Virginia or North Carolina Piedmont regions, so it is not possible to speculate about Halifax County's Anglican gentry. Nevertheless, there is no reason to assume that other factors explain the hall-and-chamber plan used by the Halifax gentry. For example, the comparison of landholdings show comparable wealth between the Tidewater and the Halifax County gentry. Further, although Halifax County was more recently settled, there is no reason to assume that residents of Halifax County were more isolated and therefore more immune to the influence of Tidewater gentry culture, or that they were less aware of the social and economic hierarachies within their community and other communities. See Richard Beeman, *Evolution of the Southern Backcountry*; Charles Farmer, *In the Absence of Towns: Settlement and Country Trade in Southside Virginia, 1730–1800* (Lanham, Md.: Rowman and Littlefield, 1993); Turk McCleskey, "Rich Land, Poor Prospects: Real Estate and the Formation of a Social Elite in Augusta County, Virginia, 1738–1770," *Virginia Magazine of History and Biography* 98 (3) (July 1990): 449–86.

11. Turk McCleskey asserts in his study of Augusta County that newly settled parts of Virginia were deliberately structured to replicate the social and economic order of the Tidewater. Speculators and surveyors carefully controlled access to land and thus ensured that westward expansion could be had without the social upheavals that accompany spontaneous migration. See Turk McCleskey, "Rich Land, Poor Prospects." This scenario was played out in Halifax County where an Anglican gentry emerged early and continued to dominate political affairs into the 1790s. A comparison between the vestry book of Antrim Parish and Halifax County court records reveals that, between 1752 and 1797, all of the county clerks, justices, burgesses, and, later, state delegates were members of the Anglican Church.

12. J. Stephen Kroll-Smith, "Tobacco and Belief: Baptist Ideology and the Yeoman Planter in Eighteenth-Century Virginia," *Southern Studies* 21 (4) (Winter 1982): 353–55.

13. Kroll-Smith, "In Search of Status Power," 159–60.

14. Ibid., 161–62.

15. Ibid., 163

16. Ibid., 166.

17. Kroll-Smith, "Tobacco and Belief," 359–62; Roanoke Association Minute Book 1789–1831, MSS, Virginia State Library and Archives.

18. Kroll-Smith, "Tobacco and Belief," 368. The Baptists were not given to writing down their sermons and thus little survives of specific documents that might shed light on how they used the Bible to articulate their beliefs. The Rev. John Williams, however, kept a notebook from May 7, 1771, to Sept. 15, 1771, in which he recorded eighty sermon texts. Kroll-Smith analyzed these texts to determine a central theme. Each text was examined for its figurative or literal emphasis, its use of per-

sonal pronouns, and the presence or absence of in-group or out-group emphasis. A literal emphasis suggests an immediate impact on the listener. Personal pronouns would lead listeners to personalize the message. Finally, an in-group emphasis, according to sociologists, suggests a new criteria for social bonding. Kroll-Smith found that fifty-eight texts address the idea of new birth. Sixty-four are literal appeals, and only sixteen are figurative. The second-person singular and first-person plural are used thirty-nine times, while the third-person singular is used only ten times. Twenty texts address the question of in-group, out-group criteria.

19. The wealth structure of Halifax County represents the year 1785 and was calculated by combining the land tax lists from 1782 to 1785. Before 1785 only land transactions were recorded for each year, making it necessary to combine the tax lists to determine who owned land in 1785. The Personal Property Tax of 1787 listed the number of slaves owned by each head of household. James Bates described the buildings on the properties of Oliver and Richardson in his 1785 tax list.

20. Rhys Isaac, "Evangelical Revolt: The Nature of the Baptists' Challenge to the Traditional Order in Virginia, 1765 to 1775," *William and Mary Quarterly* 3d ser., 31 (July 1974): 345–68. Kroll-Smith argues that previous historians stereotyped the Baptists as lower-class landless poor on the basis of contemporary (and biased) observers. Kroll-Smith's examination of the real and personal property tax lists, wills and inventories, and tithable lists of four congregations in Lunenburg, Chesterfield, Lancaster, and Albemarle Counties shows that their members were middling class. See Kroll-Smith, "Tobacco and Belief," 88–95. There is a direct connection between the Baptists' beliefs and their actions. On ideologies, Clifford Geertz has said that "ideologies render otherwise incomprehensible social situations meaningful, then so construe them as to make it possible to act purposefully within them, which accounts both for their highly figurative nature and for the intensity with which, once accepted, they are held." Cited in "Ideology as a Cultural System," in *Ideology and Discontent,* ed. D. E. Apter (New York: Free Press, 1964), 64.

21. Isaac, "Evangelical Revolt," 353. For a discussion on how the emotions of the gentry affected their familial and social interactions, see Jan Lewis, "Domestic Tranquillity and the Management of Emotion among the Gentry of Pre-Revolutionary Virginia," *William and Mary Quarterly,* 3d ser., 39 (Jan. 1982): 135–49.

22. Isaac, *The Transformation of Virginia,* 162–63. The quote is from John Williams, Journal, MS, May 10, 1771, Virginia Baptist Historical Society, Univ. of Richmond. The Baptists were not the only sect to be persecuted by the gentry. Thomas Coke, an English cleric authorized by John Wesley to organize a Methodist church in Southside Virginia, was driven out of Halifax County in 1784 by an armed mob when he preached abolition. One woman offered fifty pounds to anyone who could catch and horsewhip Coke. One man pursued Coke out of the county with the intent of killing him. By 1788, however, Coke returned to a very different scene in Halifax County. When he arrived, he was warmly received by all of the "great people of the county," including five colonels and his assassin-turned-convert. See Sylvia R. Frey, *Water from the Rock: Black Resistance in a Revolutionary Age* (Princeton: Princeton Univ. Press, 1991): 245–51. The Roanoke Baptist Association also grappled with the issue of slavery in one of its circular letters. No agreement could be reached, however, on what to do about members who held slaves, and the authors freely admitted that in the face of such division, the best advice they could offer was that masters should treat their slaves with kindness. This lack of consensus over the issue of slavery supports Kroll-Smith's argument that the Baptists appealed to the middling planters of Virginia, many of whom owned slaves.

23. Robert B. Semple, *Rise and Progress of the Baptists* (Richmond, Va.: Pitt and Dickenson, 1894), 20–21; Antrim Parish Vestry Book, MSS, Univ. of Virginia Library, Special Collections, Charlottesville, Virginia.
24. Roanoke Baptist Association Minute Book, MSS, Virginia State Library and Archives, Richmond, Virginia. Accession no. 23600. At each meeting of the association since its inception, members were asked to submit "materials" toward the writing of a history of the Baptists in Virginia. The fact that the Baptists were already trying to write a history of their progress points to a self-awareness and a sense of "arrival" as a faith to be reckoned with. No longer officially persecuted, the Baptists were ready to make their bid for social hegemony in the religious vacuum left by Disestablishment. Writing their own history and telling their own story was an important step toward filling this void.
25. Isaac, "Evangelical Revolt," 354–55.
26. James Hunt Account Book, MSS no. 17,204. Library of Congress. Jonathan Farris brought this source to my attention.

CHAPTER 3

Bernard L. Herman

The Embedded Landscapes of the Charleston Single House, 1780–1820

C. C. Hines, a representative of the Philadelphia-based Insurance Company of North America, reported from Charleston in 1860: "There are more little, old, odd, awkward buildings here than I ever saw in one town before! Brick with tile roofs prevail tolerably well peppered with frames here & there. . . . Dwellings do not *look* so well as one would expect to see in so large a town."[1] Like many other visitors before and since, Hines was struck by the peculiarities of Charleston's urban landscape. "Old," "odd," and "awkward" are terms that evoke a sense of a local architecture which is at once curiously exotic and disquieting. Moreover, Hines extended these adjectives to the whole of the city and not just to one or two specific buildings. Hines concluded that the architectural landscape was a paradox. Charleston was large enough and old enough to warrant the expectation of an affluent cosmopolitan culture; the impression given by the city's houses, however, suggested outdated manners and architectural constraint.

A prominent town house form that shaped Hines's impressions was the Charleston single house. Its distinctive features included a gable-end orientation to the street, a walled or fenced lot, and multiple outbuildings packed into a deep, narrow rear yard. The single house, more than any other Charleston building type, remains the urban dwelling that distinguishes the city's architectural character. But it also remains little understood. Why did the form develop? How did it compare to other Charleston town houses? How did it work as residence and statement of social order and economic values? To address these questions requires us to examine the dramatic rise of the single house and its defining impact on the streetscapes of late-eighteenth- and early-nineteenth-century Charleston.

Like Hines, we observe and then learn from

the buildings and environments we study. The use of architecture as evidence enables us to introduce new questions into the domains of social and cultural history, not to mention the "old" architectural history. Vernacular architecture studies approach buildings as the products of human interaction culturally. It combines the methods and perspectives of historical archaeology, cultural geography, social history, and folklife studies. We are engaged in a kind of above-ground excavation that seeks pattern through the rigorous recording of objects situated in multiple contexts. On one level, context is purely material: we seek to describe the object or site in terms of its physical attributes—material, fabrication, ornamentation, form, and color. On a second level, context consists of place and time. On a third level, our contextual investigations are cultural—we seek to evaluate the object or site in multiple domains including those identifying proxemic, functional, communicative, and symbolic interactions. Thus, contextual considerations begin with the "material" part of material culture and work toward the interpretation of culture.

Few house types are more closely identified with a particular place than the single house is with Charleston (fig. 3.1 and fig. 3.2). Basic characteristics of the single house have been identified by a number of observers. According to its most meticulous student, Gene Waddell, the essential single house is "two or more stories of the same plan with a central stair hall between two rooms on each floor and an entrance opening directly into the hall" (fig. 3.3 and fig. 3.4).[2] Waddell continues: "a Charleston Single House is a separate, multi-story dwelling one room wide and three across including a central entrance and stair hall. It also typically, but not necessarily, has its narrow end to the street, a piazza along one of its longer sides, and back wall chimneys."[3] Students of the single house tradition, however, typically emphasize the house with little regard for its larger, immediate contexts of lot, neigh-

Fig. 3.1. Charleston Single Houses, Hassel Street, Ansonborough, Charleston, South Carolina. Street elevations. Built c. 1840 to replace earlier houses lost in the fire of 1838, the Hassel Street dwellings represent the full development of the single house form as it appeared by the mid-nineteenth century. David L. Ames.

bors, and interiors. One author, discussing the single house, illustrates a facsimile of an eighteenth-century plan of the Pringle House on Tradd Street, with the notation that the piazzas, for some reason (possibly for clarity), have been expunged.[4] Also shorn from the house are all the other amenities such as outbuildings and gardens. But, as the Pringle House plat and many others like it suggest, the Charleston single house is not just a dwelling. Rather, the dwelling proper is only one element within the entire city lot with all of its architectural and landscape amenities. The Charleston single house, in fact, can be un-

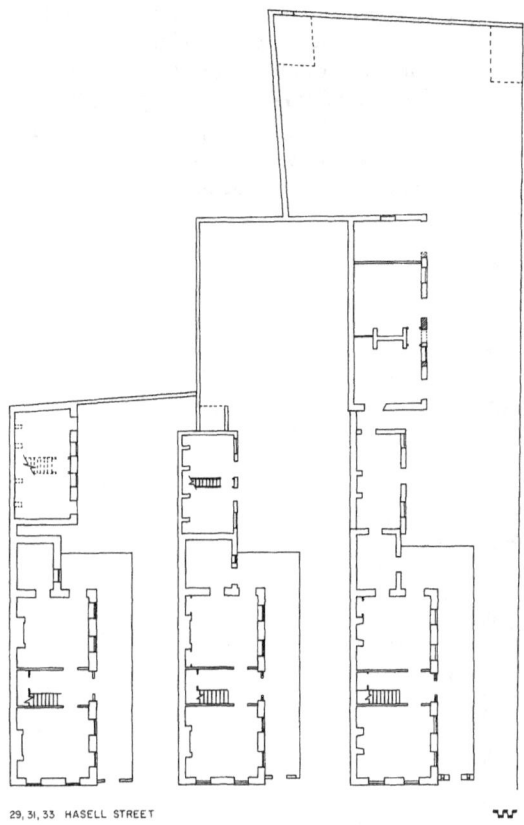

Fig. 3.2. Charleston Single Houses, Hassel Street, Ansonborough, Charleston, South Carolina. First floor and lot plans. Drawing courtesy of Gabrielle M. Lanier.

derstood best not as a building type, but as an architectural strategy focused on the maintenance of complex social relationships.

The Charleston single house provides an opportunity to apply the idea of embedded landscapes—a concept developed out of Ian Hodder's work in contextual archaeology and Dell Upton's interpretations of eighteenth-century Virginia parish churches and houses.[5] Hodder draws a distinction between two types of contextual meaning. The first type, he notes, "refers to the environmental and behavioural context of action" where the meanings invested in an object are discovered "through placing it in relation to the larger functioning whole." Second, Hodder continues, "context can be taken to mean 'with-text', and so the word introduces an analogy between the contextual meanings of material culture traits and the meanings of words in a written language." Hodder's contextual archaeology recognizes the "situated" nature of artifacts not only in time and place, but as importantly within relational fields of "meaning content" or discourse. The idea of embedded landscapes also builds from Upton's ideas of movement and the experiential dimension of objects. The plantation landscapes of colonial Virginia "embodied the principle of movement." As people moved through parish churches, courthouses, and the plantation countryside, they encountered an array of landscape experiences that both affirmed and contested social relationships within the larger community. As Upton remarks on the plantation house, "More important than being in a certain room was the route taken to get there, or how far along the formal route one progressed." Movement in these settings, whether processional or segmented, defined not only individuals but the structure of plantation society. Thus, the notion of embedded landscapes recognizes first how artifacts and their settings function as sites for the exchange of symbolic actions and, second, how the content of those actions reflected in the material world remain open to negotiation and multiple, intersecting interpretive possibilities.

Within a framework of embedded landscapes, we can study and interpret buildings as individual objects, as representatives of a type, or as ensembles.[6] The embedded landscape approach also provides for the study of the spaces and interstices within and between buildings, especially the kinds of spaces where action and interaction occur and relationships are defined in ways that socially and symbolically unify and divide people. For example, Lena Orlin discusses the sixteenth-century Tudor long gallery as an archi-

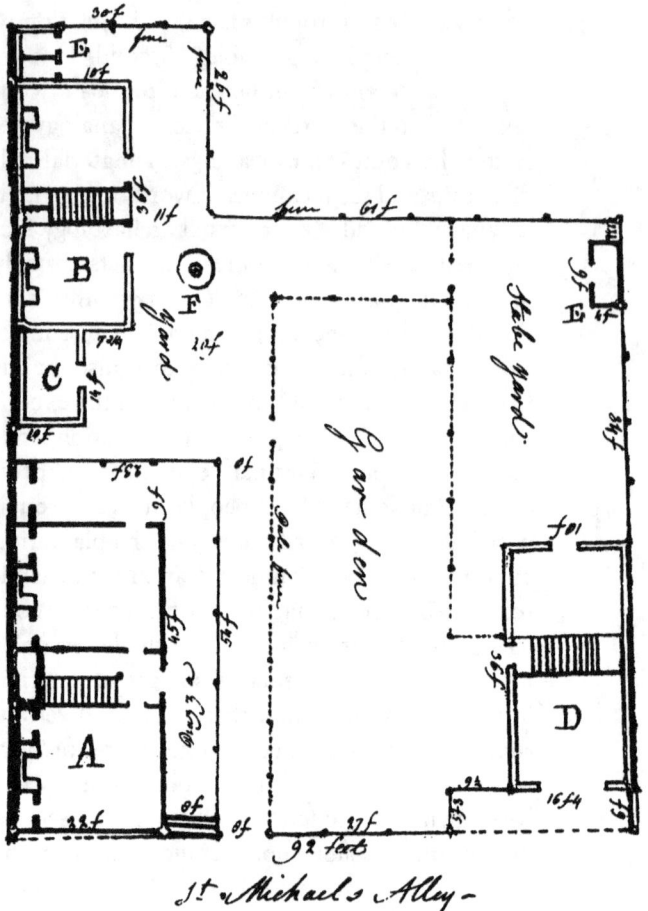

Fig. 3.3. Charleston Single House Lot Plan. 176 Meeting Street (late eighteenth century), insurance survey from Aetna Collection, RG 4 (Advertising and Public Relations Department), Series: Historical Files, South Carolina Folder. Courtesy of Cigna Archives, Philadelphia, Pennsylvania.

Fig. 3.4. Charleston Single House Lot Plan. Elijah Hall Bay House (c. 1780), corner of Meeting Street and St. Michael's Alley, survey plat no. 515 from McCready Plat Collection, City of Charleston, Charleston, South Carolina.

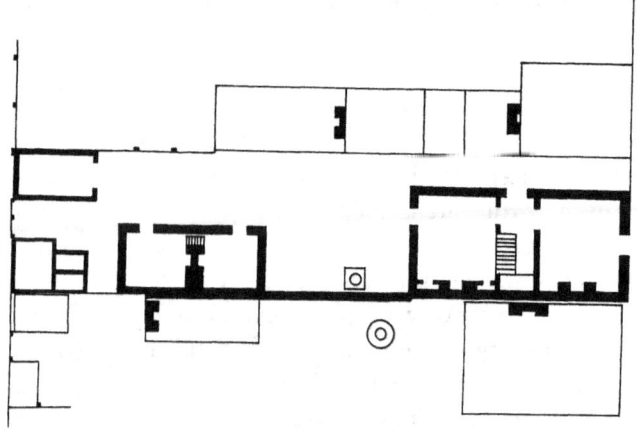

tectural space where people could be observed and yet maintain the privacy of visible, whispered conversations.[7] Similarly, prosecution witnesses in the trials following Denmark Vesey's foiled slave insurrection testified to seeing slaves converse in the street, on the wharves, in shops, and yards behind their masters' houses. Benjamin Hammett recounted the confession of his slave Bacchus: "Perault, when hauling cotton from my store, told Bacchus in the yard secretly that he wanted him to go to the Society with him." The society in question was composed of Denmark Vesey, Monday Gell, Smart Anderson, and other figures central to the planned revolt. Similarly, slave owners labored under the impression that their knowledge of their slaves' actions was complete. A white defense witness for Billy Robinson testified, "I live in a house in Elliot Street—there are two rooms on a floor the front occupied by Mr. Howe—the back by me—Billy occupies a room above the Kitchen and no one can go into his room without passing through my Kitchen—I never saw Perault go into Billy's room or into my Yard." What the testimony in these cases and many others like them underscored for Charleston's white population was their vulnerability. They saw conversations, but did not hear; they looked into their yards and kitchens, but did not see. The porous nature of urban places and their lack of control over the interstices of the city ultimately frightened Charleston whites as much as the betrayal they perceived in the plot.[8]

The idea of embedded landscapes also enables us to wrest landscape studies free from purely geographic considerations. Some embedded landscapes, for example, are defined not by place, but by mutual interests. Thus, the eighteenth-century mercantile landscape, particularly in the interior organization and furnishing programs for merchant houses, provided for the maintenance of economic and social ties throughout the North Atlantic rim and beyond. Other embedded landscapes signified deeply conflicted social and economic relationships in which pretended acquiescence alternated with acts of resistance. Leland Ferguson's study of slave life and material culture on South Carolina's Low Country plantations, for example, reveals the many ways in which slaves temporarily claimed for their own uses marginal spaces away from their owners' surveillance.[9] Thus, slaves established meeting places in the woods for worship, society, and refuge. The vulnerability of the larger landscape to ephemeral black claims, no matter how fleeting, was far more unsettling to white slave holders than the prospect of established slave settlements that could be overseen and regulated. Historian Rhys Isaac, in his study of eighteenth-century Virginia, described the same quality of embedded plantation landscapes where issues of social authority and vulnerability were periodically inverted.[10] The following discussion outlines two architectural contexts developed from the process of looking at the Charleston single house within a framework of embedded landscapes: the formal parlor and the overall organization of the house lot. The embedded landscapes of the parlor and the single house building and yard complex show that the single house functioned both to promote Atlantic mercantile culture and to express and enforce social hierarchy in a black majority urban slave society.

On the interior, the most formal room in the Charleston single house of the late eighteenth century was the drawing room, also known as the parlor or "best room." The location of the "best" room in the single house—a room identified through a close examination of internal finishes—followed one of two primary choices: either on the first or second floor, but always in the front or "street" side of the house. The choice of location relates directly to the overall functions of the house. The single houses along Church Street, for example, generally placed the drawing room on the second floor and over a ground floor office or shop which could be entered directly from the street. Sociability literally and symbolically occupied a space above commercial endeavor. The pattern of placing the best room in the house on the second floor was shared throughout the urban culture of the North Atlantic rim, expressed in a variety of regionally and even locally identifiable house plans and styles ranging, for example, from the several designs adapted to town houses in cities like Philadelphia, Baltimore, Alexandria, London, Bristol, and Hull.

The second placement choice for the best room was in the first or ground floor front of the house. In eighteenth-century Charleston, the single houses where this option was most commonly exercised stood away from the commercial center of the city and along its predominantly residential fringe, for example, Orange and Legare Streets. Here builders of houses without commercial functions brought the best room down into a more intimate relationship with the street—a choice which speaks to the possibility of early neighborhoods defined by shared status rather than by a topographical proximity to trade or work.[11]

What did these drawing rooms look like, and more importantly how were their architectural values related to each other? The interpretive strategy of intrasite/intersite analysis (drawn from historical archaeology) provides a means for looking at the sociology of the best room in terms of its relationships to other domestic spaces within the house (intersite analysis) and to other comparable spaces in other dwellings (intrasite analysis).[12] Thus, we are addressing the proxemics and textures of the parlor in two contexts: the house and the city. These contexts are interconnected and reflect the movement of people as they encountered these spaces throughout the city. The experience of those architectural settings was nuanced by slavery, family, gender, status, wealth, community, and cosmopolitanism. Still, despite the variety of experience and perspective and the fleeting vagaries of fashion, there is an identifiable architectural pattern to the parlor.

Taken together, 90 and 94 Church Street in Charleston enable us to look at the appearance and placement of the parlor within the single house from the mid-eighteenth through the early nineteenth century (fig. 3.5 and fig. 3.6). The two houses (90 and 94 Church Street) were constructed in 1759 and 1760 as three-and-a-half story, center-passage plan dwellings with ground floor front commercial rooms entered directly from the street. The mid-eighteenth-century lot arrangement at 90 Church included a two-story quarter-kitchen, a domestic service building typically containing a kitchen and wash house on the ground floor, and a number of slave apartments upstairs. The lot at 94 Church included a narrow passage behind the house providing access to the neighbors' back-buildings on the interior of the block.[13] Although neither building individually retains all of its first period interior finishes, together they provide an overall impression of how early single houses were decoratively and functionally considered. The Leger House at 90 Church was provided with a

Fig. 3.5. Peter Leger House (90 Church Street), c. 1759–60; Alexander Christie House (92 Church), c. 1805–7; Cooper-Bee House (94 Church Street), c. 1760–65. Church Street elevations. Developed individually, these single house lots represent building activity ranging from the mid-eighteenth through the early nineteenth centuries. David L. Ames.

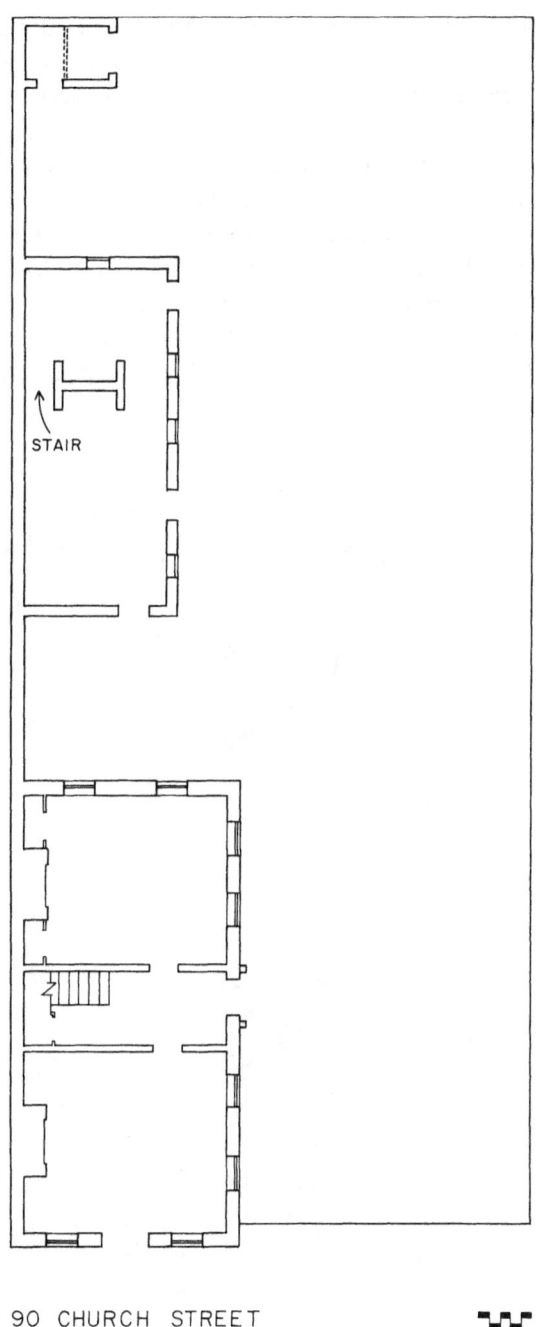

90 CHURCH STREET

Fig. 3.6. Reconstructed c. 1760 plan of 90 Church Street. Drawing courtesy of Gabrielle M. Lanier.

Fig. 3.7. Single House at 90 Church Street. First-floor front "office," or commercial room. Built with a door leading directly from the street into the first-floor front room, 90 Church Street represents single houses that incorporated both commercial and domestic functions.

fully paneled heated office or counting room (fig. 3.7).[14] The stair in both buildings was an open string arrangement, and, in the case of the Cooper House at 94 Church, it was finished with heavily-turned balusters, paneled soffits, and elaborately carved cornice. In the progression of spaces that extended from the street to the outbuildings in the yard, the plainest ground-floor spaces in the main block of both houses were the paneled dining rooms that stood between the entry passage and the dooryard shared by the dwelling and the kitchen. On the second floor, the hierarchy of rooms ran from the front best parlor overlooking the street below (and, as in the Cooper House, provided with a small balcony), the passage and stair, and to a rear dining-room chamber looking out onto the backbuildings, service yard, and garden. The third floor, considerably less finished than those below, contained two secondary sleeping chambers. The creation of a spatial and functional hierarchy which combined commerce, social life, and domestic operations into a functionally and symbolically effective building bound the Church Street houses and others like them together into a larger urban landscape.

The parlor or drawing room reflected the highest degree of aesthetic investment in an interior hierarchy of finishes that visually conveyed the relative importance of individual rooms.[15] In the single house, the placement of the parlor or drawing room at the front of the house juxtaposed the most formal room with the public world of the street. In all instances, however, that juxtaposition was mediated by contrived paths of access. For single houses where the best room occupied the second-floor front, access could be gained only by entering the house through a formal entrance facing the street, down the piazza, passing through a second formal entry into the stair passage, and ascending the stairs to the upper floor. In comparable dwellings where the best room occupied the ground floor, access was regulated through a route leading from street to piazza to entry to parlor. Both routes required the privilege of invitation or intimate familiarity. Within the house itself, the best room defined one extreme of a hierarchical spatial text glossed with ornament. No visitor could mistake the best room for a front office, chamber, or everyday back dining room. That hierarchy was articulated only through the visual relationships between the rooms. The quality of detailing in the best rooms might differ from house to house, but within each house the hierarchy of detail clearly communicated decorative and social hierarchy.

Following a comparative reading of multiple houses, we can explore the architectural evidence of parlor culture and its general currency in and beyond Charleston. The second-floor drawing room of the Peter Bocquet House on Broad Street in Charleston, for example, finds its equivalents in the best rooms of houses on Legare, Church, and Broad Streets (fig. 3.8). At the same time, the quality and type of finish evident in the Bocquet House speaks directly to a transatlantic culture of mercantilism and fashion observed, for example, in the Blaydes family house in Hull, England (fig. 3.9). Those same concerns are reflected again in the con-

Fig. 3.8. Peter Bocquet House, 95 Broad Street. Second-floor drawing room interior, c. 1770–72. Like the majority of Charleston's eighteenth-century single houses, the Bocquet House placed the best room on the second floor directly over the business premises below.

Fig. 3.9. Blaydes House, High Street, Hull, England. Built in the early eighteenth century, extensively enlarged in the mid-eighteenth century, and remodeled to a lesser degree in the early nineteenth century, the Blaydes House retains a larger portion of its second-period interiors. The mantel and overmantel shown here are located in a first-floor reception room. Courtesy of the Royal Commission on the Historical Monuments of England © Crown Copyright.

Charleston houses. Composed of a mixture of resin, glue, linseed oil, and whiting steamed, beaten into a stiff paste, and pressed into molds, composition ornament elements were applied to woodwork ranging from door casings to mantels.[17] Scenes depicting classicized rustic dances, individual figures draped in Grecian costume, or decorative elements based on floral swags, garlands, baskets of fruit, and sheaves of wheat provided a coherent and broadly continuous backdrop for best rooms throughout the late-eighteenth-century North Atlantic world. The overall effect is dizzying; we start to see the interiors of the houses as artifacts both of local society (defined by place and class) and a more diffuse Atlantic community (defined by exchange relations, emulation and mutuality, and the knowledge of manners). Thus, the embedded landscapes of early Charleston town houses possess local outsides and global insides.

The furnishings of the drawing room or parlor reflect an archaeology of etiquette revolving around competitive and convivial exchange relations—most of which was regulated by the rules of polite discourse. Francis Simmons's estate inventory for his house on Legare Street lists the furnishings of the second-floor drawing room: card tables, tea table, fourteen cane-bottom chairs, three settees, carpet, and accents such as chimney ornaments described as "elegant." Angus Bethune's front parlor overlooking Broad Street held fourteen mahogany chairs, two card tables, tea tables, and sofa. At least one painting graced the wall, while plated candlesticks and chimney ornaments attested to the affectations of a culture of refinement. Card tables, however, were not just objects of polite discourse—they were an arena for the complex competitive world of trade and social rank in a society where the distance between the counting house and the dining table was minimal. Visitors and residents knew the rules and understood the visual and material world which often encoded those rules.

Merchants in other cities furnished their par-

temporary parlors of northern New England. Even as tastes change, style (what Upton defines as "a system of common understanding, within which the active participants of a society can operate in a coordinated manner, however imperfect that coordination might be") remains constant.[16] The use of composition or stucco ornament in Charleston parlors of the late eighteenth and early nineteenth centuries, for example, finds precise analogs in comparable parlors in distant cities as well as in other lors in comparable ways. Joseph Spear, a Baltimore merchant who specialized in supplying shipboard diets with "navy Bread," lived in a three-story rowhouse two rooms deep and entered by a stair hall to one side.[18] The "Front Room Down Stairs" reflected his intention of using this space as the formal heart of the house. In his drawing room he placed a dozen mahogany chairs, two card tables, tea table, and sofa along with other lesser objects. Again, furnishings describe three modes of competitive social discourse: card playing, tea ceremonies, and conversation. Similarly, in the houses of eighteenth- and early-nineteenth-century Portsmouth merchants, ample evidence survives providing us with a sense of the internal architecture, furnishings, and sociology of the house. The house of Margaret and Thomas Manning incorporated architectural elements that reflected both local preference and cosmopolitan taste.[19] The exterior of the Manning House more closely followed the precedent set by other local merchant mansions raised in the late colonial period. With its plain clapboard exterior, heavy frame skeleton, hipped roof, and kitchen ell, the center-passage plan Manning House kept to local custom in its use of materials, plan, and its orientation to the street and nearby waterfront. The interior rooms included a parlor furnished with a heavily molded mantel highlighted with carved floral festoons, entry with an open stair, and paneled dining room and kitchen fireplace walls. The Mannings' parlor furnishings included carpeting, card tables, gilded mirror, ten chairs, two settees, and a sofa. Branched candlesticks, chimney ornaments, brass andirons, and other decorative items completed the parlor setting. Although architecturally less elaborate, the dining room both continued and combined the material display of commerce and sociability. A secretary and worktable stood alongside a sideboard, pembroke table, a set of ten leather-bottom chairs, and an extensive array of china and glassware ranging from a japanned knife tray to a silver-edged coconut cup.

In Norfolk, Virginia, merchant Moses and Elizabeth Myers's large brick house, erected in 1796, similarly connected local design preferences with those of the larger Atlantic trading community.[20] The ornate composition ornament in the Myerses' drawing room and adjacent salonlike passage echoed the Mannings' earlier architectural sensibility. Where the Mannings commissioned ornately carved mantelpieces for their parlor and the best chamber above, the Myerses drew on the late-eighteenth-century craze for composition ornament. Their parlor mantel was graced with applied swags, bosses, and classical figures. In terms of furnishings, the Myerses' parlor, like the Mannings', followed a similar pattern of card tables, seating furniture, and appropriately tasteful decorative details, based in large measure on the visual language of Neoclassicism. Philadelphians Stephen and Mary Parrish Collins pursued exactly the same strategy: a best room located on the second floor at the front of the house and furnished with the same forms of competitive entertainment and conversation: card tables, mahogany chairs, sofa, and ornaments such as glass candlesticks and "Chinese Jars."[21]

The continuities suggested by these furnishing strategies were reflected in the architectural detail of houses and translated into social exchange that extended beyond the best room. The dining room and parlor, for example, offered an important venue for face-to-face negotiations, one where the competitive culture of trade was expressed through the rituals of sociability.[22] The dining room table provided the arena for one aspect of these competitive exchanges, one in which the tabletop metaphorically functioned as a representation of the city itself. As prescribed in the popular literature of genteel society, the dining table offered a regular rectangular, or sometimes oval, field free from irregular topography and previous constructions that marred the city proper.[23] The table was divided into place settings equally distributed around its perimeter. Public points defined by serving dishes, candlesticks, and centerpieces were interspersed with individual places. The host and hostess occupied opposing ends of the table, and their company (often all men) was placed between them. In theory all the guests enjoyed equal access to the trade of the table and the transactions associated with conversation and etiquette. In reality, preferred seating (expressed, for example, in proximity to the host's seat of power) defined a topography of unequal access and authority.

The dining table, like the city plan, was a scene for exchange relations. Both were settings where objects were set in social motion. How individuals comported themselves in the parlor or counting house depended on a thorough knowledge of the rules of material as well as verbal discourse. Success was determined by the diners' ability to negotiate and conclude "trade" in an arena of competitive display that embraced domestic objects ranging from chairs to ceramics. Once seated at the table, or once standing in the counting house or on the vendue range, the ability to perform socially and commercially (and the two were not very far apart in the eighteenth-century Atlantic world) distinguished the players and provided the means to ascendancy or downfall. The flow of conversation along the lines of acceptable topics, the use of wit without resorting to insult or crassness, the ability to substantively inform and amuse enabled the dining-room participants to compete at the table. Similarly, the knowledge of how to eat—using the soup spoon for soup, accepting service, and even chewing—further defined the place of the individual in a competitive context which required knowledge as well as ability. The rituals of the dinner table mirrored the world of trade in the process of negotiation. Success in trade arose in part from the ability to negotiate advantage, a process in the counting house that drew on a complex knowledge of markets, profits, and competitors, as well as the forms of etiquette. Success at the dining table also reflected a similar competitive desire for gaining social advantage, but here the mannered skills and subtleties of sociability superseded knowledge of the marketplace. As two elements in an embedded landscape, the architectural settings and actions of trade and table informed and reinforced each other.

The connections suggested between tabletop and the plan of the mercantile city, however, do not stop with these comparisons. We need to mention two other key types of tables—those for tea and those for gaming. The connection between dining table, counting house, and card table is easy to establish.[24] The players situate themselves symmetrically around the perimeter of the card table and either play individually or in partnerships. The language of bidding, betting, bluffing, counting, and winning or losing are all those associated with the language and practice of trade. Unlike the dining table with its hierarchy of seating, the card table provides equal access to a field of competitive action. Here the focus of attention is more on the transactions of gaming and less on the niceties of dining etiquette and conversation.

Tea table topography, however, represents an entirely different terrain.[25] No less competitive and requiring considerable prior knowledge and ability to perform, the tea table appears to have been the domain of women. What distinguishes the tea table is its conspicuous asymmetry and social imbalance when in use. The circular table provided a pedestal for display where tea pot, creamer, sugar bowl, tea canister, cups, saucers, sugar tongs, and spoons were all set out for admiration. Their placement, while artful, did not provide for equal access to a field of discourse. Tea drinkers did not sit around the tea table in the same way that guests occupied their places at a dining table or in the manner that players faced each other across a card table. Instead, the hostess occupied a chair placed slightly askew to the center of the table and served her guests from a very different attitude of resident authority. Guests sometimes occupied chairs near the tea table or stationed themselves on chairs and settees around the parlor. The overall effect was one of studied casualness where the culture of the salon prevailed. In the world of urban exchange relations, the tea table and its array provided a field for the competitive trade in intimacy and manners. The emphasis on casual display by both hostess and guests relied on a sensibility that reified etiquette and social knowledge. Like gaming and dining, taking tea tended to occur in an architecturally constant setting defined by the best rooms in the house. The interior detailing of the parlor, drawing room, and dining room, then, possessed the quality of a landscape where major topographical features remained the constant setting for shifting forms of social relationships.

The ways in which different table top "terrains" intersect with one another and with the larger worlds of house and city remain largely unexplored. The material differences between the organization, appearance, and placement of dining, card, and tea tables suggest social as well as functional distinctions. Each offered a different "terrain" demanding different discursive skills; each realized its larger significance only when in use. The sociology of use, however, remains unresolved. Tea, as social behavior, changed through the eighteenth century. Largely the domain of women in the colonial period, the domain of the tea table opened to men in the early national period. But, even as men increasingly participated in taking tea as a heterosocial event, the seat of authority remained feminine.[26] Card playing in the home provided a considerably less gendered field for the display of social knowledge. "Card playing," observed Gerald Ward, "fulfilled a significant role in the relationship between the sexes. Card parties were often mixed, and the games allowed women to compete with men on equal terms, an otherwise rare occurrence."[27] Formal dining also changed in the post-Revolutionary decades, and dinners where women conversed shoulder to shoulder with men became more common. Variation and change in the sociology of tea, card, and dining tables suggest larger changes in the early American urban landscape where social life may not have been so rigidly divided as we suppose.

Investigations of the parlor and its social *topos* reveal only one embedded landscape of the Charleston single house. The second landscape introduced here focuses on the whole of the Charleston single house lot. The notion that Charleston lots take on the aspect of urban plantations is wonderfully introduced by Richard C. Wade, who observes that the single house "'compound' was the urban equivalent of the plantation. Like its rural analogue, it provided a means of social control as well as of shelter; it embodied the servile relationship between white and black; and it expressed a style of living appropriate to its setting."[28]

The extended single house plan consisted of a series of interconnected functional zones that communicated with one another and with the street via a number of routes (fig. 3.10). The main house abutted but did not front the street. Access from the street into the single house, therefore, followed one of two routes: from the sidewalk onto the piazza or from the sidewalk or street and down the carriage way. The piazza route led to the main and most formal entry into the stair passage, to a secondary entry into the breakfast room, or to a set of steps at the far end of the piazza which led down to the dooryards of the backbuildings. While these two options directed traffic of varying levels of formality and familiarity directly into the house, a third, the carriage way, provided a different avenue of access. The carriage way, admitting both wheeled and pedestrian traffic, led into the single house compound at street level. Pedestrians—slaves, for instance—

Fig. 3.10. View from the Single House Yard toward the Street. Access in and out of the single house compound included the carriage way and piazza. David L. Ames.

entering by the carriage way literally passed beneath the gaze of the occupants of the main house as they went about their business at the rear of the house or among the backbuildings (fig. 3.11). Carriages or horses carrying social equals entered nearly at eye level with the piazza. Passengers and riders stopped at the rear steps, stepped down into the yard, then up onto the piazza, and back toward the main entry. This mode of entry was only slightly less formal than entry from the sidewalk. In all instances the organization of the single house unit ran from street to backyard wall in a pattern of decreasing formality, declining architectural detail and finish, and increasing dirtiness. Similarly, single house organization shifts from predominantly social to predominantly utilitarian spaces.[29] These linked domestic spaces existed in and defined a highly stratified and processional urban plantation landscape.[30] In this world of symbolic stature, the slave's eye-view of the "big" house spoke to very different relationships and forms of movement than those defined by the master's and mistress's guests and business associates.

What has only been suggested here is the interpretive potential of the single house from the perspective of the slave quarter. The typical Charleston quarter of the late eighteenth century consisted of a two-story building with either a center or back wall chimneys. Ground-floor spaces were dedicated to cooking and washing functions. Upstairs, based on the little surviving architectural evidence we have, the quarter was divided into a number of living units including what appear to be common heated spaces and much smaller (in one instance only seven feet square) sleeping chambers. Windows were simply shuttered and left unglazed. The cramped slave living spaces seem to have served as little more than uncomfortable sleeping closets. For slaves the most likely arenas for social exchange included the work spaces in kitchens and wash houses, work yards, and the interstices of the city ranging from market stalls to riverside wharves.

Fig. 3.11. Backbuildings, Aiken-Rhett House, Elizabeth Street, Charleston. Built and enlarged during the first half of the nineteenth century, the Aiken-Rhett backbuildings compose a yard of two facing ranges. On the left are the kitchen, washhouse, and storage rooms with second-story quarters; on the right stand the carriage house and stables with second-story quarters and hay loft. David L. Ames.

What we have only begun to surmise, however, is how African-American space worked in the embedded landscapes of Charleston. For example, in the years after Denmark Vesey's revolt in 1822, the black majority's ability to move through the city increasingly drove a fearful white population to seal those cracks and contain physical movement, sight, and sound. Betrayed as much by urban space as their slaves, white Charlestonians constructed new masonry garden walls to replace old wooden fences and sealed rear doors and window openings that communicated with alleys and neighbors' yards.

Still, the Charleston single house lot did not simply ape a low-country plantation landscape. Plats of early Charleston illustrate a third set of embedded landscape relations that look outward to the trading world of the Atlantic. Many of the houses located along East Bay and its side streets possessed backlots occupied not by quarters, stables, and gardens, but by two- and three-story brick warehouses. Even the most sophisticated town house projects like Vanderhorst Row included one or two domestic support buildings close to the house and then ranks of commercial buildings crowding the expanse between kitchen and waterfront. The possible forms of the urban plantation associated with the Charleston single house reconciled the mercantile landscapes of the port city in yet another context. The urban complex, defined by the whole of the single house lot in all its possibilities, linked the local to the global in complex ways. In Bristol, for example, eighteenth-century town houses presented the face of regular brick terraces popularized in London. Typically these houses incorporated an entry that contained the stair to the upper stories as well as providing passage to the lot behind the dwelling. The organization of the domestic and working environments behind the Bristol town house extended into a number of divided and discrete spaces and buildings. Here, covered passages or piazzas connected the back of the house to separate kitchens that backed onto work yards furnished with stables, storehouses, and privies. Unlike the Charleston single house, the image the Bristol town house projected at the street resonated with the metropolitan culture of the capital city, but the organization of the houselot found its counterparts in provincial urban ports like Charleston.

Exploring the embedded landscapes of Charleston through the example of the single house is a process that begins with looking at buildings. Through the close examination of construction, plan, and ornament, we begin the process of using buildings to help us ask questions about context and landscape. How do the spaces contained and defined as house, table, yard, and city intersect as symbolically nested environments? The questions that buildings raise are those that address material realities of physical movement, decorative hierarchy, and functional space—realities that are dynamic, not static. The social and symbolic dynamics of buildings are about people and about how people organized aspects of their world through objects and their use. Thus, the discovery and interpretation of embedded landscapes cannot rely on architectural evidence alone. To reclaim and understand historic environments demands evocation of past lives reflecting diverse experiences ranging from Billy Robinson's kitchen quarter to Peter Bocquet's drawing room. The placement and appearance of dwellings, rooms, and yards find meaning through the ways in which their inhabitants furnished and used those spaces and the varying status and circumstances surrounding the embedded landscapes of everyday life. Thus, the Charleston single house yields the substance, messiness, complexity, and often conflicted sensibilities we seek to study and comprehend in vernacular architecture.

Notes

Special thanks are due to the many individuals in Charleston who have provided access to their homes and businesses and suggested new research directions. Their generosity in sharing their time and buildings is the proof of southern hospitality. I owe a world of gratitude to David and Lucinda Shields, Martha Zierden, Jonathan Poston, Louis Nelson, and Carter Hudgins. For help in other cities referred to in this essay, my deepest appreciation is extended to Robin Thornes, Marcia Miller, Holly Mitchell, Suzanne Rosenblum, Richard Candee, Roger Leech, and Gabrielle Lanier. Sally McMurry's thoughtful editing greatly improved this essay.

1. Letter, C. C. Hines to E. G. Ripley, Apr. 16, 1860, from Charleston South Carolina. Aetna Collection, RG 4 (Advertising and Public Relations Department), Series: Historical Files, South Carolina Folder. Courtesy Cigna Archives, Philadelphia, Pennsylvania.
2. Gene Waddell, "The Charleston Single House: An Architectural Survey," *Preservation Progress* 22 (2) (Mar. 1977): 4–8.
3. One of the most detailed descriptive treatments of a Charleston single house is Harriet P. and Albert Simons, "The William Burrows House of Charleston," *Winterthur Portfolio, III* (Winterthur, Delaware: Winterthur Museum, 1967), 172–203.
4. Mills Lane, *Architecture of the Old South: South Carolina* (New York: Abbeville Press, 1989), 70–72.
5. Ian Hodder, *Reading the Past: Current Approaches to Interpretation in Archaeology* (Cambridge: Cambridge Univ. Press, 1986), 118–46; Dell Upton, *Holy Things and Profane: Anglican Parish Churches in Colonial Virginia* (New York: Architectural History Foundation, 1986), 205–19.
6. These approaches have been demonstrated in other works on other architectural traditions. The concept of house types, for example, is a mainstay in Jay Edwards, "The Origins of Creole Architecture," *Winterthur Portfolio* 29 (2/3) (Summer/Autumn 1994): 155–89. The ensemble model is advanced in John Vlach, *Back of the Big House: The Architecture of Plantation Slavery* (Chapel Hill: Univ. of North Carolina Press, 1993), 193–94.
7. Lena Cowen Orlin, "The Tudor Long Gallery and the Progress of Privacy," lecture, department of English, Univ. of Delaware, Newark, Delaware, Sept. 20, 1995.
8. Edward A. Pearson, "Designs Against Charleston: The Trial Transcript of the Denmark Vesey Conspiracy of 1822," MS in preparation.
9. Leland Ferguson, *Uncommon Ground: Archaeology and Early African America* (Washington, D.C.: Smithsonian Institution Press, 1992).
10. Rhys Isaac, *The Transformation of Virginia, 1740–1790* (Chapel Hill: Univ. of North Carolina Press for the Institute of Early American History and Culture, 1982), 323–57.
11. Studies on the relationship of occupation and status related to places of residence and work are explored in Richard M. Bernard, "A Portrait of Baltimore in 1800: Economic and Occupational Patterns in an Early American City," *Maryland Historical Magazine* 69 (4) (Winter 1974): 341–60; Nan A. Rothschild, *New York City Neighborhoods: The Eighteenth Century* (San Diego: Academic Press, 1990); Mary Schweitzer, "The Spatial Organization of Federalist Philadelphia," *Journal of Interdisciplinary History* 34 (1) (Summer 1993): 31–57. In these studies and others exploring similar evidence and issues, there is little sense of the architectural context.
12. William Turnbaugh and Sarah Peabody Turnbaugh, "Alternative Applications of the Mean Ceramic Date Concept for Interpreting Human Behavior," *Historical Archaeology* 11 (1977): pp. 90–104.
13. Information on the three Church Street properties is contained in an excellent continuing series of newspaper articles, "Do You Know Your Charleston," by Robert P. Stockton, on the history of Charleston

property and architecture. See "'Bee House' Improperly Named," *Charleston News and Courier*, Jan. 28, 1980; "Dubose Heyward Lived Out Back," *News and Courier*, Feb. 12, 1979; and "'Single House' Is St. Philip's Rectory," *News and Courier*, Feb. 5, 1979. All articles are contained in the research files of the Historic Charleston Foundation. I am grateful to Jonathan Poston and Thomas Savage for sharing this material.

14. The amenity of the heated and decoratively treated commercial room in the Leger House was not found in all single houses with commercial spaces. Many more likely had simple board paneling and shelving and no fireplace. An example of the latter feature is at 77 Church Street.
15. Edward Chappell, "Looking at Buildings," *Fresh Advices: A Research Supplement* (Nov. 1984): i–vi.
16. Upton, *Holy Things and Profane*, 101–2.
17. Carl R. Lounsbury, *An Illustrated Glossary of Early Southern Architecture and Landscape* (New York: Oxford Univ. Press, 1994), 89–90. Mark Reinberger's continuing work on the history of eighteenth-century composition ornament fully explores both the technology and application of this decorative material.
18. Joseph Spear inventory, Baltimore County, Maryland, Inventories (1809–11), no. 26, Oct. 27, 1810, 474–75.
19. Thomas Manning Estate, Docket 9908 (1819), Rockingham County Recorder of Wills, Exeter, New Hampshire.
20. Indenture between Moses and John Myers and William B. Lamb and Richard Drummond, trustees, Deed Book 18 (1820), 11–12, Recorder of Deeds, Norfolk, Virginia.
21. Stephen Collins inventory, File 98, Book X (1794), 140, Philadelphia Probate Records, Philadelphia, Pennsylvania.
22. For British parallels, see Peter Borsay, *The English Urban Renaissance: Culture and Society in the Provincial Town, 1660–1770* (Oxford: Clarendon Press, 1989); Dan Cruikshank, *Life in the Georgian City* (London: Viking Press, 1990); Sylvia Collier and Sarah Pearson, *Whitehaven, 1660–1800: A New Town of the Late Seventeenth Century; A Study of Its Buildings and Urban Development* (London: Her Majesty's Stationery Office, 1991).
23. Barbara G. Carson, *Ambitious Appetites: Dining, Behavior, and Patterns of Consumption in Federal Washington* (Washington, D.C.: American Institute of Architecture Press, 1990), 103–35; Mark R. Wenger, "The Dining Room in Early Virginia," in *Perspectives in Vernacular Architecture, III*, ed. Thomas Carter and Bernard L. Herman (Columbia: Univ. of Missouri Press, 1989), 149–59.
24. Benjamin A. Hewitt, *The Work of Many Hands: Card Tables in Federal America, 1790–1820* (New Haven: Yale Univ. Art Gallery, 1982). For the etiquette and rules associated with card playing, see especially Gerald W. R. Ward, "'Avarice and Conviviality': Card Playing in Federal America," in Hewitt, *The Work of Many Hands*, 15–38.
25. Rodris Roth, "Tea Drinking in Eighteenth-Century America: Its Etiquette and Equipage" (1961), reprinted in *Material Life in America, 1600–1860*, ed. Robert Blair St. George (Boston: Northeastern Univ. Press, 1988), 439–62; Diana diZerega Wall, *The Archaeology of Gender: Separating the Spheres in Urban America* (New York: Plenum Press, 1994), 122–25, 138–44. For an excellent archaeologically based study of the material culture of Charleston's eighteenth-century urban elites, see Martha Zierden, "Just Imported: The Archaeology of Urban Life in Eighteenth-Century Charleston," paper read at the Society for Historical Archaeology annual meetings, Washington, D.C., Jan. 6, 1995.
26. David S. Shields explores the social history of eighteenth-century tea and tea table society in "Tea Tables and Salons," in *Civil Tongues and Polite Letters* (Chapel Hill: Univ. of North Carolina Press, forthcoming).
27. Ward, "Avarice and Conviviality," 29.

28. Richard C. Wade, *Slavery in the Cities: The South 1820–1860* (New York: Oxford Univ. Press, 1964), 61.

29. James Deetz summarizes Lewis Binford's tripartite definition of function in his *In Small Things Forgotten: The Archaeology of Early American Life* (Garden City: Anchor Press/Doubleday, 1977), 50–52. A parallel discussion appears in Jon Goss, "The Built Environment and Social Theory: Towards an Architectural Geography," *Professional Geographer* 40 (4) (1988): 392–403.

30. Wade, *Slavery in the Cities,* 55–79. Dell Upton's treatment of articulated, processional landscapes in colonial Virginia provides a vital sense of the types and meanings of physical movement in hierarchical landscapes. See "White and Black Landscapes in Eighteenth-Century Virginia," reprinted in *Material Life in America,* ed. Robert Blair St. George, 357–69; see also Chappell, "Looking at Buildings," which offers a more intimate means of identifying hierarchical landscapes contained within houses.

CHAPTER 4

Carl Lounsbury

The Dynamics of Architectural Design in Eighteenth-Century Charleston and the Lowcountry

On June 22, 1753, James Glen, the royal governor of South Carolina, convened a meeting of members of the King's Council and Commons House of Assembly to observe the anniversary of King George II's accession to the throne with a grand ceremony. The crowning moment of the day occurred when these distinguished leaders of the colony gathered at the northwest corner of Broad and Meeting Streets in Charleston to lay the cornerstone of the first provincial statehouse.[1] Work progressed slowly due to a shortage of funds to finance the rapidly escalating cost of this undertaking, but when officials moved into this two-story brick structure three years later, they took great satisfaction in knowing that they had completed one of the grandest public buildings erected in the American colonies. Its English Palladian form and detailing asserted the refined tastes of its provincial builders and provided an appropriate setting for the formal rituals and ceremonial activities that punctuated the rhythm of public life in the colony.

Yet, this public accomplishment was short-lived. The statehouse and much of the city suffered damage during the Revolution. The destruction and humiliation wrought by the British occupation of Charleston was followed after the war by the decision in 1788 to remove the state government to the upcountry village of Columbia. Shortly thereafter, a further blow was struck when the statehouse burned.[2] In the early 1790s, the building became the Charleston County Courthouse as a third story was added to the old walls and the interior refitted. Although the building served as the center of legal life in the city for the next two hundred years, its earlier form was severely altered and the original plan concealed by several generations of renovations and two large additions.[3] By the time Hurricane Hugo damaged the courthouse in 1989, the early history of the building had been so forgotten that no one was certain whether anything had survived of the old statehouse. The Hugo disaster provided the opportunity for a systematic study of the fabric and associated documents, which rescued the building's architectural and cultural history from its long obscurity.[4] With a firm commitment to revive the fortunes of this civic institution, the Charleston County Council undertook to restore the courthouse to its late-eighteenth-century appearance.

Charleston's architecture is deceptively familiar. Like the courthouse, it has been encrusted with legend, but much remains unexamined. The distinctive urban environment is well known, attracting many thousands of visitors annually, but the historic development of a cityscape defined by walled lots, narrow frontages, and tiered piazzas is less familiar. The plans and rich detailing of a few dwellings, such as the Miles Brewton House and the Nathaniel Russell House, are icons in the history of early American architecture. However, as the story of the statehouse suggests, most of Charleston still needs thorough field and documentary research. The first serious investigation of Charleston's architectural heritage began in the late 1910s and flourished for more than two decades as local architects and historians measured many of the great landmarks, plumbed private and public archives for building documents, and published their findings in a series of articles and

Fig. 4.1. The Charleston County Courthouse, 1883. This view of the courthouse shows it as it was reconfigured following the fire of 1788 and prior to its first major renovation in 1883. Courtesy of the Historic Charleston Foundation.

books which established the boundaries of architectural discussion for the next half century.[5] Although well illustrated, they lacked interpretive analysis and had a limited perspective. Much of the writing from the 1920s and 1930s described in the narrowest terms the stylistic development of Charleston according to national patterns. As might be expected of their time and place, they concentrated on the great colonial and antebellum dwellings south of Calhoun Street and the mansion houses standing along the Cooper and Ashley Rivers and their tributaries but ignored vast areas of the urban and plantation environment. Stores, warehouses, postbellum dwellings, slave houses, and kitchens received little notice.

Without a flourishing research institution or university in the area with a cadre of scholars and graduate students mining the wealth of documentary and field evidence, few added fresh perspectives to Charleston's architectural history in subsequent decades. Given this background, any new work must begin by re-examining many old assumptions. What has been written in recent years echoes or refines but seldom questions the basic premises underpinning the work of the pioneering generation of scholars.[6] For example, many have argued for a Caribbean source for the brightly colored stuccoed exteriors. This belief affected twentieth-century preservation activities in the city. During the 1930s, the restoration of a number of houses on East Bay Street—now known as Rainbow Row—was guided by this colorful notion of a Caribbean influence. But when did buildings such as these, and St. James Church, Goose Creek, receive their first coat of stucco? Completed by Barbadian immigrants by 1717, St. James was originally brickfaced and only later stuccoed.[7] Charles Fraser's sketch of the church in 1800 is tantalizingly confusing. Did he portray the red bricks set off by jambs, quoins, and cornice painted white or had the brickwork by that point been roughcast and painted red? If it were still brick-faced in 1800, one can only wonder about the lingering effects of Barbados on third- and fourth-generation native South Carolinians.[8] This is not to dismiss the earlier use of stucco in Charleston and the lowcountry. In 1768, scarcely a dozen years after its completion, the statehouse had a coat of stucco applied over its finely detailed brickwork which had featured rubbed jack arches.[9] What needs careful documentation is the advent of this fashion for roughcast. Stucco and Roman cement were less expensive means of imitating the more prestigious material of stone, and Charlestonians certainly took to this trend with great zeal, as an Englishman noted in a visit to the city in 1774. By then, the statehouse, St. Michael's Church, and the nearby guardhouse were "plaistered over so well on the outside to imitate stone that I really took them all for stone buildings at first." Both Broad and Meeting Streets contained "many large handsome modern built brick houses also some of brick inside and plaistered over on the outside so as to imitate stone very well."[10] It seems likely then that colonial Charlestonians selected more subdued tones for their decorative stucco than twentieth-century restorations would suggest.

Another long held but unexamined assumption is that the Charleston piazza derived from Caribbean sources. South Carolinians did construct open-sided porches or piazzas by the 1730s, but were they adopting a form developed by Caribbean settlers? Was there any correlation between the form's appearance in the two regions? Certainly trade relations and social networks between the two regions were strong throughout the colonial period, but there is no intrinsic reason to suppose that the architectural influences operated in only one direction; indeed, building materials and house frames were shipped from the mainland to the islands.[11] On the Caribbean side of the equation, scholars still lack the type of fieldwork necessary to answer critical questions about the chronological appearance of stucco and piazzas. The question of Charleston's architectural inheritance and legacy clearly begs closer scrutiny, especially for the formative period of the mid-eighteenth century.

Architectural Design in Charleston and the Lowcountry

Fig. 4.2. St. James, Goose Creek, Watercolor by Charles Fraser, c. 1800. Courtesy of the Gibbes Museum of Art, Charleston.

Much of the culture that gave Charleston and the lowcountry such a distinctive character was fashioned in the forty years between Bishop Roberts's painting of the Charleston waterfront in the late 1730s and the occupation of the city by the British during the Revolution. As the plantation system matured during the 1730s, wealth flowed into the colony at an unprecedented level, partly generated by a dramatic increase in the production of rice and the introduction of indigo.[12] By the time of the construction of the statehouse in the 1750s, these exports had made many planters among the wealthiest people in British North America. On the eve of the Revolution, the per capita wealth of Charleston was as much as four times that of people living in the Chesapeake and close to six times higher than that of the inhabitants of New York and Philadelphia.[13]

Agricultural prosperity transformed the city of Charleston. The surge in agricultural exports was accompanied by the introduction of a variety of imported goods that soon turned luxury items into necessities. Charleston was the entrepôt for this highly productive hinterland and had become a community where modest fortunes could be made catering to the needs of the planter plutocrats. Doctors, lawyers, and schoolmasters enriched the fabric of urban life as men of taste and education saw their skills and services in increasing demand. Merchants flocked to the city to establish wholesale and retail trade connections with firms in London, Bristol, and Glasgow and subsidiary stores deep in the Carolina backcountry.

Planters, provincial officials, and professionals found Charleston's shops filled with items ranging from imported ceramics, tea, and books to locally produced furniture and coaches.

Like few other cities in America, Charleston acted as a magnet, drawing the rich and powerful as well as the poor and enslaved. Besides the lure of consumer goods, planters were attracted to the city for many other reasons, not the least of which was the quest for political power. Clustered almost entirely in Charleston, the offices and courts of the provincial government so dominated the colony that few local institutions emerged that could serve as counterweights. The way to power in South Carolina was not through the county court or parish vestry, as in Virginia or Maryland, but through a position in the provincial government or elected assembly. More than any other British colony on the American mainland, Charleston functioned like an old medieval city-state.[14]

Commerce and politics may have dominated the talk of taverns and dining rooms, but Charleston also offered its inhabitants and visitors many social and cultural diversions. The pursuit of pleasure by the provincial elite spawned a host of new public activities and forms of entertainments. Theaters, music concerts, assemblies, clubs, and other social events enriched the cultural life of the community. In 1773 a young Bostonian, Josiah Quincy, carefully recorded in his diary the details of a very rich and active social world far more brilliant than that of his native city. Quincy spent much of his time dining in great houses, drinking fine wines, toasting the beauties of the city, and talking politics. On other occasions he attended balls and assemblies where he noticed the women and men "dressed with richness and elegance uncommon with us."[15] Public walks, long rooms, libraries, and museums provided places and opportunities for members of polite society to display their charms, beauty, and good breeding and to find suitable matrimonial partners. Over time, marriage alliances cemented the bond between planters, merchants, and professionals, creating a self-conscious elite society.

The concentration of wealth in the city naturally affected the habits of its citizens. As another eighteenth-century visitor observed:

> the manner of the inhabitants of Charleston are as different from those of the other North American cities as are the products of their soil. The profitable rice and indigo plantations are abundant sources of wealth for many considerable families, who therefore give themselves to the enjoyment of every pleasure and convenience to which their warm climate and better circumstances invite them. Throughout, there prevails here a finer manner of life ... there were neither domestic circumstances to stand in the way nor particular religious principles, as among the Presbyterians of New England or the Quakers of Pennsylvania, to check the enjoyment of good living. So luxury in Carolina has made the greatest advance, and their manner of life, dress, equipages, furniture, everything denotes a higher degree of taste and love of show, and less frugality than in the northern provinces.[16]

Charleston was not a strange and hedonistic Southern version of Boston or Philadelphia, but a city whose social patterns and development more closely followed the trends characteristic of most eighteenth-century British provincial cities. The activities and cultural institutions established by polite society in Charleston in the third quarter of the eighteenth century had similar counterparts in York, Norwich, Bristol, and a host of smaller provincial cities in England and Scotland, where horse races, concerts, theaters, fraternal and social clubs, and scientific societies enriched the fabric of urban life.[17] The economic and cultural maturation of South Carolina elite society in the late colonial period is what historian Jack P. Greene has described as the process of social replication or Anglicization. After a period of growing acculturation when colonists adjusted the slave-based plantation economy to lowcountry conditions, the emerging elite displayed a strong desire to replicate British society in South Carolina and began to take pride in the extent to which it was coming to increasingly resemble the metropolitan culture of London.[18] Eliza Lucas's observation that "the people live very Gentile and very much in the English taste" was echoed by countless others.[19]

One of the most striking manifestations of this social replication of metropolitan culture was the substantial investment in the reshaping and refining of the architectural fabric of the city since, in the eyes of contemporaries throughout the Anglo-American world, a town's physical form was the most conspicuous sign of its prosperity and power, expressing the social and cultural aspirations of those who resided there. Grand public buildings were simply the most obvious indication of this process. The simultaneous construction of the statehouse and St. Michael's Church formed one of the most impressive civic squares in British America. Unlike the hybrid form of the capitol in Williamsburg or the awkward provincialism of the statehouses in Philadelphia and Boston, the South Carolina statehouse, with its projecting pedimented central block, stood squarely in the Palladian fashion, which characterized the assize courts and assembly rooms in leading provincial English towns. The transatlantic antecedents of the Charleston statehouse are readily apparent in its function and classical details. The scale, form, massing, and detailing of shire halls and other civic buildings provided Charlestonians with vivid images of civic architecture. Most were two or three stories tall and stretched from five to eleven bays in length, with a massive door or projecting pediment usually accentuating the center of the building. A mixture of rich details—compass-headed windows, niches, cupolas, coats of arms, rustication, and arcades—imbued these public buildings with a conspicuous degree of architectural pretension.

How these English public building prototypes were translated into a formal design for workmen to follow on the building site remains unknown, since no drawings or specifications for the statehouse's construction survive. As William Rigby Naylor's 1767 drawings for the Exchange exemplify, there were a number of master builders working in Charleston who were more than capable of devising a plan and perhaps an elevation for the statehouse. Yet, even drawings such as these do not necessarily reveal the individual or source responsible for the design. It is more than likely that the actual design decisions emerged from the deliberations of a building committee. Composed almost entirely of members of the provincial assembly, the statehouse building committee simply appropriated recognizable architectural forms whose symbolic attributes would have been quickly understood in any part of the English empire.[20] Many of the commissioners had considerable experience in this new architectural vocabulary. For example, in the mid-1740s, Charles Pinckney formulated a plan and estimated the costs of an imposing two-story brick dwelling on Colleton Square facing the Cooper River. With its engaged pilastered portico and Venetian window lighting the stair landing at a right angle to the entrance hall, Pinckney's house was one of the first in the city to embody many of the English Palladian features that were to be repeated in the statehouse design.

No account or minutes of the building commission survive, so it is difficult to ascertain the precise role of each member or to suggest which one of them (or any other individual) was responsible for the design of the structure. Throughout most of the American colonies in the late colonial period, the design of public buildings was often the result of collective decisions. Generally, a committee would decide upon the size, plan, number of stories, materials, and placement of doors and windows, with the details developed in

Fig. 4.3. Courthouse, Warwick, Warwickshire, 1725.

consultation with the builder (or "undertaker," as he was known in the eighteenth century). Secondary decisions were then made about interior and exterior finishes, leaving the details of execution more or less in the hands of the professional builders and individual craftsmen who carried out their work in the customary fashion of the city or region.

In the overall design, there was little to distinguish the statehouse from the formulaic pattern of public and country house architecture that had flourished in Great Britain for more than a quarter of a century. In this broader context, the severely plain, two-story rectangular block set off in the center by a projecting three-bay pediment fit comfortably into prevailing English architectural fashion. Only the absence of a rusticated ground floor and the lack of carved or molded detailing around the apertures marked the structure as a modest provincial interpretation of metropolitan taste. Yet, in the context of the American colonies, it was indeed a landmark, heralding a more sophisticated application of design ideas in public building.

If the public buildings of Charleston emulated the best of British provincial design, the form of the city's dwellings began to respond to local circumstances. At no time did Charlestonians mistake their society for a mirror of London, for Charleston society had been profoundly conditioned by the novel physical environment of the New World as well as by the peculiar economic and social conditions which had emerged in three or four generations of settlement.[21] Fueling the wealth of the elite of Charleston was a plantation culture based on the exploitation of a large enslaved population of African laborers. This vast black presence defined for white South Carolinians a social order that was manifestly different from any English precedent. It also helped shape a remarkably distinctive plantation and urban landscape.

Charleston's domestic architecture in the eighteenth century was a complex and continuous interaction between local experience and metropolitan ideals. From the 1740s through the early national period, the city was thoroughly transformed. Bishop Roberts's late 1730s view of the port depicts a densely packed urban scene with large dwellings, warehouses, and stores rising two and three stories. If the topography illustrated in a contemporary map is still familiar, the buildings shown in Roberts's painting are scarcely so. The features which are characteristic of Charleston architecture today—houses with narrow frontages and multistory piazzas—are nowhere to be seen. Instead, buildings of five, seven, and even ten bays line Bay Street; shallow, bracket-supported balconies open from second-story doorways; and dormers light the garrets of Dutch and M-roofs. A few buildings have curvilinear gables. The buildings painted by Roberts represent a period of architectural experimentation, a period of creolization when new forms and new materials, such as tabby walls and cypress wainscotting, were employed by the inhabitants of Charleston and the surrounding countryside.[22] Some of these conventions were cast aside—for example, the broad fronted alignment of buildings toward the street. Others were given up as fashioned dictated—the use of M-roofs for example. A small number, however, continued in use and became part of the lowcountry building tradition even while losing favor elsewhere.[23]

Bishop Roberts captured the Charleston cityscape at a moment when all was about to be swept away—by fire and fashion. Fires certainly destroyed most of what is depicted in his view of the port from the Cooper River. These buildings were not replaced in kind, but by something entirely new. Merchants, planters, and professionals began to construct dwellings, service buildings, and shops whose orientation and plans clearly articulated new sensibilities about interactions among family and guests, servants and masters, shopkeepers and customers. Foremost was the emergence of a domestic plan and lot arrangement that was to dominate Charleston for a century and a half. The *single house,* as it came to be called in the late eighteenth century, stood two or more stories and contained a center-stair passage flanked on either side by a single depth of rooms.[24] The dwelling's shorter end fronted the street and usually had a piazza of one or more stories stretching across the long entrance facade. At the back of the house stood service structures such as kitchens, stables, wash houses, and

Fig. 4.4. Bishop Roberts, *Prospect of Charles Town,* c. 1739, Engraving by William Toms. This partial view of the Charleston waterfront depicts Bay Street from Granville's Bastion in the south to the Council Chamber at the head of Broad Street. The panorama of the port continues northward just past St. Philip's Church. Courtesy of the Colonial Williamsburg Foundation.

slave quarters. A walled or railed fence enclosed this urban compound whose entrance was accentuated by gate piers. Entrance to the house was through a frontispiece which gave access onto the piazza. Halfway down the piazza, a doorway opened into the stair passage. As Bernard Herman has observed, the form of the single house responded to a combination of local circumstances: merchant and planter families sought to cement their position in society by erecting well-fashioned houses, developmental pressures created narrow deep lots, a warm climate encouraged the use of open but formal porches for semipublic activities, and walled enclosures provided garden privacy and helped regulate the movement of slaves and outsiders in this domestic setting.[25]

Even as the form of Charleston residences was emerging as a distinctive regional type, in terms of furnishings and ornamentation, Anglicization still prevailed. Because it was a port, Charleston had direct access to new architectural ideas promoted in design books (which were stocked by the city's booksellers) and in the buildings seen by the merchants and planters who frequented London, Bristol, and Glasgow on a regular basis. Pouring into the city as well were costly imported materials like marble chimneypieces, Delft hearth tiles, and Central and South American mahogany, along with a steady stream of highly skilled British tradesmen who sought their livelihood in a rich, bustling community. The intricately carved chimneypieces found in dozens of dwellings throughout the city exemplify the skills of a number of London-trained immigrant craftsmen who found an appreciative clientele eager for the latest in metropolitan fashion.[26]

Charleston provided the opportunity to construct bold, classically inspired buildings on a scale that few other American cities could match. The South Carolina planter elite, unlike its counterparts in Virginia and Maryland, chose to make the capital its primary place of residence, electing to spend only short intervals of time on country estates. Residing in town for extended periods, the great planters and their merchant suppliers maintained opulent urban residences, for it was here, in the city, that the notion of style mattered most.[27] The imported materials and fine detailing of dwellings such as merchant Miles Brewton's house had few rivals elsewhere in the colonies. According to Josiah Quincy, Brewton's house was "said to have cost him 8000£ sterling" and contained, besides the carved woodwork of the London-trained Ezra Waite, "the grandest hall I ever beheld, azure blue satin window curtains, rich blue paper with gilt, mashee borders, most elegant pictures, excessive grand and costly looking glasses."[28] It is no accident, then, that building in this city was more Anglicized, more substantial, and more embellished, than any other city in the entire South.

This provincial architecture was not a diminished image of metropolitan design ideas, diluted or distorted by ill-trained artisans unable to comprehend the sophistication and complexity of the original forms.[29] Rather, it drew selectively from local and metropolitan customs. As Dell Upton has argued, colonists carefully chose those aspects of the metropolitan corpus which suited their own particular needs and desires.[30] Academic design concepts did not displace local patterns but became intricately woven into the native building tradition, creating distinctive regional forms. Many features of this eighteenth-century academic architecture, such as rubbed brickwork, hipped roofs, and oval windows, merged with local elements and practices from the previous century so that the great houses and public buildings constructed in the late colonial period were blends of Anglo-Georgian ideals and Creole building practices.

In colonial Charleston, features such as piazzas, wooden shingles, and beaded weatherboards set the city apart from Georgian London. Social conditions, levels of wealth, access to materials, technological capabilities, craft skills, climate, and topography shaped its response to building forms. The process of designing, building, and furnishing a dwelling was a complex one involving the participation of dozens of people in various and ever-changing combinations and circumstances. Small elements such as a window architrave or even more complex ones such as a chimneypiece or paneled door may show few variations from examples illustrated in imported builders' books, but their execution, treatment, and combination with other elements almost invariably reveal local or regional patterns. Architrave moldings, balusters, and other Georgian details might attest to the superficial resemblances of dwellings in eighteenth-century Bristol and Charleston, but differences in materials, construction, scale, plans, and the arrangement of buildings in the landscape made the architectural character of the two ports as distinct as the accents of their inhabitants.

Regional variations remained a part of the building process because much of the design and fabrication of buildings was left in the hands of skilled craftsmen. The thousand and one decisions about any building—the finish of a piece of material or the detailing of a staircase—continued to be resolved by craftsmen on site. Although building specifications grew in their list of particulars as clients indicated their choices of treatments and details, many fundamental as well as minor elements were left to the traditional rules governing the execution of workmanlike craftsmanship. Contracts may have required good, well-fired bricks and hard lime mortar, but rarely did they specify types of brick bonding, mortar-joint widths and finishes, or range of brick colors. It was understood from long-standing experience what was expected, and any variation from time-honored practices of a particular locality required explicit explanation. Thus, the monochromatic brickwork in Charleston in the late colonial period distinguishes it from the characteristic penchant for variegated surfaces in the Chesapeake. Each region had evolved its own standards of practice. What was not spelled out was left to custom, so that tradition continued to shape the form and finish of most buildings erected in early America.

The interplay between outside ideas and local building practices can be seen at Pompion Hill, a brick chapel of ease erected between 1763 and 1765 in the parish of St. Thomas, Berkeley County. It is a building of mixed pedigree. Compared to a contemporaneous 20-by-30-foot log church in neighboring St. John's Parish, Pompion Hill, measuring 36 by 48 feet, must have seemed the height of fashion.[31] Contrasted with English parish churches of the period, its parochial origins are unmistakable. From a topographical view, its solitary location on the bluff overlooking the East Branch of the Cooper River more than twenty miles northeast of Charleston would be unusual in much of America and Britain but common in the lowcountry.[32] There are isolated English churches, but their secluded positions usually derive from a very different set of historical circumstances. Many of these isolated churches are the parish churches of now deserted medieval villages or appendages of a great estate, such as St. Mary's, Avington, Hampshire (1768).

Fig. 4.5. Pompion Hill Chapel, St. Thomas and St. Denis Parish, Berkeley County, S.C., 1763.

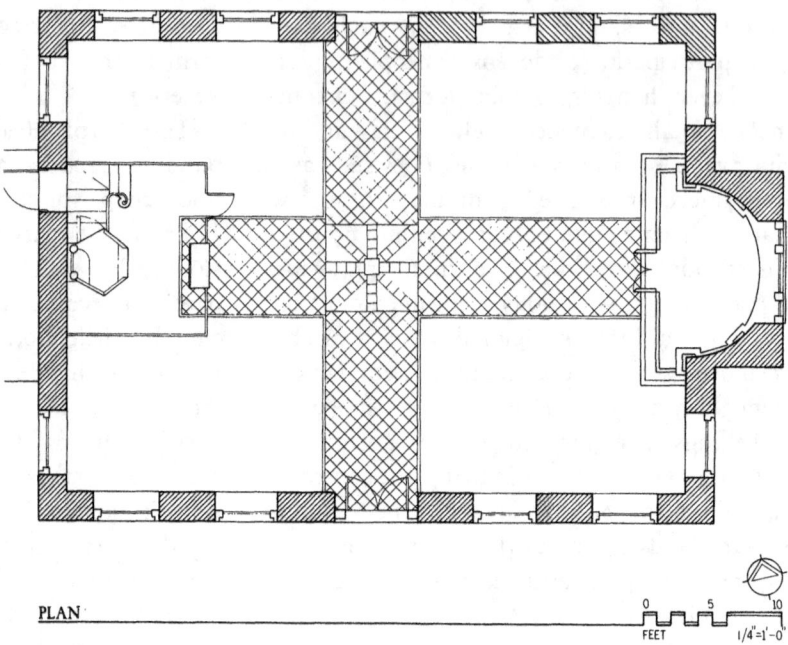

Fig. 4.6. Plan of Pompion Hill Chapel.

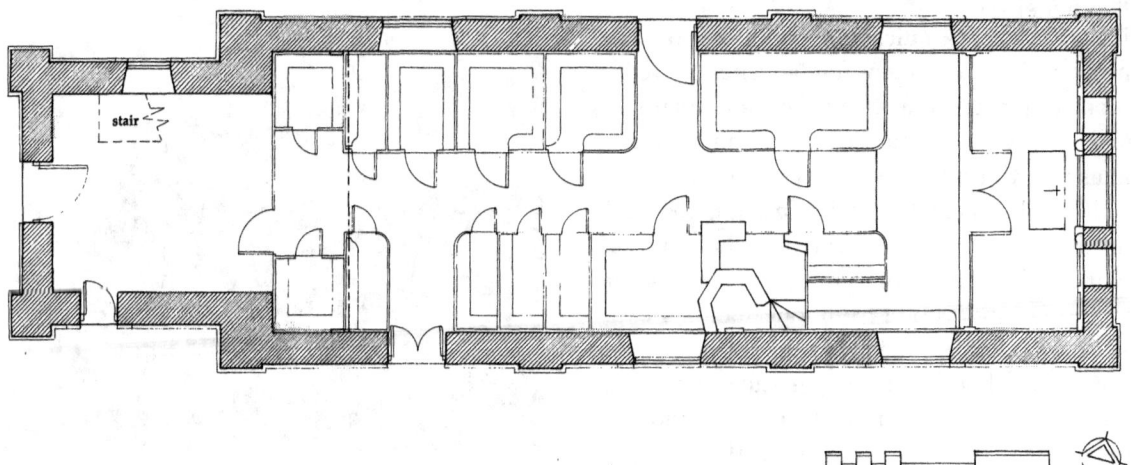

Fig. 4.7. Plan of St. Mary's Church, Avington, Hampshire.

Inside Pompion Hill, the form and enriched carving of the pulpit drew inspiration from the plates of Batty Langley's *Workman's Treasury of Designs,* which was first published in 1740 and had wide currency in the American colonies.[33] Whereas English pulpits of this period were fabricated out of oak, walnut, or Baltic pine, at Pompion Hill craftsmen used a local material to construct a "genteel Pulpit of Cedar."[34] The similarities with polygonally shaped pulpits in other Anglican churches such as St. Mary's, Avington, are unmistakable and underscore the universality of many design details in the eighteenth-century Anglo-American world.[35] Yet, the rectangular layout of Pompion Hill Chapel, with the Langley-derived pulpit standing in the west end opposite the chancel, its two entrances placed in the center of the longer north and south walls, and the nineteenth-century benches facing each other across a central aisle, is much more akin to a dissenting meeting house plan than the linear Anglican arrangement of Avington Church.

On the exterior, the absence of a dominant west tower accentuates Pompion Hill's affinity with the meeting house form, and it is only the Venetian window in the east wall of the shallow chancel which reveals its Anglican affiliation and ecclesiastical orientation. The oxeye and compass-headed windows follow contemporary Anglo-American public building practices, but the brickwork, mortar joints, and transomed shutters are unmistakably South Carolinian. Clearly, the form of Pompion Hill Chapel derived from the amalgamation and interaction of homegrown and academic sources. It was this rich blend, not the individual ingredients, that made Pompion Hill Chapel, in the eyes of one of its contemporaries, "one of the best country churches in Carolina."[36]

As Pompion Hill Chapel suggests, this imaginative interplay between regional traditions and metropolitan influences was firmly embedded in Charleston and lowcountry architecture by the middle of the eighteenth century. Searching contemporary English architectural books for design precedents for public building forms or the enriched woodwork found in grand domestic rooms may be a useful exercise in connoisseurship, but can lead to a serious misreading of the nature of the design process. Looking at buildings in this manner only promotes an anachronistic and artificial distinction between high-style and vernacular building, a perspective as distorted today as it was alien to contemporary builders of the South Carolina statehouse.[37] Such discrete categorizations encumber our understanding of the complexity of the colonial building process in Charleston, the lowcountry, and the rest of early America.

Notes

The opportunity to study the Charleston County Courthouse with my colleagues Willie Graham and Mark R. Wenger of the Architectural Research Department at the Colonial Williamsburg Foundation and Brown Morton of Mary Washington College induced us to take a closer look at the buildings and documents of eighteenth-century Charleston. The following observations about the state of architectural research in this area grew out of that study and were presented as a keynote address at the annual meeting of the Vernacular Architecture Forum in 1994. I am very grateful to Jonathan Poston of the Historic Charleston Foundation for his encouragement of our research, his reading of the earlier version of this chapter, and the kind hospitality shown to all of us during our many visits to Charleston over the past decade.

1. After the cornerstone was laid, Governor Glen and his entourage retired to John Gordon's tavern at the northeast corner of Broad and Church Streets for dinner and toasts to celebrate the occasion. See *South Carolina Gazette,* July 2, 1753.

2. *Columbian Herald,* Feb. 7, 1788.
3. Although the historical importance of the courthouse was acknowledged by Charlestonians throughout the nineteenth and twentieth centuries, few were inspired by the building. In her 1945 study of Charleston, Beatrice St. Julien Ravenel noted that most critics agreed with the verdict passed on the building nearly a century earlier, which was attributed to the antebellum novelist and native Charlestonian William Gilmore Simms: "It is content to be big, solid, square, and lofty, serving its purposes, and making no fuss, and challenging no man's admiration" (*Harper's Magazine,* June 1857). Quoted in Beatrice St. Julien Ravenel, *Architects of Charleston* (Charleston, 1945; rev. ed., 1954; reprint, Columbia: Univ. of South Carolina Press, 1992), 75.
4. For an account of that investigation, see Carl Lounsbury, Willie Graham, Mark R. Wenger, and W. Brown Morton, *An Architectural Analysis of the Charleston County Courthouse,* unpublished report for the Historic Charleston Foundation, August 1991.
5. Published in 1917, Alice and Daniel Huger Smith's *The Dwelling Houses of Charleston* (Philadelphia: J. B. Lippincott Company) was one of the first efforts to chronicle the history of Charleston's architecture. Antiquarian in tone, Harriette Kershaw Leiding's *Historic Houses of South Carolina* (Philadelphia: J. B. Lippincott Company, 1921) featured buildings from the entire state and included evocative drawings by Alfred Hutty. The most visually detailed early study was *The Early Architecture of Charleston,* edited by two local architects, Albert Simons and Samuel Lapham Jr. The first edition was published in New York in 1927 by the Press of the American Institute of Architects under the title of *The Octagon Library of Early American Architecture, Volume I: Charleston, South Carolina.* Generously illustrated with photographs and measured drawings but containing little analytical text, the volume drew attention to the finest houses and public buildings to survive in the city, many of which had been or were to be renovated by the authors' architectural firm. In 1938 Charleston historian Samuel Gaillard Stoney, along with Simons and Lapham, published *Plantations of the Carolina Low Country* under the auspices of the Carolina Art Association. Stoney described the important plantations and churches and the families associated with them in the area surrounding the city. Measured plans and detail drawings by Simons and Lapham and evocative photographs by Frances Benjamin Johnston and Ben Judah Lubschez and others accompanied Stoney's brief survey of the historical and architectural developments of the region. Unfortunately, Stoney provided little documentation for the dating of the buildings in his survey. The last major work of the period, *Architects of Charleston,* appeared at the end of World War II and surpassed previous studies in its attention to archival sources. A leading member of the city's nascent historic preservation movement in the 1930s, Beatrice St. Julien Ravenel produced a documentary history of the careers of the city's principal architects and builders of the eighteenth and nineteenth centuries.
6. See, for example, Mills Lane, *Architecture of the Old South: South Carolina* (Savannah: Beehive Press, 1984). In a solidly researched study with much new information, Kenneth Severens elaborated on the traditional perspective in *Charleston Antebellum Architecture and Civic Destiny* (Knoxville: Univ. of Tennessee Press, 1988). His study of civic rather than domestic architecture in the antebellum period called attention to several previously ignored buildings.
7. In 1727, the parish minister wrote that "St. James Goose Creek is built of brick cornered with plaister work in imitation of Hewed Stone, as are 3 Door Cases Wst No & So and 9 handsome arched Windows are plaistered answerably" (Rev. Richard Ludlam to the Secretary of the Society for the Propagation of Gospel, SPG Letterbook A, XX, Fulham Palace, London, Dec. 12, 1727). Originally, the walls were carefully laid in Flemish bond with decoratively finished mortar joints.

8. In 1810 the vestry of St. James advertised that it would "receive proposals for ROUGH-CASTING their Parish Church." Whether or not this was the first time the entire building was stuccoed is unknown. See *Charleston Courier*, Sept. 26, 1810.
9. In 1768 Peter and John Horlbeck received £1,250 for "Rough Casting the State House." *Journal of the Commons House of Assembly* No. 37, Part 2, 526–27, Feb. 23, 1768, Columbia, South Carolina Department of Archives and History.
10. "Charleston, S.C., in 1774 as Described by an English Traveller," reprinted in *The Colonial South Carolina Scene: Contemporary Views, 1697–1774*, ed. H. Roy Merrens (Columbia: Univ. of South Carolina Press, 1977), 282.
11. It seems unlikely that the earliest white settlers to South Carolina from Britain's West Indian colonies such as Barbados were familiar with the piazza. Immigration from this area fell to a trickle by the first decades of the eighteenth century, a full generation before the advent of the piazza in the lowcountry. On the relationship between the West Indies and South Carolina, see Jack P. Greene, "Colonial South Carolina and the Caribbean Connection," in his *Imperatives, Behaviors, and Identities: Essays in Early American Cultural History* (Charlottesville: Univ. Press of Virginia, 1992), 68–86. For an overview of the issues involved in the study of Caribbean architecture, see William Chapman, "Irreconcilable Differences: Urban Residences in the Danish West Indies, 1700–1900," *Winterthur Portfolio* 30 (Summer/Autumn 1995): 129–33.
12. John J. McCusker and Russell R. Menard, *The Economy of British America, 1607–1789* (Chapel Hill: Univ. of North Carolina Press, 1985), 179; Kenneth Morgan, "The Organization of the Colonial American Rice Trade," *William and Mary Quarterly*, 3d ser., 52 (July 1995): 433–52.
13. Greene, "Colonial South Carolina and the Caribbean Connection," 83.
14. For a study of the cultural and political life of Charleston during this period, see George C. Rogers Jr., *Charleston in the Age of the Pinckneys* (Columbia: Univ. of South Carolina Press, 1980); Walter J. Fraser Jr. *Charleston! Charleston!: The History of a Southern City* (Columbia: Univ. of South Carolina Press, 1989).
15. Mark A. DeWolfe Howe, ed., "Journal of Josiah Quincy, Junior, 1773," *Proceedings of the Massachusetts Historical Society* 49 (1915–16): 441–51.
16. Johann David Schoepf, *Travels in the Confederation [1783–1784]*, 2 vols., trans. and ed. Alfred J. Morrison (New York: Burt Franklin, 1968), 2: 167–68.
17. The best summary of the development of English urban culture in this period is Peter Borsay, *The English Urban Renaissance: Culture and Society in the Provincial Town, 1660–1770* (Oxford: Clarendon Press, 1989).
18. Jack P. Greene, *Pursuits of Happiness: The Social Development of Early Modern British Colonies and the Formation of American Culture* (Chapel Hill: Univ. of North Carolina Press, 1988), 147–50, 168–69.
19. Eliza Lucas to Mrs. Boddicott, May 2, 1740, in *The Letterbook of Eliza Lucas Pinckney 1739–1762*, ed. Elise Pinckney (Chapel Hill: Univ. of North Carolina Press, 1972), 7.
20. The building commissioners included William Middleton, Charles Pinckney, William Bull Jr., James Graeme, Andrew Rutledge, John Dart, Othniel Beale, Benjamin Smith, and Isaac Mazyck. "Acts of the Colonial Assembly, 1749–1756, Act: 13," CO5/420, Public Records Office, London.
21. Rather than a "metrocentric approach," recent scholarship by a number of historians have explored the "interaction among component parts of imperial systems." Bernard Bailyn and Philip D. Morgan suggest that "instead of a single, coherent outward thrust by the English, the process should be seen as vastly more complicated, much more double-ended, with the colonies playing as dynamic a role as the metropolis" (Bernard Bailyn and Philip D. Morgan eds., *Strangers within the*

22. On the use of native woods in building and furniture making, see Bradford L. Rauschenberg, "Timber Available in Charleston: 1660–1820," *Journal of Early Southern Decorative Arts* 20 (Nov. 1994): 39–99.

23. The use of curvilinear gables at St. Stephen's Parish Church in the late 1760s and at St. Bartholomew's Parish Church, rebuilt after it was burned by the British during the Revolution, are two notable examples of the survival of this gable form in the second half of the eighteenth century.

24. See, for example, a contract made in 1789 to build a "dwelling house commonly called a single house" (Charleston County, S.C., Land Records, Book R).

25. For a more detailed discussion of the single house, see chap. 3 in this volume, "The Embedded Landscapes of the Charleston Single House, 1780–1820," by Bernard L. Herman.

26. One such immigrant from the British Isles was Samuel Cardy, a builder from Dublin who came to Charleston in the early 1750s. Shortly after his arrival, he was entrusted with the construction of St. Michael's Church. See Kenneth Severens, "Emigration and Provincialism: Samuel Cardy's Architectural Career in the Atlantic World," *Eighteenth Century Ireland* 5 (1990): 21–36.

27. McCusker and Menard, *The Economy of British America*, 183.

28. Howe, ed., "Journal of Josiah Quincy, Junior, 1773," 444–45. In 1769 Ezra Waite, "Civil Architect, House-builder in general, and Carver, from London," advertised his expertise in the local newspaper noting that he "has finished the architecture, conducted the execution thereof, viz.: in the joiner way, all tabernacle frames (but that in the dining-room excepted) and carved all the said work in the four principal rooms; and also calculated, adjusted, and draw'd at large to work by, the Ionick entablature, and carved the same in the front and round the eaves, of Miles Brewton, Esquire's House, on White Point" (*South Carolina Gazette and Country Journal*, Aug. 22, 1769).

29. The following three paragraphs are adapted from my introduction to *An Illustrated Glossary of Early Southern Architecture and Landscape* (New York: Oxford Univ. Press, 1994), xi–xii.

30. Dell Upton, "Vernacular Domestic Architecture in Eighteenth-Century Virginia," *Winterthur Portfolio* 17 (Summer/Autumn, 1982): 95–119.

31. A brief description of the log church appears in a letter by the minister of the St. John's Parish. Rev. Levi Durand to the Secretary, SPG Letterbook B, vol. 5, no. 249, Oct. 1, 1764.

32. No detailed study of the surviving colonial parish churches of South Carolina has been undertaken. A good beginning is Harriette Hawkins, "Icons in the Wilderness: The Anglican Churches of Rural South Carolina," (Master's thesis, Univ. of Delaware, 1983).

33. Batty Langley, *The City and Country Builder's and Workman's Treasury of Designs* (London, 1740). See particularly plate CXIV in the 1750 edition.

34. Rev. Alexander Garden to the Secretary, SPG Letterbook B, vol. 5, no. 220, May 6, 1765.

35. Both pulpits share similar ovolo molding profiles wrought from planes with blades that were no doubt manufactured in Birmingham or Sheffield. Each ogee-shaped sounding board is crowned by a dove, the symbol of the Holy Spirit.

36. Alexander Garden to the Secretary, SPG Letterbook B, vol. 5, no. 220.

37. On the detrimental effect this distinction has had on the scholarship of early American architecture, see Dell Upton, "Outside the Academy: A Century of Vernacular Studies, 1890–1990," in *The Architectural Historian in America*, ed. Elisabeth Blair MacDougall (Washington, D.C.: National Gallery of Art, 1990), 199–213.

(Note: item 21 continues at top) *Realm: Cultural Margins of the First British Empire* [Chapel Hill: Univ. of North Carolina Press, 1991], 9).

PART II

VARIETIES OF URBAN FORMS

CHAPTER 5

James Michael Buckley

A Factory without a Roof: The Company Town in the Redwood Lumber Industry

Our understanding of the built environment of North American industry has been assembled from social and architectural studies of a variety of mill villages, factory towns, and industrial cities. The bulk of this research has focused on an assortment of sites on the eastern edge of the continent; as a result, boardinghouses in Lowell, shoemakers' "ten-footers" in Lynn, and company houses in the North Carolina Piedmont have all taken their places as standard elements of the vernacular landscape.[1] By contrast, however, we know little about the social character and physical form of industrial development in other parts of the United States and Canada. Our general impression of the American West, for example, is dominated by Hollywood images of cowboys ranging freely across the prairie and hordes of independent prospectors panning streams by hand. Behind this rustic, movie-set facade, however, lies the reality of a highly mechanized, corporate-driven industrial economy centered on general manufacturing as well as resource extraction. Unlike the gradual transformation from agrarian to industrial order that many eastern regions experienced, industries in the West often bloomed suddenly in the wake of a mining rush or completion of a railroad line. These industries frequently occupied isolated sites where a single large employer could dominate work and social relations. Even in sizable cities like San Francisco, the high cost of attracting skilled workers from the East often prompted western firms to invest in advanced machinery that could take the place of human hands. It is the physical and social environment of this capital-intensive, corporate-based industry of the West that historians need to explore in greater depth.[2]

The redwood lumber industry of California is a characteristic example of western industrial development. When the first commercial loggers began to fell redwood trees on California's North Coast in the 1850s, the expansive forests of this isolated region were largely undisturbed by human impact. By the beginning of the next century, however, the thriving lumber operations of this area had thrust the North Coast into prominence as a vital part of an important national industry. The rapid economic development of this region produced a dramatically new landscape of industrial capitalism, characterized by huge processing plants, diminished forests, and a form of settlement found throughout the West: the company town. The company towns that dominated the redwood realm emerged in the late nineteenth century as the lumber industry shifted from low-tech production at waterfront sawmills to highly mechanized operations located in the backwoods. The enormous investment required for this transformation brought new forms of business ownership and new conditions of employment for workers, as giant corporations rearranged the industrial landscape in a search for greater efficiency.

Several North Coast redwood lumber companies constructed new mill communities in isolated forest locations, but the most elaborate example was completed by the region's largest lumber manufacturer, The Pacific Lumber Company. In developing the town of Scotia, Pacific Lumber enlisted architectural form in the company's effort to renegotiate the terms of labor relations in the redwood lumber industry. As the scale of redwood lumber production reached its peak in the early years of this century, Pacific Lumber's corporate managers hoped that the design of this remote community would help modernize the traditional work attitudes of their employees. Still owned and operated by its founding firm, Scotia represents a prime example of how corporations, in a variety of isolated settings in the American West, manipulated the built environment outside the workplace in an attempt to improve the industrial worker who toiled within.

The Redwood Lumber Industry on California's North Coast

The coast redwood is the world's tallest tree, with some specimens reaching heights of three hundred feet. These long-lived giants grow in coastal hills and river bottoms in a narrow band from Santa Cruz to the Oregon border. The distinctive coloring and structural strength of redwood lumber made it a popular construction material with early settlers. As Gold Rush San Francisco exhausted the supply of lumber from the redwood groves in the Bay Area, lumber merchants turned to the bountiful forests of California's North Coast, the rugged, sparsely populated region stretching across Mendocino, Humboldt, and Del Norte Counties. Humboldt Bay, located in the heart of the North Coast about two hundred miles north of the Golden Gate, soon emerged as the best harbor for ships carrying redwood cargo to San Francisco. In the 1850s, several sawmills sprang up along the waterfront in the booming city of Eureka.

Harvesting redwood lumber was an arduous process due to the enormous girth of redwood tree trunks, which often approach twenty feet in diameter. It could take as long as a week for two loggers to topple one of these titans by hand with axes and a huge crosscut saw. In the early days of logging, ox teams dragged the felled timber to streambeds, where winter floods carried the logs to sawmills on Humboldt Bay.[3]

Most of the early waterfront mills were owned by small partnerships of experienced lumbermen from New England and eastern Canada. These owners were hands-on managers, such as William Carson, who supervised his operation from the famously extravagant home he built on a bluff overlooking his mill in Eureka. Despite mill owners' close proximity to and tight control of the workplace, they did not have a strong grip on the personal space of their employees, who lived in private homes and boarding houses in existing towns.[4]

The demand for redwood lumber increased as California's cities grew in the late nineteenth century. Expanding markets encouraged mill owners to develop technological improvements that would accelerate the movement of logs out of the woods and through the mill. By the 1880s, slow-footed oxen gave way to narrow-gauge railroads and mechanized cable systems like the steam donkey. At the mill, the up-and-down frame saw was soon replaced by faster circular and band saws fed by automatic carriages.[5]

Armed with mechanized tools, woodsmen had a rapid and widespread impact on the forest. Logging railroads opened up previously inaccessible interior woods, and lumber companies began to locate their sawmills near the raw material in the forest instead of in waterfront towns. Beginning in the late 1880s, with both loggers and mill workers now employed in isolated backwoods sites, lumber companies built small communities

Fig. 5.1. View of the Jolly Giant Mill Near Arcata, California, in the Late 1870s. The mill has the casual arrangement of buildings typical of a backwoods sawmill settlement of the late nineteenth century. Courtesy of the Clarke Memorial Museum.

Fig. 5.2. Interior of a Lumber Company Bunkhouse in the State of Washington. Darius Kinsey. Courtesy of the Special Collections Division, University of Washington Libraries.

of barracks and shacks casually arranged around the mill and cookhouse (fig. 5.1). It was this bustle of human and mechanical activity in remote locations that gave the forest the appearance of what logging historian Stewart Holbrook called "a gigantic factory without a roof."[6]

Like many isolated industrial sites in the American West, these open-roofed factories attracted a "floating army" of migrant labor—men accustomed to short stints of hard work building railroads, picking vegetables, loading ships, and felling timber, with frequent changes of scenery and often with periodic bouts of drunkenness (fig. 5.2). Redwood lumberjacks had a built-in tradition of independence and transience inherited from the heyday of logging in the Great Lakes and New England forests. While the men who toiled inside the mill tended to be less peripatetic than the "timberbeasts" in the woods, strenuous work and unpleasant conditions in mechanized sawmills resulted in a high rate of work force turnover. Such labor instability proved to be a serious concern for lumber companies in the early years of the twentieth century.[7]

Western workers developed a unique labor radicalism resulting from the boom-and-bust nature of the extractive industry in the region's forests and mines. In the American West more than in other areas of the industrializing nation, suggests labor historian Melvin Dubofsky, "[m]odern technology and corporate capitalism advanced too quickly for smooth adjustment; the rapid pace of economic growth resulted in individual failures and frustrations, social breakdowns, and mob violence." As the scale of operations harvesting the West's resources increased, labor organizing by the Industrial Workers of the World (IWW) and other unions expanded and intensified in character in an effort to counter the dominance of capital. Though the isolated character of work sites in the redwood forest made organizing lumber workers difficult, labor leaders occasionally succeeded in encouraging protests against the harsh conditions of this work, culminating in the 1907 strike by more than twenty-five hundred Humboldt County redwood industry workers.[8]

At the same time that labor organizers were attempting to build potent associations of workers, the financial demands of logging railroads, steam machinery, and powerful saws caused most of the region's small partnerships to give way to consolidated corporations, which could raise the capital needed for large-scale production. By the turn of the century, many redwood lumber companies had become giant enterprises by vertically integrating operations that had previously been separately owned—logging crews, sawmills, fleets of ships, and retail lumber yards. The pressure for adequate returns on this substantial investment caused corporate managers to be less tolerant of the traditionally intractable and increasingly militant lumber worker. As a result, lumber companies began to impose a more organized structure onto casual backwoods mill villages, with spacious, ordered streets and sidewalks, substantial hotels for workers and visitors, elaborate company stores, and formal recreation facilities such as dance halls and ballfields. By constructing such company towns with better worker housing and more community amenities, lumber corporations hoped to protect their significant capital investment by attracting a more stable, dependable workforce.[9]

Scotia and The Pacific Lumber Company

The most spectacular example of this building program in the redwood forest is Scotia, a company town located about thirty miles south of Eureka. Founded in 1886 and still entirely owned and operated by The Pacific Lumber Company, Scotia has changed little from the 1920s: nestled into this bend of the Eel River are two huge sawmills adjacent to a small village center, surrounded by neat rows of well-maintained houses on several residential streets (figs. 5.3, 5.4).[10] Pacific Lumber constructed the first sawmill on the site in the mid-1880s after completing a rail line that connected the huge stand of virgin redwood in this area to the wharves of Humboldt Bay. The original mill employed about three hundred men, for whom the company built a large bunkhouse and provided about one hundred small dwellings, half of which were shared by single workers and the rest occupied by married employees with their families. Except for piped water, no indoor utilities were provided until well into the twentieth century. The residential structures, along with the cookhouse, company store, and a small hotel in a converted house, were arranged informally around the mill buildings and lumberyards. Pacific Lumber's operations soon grew so large that the company started its own ranch to feed workers, with a slaughterhouse behind the mill.

When the original sawmill burned in 1895, the company constructed a new, more substantial structure (Mill A), making Pacific Lumber the largest lumber company on the North Coast by the turn of the century. This expansion prompted a struggle for control that was eventually won by a family of Great Lakes lumber operators, who incorporated the firm in Maine in 1905. Using corporate capital raised in the Midwest, the new owners soon doubled Scotia's capacity with construction of a second sawmill, Mill B, on the opposite side of Scotia's vast log pond from the earlier mill. With the new mill in operation, the company now employed 2,000 workers. Each mill had its own bunkhouse and cookhouse, serving between 200 and 300 men; another 200 men lived in the Scotia Hotel, and

Fig. 5.3. Aerial View of Scotia, c. 1970, Looking North. The town center and main residential section lie between Mill B (1908) in the foreground and Mill A (1895) at the north end of town. The town of Wildwood (now called Rio Dell) is visible at the top of the photograph across the Eel River from Scotia. Courtesy of The Pacific Lumber Company.

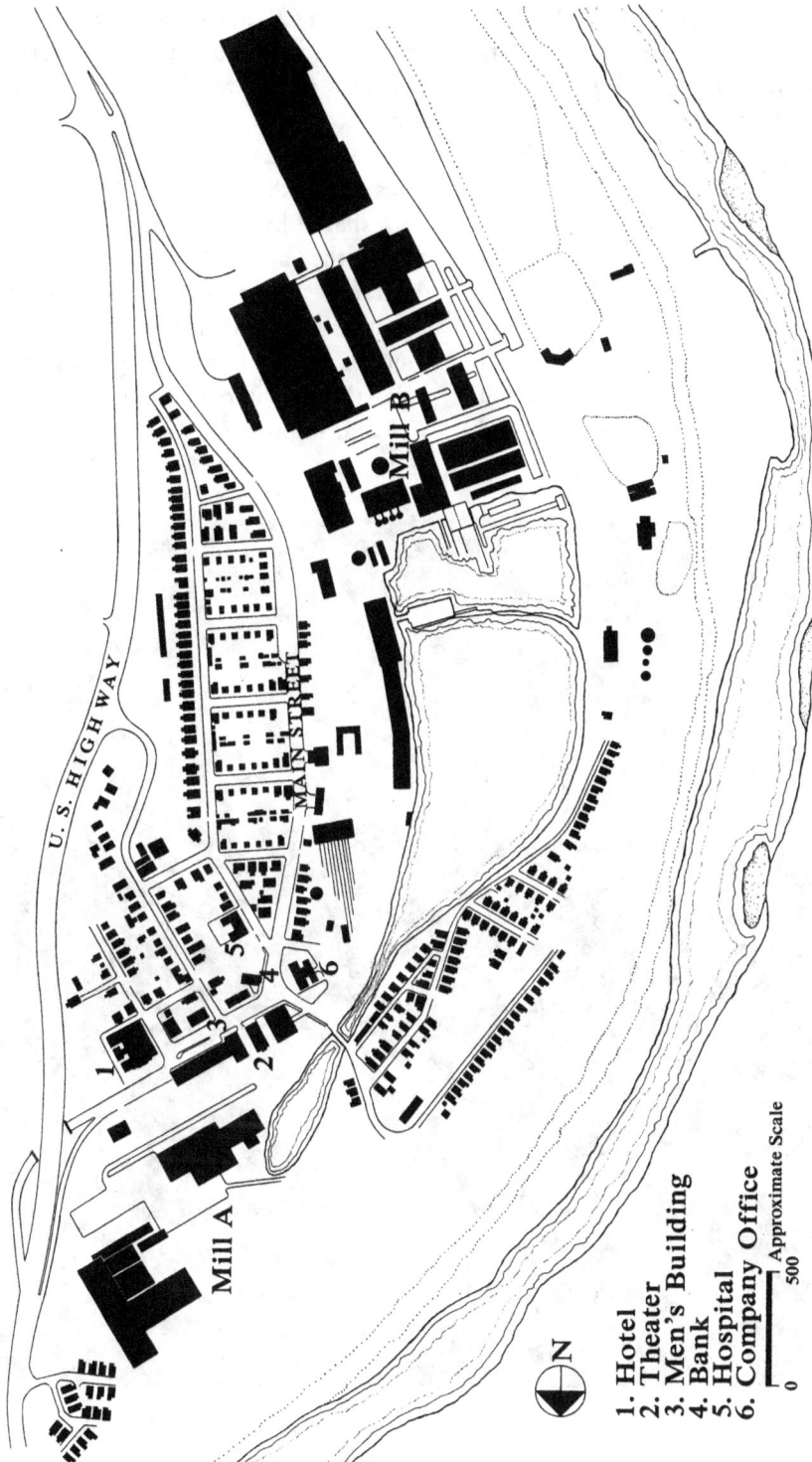

Fig. 5.4. Plan of Scotia, c. 1960. Traffic on the Redwood Highway from San Franciso traveled on Scotia's Main Street until the new U.S. Highway 101 bypassed the town in the 1950s. Drawing by Sahoko Tamagawa. Courtesy of the Humboldt State University Library.

700 more lived in the backwoods logging camps.[11] As it grew, the town largely retained its informal arrangement; there was no main thoroughfare, and warehouses, company stores, and blacksmith shops vied for space in an ill-defined central area (fig. 5.5).

With such great investments in land and plant, concerns about the effectiveness of workers became paramount for large enterprises like Pacific Lumber. While early mill owners like William Carson had practiced paternalistic oversight of their workers, the rise of the giant corporation and the economic uncertainties of the depressed 1890s severed the direct relationship between owner and worker in the new century. Corporate managers considered labor too itinerant and too unpredictable for the amount of capital these corporations were required to put at risk. Such concerns about the nature of the industrial worker were shared by major employers in other industries in the early part of this century, prompting them to develop a new approach to industrial relations. Faced with workers whose monotonous routines left them ready to slack off, strike, or quit, these employers implemented programs aimed at improving workers' output by improv-

Fig. 5.5. Scotia in 1902. View from the east with Mill A on the right. Courtesy of the Humboldt State University Library.

ing their circumstances. These programs, offered by firms such as National Cash Register, H. J. Heinz, and Procter & Gamble, included incentives like profit sharing, medical insurance, and English language classes. Business leaders termed such efforts "welfare capitalism" because they shared a common goal of improving work force stability and loyalty by increasing worker contentment. These welfare programs attempted to recast the reluctant worker into a corporate mold—in the phrase of historian Stuart Brandes, "to build a New Capitalist Man."[12]

It was this effort to shape the worker that led to the transformation of Scotia's landscape after the completion of the second mill around 1910. By the turn of the century, many elements of a company town were already in place: worker housing, churches, schools, and the ubiquitous company store, all constructed by Pacific Lumber. Over the next three decades, the firm embarked on a building campaign that would expand its industrial plant physically and at the same time use the design and development of the company town to encourage workers to operate the factory without a roof more efficiently. Pacific Lumber intended to accomplish this goal of greater worker efficiency by redesigning the casual backwoods mill village to resemble a proper country town. Prompted by the State of California's plans in the 1910s for the Redwood Highway, a motor route from San Francisco to the Oregon border that would eventually pass directly through Scotia, the firm cut a classic Main Street through the congested village center. The company constructed a new office building to anchor one side of this central space, with the existing Scotia Hotel holding down the opposite end. In the following years, Pacific Lumber assembled a series of company-owned institutional buildings around this new road to create a civic forum, a sort of billboard-in-the-round that the company hoped would advertise its compact with a new breed of stable, contented lumber workers.[13]

In 1910, the company laid the groundwork for its village center by turning a vacant storefront across from the company store into a Men's Social Club containing a library and a recreation space. The club soon expanded into the rest of the two-story building, with the upper floor given over to a broad range of community uses, including religious services, movies, and dances, and basketball and boxing matches.[14] Company records suggest that Scotia's Men's Club had its origins in a request by workers for a safe, quiet place to avoid the bars and brothels of Wildwood, the town just across the Eel River from Scotia. But it is more than coincidental that, in the same year the club opened, Pacific Lumber closed the company saloon that had been in operation since the 1880s. A. P. Alexanderson, a Swedish immigrant who started working in the Pacific Lumber mill in 1893, remembered that the company saloon was open mornings, evenings, and all day on Sunday, the workers' day off: "They were supposed to close during working hours but they could almost always get in any time of the day. There was a lot of drinking in those days. Some of the men were regular soaks, but most of them were law abiding citizens."[15] In providing its own saloon, Pacific Lumber had sanctioned drinking but hoped to gain a measure of control. By 1910, the official attitude had evolved from regulated tolerance to attempted elimination; from that point forward, sober faces—both human and architectural—were the only expressions that belonged on the town's new Main Street.

Pacific Lumber constructed buildings on the new thoroughfare for two other company institutions in the early 1910s. The firm opened a savings bank for its workers in a building next to the Mill A bunkhouse. The president of the company, C. W. Pennoyer, announced that the company's financial transactions would be handled through this institution and that workers would be paid at the company office and cash their checks at the bank.[16]

Soon after the establishment of the Men's Club and bank, Pacific Lumber enlarged the modest company store across the street from the club building into a more substantial mercantile operation. The small emporium that had met the basic needs of Scotia's early residents was replaced with a prominent commercial building appropriate to the store's augmented stock of goods. The company added a large warehouse next door, whose long front facade helped define the edge of the new central street. The stage was now set for an even more elaborate remodeling of Scotia's village center.

In 1921, Pacific Lumber carried out a substantial improvement to its operations: the dismantling of the steam power plant in Mill A and the subsequent electrification of this operation. The increased capacity of the refurbished mill required the hiring of 150 additional workers, for a total of 1,500 employees in this mill alone.[17] While preparing for this substantial investment in industrial facilities, Pacific Lumber's managers laid plans for an expansion of Scotia's social infrastructure as well.

In 1920, company officials decided to construct a new theater next to the enlarged store to house some of the clubhouse activities, and, for the first time, they called in a professional architect for help. Alfred Henry Jacobs of San Francisco designed a structure that mirrored architecturally the daily work of Scotia's residents: a palace of milled redwood lumber fronted by a portico of "natural" columns of redwood logs (fig. 5.6). For workers attending the weekly picture show, going to the movies became an odd

Fig. 5.6. Winema Theater (1920). Courtesy of the Humboldt State University Library.

sort of busman's holiday. Unlike the escapist fantasies that movie palaces of the 1920s typically offered, Scotia's theater reinforced its patrons' identification with the world of wood manufacturing. Company officials named the theater "Winema" after a Modoc Indian woman of that name who had mediated between whites and her own people in a prolonged war. A company brochure from 1929 described Winema as "an Indian maiden who devoted her life to the establishment of friendly relations between her own people and the white men." On one level, the Winema Theater's prominent position on the new Main Street indicates that Pacific Lumber wanted the building to capture the attention of town visitors; on another level, however, the story of the Indian who worked constructively with those in power suggests that the company aimed this architectural image at the resident workers as well.[18]

Shortly after the completion of the Winema Theater, company officials decided to move the bank to a new home and commissioned Eureka architect F. T. Georgeson to make an innovative visual statement about the importance of thrift (fig. 5.7). Georgeson responded with a staid Neoclassical temple appropriate for the serious business of saving, but, like the architect of the Winema, he related this activity to the central purpose of the community by surrounding the building with a portico and an engaged colonnade of raw log columns. The didactic message of this "Redwood Doric" structure is clear: save your hard-earned pennies, but do not forget where those wages came from.

The construction of the village center continued in the 1920s with two additional structures. A new hotel, the Mowatoc, replaced the old hostelry on Main Street. With its Indian-derived name and grand lobby amidst the redwood splendor, the Mowatoc imitated on a small scale the grand resort hotels of the national parks. Pacific Lumber completed its civic complex in 1929 with a new company hospital building behind the savings bank that offered medical services to workers for one dollar per month.[19]

The makeover of the casual mill village extended to Scotia's residential area as well. Like other early woods communities, the original housing in Scotia was casually fit in around the requirements of the mill. But the houses built in conjunction with the new mill around 1908 were three-, four-, and five-room cottages laid out in large, open lots on a grid plan. Connected by wooden plank sidewalks, these houses created a formal streetscape with pretensions as a proper town. Subsequent housing construction was also neatly arranged in rows of similar single-family units. This new residential landscape indicated that the idea of regularizing the workplace had spread from the mill to the domestic environment. Pacific Lumber's decision to focus on detached, single-family houses rather than row houses or apartments underscored its intention to promote the image of a stable, married worker. The pleasant rows of neat cottages in the controlled space of Scotia contrasted sharply with the roughneck environment of Wildwood, the community just across the bridge and beyond the control of the company. Since only Pacific Lumber employees could live in Scotia, the company hoped that the workers they most desired—steady, sober, and loyal—would feel rewarded by the opportunity to live in the attractive, though restricted, environment of Scotia. Though the detached family house was one way to reinforce American family values, 1920s style, there was a contradiction in the company's ideology of promoting the stabilizing influence of having one's own home without providing the opportunity to own it.

The new landscape was not only intended for the mill town; lumber companies tidied up the ragged backwoods camps as well. Instead of rough-built shanties, lumberjack cabins were lined up in highly ordered rows of whitewashed, individual living units. Prompted by progressive

Fig. 5.7. Scotia Savings Bank (1921).

state legislation in the early 1910s, lumber corporations again turned to the physical environment as a tool to improve the character of those who manned the production machines.[20] Donald McDonald, a vice-president of Pacific Lumber, applauded the work of the state's commission on camp sanitation: "The results are not measurable in dollars and cents alone. Proper conditions about the wood camps not only make for better men, but better service and in our judgement the work which has been carried on by your commission has been a distinct help, not only to the employee, but the employer."[21]

The Redwood Lumber Town in Context

While other North Coast lumber companies provided many of the same institutions, it was The Pacific Lumber Company's new town center that gave the strongest visual expression to the corporate effort to reform the worker's environment (fig. 5.8). There were many reasons behind this strategy, including the threat of union agitation throughout western forests by the IWW and other organizers, and the increasing ethnic diversity of the labor force, as Italians joined Scandinavians in the woods and mills in increasing numbers.[22] But the architectural elaboration of Scotia was not simply a defense against strikes or unseemly immigrant customs; the company's efforts indicate a deeper belief by its managers in their ability to transform labor into a partnership, to persuade the worker to become a sturdy cog in the machinery of the forest factory.

Pacific Lumber's intentions were explicit. "Make your mill town beautiful," encouraged the company's general manager, E. A. Blockinger, in a 1911 newspaper article. "Get your men loyal and keep them so. Let this replace loyalty to a union. The spirit is what you want in your men. Ten good men will accomplish as much as fifteen ordinary laborers if the spirit and goodwill is there."[23] A visitor to Scotia in 1913 described the apparent effect this strategy had on the supposedly rough-hewn lumberjack: "I walked into Scotia on a Sunday morning 14 years ago and I could see men under the influence of liquor in all directions. . . . I again walked into Scotia on a Sunday morning six months ago, and I could see well-dressed men with respectful countenances, pleasant and cheerful, and afterwards I learnt that practically everyone had a bank account. I could see bright, neatly dressed children coming from Sunday school, men and women going to church or on their way to visit neighbors."[24]

How did these "well-dressed men" and their families respond to Pacific Lumber's town-building campaign? Like most industrial workers of the era, the lumberjacks and millhands of California's North Coast left little record of their reaction to changes in the conditions of their work. Workers clearly benefited from the many amenities introduced into company towns, compared to the rough conditions of early woods mill villages, but it is difficult to tell if they chafed under the corporate grip as a result. If we measure redwood workers' contentment by the subsequent record of labor unrest, then mill owners' extra investment in company towns seems to have paid a significant dividend. In his study of Humboldt County labor, Daniel Cornford found that the redwood lumber industry during the interwar period was notable for "the serenity of labor relations."[25] The American Federation of Labor (AFL) union established among redwood workers in the period of high demand during World War I dissolved in 1923, and IWW organizers in the 1920s were frustrated by the complacency of workers; one complained that "it would take a Sherlock Holmes to find any militancy in these tame apes."[26] Even during the turbulence of California labor in the mid-1930s, led by waterfront workers in San Francisco who often handled redwood cargo from the North Coast, Humboldt County's lumber industry experienced only a brief strike in 1935 against a few companies.[27]

In the corporate board rooms of the redwood lumber industry, the development of company towns marked a change in attitude about natural resources as well as a new approach to labor relations. Like the itinerant lumberjacks who shifted from camp to camp, suggests Vernon Jensen, "[t]he lumber industry throughout most of its life has been an aggressive, ingenious, unstable migrant." The tradition of transience in the North American lumber industry is epitomized in

Fig. 5.8. Scotia's Main Street, c. 1920. View from The Pacific Lumber Company's office building at the western end of the town center during an election or political rally. The buildings include, from left to right, Winema Theater, company store and warehouse, hotel, Men's Club, and post office. The new bank building would be constructed just to the right of this view. Courtesy of The Pacific Lumber Company.

the adage that usually guided logging operations: "cut out and get out." Until the early part of this century, American lumber operators assumed that they would always find another untouched forest over the next ridge as soon as they logged out their current site. With only a twenty- or thirty-year time horizon for their forest operations, they had little reason to plan a full-fledged community that would only be pulled up when the timber gave out.[28]

But in the redwood forests of the early 1920s, according to California forest historian C. Raymond Clar, "the responsible timber men with extensive capital investments in their operations were beginning to look forward to the future of their own timber supply."[29] Pacific Lumber, with its workers comfortably settled in Scotia, became one of the earliest practitioners of modern forestry in the redwoods with reforestation efforts and an experimental nursery. The same family that had acquired the company around 1900 continued to control the firm's stock for most of this century, and these owners matched their concern for long-term labor stability with a similar interest in long-term resource management. Pacific Lumber's approach to its built environment was thus linked to a broader shift in corporate attitudes about the natural environment.[30]

Scotia represents one of many experiments in the use of architectural form to create a modern, stable industrial community. Like many other model factory towns of the early twentieth century, it reinterpreted for a new corporate leadership the earlier, paternalistic visions of individual factory proprietors like George Pullman. This idea of imposing a more modern community order on a rustic location was common in the western and southern woods at the height of lumber production in the early twentieth century. Several lumber corporations constructed well-planned company towns at mill sites in the first part of this century: Potlach, Idaho (Weyerhauser); Brookings, Oregon (Brookings Lumber Company), and Gilcrest, Oregon (Gilcrest Timber Company); Rosboro, Arkansas (Caddo River Lumber Company); Kaulton, Alabama (Kaul Lumber Company). Some towns, such as Brookings and Kaulton, were laid out by professional architects and designers; more often, the design of such communities was handled by company engineers incorporating the ideas of the new city planning profession. This forest industry experience can be compared to many other contemporaneous examples of community planning for industry in which industries seeking a modernized work force set out to build an environment to help make that happen. In several industrial communities of the early twentieth century, manufacturers attempted to use architecture to mold the work environment: Bertram Goodhue's copper mining town of Tyrone, New Mexico; the steel mill community of Vandergrift, Pennsylvania, designed by the firm of F. L. Olmsted; Earl Draper's southern mill towns; and the industrial communities constructed with federal government assistance during World War I.[31]

The isolated nature of industry in the American West offered employers an excellent opportunity to use architecture and space in their effort to build a New Capitalist Man. Pacific Lumber's attempt to create order out of the haphazard mill village represented a conscious effort to design a structured physical and social work community that would regularize the unpredictable character of labor. Industrial firms throughout North America carried out similar efforts at this time, but Scotia, with its prominent location on a major highway, served then (and endures today) as an architectural advertisement for industrial harmony in the factory without a roof.

Notes

I would like to thank Paul Groth, Dan Cornford, Diane Shaw, and Bill Littmann for their helpful comments on this paper.

1. For the selected examples, see John Coolidge, *Mill and Mansion: A Study of Architecture and Society in Lowell, Massachusetts, 1820–1865* (New York: Columbia Univ. Press, 1942); Richard M. Candee, "Architecture and Corporate Planning in the Early Waltham System," in *Essays from the Lowell Conference on Industrial History 1982 and 1983,* ed. Robert Weible (North Andover, Mass.: Museum of American Textile History, 1985); Alan Dawley, *Class and Community: The Industrial Revolution in Lynn* (Cambridge, Mass.: Harvard Univ. Press, 1976); Jacquelyn Dowd Hall et al., *Like a Family: The Making of a Southern Cotton Mill World* (Chapel Hill: Univ. of North Carolina Press, 1987). Among many other studies of eastern industrial architecture and community, see William Pierson, *American Buildings and Their Architects: Technology and the Picturesque, the Corporate and Early Gothic Styles* (Garden City, N.Y.: Doubleday, 1978); John S. Garner, *The Model Company Town: Urban Design through Private Enterprise in Nineteenth-Century New England* (Amherst: Univ. of Massachusetts Press, 1984); Anthony F. C. Wallace, *Rockdale: The Growth of an American Village in the Early Industrial Revolution* (New York: Knopf, 1972).

2. On Western American industrial development, see Patricia Nelson Limerick, *The Legacy of Conquest: The Unbroken Past of the American West* (New York: W. W. Norton, 1987), 97–133; William Cronon, "Kennecott Journey: The Paths Out of Town," in William Cronon et al., eds. *Under an Open Sky: Rethinking America's Western Past* (New York: W. W. Norton, 1992); William G. Robbins, *Colony and Empire: The Capitalist Transformation of the American West* (Lawrence: Univ. Press of Kansas, 1994), 61–82. For gradual versus sudden industrial development in the eastern and western United States, compare, for example, Jonathan Prude, *The Coming of Industrial Order: Town and Factory Life In Rural Massachusetts, 1810–1860* (New York: Cambridge Univ. Press, 1983) Prude with Rodman Wilson Paul, *Mining Frontiers of the Far West, 1848–1880* (New York: Holt, Rinehart, and Winston, 1963). For specific industrial sites in the West, see James B. Allen, *The Company Town in the American West* (Norman: Univ. of Oklahoma Press, 1966).

3. On early redwood logging, see Howard Brett Melendy, "One Hundred Years of the Redwood Lumber Industry, 1850–1950," (Ph.D. diss., Stanford Univ., 1952), 28–55; Lynwood Carranco, *Redwood Lumber Industry* (San Marino, Calif.: Golden West Books, 1982), 17–41. For the early history of Humboldt County, see Owen C. Coy, *The Humboldt Bay Region, 1850–1875* (Los Angeles: California State Historical Association, 1929).

4. See Daniel Cornford, *Workers and Dissent in the Redwood Empire* (Philadelphia: Temple Univ. Press, 1987), chap. 6; Benjamin Sacks, *Carson Mansion and Ingomar Theatre: Cultural Adventures in California* (Fresno, Calif.: Valley Publishers, 1979).

5. See Thomas R. Cox, *Mills and Markets: A History of the Pacific Coast Lumber Industry to 1900* (Seattle: Univ. of Washington Press, 1974), for growth of the lumber market in California and the Pacific Rim. On woods operations, see Stewart H. Holbrook, *Holy Old Mackinaw: A Natural History of the American Lumberjack* (New York: Macmillan, 1938), 180–86; Melendy, "One Hundred Years," 28–55; Lynwood Carranco and John T. Labbe, *Logging the Redwoods* (Caldwell, Idaho: Caxton Printers, 1975). On redwood mill technology, see Carranco, *Redwood Lumber Industry,* chap. 5; Melendy, "One Hundred Years," 56–70; on sawmill technology in general, see Carl R. Lounsbury, "Wild Melody of Steam: The Mechanization of Building Materials, 1850–1890," in *Architects and Builders in North Carolina: A History of the Practice of Building,* ed. Catherine W. Bishir et al. (Chapel Hill: Univ. of North Carolina Press, 1990); Ralph Clement Bryant, *Lumber: Its Manufacture and Distribution* (New York: John Wiley and Sons, 1922).

6. Holbrook, *Holy Old Mackinaw,* 186. On redwood logging camps, see Melendy, "One Hundred Years," 31–33.

7. Labor historian Vernon Jensen suggests that sawmill workers were usually "psychologically and socially distinct" from the men who felled trees; see Vernon H. Jensen, *Lumber and Labor* (New York: Farrar and Rheinhart, 1945), 4. On migrant labor generally, see Gregory R. Woriol, *In the Floating Army: F. C. Mills on Itinerant Life in California, 1914* (Urbana: Univ. of Illinois Press, 1992); Nels Anderson, *The Hobo: The Sociology of the Homeless Man* (Chicago: Univ. of Chicago Press, 1923); Carey McWilliams, *Factories in the Field: The Story of Migratory Farm Labor in California* (Boston: Little, Brown and Company, 1939). On lumber workers in various regions, see Holbrook, *Holy Old Mackinaw*; Robert E. Pike, *Tall Trees, Tough Men* (New York: Norton, 1967), and for turnover in northwestern mills, see Cloice Howd, "Industrial Relations in the West Coast Lumber Industry," *Bulletin of the United States Bureau of Labor Statistics* (Washington, D.C.: U.S. Government Printing Office, 1924).

8. Melvyn Dubofsky, "The Origins of Western Working Class Radicalism, 1890–1905," *Labor History* 16 (4): 154. Dubofsky limits his discussion to the mining industry of the intermontane West, but the conditions of the lumber industry in the Far West were similar. On labor organizing in the lumber industry, see Cornford, *Workers and Dissent*; Limerick, *Legacy of Conquest*, pp. 97–124; Melvyn Dubofsky, *We Shall Be All: A History of the Industrial Workers of the World* (Chicago: Quadrangle, 1969); Barney Warf, "Regional Transformation, Everyday Life, and Pacific Northwest Lumber Production," *Annals of the American Association of American Geographers* 78 (2) (1988): 326–46; Norman H. Clark, *Mill Town: A Social History of Everett, Washington* (Seattle: Univ. of Washington Press, 1970).

9. On the development of the lumber industry in Humboldt County, see Melendy, "One Hundred Years," 99–117; Cornford, *Workers and Dissent*, 151–55. On the development and structure of American corporations, see Alfred D. Chandler Jr., *The Visible Hand: The Managerial Revolution in American Business* (Cambridge, Mass.: Belknap Press, 1977). On the modernization of traditional work habits generally, see Herbert G. Gutman, "Work, Culture, and Society in Industrializing America, 1815–1919," in *Work, Culture, and Society in Industrializing America, 1815–1919: Essays in American Working-Class and Social History* (New York: Knopf, 1976); Daniel T. Rodgers, *The Work Ethic in Industrial America, 1850–1920* (Chicago: Univ. of Chicago Press, 1978); Daniel Nelson, *Managers and Workers: The Origins of the New Factory System in the United States, 1880–1920* (Madison: Univ. of Wisconsin Press, 1975).

10. On Scotia generally, see Ben Shannon Allen, "From the Penobscot to the Eel," MS, Bancroft Library, Univ. of California, Berkeley; Melendy, "100 Years"; "An Interview with A. P. Alexanderson," MS transcript of oral interview, Bancroft Library, Univ. of California, Berkeley; W. H. Wilde, "Chronology of the Pacific Lumber Company," MS, Bancroft Library, Univ. of California, Berkeley; Cornford, *Workers and Dissent*.

11. From *The Timberline,* Pacific Lumber Company newsletter, 1993, in Humboldt Room, Humboldt State Univ. Library, Arcata, Calif.

12. Quotation from Stuart D. Brandes, *American Welfare Capitalism, 1880–1940* (Chicago: Univ. of Chicago Press, 1976), 33. Labor shortages and increased product demand during World War I sped the introduction of welfare capitalism in several industries, including lumber. See also Daniel Nelson, *Managers and Workers: Origins of the New Factory System in the United States, 1880–1920* (Madison: Univ. of Wisconsin Press, 1975); Sanford Jacoby, *Employing Bureaucracy: Managers, Unions, and the Transformation of Work in American Industry, 1900–1945* (New York: Columbia Univ. Press, 1985); Gerald

Zahavi, *Workers, Managers, and Welfare Capitalism: the Shoeworkers and Tanners of Endicott Johnson, 1890–1950* (Urbana: Univ. of Illinois Press, 1988); Lizabeth Cohen, *Making A New Deal: Industrial Workers in Chicago, 1919–1939* (New York: Cambridge Univ. Press, 1990). On labor in the lumber industry, see Jensen, *Lumber and Labor*.

13. Carranco notes that the company took out a mortgage in 1913 on equipment and timber, raising funds from Chicago and Michigan banks to develop the town. See Carranco, *Redwood Lumber Industry*, 155.

14. In the 1920s, many of these activities were turned over to the Industrial Department of the YMCA, which coordinated recreation at several mill and woods operation in Humboldt County. For YMCA at Pacific Lumber, see Cornford, *Workers and Dissent*, 205. See also Jacoby, *Employing Bureaucracy*, 56–59, on the industrial YMCA in general.

15. From "Memories of A. P. Alexanderson," MS oral history, Bancroft Library, Univ. of California, Berkeley (n.p., 1956).

16. *Humboldt Times,* Mar. 5, 1910.

17. Melendy, "One Hundred Years," 205; *Humboldt Times,* May 29, 1921.

18. Jacobs, an MIT graduate who had also attended the École des Beaux-Arts, designed the Curran Theater in San Francisco in 1922. Earlier examples of the "log column" theme include exhibition buildings, such as the log structure at the Lewis and Clark Exposition in Portland (1906) and Bernard Maybeck's "House of Hoo-Hoo" for the lumber industry at the Panama-Pacific International Exhibition (1915). Resort architecture in the Far West also played on a forest architecture theme, such as Glacier Park Lodge in Montana (1913); see Ann Farrar Hyde, *An American Vision: Far Western Landscape and National Culture, 1820–1920* (New York: New York Univ. Press, 1990).

19. Cornford notes that organized labor had established its own hospital in Humboldt County and fought the efforts of the major redwood corporations to control the provision of medical services with company facilities. See *Workers and Dissent*, 176.

20. The California Legislature passed a Camp Sanitation Act in 1913 and established a Commission on Housing and Immigration to oversee camp conditions in 1915. See Cornford, *Workers and Dissent*, 206–9.

21. Quoted in Cornford, *Workers and Dissent*, 207.

22. The IWW, in fact, gained less of a following in the redwoods than AFL-based unions in the early twentieth century. Redwood lumber company managers were no doubt concerned that the even greater worker radicalism in the Pacific Northwest would spread into their camps and mills. On ethnic diversity in the Humboldt lumber industry, see Cornford, *Workers and Dissent*, 194–95. By 1910, Italians made up 16 percent of lumber workers in the vicinity of Scotia and were the largest foreign contingent in the company's work force.

23. *Pioneer Western Lumberman* 56 (July 15, 1911), quoted in Cornford, *Workers and Dissent*, 201. The company offered cash prizes of ten to seventy-five dollars for beautifying lawns and gardens. A company brochure noted: "A visitor driving through town can see easily how well the employees keep up their premises."

24. P. A. Rosetti letter to *Collier's National Weekly* 50 (Mar. 15, 1913).

25. Cornford, *Workers and Dissent*, 214.

26. From *Industrial Worker,* July 29, 1922, quoted in Cornford, *Workers and Dissent*, 211. Jensen noted in 1945: "During the past two decades the working force has changed its characteristics considerably. Formerly, many of the workers, particularly in the logging end of the industry, were homeless, migratory men. Workers are no longer as migratory as they once were.... More family men and a more stable group now work in the industry" (*Lumber and Labor,* 105–6).

27. See Frank Onstine, *The Great Lumber Strike of Humboldt County, 1935* (Arcata, Calif.: Mercurial Enterprises, 1980).

28. Jensen quoted from *Lumber and Labor*, 3. See Michael Williams, *Americans and Their Forests: A Historical Geography* (Cambridge: Cambridge Univ. Press, 1989), 216–37; Kenneth L. Smith, *Sawmill: The Story of the Cutting of the Last Great Virgin Forest East of the Rockies* (Fayetteville: Univ. of Arkansas Press, 1986), 29–31.

29. C. Raymond Clar, *California Government and Forestry* (Sacramento: California Division of Forestry, 1959), 1: 480.

30. Pacific Lumber also donated large tracts of uncut forest land for parks, working in conjunction with the Save-the-Redwoods League. Ironically, it was this dedication to long-term forest management that resulted in the preservation of the old-growth forests that are currently at issue. For an overview of the national conservation debate, see Williams, *Americans and Their Forests*, 393–459.

31. On Pullman, see Stanley Buder, *Pullman: An Experiment in Industrial Order and Community Planning, 1880–1930* (New York: Oxford Univ. Press, 1967). For specific lumber towns mentioned, see Keith Peterson, *Company Town: Potlatch, Idaho, and the Potlatch Lumber Company* (Pullman: Univ. of Washington Press, 1987); Smith, *Sawmill*; *Homes for Workmen* (New Orleans: Southern Pine Association, 1919). On company towns in extractive industries in the American West generally, see Allen, *Company Town*; Leland M. Roth, "Company Towns in the Western United States," in *The Company Town: Architecture and Society in the Industrial Age,* ed. John S. Garner (New York: Oxford Univ. Press, 1992).

Surveys of U.S. company towns include Margaret Crawford, *Building the Worker's Paradise: The Design of American Company Towns* (New York: Verso, 1995); John Reps, "The Towns the Companies Built," in *The Making of Urban America: A History of City Planning in the United States* (Princeton: Princeton Univ. Press); and Gwendolyn Wright, "Welfare Capitalism and the Company Town," in *Building the Dream: A Social History of Housing in America* (Cambridge: MIT Press, 1981). On specific towns mentioned, see Anne E. Mosher, "Something Better Than the Best: Industrial Restructuring, George McMurtry, and the Creation of the Model Industrial Town of Vandergrift, PA, 1883–1901," *Annals of the Association of American Geographers* 85 (1) (1995); Crawford, *Building the Worker's Paradise*, 174–99; Richard M. Candee, *Atlantic Heights: A World War I Shipbuilder's Community* (Portsmouth, N.H.: Portsmouth Marine Society, 1985).

CHAPTER 6

Timothy Davis

The Miracle Mile Revisited: Recycling, Renovation, and Simulation along the Commercial Strip

The Death and Life of Great American Strip Malls

As the twentieth century draws to a close, it is time to re-examine one of America's most maligned and misunderstood landscapes: the automobile-oriented commercial strip. Like its baby boomer clients, the post–World War II "Miracle Mile" is fast approaching middle age, while the 1930s roadside has advanced well into its golden years. Sparkling modern shopping centers and exuberant neon-lined strips that epitomized the automobile's influence on the American landscape and alternately outraged or titillated generations of planners and critics are now faded relics that have long since lost their ability to shock architectural puritans or provide sustenance for middle-class shoppers. Urban theorists now debate the role of "Edge Cities" and hypothesize Blade Runner/Disneyland fantasies of the future American metropolis, while affluent suburbanites spend their dollars in more glamorous retail palaces located farther out on the urban periphery or in newly renovated downtown historic districts.[1] For most Americans, the classic mid-twentieth century strip is just a nebulous zone of drab buildings and half-empty parking lots heedlessly bypassed on the way to more appealing destinations. Despite the strip's declining prominence, the tremendous amount of automobile-oriented commercial architecture produced during the mid-twentieth century ensures that it will continue to play a significant, if largely overlooked, role in the postmodern urban landscape. This essay examines the current condition of old miracle miles, bypassed approach roads, moribund motels, and down-at-the-heels strip malls in an attempt to understand the ways in which the aging process has affected the strip landscape and show

how the strip has evolved to accommodate changing economic trends, architectural fashions, and social conditions (fig. 6.1).[2]

In re-examining the strip, it is imperative to go beyond the visual analyses of the Robert Venturi camp and to get past the "problem" mentality that the strip has always posed to urban planners, who continue to bemoan the fact that American cities long ago departed from Old World prototypes. Nor should we simply romanticize the strip as a relic of the halcyon days of automobile culture, preserving certified remnants of a distantly remembered or recently invented past. "Classic" roadside architecture has no shortage of defenders, after all, as the rapid growth of the Society for Commercial Archeology, the cult of the diner, the sanctification of Route 66, and the "Great Shopping Center Debate" in the pages of the Society of Architectural Historians preservation newsletter have recently shown.[3] During the course of the last decade or so, mid-twentieth-century commercial landscapes have developed an enthusiastic following among both popular and academic audiences. Elegiac pictures of old diners and drive-ins appear in coffee-table books, magazine articles, and museum exhibitions, while even the most respectable architectural journals and academic presses publish extended scholarly investigations of automobile-oriented shopping centers, "It Happened One Night" tourist cabins, Walter Dorwin Teague

Fig. 6.1. Delwood Plaza, Austin, Texas.

Texaco stations, and other examples of once-ostracized roadside architecture.[4] Federal and state preservation bureaucracies have eagerly lent their imprimatur to this movement, endorsing national register nominations and providing technical and administrative assistance to help preserve and restore select examples of mid-twentieth-century roadside development.

Most commercial architecture aficionados focus on pre–World War II artifacts from the folksy "Mom and Pop" era of roadside development, though the exuberant excesses of the 1950s Miracle Mile, the modest beginnings of the shopping mall era, and the origins of franchised America are acquiring ardent devotees. Advertisements for "collectable" plates featuring golden-arched McDonald's appear in the pages of *Parade* magazine, while the popular press eagerly fuels the flames of baby boomer nostalgia, appealing to the collective memory of aging boomers with provocative headlines such as "Will Future Generations have any physical record of the era of Green Stamps and Golden Arches?"[5] As nostalgia works its way up through the decades at an ever-increasing pace, it seems inevitable that even the bland roadside architecture of the 1960s and 1970s will experience its share of misty-eyed romanticism, commercialized revivalism, and academic endorsement. The youth-oriented pop culture industry has already tired of the 1950s and is profitably marketing the 1960s and 1970s to today's Generation Xers, who view bell-bottoms, VW Beetles, and shag haircuts as quaint relics of a more innocent and authentic era. Thanks to cable television reruns, the California Ramblers and Contemporary tract homes of *Bewitched* and *The Brady Bunch* are well on their way to replacing the Colonial Revival suburbs of *Leave It to Beaver* and *Dennis the Menace* as the Virgilian landscape of America's lost golden age. Given academia's tendency to follow the whims of popular culture at a dignified but not-too-distant remove, it seems likely that stripped-down Texaco stations, mansard-roofed McDonald's restaurants, multiplex cinemas, and Wal-Marts will soon metamorphose into master's theses and National Register nominations before reaching their apotheosis as lushly printed John Margolies monographs.[6]

But nostalgia is not a terribly important reason to value a landscape. Selective historical preservation tends to be an elitist activity that mummifies exemplary buildings or turns them into upscale commercial boutiques, epitomizing the middle-class penchant for embalming a sanitized past rather than accepting a messy and complicated present.[7] One need only compare the franchised homogeneity of Washington's highly praised Cleveland Park "Park and Shop" renovation with the messy vitality of nearby unrenovated strips for a demonstration of the gentrified sterility that can result from well-intentioned restoration efforts. Yet some degree of historic preservation is undoubtedly desirable, if the goal of the movement is to provide a comprehensive architectural record of American culture. A Stanley Mestal McDonald's, a Mies van der Rohe-knock-off bank, or a megalithic suburban Sears store is probably as telling an artifact of the baby boom years as revitalized main streets and well-manicured courthouse squares are of earlier periods. The process of preserving relatively recent commercial architecture is already underway, in fact, as the Smithsonian collects old diners, McDonald's fans fight to preserve vintage golden arches, and preservationists organize to save 1950s motels and shopping centers.[8] In 1995 the National Park Service and a host of other preservation-oriented organizations sponsored a major conference dedicated to "Preserving Resources of the Recent Past." This gathering featured presentations on subjects ranging from the restoration of glass curtain walls and Lustron houses to the preservation of cold war missile silos and the documentation of 1960s subdivisions.[9] The classic roadside triumvirate of gas stations, tourist cabins, and drive-in restaurants received a chorus of acclaim, suggesting that these long-derided structures are well on their way to replacing Arts and Crafts bungalows and Art Deco storefronts as the latest objects of preservationists' populist fancies.[10]

While the preservation of outstanding roadside relics is undoubtedly a worthwhile activity, it is also important to consider how the unreconstructed strip contributes to the everyday lives of its current users. In order to do justice to the strip's role in contemporary American culture, one needs to go beyond the preservationists' artifactual fetishization, forgo the condescending wit of architectural theorists, and view the aging strip landscape with the empathy of urbanists such as Jane Jacobs, who pleaded the case for old, ugly, and ordinary buildings and chaotic mixes of uses and spaces; not for their own sake, but because they added opportunity, variety, and vitality to the urban landscape—even though these buildings were put to uses that might not always conform to middle-class ideas of beauty, morality, and good taste.[11] Lauding the preservationists' immaculate relics is a bit like oohing and aahing over the carefully screened selections of a pricey vintage clothing boutique, while ignoring the fact that many people make do—out of necessity, rather than choice—with the frayed but functional polyester castoffs that fill the dingy aisles of Goodwills and Salvation Army stores. In much the same way, the cheap, ugly, out-of-fashion buildings found along aging commercial strips provide opportunities for marginal tenants and shoestring entrepreneurs to secure a foothold in the postmodern metropolis. A closer look at the hand-me-down landscape that has developed between the old commercial centers and thriving suburbs of practically every North American city reveals the ingenious manner in which a wide range of businesses and individuals have appropriated and adapted these architectural cast-offs to serve their social and economic needs (fig. 6.2).

Jacobs's call for the preservation of old and ordinary buildings usually brings to mind the iron-fronted commercial buildings, charming rowhouses, and crowded ethnic neighborhoods of nineteenth-century Manhattan and other dense, long-established metropolises. We need to look with equal tolerance at the aging miracle miles that make up the frayed edges of the contemporary urban fabric. It may seem like an audacious leap to

Fig. 6.2. Strip Mall Church and Thrift Store, Lexington Park, Maryland.

expand Jacobs's respect for older, affordable, and easily available buildings from the cozy confines of pedestrian cities to the sprawling automobile-oriented landscapes of the twentieth-century North American city, but in this day and age, declining strips, derelict gas stations, and moribund shopping centers provide a similar haven for those at the lower end of the economic ladder. Jacobs, the consummate urbanite, might not relish the comparison, but the miracle mile, like lower Manhattan during the early and mid-twentieth century, has become the landscape of first and last resort for an increasing number of immigrants and lower-income Americans. Fledgling entrepreneurs recycle old strip mall storefronts and abandoned gas stations to avoid the high rates of gentrified downtown marketplaces or upscale malls; semipermanent renters live in decrepit motels and motor courts because they cannot afford conventional housing; immigrant communities transform outmoded shopping centers and aging subdivisions into thriving ethnic enclaves. In many cases, these new inhabitants are quietly converting barren and forsaken automobile-oriented wastelands into vibrantly humanized and strikingly heterogeneous places. While urban planners focus their energies on reviving the past and predicting the future, earnestly promoting "neotraditionalist" design or weaving fantasies about the brave new world of cyberspace—even as the more conscientious among them bemoan the elitist homogeneity of these ersatz environments—the ubiquitous strip is quietly evolving into a richly multicultural landscape that reflects the changing ethnic and economic character of late-twentieth-century American society.

Recycling: The "Vernacularization" of the Commercial Strip?

The reasons for the decline of the strip are well-known to most students of the American landscape.[12] With the spread of gigantic malls and ever-larger discount retailers, most "miracle miles" long ago ceased to appear very miraculous. The enclosed malls that proliferated in the 1960s and 1970s offered ample parking, huge selections of merchandise, and constant air-conditioned comfort, amenities most older strip centers could not provide. In similar fashion, the old turnpikes and boulevards that served as the primary thoroughfares of the mid-twentieth-century strip could rarely be upgraded to compete with modern, limited-access expressways. Mounting congestion made shopping and commuting along the original strips increasingly unattractive. The commercial and residential tissue surrounding these atrophied arteries began to decay as businesses moved to more upscale locales and new bypasses were constructed to reach the upgraded retail and residential spaces of the much-heralded Edge Cities. Another important but largely overlooked reason for the accelerating deterioration of the postwar strip is that the original owners of many roadside businesses were members of the Depression/World War II generation; by the 1980s, many were retiring for age- and health-related reasons. Commercial realtors encountered problems finding replacements to take over marginally profitable small businesses that often required considerable investment to refurbish to competitive standards. When storefronts went unrented, commercial decline was often compounded, as customers were dissuaded from patronizing remaining businesses by the accumulating aura of dereliction and decay. A similar phenomenon occurred in many of the residential developments surrounding postwar strips and shopping centers. Many original inhabitants of these modest subdivisions began to die or move away. Tiny tract homes that looked good to returning veterans desperate for any sort of housing were scorned by middle-class suburbanites, but they appealed to lower-class and immigrant residents, who moved in and transformed neglected neighborhoods into working-class and ethnic enclaves. These demographic changes may have contributed to the decline of traditional businesses and dissuaded upscale development, but they provided a fertile environment for the development of new enterprises and specialty stores catering to the changing class and ethnic makeup of the surrounding neighborhoods.[13]

This process of socioeconomic succession is gradually replacing what might be called the "First Generation" strip landscape with a new mix of establishments and owners that reflects the ongoing evolution of American urban culture in much the same way the transformation of traditional downtowns did several generations earlier (fig. 6.3). The bare-bones Colonial Revival and modernist architecture of most strip developments provides a ready medium for small-scale recycling and creative adaptation. Generic facades and malleable open plans are ideally suited to repeated remodelings and a wide variety of uses. The names and types of stores may change repeatedly, but the strip mall's interchangeable retail spaces afford the same sort of utilitarian flexibility as nineteenth-century cast-iron storefronts or the rental stalls of traditional urban markets. While some shopping centers have been completely transformed, many hand-me-down strip centers contain a mixture of older businesses, new shops, and empty storefronts. During the early 1990s, a languishing 1950s shopping center in Austin, Texas, housed a variety of older enterprises including chiropractors, locksmiths, traditional beauty salons, second-tier supermarkets, a Goodwill thrift store and a health clinic, along with an eclectic array of recent arrivals typified by a New Age emporium called "The Crystal Connection." An even more modest Austin strip center contained a sewing machine repair shop, a saw sharpener, and the venerable "Betty's Jewelry," together with a selection of newer enterprises including an alternative record outlet and two vintage clothing stores specializing in cast-offs from the 1950s and 1960s. In another form of "adaptive reuse," as preservationists would call it in more genteel surroundings, several moribund neighborhood shopping centers around Austin were converted into office buildings; overhead was minimal, and the ample parking facilities eliminated a common headache for small business operators and employees. While the low rents of down-at-the-heels strip malls ex-

Fig. 6.3. Strip Mall Succession, Ballston, Virginia.

ert obvious appeal for shoestring businesses, the laissez-faire attitude—or outright neglect—that often characterizes the management of marginal shopping centers can be attractive to small entrepreneurs. Shopkeepers in one older commercial strip located in a neighborhood of postwar tract homes said they preferred the location not only because it was more affordable, but because it gave them significantly more freedom to personalize their shops and set their own business hours than a large mall would allow. They also spoke of the strong sense of community shared by neighboring small business owners.

Aging supermarkets—especially those that are no longer so super nor so marketable in terms of square footage, location, or decor—are another form of readily recycled commercial architecture. Old supermarkets are especially attractive to cost-conscious enterprises requiring considerable space. Thrift stores, furniture outlets, recycling businesses, aerobics parlors, day-care centers—even churches—are taking advantage of defunct supermarkets to satisfy their need for spacious, low-cost quarters. State and municipal governments have recognized that cast-off supermarkets are both more affordable than new buildings and ideally located for providing community services. Austin converted an old Safeway into a Health and Human Services building and pressed another empty supermarket into service as a community college. Evanston, Wyoming, remodeled its decommissioned Safeway into a public library. Many communities have begun to locate municipal offices in new and old strip malls to save money and provide better access for time-pressed, automobile-dependent citizens.

Another legacy of the miracle mile's decline that has proven a boon to small businesses is the surplus of obsolete full-service gas stations, which became bargain spaces when oil companies began selling them off in the 1970s. Old gas stations are perfectly situated to serve automobile traffic and just the right size for many independent businesses and franchises. Predictably, many turn into automobile-related enterprises such as muffler shops, tune-up centers, and window-tinting establishments. Their convenient designs and locations make them well suited for other drive-in businesses such as dry cleaners, video stores, barbecue stands, and florists. Several Washington-area entrepreneurs have discovered that the old service bays make excellent showrooms for displaying carpet remnants. Atlanta's fashionable Buckhead district boasts a chic restaurant and a "Zen center" housed in former gas stations. A group of counterculture entrepreneurs in Jackson Hole, Wyoming, transformed an old garage into a teak-and-redwood hot-tubbing emporium. Perhaps the most outstanding example of cast-off service stations serving as stepping stones for economic advancement is the tie-dyed-rags-to-riches story of Ben and Jerry's ice cream, which started out as a shoestring operation in a remodeled gas station before expanding into a nationally prominent corporation (fig. 6.4). Starbucks, the voracious Seattle-based coffeehouse empire, has begun to colonize abandoned service stations and similarly underutilized roadside structures as the company expands from its urban base in search of new markets to conquer with its overpriced caffeine concoctions. Few businesses enjoy the meteoric success of a Ben and Jerry's or a Starbucks, but small businesses housed in secondhand gas stations are providing hope and sustenance to a diverse population of low-budget entrepreneurs throughout the country. Municipalities have also taken over old gas stations, using them for police substations and public works garages. While vintage gas station aficionados may cringe at the resulting modifications, the basic structures are being maintained and put to productive use, rather than demolished for fast-food franchises or parking lots.

The empty parking lots of abandoned gas stations and other defunct strip businesses, mean-

Fig. 6.4. Original Ben and Jerry's in Former Gas Station, Burlington, Vermont. Courtesy of Ben and Jerry's.

while, provide the sort of free common space that is increasingly unavailable or tightly controlled in modern urban environments. As highly visible display spaces, they serve as temporary showrooms for a wide variety of fly-by-night entrepreneurs, who—with or without permission—use these prime locations to sell everything from laser art and Elvis tapestries to sunglasses, stuffed animals, oriental rugs, and seasonal produce. Some of these temporary stands are staffed by underpaid employees of larger commercial operations, but many are operated by independent vendors selling whatever they can get their hands on. A few of these freelance businesses even put down roots and lease or purchase their locations. The operator of Austin's Corner Mall claimed he started out "with nothing but a half a dozen Mexican dresses and a dream," selling from a van parked in abandoned gas stations. He eventually remodeled a failing barbecue joint to serve as the main showroom for his bewildering collection of carpets, clothes, skulls, banners, and flea market trinkets, but still maintains a force of temporary employees who hawk his wares in empty lots around town. Another Austin entrepreneur leases an abandoned service station to display a constantly changing array of secondhand merchandise ranging from household items and office furniture to used cars and refrigerators. A similar gas station flea market in Clarendon, Virginia, ekes out a tenuous existence beneath a gigantic banner urging developers to transform the site into a gleaming new office building. On the other side of town, a former gas station operator shuttles between several defunct garages selling a seasonally varying assortment of seedlings and nursery stock, watermelons and fresh vegetables, Halloween pumpkins, and Christmas trees.

While it has rarely been considered a residential landscape, the strip has also become a permanent or semipermanent home for a large and growing population of less-affluent Americans. Like the traditional Single Room Occupancy hotels (SROs), whose elimination in the name of progress dramatically increased downtown homelessness, cheap motels along old highways provide affordable refuge for welfare recipients, migrant workers, and other people who cannot scrape together the security deposits and first-and-last-month's rent that are the price of admission to today's conventional housing market. In this respect, the down-at-the-heels strip has inherited many of the functions of the older urban skid rows described by Berkeley geographer Paul Groth.[14] Along with cheap lodgings, the strip provides an array of services geared toward the needs of single men, day laborers, and families down on their luck.[15] Pawn shops, check cashing services, liquor stores, laundromats, and thrift shops abound in old shopping centers and declining strips. Budget mini-storage compounds take the place of the storage lockers that gave itinerant workers a place to store their goods in the old urban skid row. Storefront churches and soup kitchens, both traditional skid-row establishments, have appeared in marginal strip centers in many towns. Plentiful discount auto part stores help the poor nurture aging vehicles, which can often be seen languishing in various stages of disassembly in the courtyards of weekly rent motels. Ironically, many residents of this quintessential American automobile landscape cannot afford to own or maintain a car. It is an increasingly common yet vaguely disturbing sight to see pedestrians—mostly young, mostly immigrant, mostly poor, often with babies and small children—walking along desolate stretches of commercial strips designed expressly for automobile use.

Motel courts and old shopping center parking lots frequently serve as open-air labor markets, where temporary employers come to find cheap workers. Contractors' vans and pickup trucks cruise by throughout the morning to pick up day laborers. Tensions occasionally arise when these labor markets are located in transitional areas, where groups of unemployed dark-skinned men hanging out in public raise fears among more traditional middle-class suburbanites. While motels and strip developments might seem unlikely environments for the development of community spirit and the maintenance of class or ethnic identity, parking lots and motel courtyards can assume important roles for those who frequent them and transform the generic automobile-oriented spaces into subtly differentiated and personalized places. As in the older urban laborer districts, a sense of community often develops among people who share the same environment and circumstances. While some residents shun contact behind locked doors, cramped motel rooms encourage residents to socialize in outdoor common areas, contributing to the village or campground atmosphere of many transient motels. People may reside in the same motel for weeks, months, or even years, developing close ties with their neighbors. Just as likely, they may drift from one motel to another as their financial situations or social behavior varies.[16]

Inevitably, the decaying strip has replicated skid row's function as a place to pursue illicit pleasures. Motels have always functioned as convenient assignation spots. With the decline in business from "respectable" travelers, many have become havens for drug dealing and prostitution. The crackdown on urban red-light districts has driven many sex businesses to the suburbs, where the strip's cheap rents, anonymity, and ease of access creates a hospitable environment for video arcades, massage parlors, pornography stores, and strip joints. The shortage of traditional SROs has led some cities to use run-down motels as temporary housing for homeless people and other social services clients. Participants in a New York City program expressed a preference for strip motels in the outer boroughs over the dingy corridors and threatening surroundings of conventional downtown shelters. Transferring homeless shelter residents from gentrifying urban districts with well-organized neighborhood associations to sparsely settled suburban strips has also proven politically expedient, though strip businesses are becoming increasingly resistant to this practice. The proprietors of more upscale establishments, backed by local "concerned citizens," have attempted to eliminate older motels, blanketly characterizing them as dens of immorality, vice, and violent crime.[17] Dallas, for example, tried to impose exorbitant licensing fees on motels with fewer than eighty beds, which would have put many independent motels out of business and forced hundreds of residents out on the street or into already overburdened homeless shelters.[18] Until society performs a better job of providing low-cost housing alternatives, eliminating marginal motels along old commercial routes will only increase the homeless population and attendant problems.[19]

The secondhand strip further resembles the older districts of traditional cities in that it provides a welcome haven for ethnic immigrants. While earlier immigrants often flocked to densely settled urban enclaves like New York's Lower East Side, Boston's North End, or big-city Chinatowns, many modern immigrants bypass dangerous and congested downtowns and head straight for the cheap suburbs along old miracle miles, where the low rental rates of aging motels, tract housing, and apartment complexes provide ample opportunity for ethnic neighborhoods to develop, and the thriving low-wage service industry provides plentiful and loosely scrutinized job opportunities. The strips in these areas are often lined with ethnic businesses housed in both new and recycled buildings. East Los Angeles is perhaps the most extensive example of the phenomenon. At a smaller scale, McKee Boulevard in San Jose, California—a classic "Miracle Mile" if ever there was one—is flanked with old shopping centers and gas stations bearing new advertisements in Spanish and various Asian languages. The old miracle miles running through the northern Virginia suburbs of Washington, D.C., are renowned for their Asian markets and restaurants—many of which are located in recycled shopping centers. "Colonial Village," a modest brick and wood 1930s shopping center in Arlington, Virginia, built in association with the nearby Colonial Revival apartment complex, now hosts a variety of small businesses ranging from a traditional barber shop and an upscale bistro to a topless bar, a Latino market, and Vietnamese, Cambodian, Thai, and Afghani restaurants. The Eden Shopping Center, a starkly modernist complex located farther out along the same boulevard, has become almost entirely Vietnamese (fig. 6.5). The classic U-shaped center is anchored by a conventional Ames discount store, but the nondescript arcades are adorned with signs announcing at least eight Vietnamese restaurants, seven Vietnamese jewelers, a large Asian supermarket, and an assortment of Vietnamese variety stores, dress shops, video outlets, travel agencies, night clubs, and billiard parlors. Unlike many mainstream strip malls, the Eden shopping center often bustles with pedestrian activity, as couples, families, and groups of young people wander from store to store or lounge about the cafes and clubs. On the other side of the nearby highway, a new postmodern shopping complex catering to more affluent subdivisions appears comparatively dull and lifeless. The cheap rentals and storefronts in older strip malls throughout the northern Virginia and Maryland suburbs have also spawned linear barrios that are home to some of the area's highest concentrations of Latin American immigrants. This has produced innumerable Latin American specialty stores along with several revived shopping centers dominated by Spanish-speaking businesses (fig. 6.6). The transformation of these iconic American landscapes has been so profound that one half expects to find ardent defenders of vintage commercial architecture protesting against the pungent aromas of foreign foods that emanate from Colonial Revival malt shops and Happy Days hamburger palaces, just as the founders of the Society for the Preservation of New England Antiquities denounced the temerity with which Boston's Italian immigrants enveloped Paul Revere's house in a haze of garlic and onions.[20] The suburban ethnic strip phenomenon is so pervasive in some regions of the country that it may seem unremarkable, but the appropriation and revitalization of these quintessentially "white bread" miracle miles provides striking evidence of the resilience and adaptability of a mid-twentieth-century

Fig. 6.5. Eden Shopping Center, Arlington, Virginia.

Fig. 6.6. Multicultural Strip Mall, Arlington, Virginia.

commercial landscape that was once roundly criticized for its formulaic homogeneity and bourgeois sterility.[21]

Does all this recycling and adaptation mean the aging commercial strip has become a vernacular landscape? After all, most of these motels and shopping centers were expressly designed to replace the chaotic heterogeneity of downtown shopping districts, seamy auto camps, and eclectic roadside architecture with controlled and homogeneous planned environments. In their original incarnations, the shopping centers, motels, and franchised architecture of the classic mid-twentieth-century strip would seem to epitomize J. B. Jackson's characterization of the modern, post-vernacular landscape as the systematic creation of professional designers intent on establishing order, beauty, and stasis. If one considers vernacular to be a function of use rather than of structure or original intent, however, the hand-me-down strip resembles a classic vernacular landscape. Older strips have taken on exactly the qualities of informality, adaptability, impermanence, and relative freedom from authority that Jackson argued were essential attributes of the vernacular landscape. While postwar strip architecture may be largely undistinguished and insubstantial, its availability and malleability provides a ready source of raw material that enables

people to exercise the "inexhaustible ingenuity in finding short term solutions" and "unending patient adjustment to circumstances" Jackson identified as defining characteristics of the vernacular landscape. Driving along the aging strips encountered on the outskirts of most American cities, one can easily view the miles of empty parking lots, shabby motels, and dowdy shopping centers interspersed with occasional pockets of regeneration and activity in the terms Jackson applied to the vernacular landscape of medieval Europe, "a scattering of hamlets . . . islands in a vast sea of waste and wilderness, changing from generation to generation, leaving no monuments, only abandonment or signs of renewal."[22]

Renovation

In addition to this recycling from below, a parallel process of upscale renovation is having as profound an effect on the mid-twentieth-century strip landscape. Many long-stagnant strip malls and roadside establishments are being renovated or entirely replaced by large businesses and major developers. There are several factors behind this recycling from above. By the 1980s, the mall juggernaut that swept across the American countryside from the late 1950s through the 1970s finally began to lose steam. Enclosed mall construction dropped off as commercial real estate specialists discovered consumers were tired of trudging across gigantic parking lots and negotiating increasingly large and confusing complexes. Traditional strip malls were suddenly heralded as ideal for time-pressed modern shoppers, since they allowed motorists to drive within a few feet of a store, jump out and make a few quick purchases, then get back on the road to another destination. The time-saving appeal of strip malls was cast as increasingly significant given the rapid growth of two-worker and one-person households. Since older strip malls were generally located along heavily traveled routes, developers believed that customers could be lured back by producing visually inviting alternatives to the drab storefronts and fortresslike facades of postwar shopping centers. With increasingly strict zoning laws and environmental regulations complicating new construction efforts, another important reason for the revival of older shopping centers is that developers can often refurbish or rebuild existing complexes with minimal paperwork or planning board review.[23]

Ironically, the principal style adopted for most upscale strip mall renovation has been a popularized version of academic postmodernism, which supposedly owes its derivation to the exuberant roadside architecture displaced by the austere facades of mass-market modernism. In their haste to inject "character" into stripped-down storefronts, and/or to reinvoke the faded funkiness of surviving roadside establishments, developers have experimented with a panoply of approaches, ranging from detailed restorations of historic roadside structures to fanciful evocations of Art Deco and old-fashioned strip architecture to mile after mile of mass-produced postmodernist clichés. Pediments, columns, lattices, whimsical appliqué, vague historicism, subdued pastels, and sensitive red brick spread throughout the American commercial landscape during the 1980s, both in new construction and in the rehabilitation of aging strip centers. While the results might be more visually interesting than the preceding generation's minimalist boxes, postmodernism's domination of the current commercial landscape provides a strikingly similar illustration of the dangers of a too-successful architectural theory. Despite its superficial stylistic diversity, the relentless postmodernification of the last two decades rivals the often-criticized modernist movement in its sweeping homogenization of the American built environment.

Even modest businesses have appropriated postmodern motifs and materials to capitalize on the resurgence of the strip. The mass production of the colorful all-weather awnings associated with the festival marketplace craze spawned a wave of low-budget renovations in otherwise lackluster shopping centers. One Austin strip mall was revitalized when its owners wrapped the building with a bright blue awning that injected a splash of color into the bland stripscape, visually harmonizing an assortment of shops that had grown increasingly drab and heterogeneous over the years. This minor renovation drew several businesses from the unreconstructed shopping center across the street. Another down-at-the-heels commercial strip in Austin received a number of design awards for remodeling its mundane facade with playful neon signs, pastel pergolas, and other stock postmodern embellishments. Even some of the strip's more dubious establishments have caught the renovation bug. One Austin massage parlor tidied itself up to resemble a tasteful suburban cottage with white shutters and well-trimmed shrubbery, while the city's most notorious video arcade discarded its garish outdoor advertising in favor of a discreet sign and subdued pastel exterior, simultaneously replacing its dingy arcades with a clean, well-lighted interior replete with potted plants and tasteful gray carpets. Postmodernism's embrace of eclecticism also bestowed legitimacy on the strip's signature displays of architectural exuberance, which never really disappeared despite the blandishments of modernist critics and other self-appointed arbiters of architectural taste. New and old versions of Venturi's ducks and decorated sheds can still be found along the revitalized commercial strip, though vintage fifty-foot-tall milk bottles and neon-encrusted hamburger stands may now specialize in spicy burritos or Chinese takeout. New materials and technologies provide today's roadside merchants with an array of architectural options beyond the wildest dreams of earlier entrepreneurs. Las Vegas, of course, continues to lead the way in roadside theatrics. The erupting volcanoes, life-size sphinxes, and simulated pirate

Recycling, Renovation, and Simulation

ships of the latest wave of casino-building make Caesar's 1950s centurions seem tame and tasteful by comparison.

Simulation

While most strip mall renovators simply spice up bland facades with a few Gravesian garnishes, others engage in the literal simulation of early roadside architecture, either through "authentic" historic preservation or the creation of new "old" buildings recalling the strip's glory days. Restaurateurs have discovered that aging baby boomers long to recapture their lost youth by dragging their children into over-priced eateries designed to evoke the diners and drive-ins of American Graffiti days. These establishments are often quintessential simulacrae, unabashed fictions invoking models that never existed.[24] Like Disneyland and the movies, they are bolder, better, and more dependable than the imperfect originals they ostensibly emulate. The simulated diners popping up throughout the country are no longer greasy spoon ptomaine factories, but carefully crafted evocations of greasy spoons, with more chrome and less cholesterol. Their stainless steel walls might be crowded with tokens of 1950s excess, and they offer the obligatory Mom's meat loaf and Blue Plate Specials, but their menus are tempered with eggbeaters™ omelets and wide selections of salads and nouvelle fare. Their clientele, meanwhile, is decidedly upscale; their parking lots are filled with expensive foreign cars and gleaming sport utility vehicles, since the exorbitant prices drive the old diner crowd to McDonald's and other affordable eateries.

Some of these establishments strive for the illusion of authenticity, while others revel in their ability to depart from the limitations of any one particular era of roadside chic. Chevy Chase's realistic-seeming American City Diner's claim to authenticity rests on the fact that it was built by Kullman Industries, one of the few surviving original diner manufacturers. Yet, the American City Diner is not actually an old diner, but an amalgam of newly minted dineresque elements conjured out of vintage photographs from the 1940s. To contribute to the period ambiance, the owners erected a matching neon sign and reproduced a 1937 billboard (also based on a photograph) on the wall behind the diner.[25] Austin's Majestic Diner, in contrast, was designed to be decidedly "hyperreal." Its eclectic combination of motifs makes no pretense of obeisance to historical prototype (fig. 6.7). It merges classic suggestions of diner-ness with a cool Miami Vice stucco-deco palette and margarita bar informality, topping the whole thing off with a Jetsonesque flourish to create a baby boomer icon unlike anything ever seen by Ozzie and Harriet. Just up the street, the same restaurateurs created a slightly more affordable family-style eatery that ironically appropriated the "Wagon Wheel" theme of the neighboring trailer court. This brick, stone, and wood cowboy-chic burger joint is accompanied by a hot-dog annex coyly housed in a vintage Airstream trailer. Elsewhere in Austin, a futuristic 1950s glass box coffee shop underwent an expensive remodeling to become a "classic" sombrero-shaped Mexican restaurant. The vintage roadside restaurant craze has spawned a number of bemus-

Fig. 6.7. Majestic Diner, Austin, Texas.

ing hybrids, where old, new, and new-old are mixed in a postmodern hall-of-mirrors. Threadgill's, an "authentic" gas station-cum-restaurant located on one of Austin's major miracle miles, has undergone a number of renovations over the years. Most recently, a brand new stainless steel diner was grafted onto the main structure, which was refurbished with "period" lettering and further embellished with meticulously restored antique gas pumps. Perhaps the ultimate manifestation of the slippery relationship between reality, imitation, and simulation is a proposal from the McDonald's corporation to dismantle the last original McDonald's in Downey, California, and scatter its signature components among the chain's other stores. Will the dismembered arches join the profane ranks of detached signifiers competing with newer, and perhaps better, evocations of the roadside past, or will they function like relics of the true cross, reverently curated to traffic in the magic of the real?[26]

Gentrification and the Vernacular Strip

Is the traditional commercial strip in danger of following the course of other "rediscovered" landscapes in becoming preserved, renovated, and commercialized beyond the reach of less-affluent Americans? The gentrification of rundown miracle miles has begun to displace marginal tenants in much the same way the redevelopment of traditional downtowns eradicated the independent businesses, low-income residents, and urban ethnic communities that gravitated to these areas when the middle-class abandoned them for the suburbs. The fate of one of Austin's oldest classic strip malls demonstrates several potential downsides of strip gentrification. Constructed shortly after World War II, Delwood Plaza was the first modern strip mall in Austin. By the mid 1980s, however, it was decidedly down-at-the-heels. Many storefronts were vacant. Others were occupied by a ragged assortment of downscale establishments, including a five-and-dime, an old fashioned barber shop, a cheap lunch counter, a paint store, and a beauty college. Delwood Plaza occupied a prime commercial location next to a major expressway entrance, however. Fiesta Markets, a developer of monster "hypermarkets," bought not only the strip mall, but a defunct motel to the north and a low-income apartment building to the east. The company evicted the family-operated, full-service gas station that had occupied the corner for decades and razed all the buildings to construct a superstore engulfing several city blocks. A few proprietors refused to be bought out and hung grimly on to the end of their leases, even though the new developers aggressively bulldozed the surrounding storefronts. Typically, Fiesta adopted a postmodernized strip mall configuration. The original Delwood Plaza sign, a garish metal-and-neon protuberance, was torn down and tastefully reinvoked in sensitive red brick. To compete with this, the supermarket on the other side of the highway launched a major renovation that included the remodeling of its starkly modernist complex, which was part of the first modern plaza-style shopping center in the Austin area. Its pure geometric architecture and spare concrete courtyard were postmodernized with comforting green lawns and a whimsical appliqué of pastels and pediments, while an implausible reproduction of a nineteenth-century farmhouse appeared in the parking lot to house a convenient drive-in bank. There was no organized opposition to either of these projects, though they evicted a number of established small businesses and destroyed two of the most historically significant mid-twentieth-century commercial landscapes in Austin.

From the preservationist's point of view, a late-1930s shopping center in Silver Spring, Maryland, appears headed toward a slightly more propitious fate, due in large part to its attractively streamlined facades. In 1988 the Art

Fig. 6.8. Reprieved Shopping Center, Silver Spring, Maryland.

Deco Society of Washington spearheaded a campaign to list the physically and economically deteriorating structure on the National Register of Historic Places (fig. 6.8).[27] Developers claimed there was no way to make the original building economically viable, so planners have agreed to let most of the complex be destroyed as long as the refurbished facade is retained to serve as a quaint vestibule fronting a gargantuan shopping and entertainment center. Saving this superficial vestige of the golden age of commercial architecture represents a strategic synthesis of savvy marketing and conspicuously "responsible" development. The charming Art Deco facades will provide megamall shoppers with a comforting reminder of a bygone era, when Silver Spring and other American suburbs exuded confidence in the promise of the motor age but retained—at least in retrospect—much of the scale, pace, and cultural homogeneity of traditional small-town life. The Sierra Club and several local environmentalist groups even endorsed the project as an ecologically friendly alternative to building the new supermall on undeveloped land. While preservationists fight to save a few square yards of streamlined stucco and environmentalists applaud the project's minimal impact on the ecosystem of the Chesapeake Bay, little concern has been expressed about the fate of the small shop owners displaced by the mall, or of the megamall's impact on area residents who might be more concerned with retaining access to low-cost goods and services than with frequenting upscale boutiques and indoor wave parks. Current tenants, including a small secondhand store, a dress-alteration shop, a Jamaican restaurant, and similar marginal enterprises frequented by the area's growing immigrant population will be left to find new accommodations beyond reach of gentrification. One angry, soon-to-be-displaced merchant accused local planners and business leaders of being star-struck by overly optimistic projections of potential profits and tax revenues, cynically dismissing the existing tenants as "expendable minority and other small businesses who in the larger scheme of things really don't matter." Complaining that mall proponents were manipulating public opinion by presenting the area as a domestic "Beirut" full of bombed-out buildings and threatening inhabitants, rather than as a resilient neighborhood struggling to make do with limited resources, he observed, "They see dark and potentially dangerous streets, where we see a community that has complained for years of poor lighting. They see a community full of vagrants where we see a handful of down-on-their-luck homeless people named Mike, Gerald, and Lucille.... They see a community that can't seem to get it together, while we see a community dominated by landlords who refuse to even put a fresh coat of paint on their empty buildings so as to make the general area more inviting." County officials formally endorsed the project, which was slated to get underway as soon as the developers could muster sufficient funding.[28]

It is unrealistic to expect to preserve every relic shopping center and vintage gas station, or to protect every marginal business from the forces of gentrification. There are compelling arguments for replacing buildings that have deteriorated to the extent they present legitimate hazards to their surroundings. As the preceding characterization of Silver Spring suggests, the sort of physical and social devastation commonly associated with derelict pockets of the inner city is beginning to appear in postwar suburbs and commercial developments. The case of Tulagi Place, in Lexington Park, Maryland, provides a striking illustration of this phenomenon (fig. 6.9). The Tulagi Place shopping center was developed in the late 1940s and early 1950s to accompany a small subdivision of modernist duplexes, which provided housing for civilians working at a rapidly expanding naval base. The shopping center contained a movie theater, a supermarket, a furniture store, a motel, and a restaurant, along with several other small businesses. The shops were housed in several typically undistinguished modernist brick and glass boxes. When the housing development and the shopping center were new, they bustled with activity and attracted attention from the Washington *Evening Star,* which praised the complex as "thriving" and "well-ordered."[29] During the 1960s and 1970s, however, as the surrounding area developed more attractive housing options, the tiny duplexes of the original subdivision fell into disfavor. By the 1980s the development served primarily as cheap rental housing for low-income families. The Reagan-era defense buildup created a second economic boom that spawned a new wave of commercial building just north of the original center. The ample parking, nationally advertised franchises, and other amenities offered by these sprawling strip malls easily lured shoppers away from Tulagi Place. Both the surrounding neighborhood and the old shopping center began to deteriorate. Many businesses closed their doors. The hotel became a haven for drug dealers, addicts, and transients. A fire gutted the movie theater, closing the adjacent motel and accelerating the center's economic decline. By 1994 the only paying occupants were a barber shop, two storefront churches, a soup kitchen, a laundromat, a thrift store, and a small cafe. The supermarket that anchored one end of the complex also remained, but announced plans to relocate. Open motel rooms, dark, empty corridors, and the fire-gutted hulks of the movie theater and several nearby tract homes presented a landscape of squalor and menace of the sort more commonly associated with the South Bronx than with a model postwar planned community nestled around a prim modern shopping center. The county commissioners declared the complex a "fire-ridden, rodent-infested slum" and announced plans to tear the area down and redevelop it into "Tulagi Town Center," a pristine composition of generic postmodern office/retail blocks. Commendably, the local planning commission invited local input in the redevelopment process by placing design drawings in the local library along with a notebook for comments. They even expressed a desire to encourage marginal businesses through low-cost loans. As of

Fig. 6.9. Derelict Strip Mall, Lexington Park, Maryland.

this writing, the project remains on paper. It is unclear, however, just where the soup kitchen, the storefront churches, or the homey little local cafe will fit among the postmodern crystal palaces portrayed in the planners' sanitized community center.[30]

Striking a balance between the demands of developers, preservationists, and marginal tenants will always pose a difficult problem. While Lexington Park officials had legitimate public health and safety concerns to bolster their case for wholesale redevelopment, many aging shopping centers are structurally sound and socially valuable, even when they are not particularly attractive or economically vibrant. Preservationists are likely to praise the Silver Spring solution and other examples of upscale adaptive reuse as desirable means of preventing the wholesale destruction of historic commercial architecture; developers will argue that completely new or elaborately renovated buildings are more commercially viable than the outmoded originals. Both groups are probably right. There are other ways of evaluating the aging strip's contributions to urban culture, however. While the renovations and simulations springing up along once-neglected commercial corridors may win design awards, placate preservationists, and create visually attractive environments that generate higher profits for developers, the intention of this essay has been to suggest that society should not judge landscapes aesthetically, nostalgically, or on

Fig. 6.10. Vendor in Abandoned Gas Station, Austin, Texas.

purely economic grounds, nor as immutable historical artifacts deserving eternal preservation for their own sake, but in terms of the way they function for the people who use them on a regular basis and who depend on the services and opportunities they provide. One hopes the urge to homogenize, pasteurize, and commercialize the built environment that has turned many renovated downtowns into sterile, culturally and economically segregated theme parks will not destroy the strip's ability to function as a landscape of opportunity and refuge for its current broad array of users (fig. 6.10). For the time being, at least, the sheer physical extent of the postwar commercial landscape mediates against complete capitulation to corporate hegemony and bourgeois homogeneity. As one sector is renovated, another will undoubtedly decline in value, and low-budget businesses and tenants will gravitate there. There are already signs that the first generation of enclosed malls is starting to fall out of favor with major retailers and middle-class shoppers. Smaller malls throughout the country are beginning to experience economic hardships and an exodus of desirable tenants. Perhaps these forsaken malls will eventually open their doors to those displaced by the gentrification of the miracle mile. The mall itself—the apotheosis of automobile-oriented retail architecture—might then become the next vernacular commercial landscape, at least until today's twenty-somethings wax nostalgic and resurrect its food courts and video arcades to their former glory. Meanwhile, the aging strip, with its frayed edges, threadbare corners, stains, rents, tears, and patches, continues to function as a vital component of the urban fabric. It needs to be understood not simply as a repository of quaint commercial architecture to be preserved for nostalgic purposes, nor as a persistent blight to be eradicated in the name of moral or aesthetic improvement, but as a resilient vernacular landscape that continues to evolve in response to the needs of people who use it and depend on it (fig. 6.10).

Notes

1. The classic interpretations of the mid-twentieth-century commercial strip, pro and con, are Robert Venturi's *Learning from Las Vegas: The Forgotten Symbolism of Architectural Form* (Cambridge: MIT Press, 1977) and Peter Blake's *God's Own Junkyard: The Planned Deterioration of America's Landscape* (New York: Holt, Rinehart and Winston, 1964). The best historical overview of the evolution of the automobile-oriented commercial strip is Chester Liebs's *Main Street to Miracle Mile: American Roadside Architecture* (Boston: Little, Brown, and Company, 1985). *Washington Post* reporter Joel Garreau called attention to the increasing prominence of suburban mini-cities in *Edge City: Life on the New Frontier* (New York: Doubleday, 1991); for a look at the broader context of this phenomenon, see Robert Bruegmann and Tim Davis, "New Centers on the Periphery," *Center: A Journal for Architecture in America* 7 (1992): 25–43. Michael Sorkin, ed., *Variations on a Theme Park: The New American City and the End of Public Space* (New York: Hill and Wang, 1992), represents another popular academic view of the contemporary American city as postmodern, "ageographical," and based on sinister forms of artificiality, surveillance, and capitalist control.

2. This article is based on fieldwork in numerous American cities, including Austin and San Antonio, Texas; San Jose, California; Atlanta, Georgia; and the greater Washington, D.C., metropolitan area. Due to the protean nature of these landscapes, many of the sites described here may have changed dramatically by the time this essay is published.

3. Among the many recent books to venerate Route 66 as America's preeminent automotive pilgrimage are Michael K. Witzel, *Route 66 Remembered* (Osceola, Wisc.: Motorbooks International, 1996), and Michael Wallace, *Route 66: The Mother Road* (New York: St. Martin's Press, 1990). For the "Great Shopping Center Debate," see Richard Longstreth, "The Lost Shopping Center," *The Forum: Bulletin of the Society of Architectural Historians Committee on Preservation* 20 (Oct. 1992): n.p.; Mike Jackson, "Response to 'The Lost Shopping Center,'" and Ronald Lee Fleming, "Saving Shopping Centers: An Owlish View, or, Giving a Hoot for Enhancement," both in *The Forum* 21 (Apr. 1993): n.p.; Rebecca Shiffer, "The Shopping Center Saga Continues," and Richard Striner, "Some Answers for Ronald Lee Fleming," both in *The Forum* 22 (Apr. 1994). This tempest in the preservationist teapot pitted the forces of taste, decency, and "traditional standards" against vulgarians intent on breaching the gates with presumptuous National Register nominations and political agitation aimed at protecting endangered shopping centers such as the Shopper's World complex in Framingham, Massachusetts.

4. John Baeder helped get the roadside architecture craze rolling with his paintings and popular publications, such as *Diners* (New York: Harry N. Abrams, 1980) and *Gas, Food, and Lodging: A Postcard Odyssey through the Great American Roadside* (New York: Abbeville Press, 1982). For a demonstration of the growing popularity of motor-age landscape scholarship and historic preservation, see "Cultural Resources of the Recent Past," *CRM Thematic Issue* 16 (1993), and Jan Jennings, ed., *Roadside America: The Automobile in Design and Culture* (Ames, Iowa: Iowa Univ. Press, 1991). On gas stations, see Donald Vieyra, *"Fill 'er Up": An Architectural History of America's Gas Stations* (New York: Collier Macmillan, 1979), and John Jakle and Keith Sculle, *The Gas Station in America* (Baltimore: Johns Hopkins Univ. Press, 1994). On shopping centers, see Meredith Clausen, "Northgate Regional Shopping Center—Paradigm from the Provinces," *Journal of the Society of Architectural Historians* 43 (May 1984): 144–61; Howard Gillette, "The Evolution of the Planned Shopping Center in Suburb and City," *Journal of the American Planning Association* 51 (Autumn 1985): 449–60; and

Richard Longstreth, "The Neighborhood Shopping Center in Washington, D.C.," *Journal of the Society of Architectural Historians* 51 (Mar. 1992): 5–34.

5. Christina Waters, "Old and in the Way: Postwar Architecture Is the Valley's Latest Endangered Species," San Jose *Metro* 8, Feb. 25–Mar. 3, 1993, 16–19.

6. Photographer John Margolies succeeded Baeder as the primary popularizer of mid-twentieth-century commercial architecture. He has exhibited widely and his publications include *The End of the Road: Vanishing Highway Architecture in America* (New York: Penguin, 1981), *Pump and Circumstance: Glory Days of the American Gas Station* (Boston: Little, Brown and Company, 1993), *Home Away from Home: Motels in America* (Boston: Little, Brown and Company, 1995), and *John Margolies's Lost America Postcards* (New York: Dial Press, 1982).

7. For extended discussions of these tendencies, see David Lowenthal, *The Past Is a Foreign County* (New York: Cambridge Univ. Press, 1985); Michael Wallace, "Visiting the Past" and "Reflections on the History of Historic Preservation," in *Presenting the Past: Essays on History and the Public*, ed. Susan Porter Benson, Stephen Brier, and Roy Rosenzweig (Philadelphia: Temple Univ. Press, 1986), 137–99; and Edward Relph, *The Modern Urban Landscape* (Baltimore: Johns Hopkins Univ. Press, 1987), 218–24.

8. The spring 1994 issue of the *Society for Commercial Architecture News*, for example, contained articles lamenting the immanent demise of a Howard Johnson's, a 1960s vintage shopping mall, and a 1946 Mobil station.

9. "Preserving the Recent Past," Chicago, Illinois, Mar. 30–Apr. 1, 1995

10. A half-century earlier, critics routinely assailed the combination of gas stations, cabin courts, and "hot dog stands" as an unholy trinity of unmitigated cultural and aesthetic evil. Landscape architect Gilmore Clarke asserted that tasteless roadside development had transformed the typical American highway into a "ribbon of blight," a "shoe string of sordidness," and "an open sore." Westchester County Park Commission engineer Jay Downer characterized roadside commercial architecture as a "nauseating vulgarity of structural riff-raff" and promoted limited-access parkways as alternatives to "the panoramic hodgepodge of hot-dog dispensaries, barbecues, and so-called refreshment stands that unfold in offensive, jazzy patterns along countless mile of our American highways." Roadside improvement promoter J. M. Bennett complained that merchants were lining American highways with tasteless tourist traps "in a variety of types from mere shacks to fantastic replicas of old shoes, mammoth vegetables, Dutch windmills, wigwams, Eskimo houses and Hottentot huts, until the motorists wonder whether they are in a foreign country, the land of Oz or on the main street of Coney Island." Gilmore Clarke, "Modern Motor Ways," *Architectural Record* (Dec. 1933): 430; Clarke, "The Mount Vernon Memorial Highway," *Landscape Architecture* 22 (Apr. 1932): 179; Clarke, "Some Views on Highway Design," *Parks and Recreation* 19 (May 1936): 320; Jay Downer, "How Westchester Treats its Roadsides," *American Civic Annual, 1930*, 165–66; J. M. Bennett, *Roadsides: The Front Yard of the Nation* (Boston: The Stratford Company, 1936), 165.

11. Jane Jacobs, *The Death and Life of Great American Cities* (New York: Random House, 1961).

12. Liebs's *Mainstreet to Miracle Mile* discusses the decline of the original strip and the rise of enclosed malls and national franchises, as does William Kowinski's *The Malling of America: An Inside Look at the Great Consumer Paradise* (New York: Morrow, 1985) and Stan Luxenberg's *Roadside Empires: How the Chains Franchised America* (New York: Viking, 1985).

13. The problem with finding new tenants to take over aging businesses was raised by several interviewees and is discussed in "Classic Hojos Bypassed,

Closes," *Society for Commercial Archeology News* 2 (Spring 1994): 4.

14. Paul Groth, "Third and Howard: Skid Row and the Limits of Architecture," in *Streets: Critical Perspectives on Public Space,* ed. Zeynep Çelik, Diane Favro, and Richard Ingersoll (Berkeley: Univ. of California Press, 1994), 1–14.

15. The manner in which motels are supplanting traditional downtown hotels as havens for transients and other socially or economically marginal citizens is occasionally reported in the press, almost invariably in relation to aberrant behavior associated with motel residents. The motel's status as a refuge of last resort was dramatized in reports that the Oklahoma City bombing suspects and Frank Eugene Corder, the man who crashed a light plane into the White House in September 1994, lived in low-rent motels prior to their attacks. To emphasize the point that Corder was a pathetic down-and-outer, not a calculating assassin, the *Washington Post* reported that he had recently lost his job and separated from his wife, and was living in a "shabby motel room" in a cinder-block motel located along an old highway on the outskirts of Aberdeen, Maryland. See Debbi Wilgoren, "Pilot's Last Days Described," *Washington Post,* Sept. 14, 1994. Run-down motels have also taken the place of boarding houses and seedy hotels as emblematic locales in popular culture, rivaling trailer parks as symbolic landscapes of down-home despair in movies, music videos, and grim Sam Shepardesque tales of dysfunctionality in the heart of the American dream.

16. A *Washington Post* article about a shooting at a motel on a highway outside of Washington again focused attention on the motel-living underclass, noting that the motel in question attracted "truckers, men recently divorced, and families down on their luck." One victim was a fifty-one-year-old man who reportedly had lived at the motel with his wife and daughter for over a year. Another had been a resident for four months. The communal nature of long-term motel residency was underscored throughout the article, which reported that the shooting stemmed from an argument that began at a barbecue outside one of the rooms. The article repeatedly described the suspect, victims, and witnesses as "friends and neighbors." See Jon Jeter, "3 Killed, 1 Injured at P.G. Motel," *Washington Post,* Feb. 20, 1993.

17. Elaine Viets, "Here's Why It's Wise to Save Coral Court," *St. Louis Post-Dispatch,* Sept. 22, 1993.

18. James Ragland, "Council Makes It Easier to Seek Pawnshop, Motel Closure," *Dallas Morning News,* Sept. 27, 1990.

19. James Bennet, "For One Room, $2,250 a Month. Homeless Return to Hotels," *New York Times,* Jan. 31, 1993.

20. James Lindgren recounts SPNEA member Samuel Adams Drake's objections to the "greasy voluble Italians" of Boston's North End filling the air around Paul Revere's house with the "vile odors of garlic and onion—of macaroni and lazzaroni." Drake also complained that Italian had supplanted English as the local vernacular, so that "One can scarce hear the sound of his own English mother-tongue from one end of the square to the other." Given the prominent role of advertising signs in the roadside landscape, one wonders whether commercial architecture purists feel a similar sense of shock and despair upon encountering vintage strip buildings festooned with signs in Spanish, Vietnamese, Korean, or Afghani, with scarcely an English word in sight. See Lindgren, *Preserving Historic New England: Preservation, Progressivism and the Remaking of Memory* (New York: Oxford Univ. Press, 1995), 35–42, Drake quotation, p. 37.

21. Patrick Symmes, "Viva Suburbia: The New Immigrants Follow Jobs and Cheap Housing to the Suburbs," (Washington, D.C.) *City Paper,* Apr. 9, 1993.

22. John Brinckerhoff Jackson, "Concluding With Landscapes," in *Discovering the Vernacular Landscape* (New Haven: Yale Univ. Press, 1984), 147–57.

23. These explanations for the revival of the strip mall

are based on discussions with architects and commercial realtors in Austin, Texas, and newspaper articles such as Isadore Barmash, "For Shopping Centers, Less Is Becoming More," *New York Times,* Sept. 27, 1992; Maryann Haggerty, "The Rebirth of Run-Down Strip Malls," *Washington Post,* Oct. 22, 1994; and Margaret Pressler, "And the Mall Comes Tumbling Down," *Washington Post,* Nov. 9, 1994.

24. Jean Beaudrillard, *Simulations* (New York: Semiotext(e), 1983).

25. Pamela Scott and Antoinette Lee, *Buildings of the District of Columbia* (New York: Oxford Univ. Press, 1993), 378.

26. B. Drummond Ayres Jr., "Endangered Species: Original Golden Arches," *New York Times,* Mar. 6, 1994. Union Station in Washington, D.C., provides an additional permutation of this postmodern hall of mirrors. Newly fabricated Golden Arches frame the McDonald's outlet inside the Daniel Burnham–designed Beaux Arts train station, staking a claim for grass roots culinary authenticity against the aggressively down-home "America" cafe located in another corner of the station's grand waiting room. McDonald's has gone into the simulation business as well, reproducing the architecture and limited menu of its original restaurants in select locations, such as downtown Atlanta, where walkup customers provide the primary commercial traffic.

27. "Silver Theater and Shopping Center, Montgomery County, Maryland," National Register of Historic Places Inventory Nomination no. 88003466.

28. In Sept. 1995 the developers of the Mall of America and West Edmonton Mall floated a proposition to build a five-hundred-million-dollar shopping and entertainment complex in Silver Spring that would incorporate the facade of the historic strip mall and renovate an adjoining theater. See Margaret Pressler, "Developers Want Help on Silver Spring Mall," *Washington Post,* Sept. 9, 1995. The *Washington Post* endorsed the project in an editorial, "The Stakes in Silver Spring," *Washington Post,* Sept. 9, 1995. The support of environmentalist groups was reported in Louis Aguilar, "Environmentalists Endorse Mall, Tout Benefits of Silver Spring Site," *Washington Post,* Feb. 7, 1996. Restaurant owner H. Anthony Mapp expressed his frustrations in an op-ed piece, "Malled to Death: Big Money's Scary Vision for Silver Spring," *Washington Post,* May 5, 1996. Shortly before this volume went to press, the mega-mall backers were forced to admit they could not secure funding for their proposal. Signaling the resurgence of neotraditional strip mall development, Silver Spring now envisions a more modest redevelopment plan aimed at producing a modernistic, upscale version of the original commercial landscape it conspired to destroy.

29. "Town With Growing Pains," (Washington, D.C.) *Sunday Star Pictorial Magazine,* June 18, 1950, 4–5.

30. St. Mary's County (Maryland), Board of St. Mary's County Commissioners, "A Community Development Application for the Revitalization of Tulagi Town Center, St. Mary's County, Maryland," Submitted June 18, 1993. (The author is indebted to former St. Mary's County Historic Sites Surveyor Elizabeth Hughes for bringing this redevelopment plan to his attention.)

CHAPTER 7

Bruce Harvey

Architecture for the Future at the Charleston Exposition, 1901–1902

In August of 1885, a hurricane damaged nearly every home in Charleston. One year later, an earthquake laid waste to over one hundred additional buildings. Such widespread physical destruction matched the city's spiritual decline in this age of profound social and economic change. Charleston, once an aristocrat among southern cities, showed little energy in trying to keep pace with these changes; many of the city's youths lost hope and departed, while many of the city's elders lost hope and remained. Economic survival in nineteenth-century America, though, depended on energy and on hopes for the future. While Charleston's traditional elite enjoyed a strong commercial legacy from the city's earliest years, they continued to cherish the traditional business patterns of the antebellum era, when the cotton trade came to Charleston without extra effort on the part of merchants, and when middlemen casually arranged for its shipment.

After the Civil War, however, commercial men and farmers in the South's new upcountry towns and cities began sending more of their produce directly to the North. Charleston was left behind in this new era, as much by its laconic business spirit as by the new railroads which bypassed its port. By the 1890s, however, a group of "young men" appeared in Charleston who knew that they would have to accommodate themselves to these new conditions in order to revive the city and make it a part of the nation's commercial mainstream. Charleston's corps of progressive business leaders adopted an exposition in 1901 in the hope that it would rebuild their city, both physically and spiritually. Business leaders in other southern cities, notably Atlanta, Nashville, and New Orleans, had hosted World's Fairs with similar goals.

These new, relatively aggressive commercial leaders in Charleston also had more specific plans. In particular, they saw their exposition in

1901 as a way to stimulate activity at the city's harbor. If they could get the nation (or at least the Southeast) to come back to the port, which had been improved with federally constructed jetties in 1897, then Charleston might once again enjoy prosperity, and return to its glory days of the late eighteenth century. As the twentieth century dawned and as foreign trade became a bigger part of the nation's commerce, the Spanish West Indies represented a tremendous hope for the South's economic development. The architecture of Charleston's exposition was a crucial part of its leaders' attempt to place Charleston at the vanguard of this trade. This specific plan had only marginal success, but the imagery created by the architecture at the exposition had other, unintended meanings for the future of Charleston as it entered the twentieth century. Charleston's future, so assiduously pursued by young and progressive businessmen, would be aptly represented by these sentimental and historical buildings. The buildings, as much as the drive for modern commercial success, symbolized Charleston's future.

London had held the first international exposition, the Exhibition of the Arts and Industries of All Nations, in 1851. Expositions quickly became institutionalized as signature pieces of western Victorian culture. Fairgoers throughout Europe and America expected to see new technologies, modern innovations, and signs of the future at these expositions. At Philadelphia's Centennial Exposition in 1876, for example, the world first saw telephones; more than half a century later, at New York's 1939 World's Fair, the world began to watch television. An exposition that did not present something new was somehow suspect, only tentatively given status in the pantheon of great World's Fairs.

These fairs occasionally presented architectural innovations as well. Gustave Eiffel's Tower at the 1889 Paris Exposition comes quickly to mind, for example, along with Joseph Paxton's Crystal Palace in London in 1851, and the Trylon and Perisphere at New York's World's Fair in 1939. Public expectations for originality in the nineteenth century, however, at least in America, did not always include buildings. Instead, leading architects continued to cloak even structurally innovative buildings in traditional garb. Style was the operative concept for architecture throughout the nineteenth century, as architects chose visual details from historic buildings to bring to the viewer's imagination certain values and assumptions associated with the era in which that style originated. This type of "communication," which relied on conventional images, initially had moral overtones. Innumerable household and architectural theorists, for example, wrote books and articles proclaiming the effect of living amid beauty or ugliness, or appropriate or inappropriate styles. Many of these moral implications began to fade as the nineteenth century wore on, though, while the desire for visual associations remained. Historical styles became like a menu for architects, who in consultation with patrons chose or tailored a "look" that suited the particular purposes of the building.

This was especially the case with World's Fair buildings. Exposition planners needed temporary structures that could be erected quickly and inexpensively and that could provide large sheds with undifferentiated, open floor plans to house exhibits. While fairgoers marveled at the structural innovations of Eiffel's Tower and a greenhouse on the scale of Paxton's Crystal Palace, most expositions presented more familiar or conventional sights. The buildings provided the physical setting and context for the exhibits. The style of the buildings, however, provided the intellectual context for the exhibits and the keys to understanding them.

At the same time as London's and Paris's innovative structures come to mind, for example, the image of the World's Columbian Exposition in Chicago in 1893, the "White City," arises in opposition. Chicago's Fair introduced the concept of an overall stylistic motif for expositions, which became a way of associating the fair with a particular theme. The architects for the White City, while employing modern structural techniques, cloaked the buildings in a Neoclassical skin that projected an image of a refined urbanity and of national power and cultural authority.[1] It influenced American urban planning and architecture for a generation and more and left a powerful legacy for American exposition promoters. The southern expositions, following quickly on Chicago's heels, continued the legacy.

World's Fairs existed not only to make a profit, but also to express some message, be it about patriotism, imperial endeavors, international cooperation, or local pride. Exposition officials had various ways of spreading these messages, including widespread advertising posters and bills, promotional booklets, and access to the national press. However, they all recognized the special importance of buildings. These structures had to convey just the right message and create just the right image in order to bolster the purpose of the fairs.

Southern leaders adopted large-scale expositions during the 1890s. The previous decade had seen small yet pioneering examples, including ones in Atlanta in 1881 and 1887, in Louisville in 1886, and a larger one in New Orleans, the World's Industrial and Cotton Centennial Exposition of 1885. Atlanta kicked off a second wave with its Cotton States and International Exposition in 1895. Nashville followed suit in 1897 with the Tennessee Centennial and International Exposition. These two formed the immediate context for the South Carolina Interstate and West Indian Exposition, held in Charleston in 1901. Norfolk, Virginia, ended this string in 1907 with the Jamestown Tercentenary Exposition. Taken together, this regional burst of expositions was singular in the history of the institution and invites questions from scholars. In this poverty-stricken rural section, which only recently had endured a devastating military defeat at the hands of its own countrymen, such a burst of this new, expensive, and complex institution seems odd and unlikely.

Urban leaders in the late-nineteenth-century South used expositions to advertise their region as worthy of participating in American commercial life. Businessmen and political leaders of both parties had sought to help the South recover economically from the Civil War. An emergent southern urban business class spearheaded the campaigns to exploit the region's natural resources, develop new markets for its agricultural produce, and promote its manufacturing enterprises.[2] While they did not forsake local support, they encouraged northern investment in southern manufacturing and "respectable" immigration to the South. These leaders also adopted World's Fairs in the hopes of both celebrating and creating the kinds of development and business culture that would give the South a secure place in modern commercial America.

At one level, the South's urban leaders argued that expositions were the most efficient ways for southerners to learn about new products and techniques. While the various conventions and state and local fairs could do this, World's Fairs were something different. Expositions, which were by definition vehicles for industrial modernization and international cooperation, were their tools to alter both the reality and the image of the South. Simply hosting an exposition indicated to the outside world a trustworthy base of organizational and financial resources. This, the southern leaders hoped, would be the initial push toward a modern, stable economy in the South; once outsiders began investing in and moving to the South, southerners would be able to use these additional resources to develop attitudes and institutions that could support and maintain social and economic progress.

They also hoped that expositions would help them to overcome disagreeable regional legacies, particularly from the South's rural inheritance and from its racial problems, which hindered the region's economic development. These complex legacies help to explain the significance and function of the architecture at the expositions.

The South had long had commercial connections throughout the nation, but its manufacturing legacy was limited. Clearly, the region faced serious obstacles to industrialization, particularly in the early years after the Civil War. The war devastated the region's infrastructure, as farm animals, machinery, and buildings, along with the region's networks of roads, canals, and railroads, suffered. This physical destruction accompanied the immense loss of life, including over one-fifth of the South's adult white male population. Many of those who survived lost their life savings when the Confederate bonds and currency collapsed after the war. Agricultural production dropped precipitously, providing little income for investment.[3] Declining morale accompanied all of these losses, allowing for little of the ebullient confidence that powered northern industrialization and commercial strength.

Other internal factors came into play as Reconstruction moved toward a close. Southern health, education, and infrastructure were plagued by problems, while a lack of factory experience among the people did little to demonstrate industrial competence to potential outside investors.[4] While these internal conditions improved during the 1880s and 1890s, the South's image presented another, perhaps deeper, problem. Northern businessmen had reservations about many aspects of the South, from the region's lack of manufacturing experience to its violence and apparent lack of stability. Southern leaders also had to outrun the legacy of treason, that theirs was a disloyal section, filled with citizens devoted more to their own states than to the Union. At a less virulent level, the South had the reputation as a land of carefree, colorful individuals. Southerners were rural people who lacked the necessary discipline to run a tight industrial ship. The South was pleasing enough to contemplate as a vacation spot, but southern enterprises were a different matter. Expositions, many southern leaders came to believe, were the only institutions powerful enough to overcome such obstacles.

Charleston illustrated all of these problems. The city's history from the Civil War to the early twentieth century was indeed a sad one. Beset by natural destruction, the city's business leaders lacked the tradition of commercial vitality and aggressiveness that characterized such cities as Nashville and Atlanta. Charleston's elite did little to inculcate such a "greedy" spirit. The city's traditional commercial leaders had relied for generations on the drawing power of the city's excellent harbor, and showed little inclination to change. The city had long served as a commercial and social entrepôt, acting as the conduit for the rice plantations of lowland Carolina and the cotton plantations of the midlands and upcountry. The city had also been a center of social life, serving as the seasonal residence for plantation owners and rice and cotton brokers, who built the magnificent single houses in the eighteenth and early nineteenth centuries. These plantation owners and their business middlemen had generated a leisurely way of life known as the Charleston Style.

This was a commercial and social heritage which did little to foster an aggressive attitude among its leading residents, who maintained an aristocratic distrust of trade. The Civil War resulted not only in physical destruction and loss of life, but also helped to usher in a new way of doing business throughout the South. Merchants backed by northern credit set up shop in the new towns and cities of the upcountry South, and provided funding for poverty-stricken farmers. These merchants then saw to the marketing of the cotton, which they increasingly sent north along the railroads which extended into the South.[5] The ports of Baltimore and New York at the ends of these trunk lines flourished, while Charleston, unwilling to accommodate itself to the new conditions, withered. Before the Civil War, for example, the city's merchants had managed to stop the new railroads from reaching the wharves. The lines instead stopped several blocks away, forcing the goods to be transported to the wharves by drays for an extra charge. This situation continued into the late nineteenth century, and, as the end of the century approached, Charleston's port attracted decreasing portions of the nation's trade in imports and exports. It grabbed only 0.37 percent of American foreign commerce in 1900, behind such cities as Norfolk, Savannah, Wilmington, and Newport News.[6]

Manufacturing enterprises fared little better than the city's commerce after the war. The little investment capital that Charleston's leaders possessed often went to upstate textile mills and to the rising southern cities. Some Charleston investors had attempted to form a textile mill in the city in the 1880s, but it quickly collapsed as the result of difficulty in finding both money and workers. The discovery of phosphate deposits along the Ashley River in the 1870s and 1880s promised great returns for fertilizer manufacturing, but when miners found richer deposits in Florida and Tennessee in the 1890s, Charleston's business and reputation again declined.[7] The city reported 566 manufacturing establishments in 1890, with a total capital investment of over $7 million; Atlanta's 410 manufacturers, by comparison, had been able to attract nearly $10 million.[8] Francis Carey, a prominent Baltimore industrialist who had investments in Charleston, spoke bluntly of the city's business image in the 1890s. In a letter to a Charleston businessman, he claimed that "many difficulties exist in Charleston which exist in no other town of its size in the matter of any business enterprise of any kind."[9]

Not all of Charleston's businessmen were content to witness the city's decline. Throughout the 1880s and 1890s, the city's rising leaders sought to bring Charleston into line with the nation's burgeoning economy. They often had backgrounds outside the city, and came to success in less traditional lines of trade such as groceries, lumber, and other supplies, as well as in the railroads. Some, including Frederick Wagener, the president of the Exposition Company in Charleston, were foreign by birth, while many others were from the North. They generally focused on two aspects in their attempts to strengthen the city: the need for a new and aggressive business spirit, and the revival of the city's excellent harbor. As early as the 1880s, a Chamber of Commerce committee blended these themes by calling for a more active trade with the West Indies. The city, the authors argued, should act as the port of import and export between the West Indies and the vast productive capacity of the American West. Other cities had been more "vigorous" in seeking this foreign trade, the committee reported, but all was not lost: it would merely "be a work of time and labor" to persuade western merchants to ship their goods through Charleston. They used the pamphlet to sound a call to arms, as they noted that "it will take some time also to secure that co-operation within the State which is indispensable to our success."[10] But few of the city's established leaders, who still controlled much of the city's capital, responded to their call.

Nevertheless, many of Charleston's younger leaders continued to push the city forward into national and international markets. They attempted several times to form commercial organizations, in the hope of taking leadership from the moribund, century-old Chamber of Commerce. Most of these attempts soon lapsed into genteel social gatherings.[11] They finally succeeded in 1894 with the Young Men's Business League (YMBL), which quickly set up a Charleston Freight Bureau and served as a gadfly to the city's more entrenched leadership. Fundamentally, they claimed, the city needed new men and more money, but its leaders would also have to prove Charleston worthy. "Now is the accepted time," claimed the *Evening Post* in early 1900, "to demonstrate the fact that the commercial enterprise of the city is not all stored away in the different cemeteries."[12]

The YMBL also provided the leadership for the new Exposition. John Averill, a northern-born Confederate veteran and agent for a number of southern railroads, first suggested that the city host an industrial exposition in October 1899.[13] Charleston's "Young Men," having seen the success of expositions in Atlanta and Nashville, quickly took up the call. They found the lures of increased population, greater investments, and a reinvigorated community spirit enticing. As W. H. Welch, president of the YMBL, observed: "The projectors of this Exposition appreciating of the immediate need of some movement which would infuse new life and activity into our city, conceived the idea that an Exposition would produce better results at less cost than anything which we could do."[14]

The expositions in Atlanta, Nashville, and Charleston clearly arose from different local traditions and purposes. As with leaders in the other two cities, Charlestonians had to find a niche for themselves, a way for their city efficiently to fit into the nation's commercial currents. These promoters saw architecture as a key factor that would both draw people to the fair and, more subtly, project its underlying message. The architecture at the different southern expositions indicated a range of options in the southern attempts to fit into the American commercial mainstream.

Atlanta's 1895 exposition presented a vaguely Romanesque style (fig. 7.1). Bradford Gilbert, a New York architect whose works included railroad stations, office blocks, and a skyscraper, designed most of the buildings.[15] His use of the Romanesque came in part from his recommendation that these buildings, with their relatively simple plans and outlines, would be a cost-effective solution to the problem of large, temporary exhibit buildings. However, it also suggested the desire by Atlanta's businessmen to be seen as *au courant* with America's commercial trends. As reflected in its promotional literature and in its various buildings, Atlanta was not just a southern city trying to make its mark. Instead, its leaders argued re-

Fig. 7.1. Agricultural Building, Cotton States and International Exposition, Atlanta, 1895. From Walter G. Cooper, *The Cotton States and International Exposition and South Illustrated* (Atlanta, 1896).

peatedly that the city was already a full-fledged partner, capable of leading the rest of the South into the nation's commercial and industrial life. The ethereal classicism of the antebellum South thus gave way in Atlanta to the modern, commercial, vigorous, Richardsonian Romanesque.

Nashville's promoters in 1897 returned to the classical and commissioned several local architects to carry out the work of the Tennessee Centennial Exposition.[16] The administration's decision to create a full-scale replica of the Parthenon was only the most ambitious example of the fair's motif, as the classical heritage spread to nearly every building on the grounds (fig. 7.2). This return to classicism stemmed in part from the exposition's origins as a patriotic celebration of the state's centennial anniversary. Businessmen soon picked up on the idea, and promoted it both as a patriotic exercise and as a modern industrial exposition. In their promotional literature, the Centennial's officials emphasized the city's longstanding motto as "The Athens of the South," which helped explain the classical style of architecture. The motivation for this style was not just local pride, though, as they appealed to a more broadly American past. Through repeated calls to patriotism and virtue, they sought to recall the early years of the American Republic. "Colonial" to the leaders of the Tennessee Centennial meant something other than a specific time. Instead, in their eyes, colonial meant the last era when all sections of the country worked together for a common purpose.[17] Colonial also referred to the era when classically derived architecture provided unifying symbols for the new nation. In the face of pervasive sectional tension and distrust lingering from the Civil War, they claimed that it was now time to reassert such a unity. They appealed to what they saw as a past of national harmony, symbolized by an architectural heritage that all sections could claim.

The South Carolina Interstate and West Indian Exposition, held from December 1901 through June 1902, presented another option for fitting into the national mainstream. Patriotism was not at issue here, as in Nashville, nor was a booming intrastate commerce, as in Atlanta. Instead, Charleston's officials looked almost exclusively to an increase in the nation's foreign trade, which they hoped would pass through Charleston. In

Fig. 7.2. Minerals and Forestry Building, Tennessee Centennial and International Exposition, Nashville, 1897. W. G. and A. J. Thuss, *Art Album of the Tennessee Centennial Exposition* (Nashville, 1898).

one sense, this was a reactionary goal; Charleston had gained prominence in the late eighteenth and early nineteenth centuries as a port for the surrounding region. The exposition's leaders sought to restore this status to Charleston. At the same time, though, they risked the enmity of a well-entrenched old-guard which disdained such modern methods of urban boosterism, even if the goal was the restoration of Charleston to its Augustan age. This tension continued throughout the exposition and affected its financing in the early months of preparation and in its aftermath. Charleston's traditional commercial elite, however, had little to do with the exposition's architecture.

The exposition's officials, after very little public discussion, hired Bradford Gilbert as the supervising architect. His role here was much larger than it had been at Atlanta, as he designed the grounds and almost all of the buildings, and supervised all other aspects of the infrastructure, including the water, sewage, and road systems. The grounds were north of the city, on the east bank of the Ashley River that forms Charleston's western boundary. His ground plan clearly showed that he looked to Chicago's 1893 World's Columbian Exposition as a guide. Daniel Burnham, Frederick Law Olmsted, and Henry Codman had created a mix of high classical formality in Chicago's Court of Honor and a pastoral setting close to it. Gilbert adopted that division in his ground plan, and a clear spatial division to go along with it. His ground plan featured two principal sections, joined at a narrow neck. The direct opposition of these two, the natural and the artificial, he hoped, would help each show its individuality.

The "Nature" section was on old farmland along the Ashley River, and featured winding lanes and diverse buildings amid a picturesque layout with live oaks and magnolias. Gilbert's reliance on Olmsted's ideas of setting buildings into a naturalistic landscape and making use of the extant natural features was clear. The Natural section, he claimed, "will form a natural park of endless beauty of vista and landscape effect naturalistic [sic.] . . . a winding path of 100 feet in width will be carried underneath the overspreading live oaks along the edge of the embankment." He designed this section to contain the Art Building, the Negro Building, the Woman's Building, the various State buildings, along with less naturalistic buildings such as Transportation and Machinery.[18]

The "Art" section lay just to the southeast, on the grounds of the old Washington Race Course. In contrast to the Natural section, the Art section featured a complex geometrical design and more formal and architecturally unified buildings. Gilbert proposed to treat this level stretch of land, from which the trees had already been shorn, "artificially in such a manner as to produce the highest type of art."[19] The main buildings of the Art section most clearly reflected the exposition's dominant motif, and provided the focus of attention for the exposition. In another obvious reference to the Chicago World's Fair with its Court of Honor, Charleston's Palaces of Agriculture, Commerce, and Cotton surrounded a sunken garden and were connected by a colonnade to form a "Court of Palaces" (fig. 7.3).

Here, and in the Administration Building that connected the Art and Natural sections of the grounds, Gilbert let his imagination loose. The most striking aspect of Gilbert's role at Charleston was the wilder and more romantic style of the buildings compared to what he created in Atlanta. Gilbert's mandate was to emphasize a "southern" motif. One is hard-pressed, however, to discern anything distinctively southern in the pictures of the buildings. While the exposition promoters in both Atlanta and Nashville used the labels "southern" and "colonial" interchangeably in describing all classically inspired buildings, Gilbert's approach was markedly different and referred to the particular purposes of the fair.

Fig. 7.3. Sunken Gardens and Auditorium, South Carolina, Inter-State and West Indian Exposition, Charleston, 1901. From *Charleston and the South Carolina Inter-State and West Indian Exposition* (Boston, 1902).

While a number of the exposition's buildings showed different designs and indicated different intents and purposes, the buildings in the Court of Palaces were the most important for creating the exposition's image.

The most obvious contrast to Atlanta was that Gilbert's buildings in Charleston were so richly decorated. Domes, arcades, finials, brackets, and more dazzle and often confuse the eye. Gilbert clearly drew on a wide variety of precedents for these details. Except for vaguely Byzantine touches in the small central domes raised on polygonal, open drums, however, the precedents for these main buildings were primarily found in the Mediterranean world of the seventeenth and eighteenth centuries. Despite Gilbert's vaguely Romanesque buildings at the 1895 Atlanta exposition, one searches in vain for Romanesque or Gothic references at Charleston. Instead, Spanish and Italian styles dominated.

In plan, the three main "Palaces" were simple and nearly identical: rectangular exhibit halls, with rows of arcaded windows across the fronts on either side of grand, projecting central entrances, surmounted by central domes. The differences were primarily in the details, especially at the ends of the buildings. The South Carolina building, or the Palace of Agriculture, featured the square corner turrets which Gilbert used at Atlanta (fig. 7.4). The scalloped gable above the central entrance referred to the fashionable Mission style, which drew inspiration from Spanish colonial missions in California and Mexico. The tracery around the doors in the corner turrets showed Spanish Medieval precedents, while the more recent Italianate comes through in the brackets underneath the eaves.

The Palace of Agriculture, with its shallow domes atop the square corner turrets, pierced cupolas above the projecting central portico, and finials between the arcaded windows, was much more elaborate than its partner across the sunken gardens, the Palace of Commerce (fig. 7.5). While lacking some of the florid Italianate decorations of the Agriculture building, the Palace of Commerce showed clearer references to the Spanish Baroque, with the scalloped gables in the central portico and in the corner features and the tiled hip roofs atop the square turrets surrounding the central entrance. Many features were the same, however, including

Fig. 7.4. South Carolina Building, South Carolina, Inter-State and West Indian Exposition, Charleston, 1901. From *Charleston and the South Carolina Inter-State and West Indian Exposition* (Boston, 1902).

Fig. 7.5. Palace of Commerce, South Carolina, Inter-State and West Indian Exposition, Charleston, 1901. From *Charleston and the South Carolina Inter-State and West Indian Exposition* (Boston, 1902).

the row of projecting and sloping arcaded windows across the front, the central entrance recessed behind a screen of three arches, and the central dome on a polygonal drum.

The Cotton Palace, which had the place of honor at the head of the Court, was clearly different in elevation and detail from the two Palaces which flanked it (fig. 7.6). The entrance was much more prominent, and featured a five-bay screen with Corinthian columns rather than the three-bay arcaded entrance and a taller dome surmounted by a cupola. It also featured a simple hipped roof without separate corner treatments. This lack of corner treatments focused attention on the entranceway, which featured a scalloped gable similar to the Palace of Commerce and, flanking the portico, rounded turrets each surmounted by a shallow dome with a small cupola. The central dome, dominant horizontality, and Mediterranean-influenced row of arcaded windows across the front provided connections to the other buildings on the Court of Palaces. The more elaborate entrance, however, together with the taller dome and the building's placement at the head of the Court of Palaces, indicated the importance of the building and the centrality of cotton for the exposition, for Charleston, and for the South.

The range of European—particularly Spanish and generically Mediterranean—stylistic references worked against the notion that these buildings could be considered "southern" in any technical sense. These styles had become increasingly fashionable for residential and commercial architecture by the 1890s and early 1900s, particularly in the Southwest and in Florida. These Mediterranean-influenced styles can no more be called southern than can Greek or Roman Revival styles. The connection between the look of Charleston's principal exposition buildings and modern American commerce appears even more strained. The connections, however, worked in two important ways.

The title of the fair itself suggests one way: the South Carolina Interstate and West Indian Exposition. South Carolina's upstate textile mills provided a strong manufacturing base for the state, and Charleston's exposition leaders recognized that they would need extensive support from the mill owners. The exposition was, in large part, an attempt to encourage these upcountry manufacturers to patronize Charleston's port, and

Fig. 7.6. Cotton Palace, South Carolina, Inter-State and West Indian Exposition, Charleston, 1901. From *Charleston and the South Carolina Inter-State and West Indian Exposition* (Boston, 1902).

their lure was the West Indian trade. The Caribbean islands, Charleston's promoters argued, would be a lucrative market for the abundant produce of textile mills in South Carolina and the surrounding states.

As early as February 1900, the officials proposed a central cotton palace "in which will be shown as it were, a cotton seed and what comes from it." Already their plan was to "make the cotton exhibit a practical exposition of the cotton and cotton seed industries in order that substantial and profitable results may follow."[20] Daniel Tompkins, a prominent industrialist in Charlotte, North Carolina, who had long called for increased foreign trade for southern textile mills, coordinated the cotton exhibit.[21] The exhibits in the Cotton Palace came largely from these southern, mostly South Carolina, companies. The plan was to show the manufacturing potential for cotton and to emphasize what the southern mills were producing. Tompkins also helped to articulate the opportunities that the West Indies offered to the South's textile manufacturers. He wrote a letter to the Charleston *News and Courier* in favor of the exposition, which prompted an editorial response. "There is a wide market awaiting the Southern manufacturers in the West Indian countries and in South America," the editors proclaimed, "and the Exposition to be held here next year will enable the manufacturers of this and other Southern States to capture the rich trade of these countries."[22] The chief purpose of the fair, echoed the author of an exposition pamphlet, was "the promotion of more intimate commercial relations with the 70 principle West Indian Islands."[23]

The Spanish–American War in 1899 provided the immediate political context for the fair. American trade with the West Indies, particularly with Spanish-owned Cuba and Puerto Rico, had grown through the 1880s and 1890s. Total American imports and exports with Cuba, for example, reached a prewar high of $102,900,000 in 1893, before dropping to only $24,800,000 in 1898. The war drew the public's attention to these islands, though, and after their "liberation" in 1899, trade resumed quickly; by 1905, total American imports and exports to Cuba reached $124,700,000.[24] Southern business leaders were quick to note the potential profits from a renewed West Indian trade. The *Manufacturer's Record*, which catered largely to southern businesses, noted in 1899 that the results of the war with Spain would be a big stimulant to business. "Our new possessions," the writer concluded, "give us an immense area for industrial development. They give to the daring and enterprising spirits that have made America what it is a new outlet, a new and wonderful field."[25] *The Exposition*, a monthly magazine published by Charleston's exposition company, echoed this confidence. After quoting government statistics showing America's growing West Indian trade, the writer concluded by noting that "[h]ere, then, is a commerce of $100,000,000 lying at our very doors, which the friends of the West Indian Exposition have a right to say is an important item in even so great a commerce as that of the United States."[26] In this hopeful vision, Charleston's niche in America's commercial life was to handle the South's trade, particularly the products of the region's burgeoning textile mills, with the West Indies.

The architecture at Charleston's exposition both reflected and promoted this conscious hope for the future. The stylistic references formed a direct appeal to the Spanish heritage of the West Indies. It was also a way to emphasize Charleston's own legacy of West Indian ties. Indeed, the fair's officials promoted the Spanish influence on Charleston and the exposition regularly. An article in the *News and Courier,* for example, noted that Gilbert "has harmonized with our own beautiful Colonial the most effective characteristics of the old Spanish."[27] In Gilbert's own description, the Cotton Palace was "broken by various pediments, projections, domes, red-tiled roofs and turrets, in the typical Southern type of architecture in a strong Spanish-American motif of huge masses, simple and strong contour and outlines, with enrichments of terraces and sculpture at the various entrances and initial points."[28] The architectural critic Montgomery Schuyler sought to be more specific in defining the style: "At Chicago they called the style Columbian; at Buffalo they called it Pan-American. It is in fact what they call it in Charleston—the Spanish Renaissance of the Sixteenth Century."[29]

The exposition's planners backed up their buildings with attempts to stimulate local interest in and knowledge of the West Indies. Articles on different aspects of life and business in Cuba and Puerto Rico, for example, appeared regularly in the local newspapers and in the promotional literature. They celebrated Cuban independence day with a well-attended affair, and planned for a West Indian Congress as one of the very few special meetings that accompanied the exposition. This Congress was a sad failure, though, with few representatives in attendance.

The attempts by Charleston's leaders to boost foreign trade at the city's port also faltered. In 1902 the Fruit Dispatch Company of New York announced plans to set up a steamship line between Charleston and Central America, but this was a rare advance.[30] By 1905, Charleston had slipped further in its percentage of America's import trade, falling behind most of the other southern ports. While the city's economy did begin to expand during World War I, this was more a result of government activity at the Naval Base and dry dock than the West Indian trade.

This conscious effort to solicit more active foreign commerce at the port, though, was not the only way to explain the Spanish Renaissance style of architecture. The very romanticism and sentimentalism of the buildings paid tribute to, even glorified, Charleston's commercial backwardness and cultural recalcitrance. At times, comments on the exposition's romantic aspects got out of hand. In describing the administration building, for example, one writer sought to articulate what gave it a Spanish Renaissance feeling: "It is not so much the domes and facades, nor the deep tiled roof, though all these have much meaning, no doubt, but it is the doors and windows which at a glance takes us deep into the pages of some old Spanish romance. These only lack the damsel within and the cavalier without to complete the ideal."[31]

The city's noncommercial, sentimental image was at odds with the message of progress, but still found considerable sympathies in late-nineteenth- and early-twentieth-century America. By the 1890s, anticapitalist and antimodern critics had begun pointing to the perils of improvement while praising the old-fashioned. The early Colonial Revival movement of the 1880s, which focused on the rugged early settlement era, and the fascination with the American frontier provided some outlets for such feelings, while a renewed martial spirit and the increasing popularity of medieval-style romance literature provided others.[32] Charleston's traditional elite, who failed to support the Exposition even if they had offered little outright opposition, gave a local example of another type of antimodernism. As the writer of a 1905 magazine article noted, modern businessmen will never "persuade the Charlestonian to welcome with delight a horde of unidentified tourists. . . . Charleston shakes her head when approached on the subject of huge hotels which will accommodate the man with millions from the swarming centers of America."[33]

Owen Wister catered to this sentiment in his 1906 novel, *Lady Baltimore,* set in a fictionalized Charleston. He claimed an important role in the nation's moral life for this backward city. His friend Theodore Roosevelt chided Wister on this point, noting that "[y]our particular heroes, the Charleston aristocrats, offer as melancholy an example as I know of people whose whole life for generations has been warped by their own wilful [sic.] perversity."[34] Nonetheless, Wister made a strong emotional and moral appeal for the kind of backwardness that he found in Charleston. His protagonist comes to Charleston for genealogical research, and submits to the city's old-fashioned ways. The young man observes to a southern companion that "[s]uch quiet faces are gone now into that breathless, competing North; ground into oblivion between the clashing trades of the competing men and the clashing jewels and chandeliers of their competing wives—while yours have lingered on, spared by your very adversity."[35]

Charleston was indeed spared by its problems. As countless observers have discovered, here was something to treasure in a fast-paced, modern world. The city's architectural as well as commercial development continued slowly in Charleston, as it had since the Civil War. The city's most recent "building boom" before the exposition had been in the 1880s, but it left the distinctive parts of the city unchanged. The exposition itself had no discernible architectural influence on the city, nor did the gradual improvement of the city's fortunes in the early twentieth century permit massive downtown development. Indeed, little of the city's growth in the twentieth century can be attributed to the exposition itself. As a result of this relative failure, though, Charleston's future was in a way secured. The irony, therefore, is strong. While seeking acceptance according to the terms of modern, industrial America, the failure of Charleston's new leaders to overcome the city's traditional leadership allowed for other values to arise later. In 1931, for example, the city council pioneered the concept of historic district zoning as a way to protect its remarkable stock of eighteenth- and nineteenth-century buildings and their iron decorations. Tourists, many of them drawn by nostalgic and romantic wishes for a simpler and slower time, flocked to this living remnant of an earlier age, and gave the city an enduring economic base. Despite the heroic efforts of Charleston's businessmen with their Exposition, their city's salvation came in precisely the quality that they had sought to eliminate.

Notes

1. William H. Jordy, *American Buildings and their Architects: Progressive and Academic Ideals at the Turn of the Twentieth Century* (New York: Doubleday, 1972), 79; R. Reid Badger, *The Great American Fair: The World's Columbian Exposition & American Culture* (Chicago, Ill.: Nelson Hall, 1979), 63–72.
2. See Vicki Vaughn Johnson, *The Men and the Vision of the Southern Commercial Conventions, 1845–1871* (Columbia: Univ. of Missouri Press, 1992), 193–220; Eric Foner, *Reconstruction: America's Unfinished Revolution, 1863–1877* (New York: Harper and Row, 1988).
3. Foner, *Reconstruction*, 124–25.
4. For varying insights on these and other problems, see Blaine A. Brownell and David R. Goldfield, eds., *The City in Southern History: The Growth of Urban Civilization in the South* (Port Washington, N.Y.: Kennikat Press, 1977); James Cobb, *Industrialization and Southern Society, 1877–1984* (Lexington: Univ. Press of Kentucky, 1984; Chicago, Ill.: The Dorsey Press, 1989); Gavin Wright, *Old South, New South: Revolutions in the Southern Economy Since the Civil War* (New York: Basic Books, 1986).
5. For insights on this process, see, among others, Edward L. Ayers, *The Promise of the New South: Life after Reconstruction* (New York: Oxford Univ. Press, 1992), 214–309; Steven Hahn, *The Roots of Southern Populism: Yeoman Farmers and the Transformation of the Georgia Upcountry, 1850–1890* (New York: Oxford Univ. Press, 1983), 170–203; and C. Vann Woodward, *Origins of the New South, 1877–1913* (Baton Rouge: Louisiana State Univ. Press, 1951).

6. *The Foreign Commerce and Navigation of the United States,* House of Representatives, 56th Congress, 2d session, document 13, 50; Walter J. Fraser Jr., *Charleston! Charleston!: The History of a Southern City* (Columbia: Univ. of South Carolina Press, 1989), 208.
7. David L. Carlton, *Mill and Town in South Carolina, 1880–1920* (Baton Rouge: Louisiana State Univ. Press, 1982), 72–76; Don H. Doyle, *New Men, New Cities, New South: Atlanta, Nashville, Charleston, Mobile, 1860–1910* (Chapel Hill: Univ. of North Carolina Press, 1990), 79–80.
8. *Report on Manufacturing Industries in the United States at the Eleventh Census: 1890,* Department of the Interior, Bureau of the Census, 1895, Table 3.
9. Francis K. Carey to P. H. Gadsden, Nov. 2, 1899, Hemphill Family Papers, Manuscript Department, Duke Univ. Library, Durham, North Carolina. For further information on Charleston at the turn of the century, see Carlton, *Mill and Town,* Doyle, *New Men, New Cities, New South,* and Fraser, *Charleston! Charleston!* cited above; see also John Joseph Duffy, "Charleston Politics in the Progressive Era," (Ph.D. diss., Univ. of South Carolina, 1963).
10. "Charleston, South Carolina. The Advantages of the City of Charleston as a Port of Import and Export for the Trade and Commerce of the Northwestern States of the United States, and of Central and South America, The West Indies, and Europe," pamphlet, The News and Courier Book Press, 1880 (Charleston, S.C.), p. 20.
11. see Doyle, *New Men, New Cities, New South,* 159–72.
12. (Charleston, S.C.) *Evening Post,* Mar. 26, 1900.
13. (Charleston, S.C.) *News and Courier,* Oct. 3, 1899; for biographical information on Averill, see *The Exposition* 2 (Dec. 1901): 501.
14. Quoted in *News and Courier,* Dec. 2, 1899.
15. Information on Gilbert is widely scattered. His main pamphlets, *Architectural Sketches. With Sketches Applicable to Modern Structures* (by the author, 1881, 1889), and *Sketches of Public Buildings* (by the author, 1881), can be found in Henry-Russell Hitchcock, Historical Architecture Books, nos. 37 and 38. See also Gilbert, *Sketch Portfolio of Railroad Stations. From Original Designs by Bradford L. Gilbert* (by the author, 1881; 5th ed., 1895). For more general background information, see "Gilbert, Bradford L.," in vol. 2 of Adolf Placzek, ed., *Macmillan Encyclopedia of Architects* (New York: Free Press, 1982), 201; "Gilbert, Bradford," in Henry F. Withey and Elsie Rathburn Withey, *Biographical Dictionary of American Architects (Deceased)* (by the authors, 1956; facsimile ed., Los Angeles, Calif.: Hennessy and Ingalls, 1970), 233; "Gilbert, Bradford Lee," *National Cyclopedia of American Biography* (1910; reprint, Ann Arbor, Mich.: University Microfilms, 1967); obituary in *American Architect* 100 (Sept. 20, 1911): 3; F. Boyd Coons, "The Cotton State and International Exposition in the New South: Architecture and Implications," (M.A. thesis, Univ. of Virginia, 1988). Additional, scattered material may be found in *A History of Real Estate, Building and Architecture in New York City* (New York: 1898; reprint, Arno Press, 1967), 466–71; "Architectural Ethics: The Case of the Ottawa Terminal Station and Hotel," *Architectural Record* 24 (July–Dec. 1908): 293–99.
16. Nine architects or firms participated in the Centennial: Christian A. Asmus designed seven; Sara Ward Conley designed one; the firm of Gibel and Gabler designed one; Baxter J. Hodge designed one; Frank W. Kreider designed one; William C. Smith designed five, including the Parthenon; Frederick W. Thompson designed one; George W. Thompson designed one on his own and one in conjunction with Julius G. Zwicker; Zwicker alone designed two. All of these individuals can be located in the Nashville City Directories. See Herman Justi, ed., *Official History of the Tennessee Centennial Exposition* (Nashville: 1898).
17. See Drew Gilpin Faust, *A Sacred Circle: The Dilemma of the Intellectual in the Old South, 1840–1860* (Philadelphia: Univ. of Pennsylvania Press,

1977), 75; the men who comprised the "Sacred Circle" also looked to the Revolutionary era as the epitome of public virtues.
18. Bradford Gilbert, "The Architect's Story of the Exposition," *News and Courier,* Oct. 23, 1900.
19. Ibid.
20. *News and Courier,* Feb. 13, 1900.
21. See Patrick J. Hearden, *Independence and Empire: The New South's Cotton Mill Campaign, 1865–1901* (DeKalb: Northern Illinois Univ. Press, 1982), 26–28, for information on Tompkins.
22. *News and Courier,* June 2, 1900.
23. Alexander D. Anderson, *Charleston and its Exposition: Its Advantageous Position, and Industrial and Commercial Future,* pamphlet, Charleston, 1901, 3.
24. *Annual Review of Foreign Commerce of the United States,* House of Representatives, 60th Congress, 2d session, document no. 13, 33.
25. *Manufacturer's Record* 36 (Dec. 14, 1899): 17.
26. *The Exposition* 1 (Apr. 1901): 159.
27. *News and Courier,* Oct. 23, 1900.
28. Gilbert, "The Architect's Story."
29. Quoted in *News and Courier,* May 14, 1902.
30. Ibid., May 27, 1902; ibid., July 3, 1902.
31. *The Exposition* 1 (May 1901): 211.
32. See T. J. Jackson Lears, *No Place of Grace: Antimodernism and the Transformation of American Culture, 1880–1920* (New York: Pantheon Books, 1981), for an examination of this complex issue.
33. Anne Rittenhouse, "The Most Exclusive City in America," *Ainslee's Magazine* (Sept. 1905): 129.
34. Quoted in Owen Wister, *Roosevelt: The Story of a Friendship, 1880–1919* (New York: Macmillan, 1930), 251.
35. Owen Wister, *Lady Baltimore* (New York: Macmillan, 1906), 60; see William R. Taylor, *Cavalier and Yankee: The Old South and American National Character* (New York: George Braziller, 1961), for a thorough discussion of these themes in an earlier era.

CHAPTER 8

Dell Upton

The Urban Cemetery and the Urban Community: The Origin of the New Orleans Cemetery

Once Madaline Edwards, a young woman living in New Orleans in the 1840s, took a walk in Lafayette Cemetery No. 1 (fig. 8.1). As she strolled, she compared her circumstances to those of her married lover, Charley, who was then traveling in the North.

> I thought—(I trust such thoughts were not unjust nor profaning the spot to which I was going) of the difference in the lives of each [of us] at this moment, for conjecture lent her air as far as he was concerned. I thought, while I with step infirm, but heart not desponding was wending my way to the last silent abode of the dead, he was mixing in and among the millions of a crowded metropolis with the mass in the minds of whom death or sepulchres were the last to intrude themselves. While I walked slowly from one humble stone or board to another more indigative [sic] of wealth in those who reared them, reading the fond tribute of affection in the elaborate encomium or in the unostentatious name and age, that living friends had placed there as the last test of feelings that death could not arrest, he perhaps was moving in hurry from one massive piece of architecture to another of grandeur and beauty of the living, reared by their own opulence and love of approbation, and told in words too plain to be misunderstood by a mind so philosophical as his, that "we think not of death." While I stood among those weeds and willows that grew over and around those who once lived as we have done and now lie there, many even swept from the page of memory, he perhaps was walking amidst bowers and sweet scented flowers, whilst the name of one who so fondly linked the thoughts of him with every pulsation was swept at that happy hour from the tablet of his heart.[1]

Edwards's essay drew its power from two familiar images in the history of nineteenth-century American cemeteries. The first was the urban

Fig. 8.1. Lafayette Cemetery No. 1, New Orleans.

burial ground, crowded, ill-kempt, and reeking. During her visit, Edwards tells us, she thought of the graveyard scene in *Hamlet* as she asked the gravedigger about "the number made in a day, the depth, the price, unpleasant occupation as well as stench that arose from the water in the grave arising from the next graves in which lay the decomposed flesh of what had once been the object at least of a Mothers love: and I wondered if his occupation did not of necessity extend to his heart and render him callous to the sympathies of death." Charley's gay life contrasted with her own, ruined like the cemetery she walked in. The second image was that of the cemetery as a place of refuge from life's tribulations. Edwards invoked it explicitly in her conversation with the gravedigger when "I told him it was my desire to be buried elsewhere than in the holes of water he was making, not that it mattered much with me only in the fond associations my mind now bears to all that's rural and lovely in nature."[2] Edwards had in mind a rural cemetery, a kind of landscaped "natural" graveyard built outside most American cities beginning in the late 1820s. Rural cemeteries have been favored scenes for nineteenth-century travelers and modern landscape historians ever since, and have come to epitomize antebellum attitudes toward death and its settings.[3]

At first reading, then, Edwards's essay appears to be a straightforward affirmation of the romantic values of "natural" interment over those of the so-called "intramural" (within the city's boundaries) cemetery. Since the inception of the rural cemetery movement, contemporaries and historians have depicted it as a campaign to soften or naturalize death for the urban middle classes, on the one hand, and as an anti-urban gesture, on the other. The old intramural cemetery, it is said, epitomized the trials of urban life—its crowding, its eradication of identity, its assault on the senses, its threat to one's well being. In its suburban setting, dramatic siting, and apparently informal layout, the rural cemetery was a critique of the city itself, "an alternative environment" to the "efficiency of the urban grid system," or at least as a kind of "counterpoint" that rescued the city from its worst excesses.[4] As heterotopia or haven, the rural cemetery repudiated the urban burying ground.

In fact, the early-nineteenth-century urban cemetery and the rural cemeteries of the second quarter of the nineteenth-century were more similar in their rationales and their social, and even physical, structures than historians often recognize. For this reason, while Madaline Edwards invoked a familiar nineteenth-century discomfort and denial in the presence of death, she also articulated a less-often-examined view of the dead and their resting places as integral parts of the urban landscape.

This strand of antebellum thought about the cemetery and its occupants was at least as prevalent in popular discourse as the rural cemetery philosophy. Powerful traditional fears of death and reverence for the dead, recast in the new lights of science and sentimental personalism, shaped a novel kind of cemetery which redefined the relationship between the living and the dead as one between members of a single, albeit tension-racked, community. This new type of burial place, which I will call the reform cemetery, antedated and coexisted with the rural cemetery. The familiar, tomb-filled New Orleans cemeteries, such as the one Madaline Edwards walked in, so often exoticized by scholars and travelers, can most appropriately be understood as not-so-special varieties of the reform cemetery. They embodied changes taking place in many American cities at the beginning of the nineteenth century.

The traditional urban cemetery was a product of Christian practices that encouraged burial of the dead in hallowed ground around churches. Its intramural quality resulted from a common urban pattern in which land-intensive institutions such as monasteries, hospitals, asylums, and prisons were sited on relatively cheap land just beyond the periphery of the city. Most were engulfed by urban growth within a few years of their construction and replaced by newer facilities just beyond the new urbanized boundaries. Philadelphia's almshouse, for example, was built in the block between Third and Fourth Streets in 1732, moved west to Tenth and Eleventh Streets in 1766–67, and then to the west bank of the Schuylkill in 1833–34. Urban cemeteries shared in this pattern. New Orleans's first cemetery was located on the banks of the Mississippi, a second was constructed within the formal boundaries of the old city but beyond the built-up area around 1725, and a third (St. Louis No. 1) just outside the ramparts in 1789. Early-nineteenth-century reform cemeteries throughout the United States followed this pattern of location outside the developed portion of the city, as did rural cemeteries. The difference was that rural cemetery planners believed—wrongly as it happens—that they had chosen sites far beyond any possible urbanization.[5]

Although they were familiar landmarks created by the natural growth of the city, intramural cemeteries inspired considerable ambivalence in the early nineteenth century. To consider the quick and the dead as members of a single community exposed both to danger. The dead, for example, posed serious threats to those among the living who strayed too close. Traditional fears of death and the dead were magnified by new medical theories that attributed disease to the "miasmas" emanating from low, damp places like graveyards. Physicians tallied the large numbers of epidemics that seemed to begin near burying grounds.[6] The hazards posed by the dead—one's own ancestors—were reported with a sense of betrayal. In warning against visiting New Orleans cemeteries, A. Oakey Hall claimed that "[t]o many a tender frame has issued upon such occasions from the damp alleys and causeways, a death warrant which was sealed, delivered, and executed before the expiration of another month."[7]

At the same time, the living often betrayed the dead by encroaching on their resting places in continuing to use crowded public cemeteries and even in destroying cemeteries in the frenzy of urban expansion. These betrayals violated traditional beliefs about the sanctity of the corpse and the physical resurrection of the body, beliefs that defied official Christian doctrines that proclaimed the insignificance of the lifeless body. A Roman Catholic priest in New Orleans told architect Benjamin Latrobe "that the position of the coffin with the feet to the East and the head to the West, was of the first importance: because, that at the Resurrection, Christ would appear in the East, and if they were placed otherwise they would rise with their backs towards him."[8] Other folk traditions taught that respectful treatment of the body was necessary for the spirit's rest and to avoid ghostly retribution. For this reason, eighteenth-century Irish laborers and other lower-class Londoners rioted to prevent the bodies of compatriots from falling into the hands of medical dissectors.[9] Across the Atlantic, the managers and physicians of the Pennsylvania Hospital condemned "the indecent conduct of some Young Surgeons in taking up and dissecting dead bodies, [which] occasions a general uneasiness and displeasure in the minds of all humane People."[10]

The fear of death, the sense of the mutual responsibility of living and dead, and an obsession with their mutual betrayal were vividly evident in the nineteenth-century fascination with premature burial. In many of Edgar Allan Poe's tales, such as "The Fall of the House of Usher," "Berenice," "The Tell-Tale Heart," "The Black Cat," and "The Cask of Amontillado," people who were buried alive return to claim living companions before finally expiring. Poe's stories spoke to such potential readers as Philadelphian Thomas P. Cope, who noted in his diary "[a]n interesting, thrilling statement of premature interments—or, rather, of their fortuitous prevention" in a newspaper account that reported ninety-four such escapes in France in one decade.[11] Given the state of medical knowledge, premature burial was a real possibility in the antebellum era. Nevertheless, the disproportionate popularity of such stories spoke to the perilously indistinct boundary between the two halves of the urban community.

Although they were fearful of the dead, nineteenth-century Europeans and Americans were increasingly reluctant to consign their loved ones to death's finality. After the late eighteenth century, the older traditions dictating respect for the corpse were reinforced in bourgeois culture by an exaggerated sentimental attachment to the body as the vessel of individual personality. Latrobe wrote in striking psychosexual terms that "[t]hose who have lost friends, especially of a different sex from themselves, and have hearts to feel, need not be told, that whatever philosophical indifference may have existed respecting the fate of their own bodies after death, those of their friends become infinitely dear to them, and that no display of their affection is considered too extravagant or too expensive to be indulged and executed."[12]

In the light of old and new beliefs about the obligations of the living to the dead, New Orleans seemed particularly threatening. It lay below the level of the Mississippi River, with a water table that was consequently near grade.[13] Although it was possible to bury below ground in the traditional manner (and poor people always were, as Madaline Edwards's essay suggests), any excavation quickly filled with water. Observing a pauper's burial, Joseph Holt Ingraham noted that "some of the assistants have to stand upon [the coffin], and keep it down until the grave is refilled with the mud which was originally thrown from it, or it would float."[14] Likewise, Bennett Dowler had "watched the bailing out of the grave, [and] the floating of the coffin, and [had] heard the friends of the deceased deplore this mode of interment."[15]

For northerners, these scenes inspired all sorts of grisly fantasies. For them, death in New Orleans fused the corruption of the natural environment with the decadence of francophone culture. Contemplating a favorite Crescent City delicacy, John H. B. Latrobe, the architect's son, wrote that in St. Louis Cemetery No. 1, "whole rows of earthen chimneys marked the residence of the crawfish, at all times an unpleasant sight but rendered almost loathsome by its close neighborhood to the bodies of the dead."[16] New Yorker John Pintard connected environment and culture even more explicitly. He argued that "[i]t is of little consequence whether ones carcase is given prey to crayfish on land—or the catfish of the Mississipi," [sic] but it was difficult for him to imagine himself at both ends of the food chain. "[A] body is speedily devoured & transmigrated in crayfish or catfish—dressed by a French cook & feasted upon by a greasy Monk—a fair lady—a petit maitre or a savage who in their turn supply some future banquet—Heavens what a luxury! Mon Dieu, quelle sort! Give my bones terra firma I pray."[17]

Consequently, a whole constellation of traditional and recent beliefs about the fate of the body, given a local twist by Anglo ethnocentrism, drove well-off Orleanians to protect the body from watery encroachment and even natural dissolution as far as was in their power. As Benjamin Latrobe noted, "Those who can afford it enclose [the dead] in Leaden and Stone coffins, as if jealous of the appetites of the vermin to whom they might give nourishment."[18] By the 1830s, "The citizens . . . having a very natural repugnance to being drowned, after having died a natural death upon their beds, choose to have their last resting-place a dry one; and hence the great number of tombs."[19]

These were the famous above-ground tombs that have remained quintessential images of New Orleans since the antebellum era. The outsider's eye for the exotic—a kind of ingrown Orientalism—fixed on these tomb-filled graveyards as emblems and relics of francophone culture itself, unique signs of the social and environmental entropy of the Crescent City. Although urban metaphors are common in speaking of cemeteries everywhere, the complex relationship between the living and the dead was particularly poignant in New Orleans, because the abodes of the two were visually so similar to one another. For Madaline Edwards, St. Louis No. 2 was a "beautiful . . . dead City." Similarly, for visitor Frederika Bremer, as for New Yorker A. Oakey Hall, it was "really a 'city of the dead'" (fig. 8.2).[20] When Joseph Holt Ingraham visited the St. Louis Cemetery No. 2 in 1835, he observed that

> a broad avenue or street extends nearly an eighth of a mile in length; and on either side of this are innumerable isolated tombs, of all sizes, shapes, and descriptions, built above ground. . . . The tombs in their various and fantastic styles of architecture—if I may apply the term to these tiny edifices—resembled cathedrals with towers, Moorish dwellings, temples, chapels, palaces, *mosques*—substituting the cross for the crescent—and structures of almost every kind. The idea was ludicrous enough; but as I passed down the avenue, I could not but indulge the fancy that I was striding down the Broadway of the capital of the Lilliputians. . . . All were perfectly white, arranged with the most perfect regularity, and distant little more than a foot from each other. At the distance of every ten rods the main avenue was intersected by others of less width, crossing it at right angles, down which tombs were arranged in the same novel and regular manner. The whole cemetery was divided into squares, formed by these narrow streets intersecting the principal avenue. It was in reality a "City of the Dead." But it was a city composed of miniature palaces, and still more diminutive villas.[21]

At the same time, Orleanians saw the living city, with its heat, humidity, and ever-present epidemics, as a "Wet Grave." New Yorker Woodbury Langdon arrived in the city expecting to find "a glittering frog pond & grave yard."[22]

However, the urban and urban-looking New Orleans cemeteries that Madaline Edwards and her contemporaries visited were newly built, direct products of the sentimentalization of death. The scene in the city's oldest surviving burying ground, the now densely built-up St. Louis No. 1, for example, was much different in 1801 (fig. 8.3). When John Pintard visited the twelve-year-old burying ground in that year, "a broken palisade gave me admittance, during one of my solitary gambles [sic], into this melancholy enclosure—not a single grave stone marked the remains of either the noble or ignoble dead—Over some few, brick arches were turned. At the head of every grave was planted an Iron or wooden cross some of the Iron ones were indented with the names of the lifeless tenants below."[23]

The scene changed slowly. In 1819, St. Louis No. 1 struck Benjamin Latrobe as different from the cemeteries he knew from Washington and Philadelphia, but it was still not the landscape that we associate with New Orleans cemeteries. Some individual graves were built "of bricks, much larger than necessary to enclose a single coffin, and plastered over, so as to have a very

Fig. 8.2. "The French Cemetery, New Orleans, La." A nineteenth-century view of St. Louis Cemetery No. 2. Courtesy of the Historic New Orleans Collection.

solid permanent appearance. They are . . . 7 or 8 feet long and 4 or 5 feet wide, and . . . from 5 to 7 feet high. They are crouded close together, without any particular attention to aspect."[24] These low-slung, brick-built, individual tombs were common in late-eighteenth- and early-nineteenth-century cemeteries throughout the coastal South and the West Indies.[25] Latrobe also described and illustrated *fours* (oven tombs, named for their shapes) or *loculi,* niches large enough to hold a single coffin end on, and were customarily built in blocks or walls four to six tiers high.[26]

John H. B. Latrobe visited the cemetery in 1834 and left a description and a watercolor view that show a graveyard in transition, but one that is remarkably uncluttered by family mausoleums and consequently is still far from the familiar New Orleans image (fig. 8.4). A wall of *fours* stands at the right rear, where it probably forms a part of the cemetery's enclosure. The foreground, dominated by the Varney pyramid, appears relatively open, and a few iron crosses stand at the right of the view. Most of the visible graves are individual tombs of the sort his father had observed.

By the 1830s, the newer Crescent City cemeteries had begun to fill with two kinds of structures that served the double purpose of protecting the corpse from violation and of protecting the health and the sensibilities of the bereaved. The most conspicuous were the new family tombs and mausoleums that attracted Joseph Holt Ingraham's attention. To be sure, New Orleans's topography made such tombs immensely popular among the city's elite, and they took on a particularly stylish appearance after the French émigré architect J. N. B. de Pouilly arrived in the city in 1833 carrying a sketchbook filled with images culled from Paris's fashionable Père Lachaise cemetery.[27] Nevertheless, Ingraham exaggerated difference for his readers' entertainment, as all travel writers do. He could have observed similar family tombs in regions of the Gulf Coast that lacked New Orleans's topographical and cultural peculiarities, as well as in the new rural cemeteries of northern cities.[28]

Among and around the tombs were the vast banks of *fours* built in Crescent City cemeteries after the early nineteenth century. Although they were less noteworthy to outsiders than the mausoleums, they were more numerous (fig. 8.5).

Fig. 8.3. St. Louis Cemetery No. 1, New Orleans.

Fig. 8.4. John H. B. Latrobe, *St. Louis Cemetery No. 1* (1834). The pyramid prominently featured in the foreground is the Varney monument, also visible in fig. 8.3. Courtesy of the Historic New Orleans Collection.

Constructed either as part of the boundary walls of the cemeteries or as freestanding structures scattered throughout them, some *fours* were built by the city or by private-cemetery owners, while others were the property of benevolent, ethnic, and other organizations, in which case they were called "society tombs." The public *fours* were rented for a period of twenty-five or fifty years, then emptied and reused. At the fashionable new Cypress Grove Cemetery, a private undertaking of the Firemen's Benevolent Association, *fours* were sold for $50 for locations in the lower tier, and $55 for spots in the three upper tiers. By contrast, 14-by-16-foot lots sold for $82.88 to $127.68, exclusive of the cost of the mausoleum, which typically ran from $200 to $1,000.[29] In Cypress Grove, mausolea were commonly marble structures designed by de Pouilly and others of the city's most fashionable architects.

At the end of the eighteenth century, urbanites in most North American cities began to seek a more comprehensive landscape order that would allot space to all users, creating a transparent, readily recognizable mapping of the community of the dead.[30] New Orleans's *fours* applied this thinking to the cemetery, articulating the formerly undifferentiated, mostly unmarked common space of older public burying grounds

Fig. 8.5. Mid-Nineteenth-Century *Fours*, Lafayette Cemetery No. 1, New Orleans.

such as St. Louis No. 1. *Fours* extended the privilege of security and individual commemoration for the dead from the elite to a larger public increasingly disposed to demand it in republican America. Now, all but the poorest of the dead were mapped in time, by means of inscriptions, and in space, within the gridded structure of the *fours*. The latter were in turn linked to the gridded plat of the newer cemeteries, and to the street grid outside. When Madaline Edwards's former lover Charles W. Bradbury was interred in St. Louis No. 2 in 1880, his burial was located in Square Number 1 (of the cemetery), in *fours* number 2 of the fourth range along Claiborne Avenue between Conti and St. Louis Streets.[31] The clerk who recorded the interment thus mapped Bradbury securely in the space of both the living and dead cities.

New Orleans's *fours* were special cases of a new kind of American burial space that employed gridded space in the service of the clear articulation of individuality and social standing. The traditional urban cemetery had been conceived of as undifferentiated common space, but some of this communal space was commandeered by those wealthy enough to erect tombs and mausoleums and to have them tolerated. This is strikingly visible at older New Orleans cemeteries like St. Louis No. 1, where private monuments were crammed in willy-nilly as space allowed.

Beginning in 1796 with New Haven's New Burying Ground, gridded cemeteries divided in their entirety into clearly delineated, family-owned plots were built in most American cities.[32] For example, New Orleans's Catholic St. Louis No. 2 and Protestant Girod Street cemeteries were laid out with central and parallel side aisles. Within these armatures, individual tombs were given a strict alignment, following the 1822 orders of the city council instructing the city surveyor to visit the new cemeteries weekly "to give a line for the graves and tombs."[33]

Within a decade, spacious, gridded cemeteries were built at the edge of town to accommodate the rapid growth of the city. Cypress Grove, also called the Fireman's Cemetery, was the first when it opened in 1840 (fig. 8.7). By 1849, there were seven cemeteries in New Orleans other than the St. Louis and Girod Street burial grounds and the potters' field. Six of these lay along the dry Metairie Ridge four miles northwest of town.

These new cemeteries of the 1840s resembled the city in more than their architecture and planning. After passing through Cypress Grove's Egyptian-style gate, for example, visitors enter a wide lawn. In the center is the broken column commemorating Irad Ferry, a fireman killed in action in 1837 (fig. 8.6; see fig. 8.7). The society tomb of the Perseverance Fire Company stands near Ferry's monument, while the wall-built society tombs of two other fire companies flank this lawn—the Philadelphia Fire Engine Company on the left and the Eagle Fire Company on the right. The latter contains the remains of two of New Orleans's most renowned antebellum ministers, Sylvester Larned and his successor, Theodore Clapp, and their families. Thus, visitors pass through a kind of Elysian Field that celebrated the fire companies who founded the cemetery and protected the city and that is enriched by the graves of famous New Orleans clergy. Then they

Fig. 8.6. J. N. B. de Pouilly, Irad Ferry Monument (1840), Cypress Grove Cemetery.

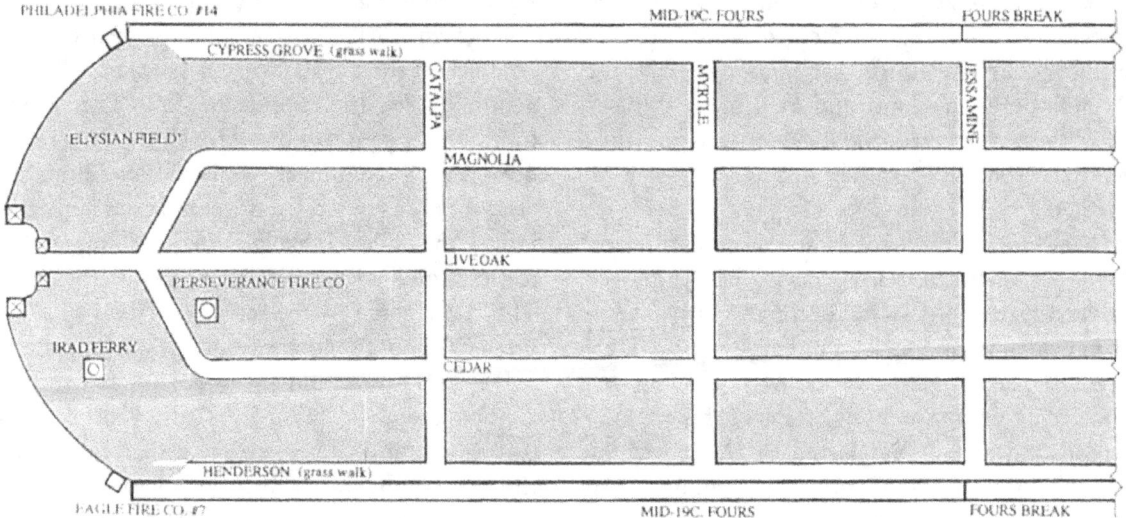

Fig. 8.7. Cypress Grove Cemetery, New Orleans. Sketch Plan. Zeynep Kezer.

reach the body of the cemetery, with its twenty-eight-foot-wide central road, Live Oak Avenue, flanked by narrower parallel streets (fig. 8.8). The tombs of many of the city's elite line the three major roads, while still-narrower pathways run along the walls, which contain the obligatory *fours*. Cross streets intersect the five main roads at two-hundred-foot intervals.

The dead city thus reproduces the social divisions and the favored spatial organization of the living city, while binding live and dead urbanites into a community that stretches unbroken through time. In a story by Madaline Edwards, two women, Irene and Caroline, visited St. Louis No. 2. Irene, a New Orleans resident, pointed out to the visitor, Caroline, that "you will see where thousands rest in more humble tenements for the City of the dead is a counterpart of that of the living, for some have gay and costly edifices whilst others are scarce sheltered from the snow or rain, but as humble as these ovens [*fours*] look after viewing the others, they are palaces compared to the thousands that fill the Potters field and other Cemetaries I have seen." Yet, while the city of the dead was intimately related to the city of the living, it is, said Irene, "only to we living friends that it matters [that there are differences in burial styles], for one reposes as sweetly as the other, and after the breath leaves our bodies it is of no consequence to us." But Irene was pleased to see "how devoted these creoles are to their dead, how sacred they hold the dust of their friends and kindred." Their devotions created a landscape within which love and sorrow could be openly and comfortably expressed for the benefit of mourner and observer. Most important, their practices "bring home to the minds of the thoughtless and superstitious that there is nothing to dread in approaching the sepulchral marble." Visitors could confront death and bereavement frankly and naturally and thus incorporate them into daily urban life.[34]

During their walk, Irene and Caroline observed the private devotions of individual mourners in decorating tombs and offering graveside prayers. In fact, New Orleans institutionalized the bonds of living and dead in a communal ritual still held on All Saints' Day each November 1. At noon on that day, nineteenth-century Catholics paraded to the cemetery for ritual prayers and embellishment of graves. The owners of tombs and *fours* lit candles, placed wreaths and garlands of flowers, and often renewed whitewash and relettered inscriptions.

It was an affair that brought together great numbers of people "of every age, color and condition." The crowds ranged from 1,000 to as many as 3,000 on a pleasant day. For some, it was a solemn occasion; for others, a festive one. But for Catholic Orleanians in general, All Saints' Day expressed the unity of the urban community through time. In the presence of the assembled multitude, the parish priest invoked rest for the souls of the dead and forgiveness for their sins and those of the living people present at the affair. For visitor J. G. Dunlap, "The whole scene is quite imposing and caused feelings of the most solemn character." The ceremonies concluded at nightfall, when the police came and the cemeteries were closed.[35]

The builders of early-nineteenth-century American reform cemeteries sought to invest the cemetery with this sense of community, while acknowledging the double-edged nature of the relationship between the living and the dead. In opening his gridded Philadelphia Cemetery (now demolished) in 1826, James Ronaldson "hope[d] that it will contribute to cherish those tender feelings that connect the living with their deceased friends." Yet, it was also a site where the distinction between living and dead was closely guarded. The gate house was a double structure. On one side was the gatekeeper's residence, which protected the dead from vandalism and desecration. On the other was the cemetery's bier house, which protected the living from the dead.

Fig. 8.8. Live Oak Avenue, Cypress Grove Cemetery.

In it the corpse was laid out for three days before burial, with a string tied around its finger and connected to a bell in the cupola. In this way, the attendant might learn if a living person was in danger of being buried alive.[36]

The stories of New Orleans's cemeteries, as well as those of lesser-known northern burial places like Ronaldson's Philadelphia Cemetery, intersect with the histories of familiar rural cemeteries such as Mount Auburn and Laurel Hill to complicate the tale of antebellum American graveyards, drawing them closer to the urban context and its spatial themes. Reform cemetery builders sought to alleviate some of the terrors of burial inside the city and to soften the abode of death with plantings and other amenities, but they found an urban spatial order to be as appropriate for maintaining individuality and clear relationships among the dead as it was for the living. These cemeteries were built close enough to the city to allow the cemetery to be a part of the daily and ritual life of its inhabitants.

This was evident in Madaline Edwards's essay occasioned by her walk in Lafayette Cemetery No. 1. She spun out a long fantasy of her own and Charley's future grave sites. Rather than lie forgotten in a swampy urban grave among those who had despised her as the mistress of a married man, Madaline wished to lie on a forest slope, with "the blue sky [as] my tomb stone, the forest oak my head-board." If Charley died first, Edwards envisioned the same sort of grave for him. There she would take their child to pay homage to its father, so that Charley might act as a kind of patron saint: "the spirit of the departed would give sanctity" to her prayer that the "pure and spotless treasure"—the child—would remain so.[37]

Yet, Madaline's vision was a surprising one. She wanted to mark Charley's grave with a "neat marble slab commemorating a few of his virtues [as] they are now unknown to the world." As time passed, after she was no longer alive to celebrate him, "the strides of improvement with another generation . . . would approach that enchanted elisium." The city would engulf the grave site, leaving the monument to "tell the tale and reveal the potency of the charm." The grave, its natural setting lost, would be transformed from a private shrine to a public monument, embedded in a new urban setting where those who were wronged or overlooked in the old city would be deservedly celebrated. Thus, Edwards foresaw a future in which the lonely, romantic grave was incorporated into an urban landscape. In the end, she conceived nature as a setting for the working out of private griefs, but accepted the urban cemetery as an appropriate instrument of sociability and as an archive of human memory.

In looking over what she had written, Madaline Edwards was "astonished to find I have gone such lengths into the imaginary," recognizing that in reality "that day may come and very soon when [Charley] will lay my last remains in a less romantic spot." She confided to her diary that "[i]f I die in Orleans, I hope to rest in the firemans," meaning the new Cypress Grove Cemetery. Ten years and a month later, long after the affair with Bradbury had ended and she had fled New Orleans, Edwards was buried in an unmarked grave in San Francisco's potters' field.[38]

Notes

1. Madaline S. Edwards, "A Walk," in *Madaline: Love and Survival in Antebellum New Orleans* (hereafter cited as *M*), ed. Dell Upton (Athens: Univ. of Georgia Press, 1996), 126. Edwards (1816–1854), a native of Tennessee, wrote two diaries and two books of essays during the years 1844–46, during which time she was the mistress of a married man, Charles W. Bradbury. Her work is informed by an acute consciousness of literal and figurative residence at the margin of urban society. All Edwards's manuscripts can be found in the Charles W. Bradbury Papers, Southern Historical Collection, Univ. of North Carolina, Chapel Hill.

2. *M*, 127.

3. On nineteenth-century American cemeteries, see David Charles Sloane, *The Last Great Necessity: Cemeteries in American History* (Baltimore: Johns Hopkins Univ. Press, 1991); and Blanche Linden-Ward, *Silent City on a Hill: Landscapes of Memory and Boston's Mount Auburn Cemetery* (Columbus: Ohio State Univ. Press, 1989).

4. David Schuyler, "The Evolution of the Anglo-American Rural Cemetery: Landscape Architecture as Social and Cultural History," *Journal of Garden History* 4 (3) (Sept. 1984): 303; Sloane, *Last Great Necessity,* 76; Thomas Bender, "The 'Rural' Cemetery Movement: Urban Travail and the Appeal of Nature" (1974); reprint in *Material Life in America, 1600–1860,* ed. Robert Blair St. George (Boston: Northeastern Univ. Press, 1988), 505–18.

5. For example, John Jay Smith, one of the founders of Philadelphia's Laurel Hill Cemetery, claimed that it was "removed beyond the probable approach of active business, or private dwellings" ([John Jay Smith], *Guide to Laurel Hill Cemetery* [Philadelphia: C. Sherman, 1844], 11).

6. Edward H. Barton, *The Cause and Prevention of Yellow Fever at New Orleans and Other Cities in America,* 3d ed. (New York: H. Ballière, 1857), 144.
7. A. Oakey Hall, *The Manhattaner in New Orleans* (1851; reprint, Baton Rouge: Louisiana State Univ. Press, 1976), 110.
8. Benjamin Henry Latrobe, *The Journals of Benjamin Henry Latrobe,* 3 vols., ed. Edward C. Carter II, John C. Van Horne, and Lee W. Formwalt (New Haven: Yale Univ. Press, 1977–80), 3: 242.
9. Peter Linebaugh, "The Tyburn Riot Against the Surgeons," in *Albion's Fatal Tree: Crime and Society in Eighteenth-Century England,* Douglas Hay, Peter Linebaugh, John G. Rule, E. P. Thompson, and Cal Winslow (New York: Pantheon, 1975), 84–85, 88, 102.
10. Pennsylvania Hospital, Board of Managers, Minutes (May 5, 1770) vol. 4: 72, Archives of the Pennsylvania Hospital, American Philosophical Society, Philadelphia.
11. Thomas P. Cope, *Philadelphia Merchant: the Diary of Thomas P. Cope, 1800–1851,* ed. Eliza Cope Harrison (South Bend, Ind.: Gateway Editions, 1978), 499.
12. Latrobe, *Journals,* 3: 246.
13. Dell Upton, "The Master Street of the World: The Levee," in *Streets: Critical Perspectives on Public Space,* ed. Zeynep Çelik, Diane Favro, and Richard Ingersoll (Berkeley: Univ. of California Press, 1994), 278–80.
14. Joseph Holt Ingraham, *The South-West. By a Yankee* (New York: Harper and Brothers, 1835), 1: 157.
15. Bennett Dowler, *Researches upon the Necropolis of New Orleans, with Brief Allusions to Its Vital Arithmetic* (New Orleans: Bill and Clark, 1850), 7.
16. John H. B. Latrobe, *Southern Travels: Journal of John H. B. Latrobe,* ed. Samuel Wilson Jr. (New Orleans: Historic New Orleans Collection, 1986), 54.
17. David Lee Sterling, ed., "New Orleans, 1801: An Account by John Pintard," *Louisiana Historical Quarterly* 34 (3) (July 1951): 231.
18. Latrobe, *Journals,* 3: 244.
19. Ingraham, *South-West,* 1: 157.
20. M, 207; Fredrika Bremer, *The Homes of the New World; Impressions of America,* trans. Mary Howitt (New York: Harper and Brothers, 1854), 2: 214; Hall, *Manhattaner in New Orleans,* 108.
21. Ingraham, *South-West,* 1: 153–55 (emphasis his).
22. Charles Joseph Latrobe, *The Rambler in North America, MDCCCXXXII–MDCCCXXXIII* (New York: Harper and Brothers, 1835), 2: 238; Woodbury Langdon, near New Orleans, to Dr. William E. Langdon, Fort Niagara, N.Y., Jun. 2, 1824, Tulane Univ. Library, Rare Books and Manuscripts Division, document M268.
23. Sterling, ed., "New Orleans, 1801," 230.
24. Latrobe, *Journals,* 3: 241–42.
25. Sharyn Thompson, "These Works of Mortuary Art: The Aboveground Tombs of St. Michael Cemetery, Pensacola, Florida," *Southern Quarterly* 31 (2) (winter 1993): 50–73.
26. Although Leonard Huber has attributed *fours* to eighteenth-century Spain, they were common features of early-nineteenth-century landscaped cemeteries in several European countries, and Latrobe's is the earliest New Orleans description I have found. See Leonard V. Huber, "New Orleans Cemeteries: A Brief History," in *New Orleans Architecture,* III, *The Cemeteries,* ed. Mary Louise Christovich (Gretna, La.: Pelican, 1989), pp. 9–10.
27. Peggy McDowell, "J. N. B. de Pouilly and French Sources of Revival Style Design in New Orleans Cemetery Architecture," in *Cemeteries and Gravemarkers: Voices of American Culture,* ed. Richard E. Meyer (Logan: Utah State Univ. Press, 1992), 137–58.
28. Sloane, *Last Great Necessity,* 22–24, 77–78; Linden-Ward, *Silent City,* 243–46.
29. *New Orleans Directory for 1842* (New Orleans: Pitts and Clarke, 1842), unpaginated advertisement.
30. Dell Upton, "Another City: The Urban Cultural

Landscape in the Early Republic," in *Everyday Life in the Early Republic,* ed. Catherine E. Hutchins (Winterthur, Del.: Winterthur Museum, 1994), 61–62, 67–79.
31. "Square No. 1 . . . Fous. N. 2 4me Rang Sur la rue Claiborne en partant de la rue Conti à St Louis," St. Louis Cemetery No. 2 Interment Book, 1877–1880, p. 306 (June 23, 1880), microfilm, New Orleans Public Library.
32. Sloane, *Last Great Necessity,* 29–34.
33. New Orleans, Resolutions and Ordinances of the Conseil de Ville (English translation), 1805–35, 7: 93 (Aug. 3, 1822), microfilm, New Orleans Public Library.
34. *M,* 205–10.
35. J. G. Dunlap, New Orleans, to Beatrice A. Dunlap, Augusta, Ga., Nov. 4, 1844, Dunlap Correspondence, 1827–69, Tulane Univ. Library, Rare Books and Manuscripts Collection, box 1, folder 3.
36. *Philadelphia Cemetery. Copy of Deed of Trust. April 2, 1827* (Philadelphia, 1827), 4.
37. Except as noted, this and the following paragraphs are based on Edwards's "A Walk," in *M,* 126–32.
38. *M,* 125.

PART III

REDEFINING WORK SPACE

CHAPTER 9

Rebecca J. Siders and Anna V. Andrzejewski

The House and Garden: Housing Agricultural Laborers in Central Delaware, 1780–1930

On a spring day in 1847, John Alston, a wealthy Quaker farmer, and James Ryan, "a colored man," met at Alston's home near Middletown, Delaware, to sign a lease agreement for a tenant house. In early January, when Ryan and his family had first moved into the dwelling, they had done so without a formal written lease; now, with the start of the agricultural season, both parties felt ready to formalize the arrangement. In return for "the sum of twenty five Dollars in work or money," Alston leased to Ryan for one year a "small tenement . . . with the garden attached" and firewood "to be cut where shown or directed." For his part, Ryan agreed to give Alston "the preference of his labor at all times . . . at the current wage of the neighborhood." Ryan also promised to limit the inhabitants of the house to himself, his wife, and their children. This lease-labor agreement provided obvious benefits to both men. Alston secured the year-round presence of a laborer for assistance with tasks tied to the seasonal cycles of planting and harvest, farm maintenance, and new improvements. Ryan acquired a place to live, sufficient land to plant a garden and keep a cow and a few pigs, firewood for heat and cooking, and the prospect of paid labor to provide cash for items his family could not grow or make.[1]

Tenant-labor agreements, such as the one between Alston and Ryan, and the houses they referred to proliferated in central Delaware throughout the nineteenth century, especially during the period from 1820 to 1860.[2] The "house and garden" appeared on the landscape and in farmers' ledgers as a visible sign of the changing relationship between farmers and laborers (fig. 9.1).[3] This new relationship resulted in part from the demographic pressures of a new labor system and from the impact of agricultural reform discourse. Prior to the end of the eighteenth century, slaves provided the bulk of the agricultural labor force needed on many farms in central Delaware. They lived either in separate quarters or in spaces such as the attics above main dwellings and kitchen wings, carrying out tasks that ranged from ditch digging, tending crops, and chopping wood to food preparation and the construction and repair of buildings.[4] Beginning in the last quarter of the eighteenth century, influenced both by religious movements like the Society of Friends and by changes in the agricultural economy, many farmers manumitted their slaves. After 1790, slaves represented only a very small portion of the labor force, comprising 5 percent or less of Kent County's total population after 1800. Unlike areas such as Virginia, which strongly encouraged newly freed blacks to leave the state, Delaware found ways to keep its free African Americans from emigrating and to employ those who filtered North.[5] Increasingly after 1800, farmers found themselves relying on a new labor force made up of free African American and poor white families who lacked the resources to purchase or tenant their own farms. While slave labor required financial and material support throughout the year, this new free labor force sought greater physical and financial separation from its employer, the farm owner or manager.[6]

The second factor that influenced the emergence of the house and garden was the increasing attention paid to agricultural reform discourse. During the late eighteenth century, gentleman farmers in both England and America began experimenting with new strategies for the improvement of crop yields and more efficient farming. Many of them published the results of their studies, sharing their information with other farmers throughout the English-speaking world. They fostered the formation of many locally based reform societies, such as the Philadelphia Society for the Improvement of Agriculture, and supported new innovations in crops, machinery, and farm buildings. Beginning in the early nineteenth century, exhausted soils and competition from western agricultural areas prompted farmers in southern

Fig. 9.1. Ridgely Tenant House, Little Creek Hundred, Kent County, Delaware. Many small house and garden dwellings like the Ridgely Tenant House lined the sides of roads throughout central Delaware in the nineteenth century. Typically these dwellings stood one and a half stories in height, with two or three bays across the front elevation. Rebecca J. Siders, CHAE, 1995.

New Castle and Kent Counties to explore the suggestions of these agricultural reform writers, diversifying their crops and moving toward a more scientific and business-like approach to working their farms. In part, these changes reflected attempts to make agricultural production both more efficient and less costly. Farmers made use of innovative machinery for planting and harvesting crops, experimented with fertilizers and crop rotation to increase soil productivity, reclaimed marsh land for agricultural use, and searched for ways to reduce the cost of labor.[7]

In response to these changes in labor and agriculture, landowners and tenants transformed the agricultural landscape with a multitude of small tenant houses scattered about on the edges of fields and farm complexes, often referred to by their owners and occupants as house and gardens. Most commonly constructed to lodge married laborers and their families, the house and garden dwelling found its greatest popularity among large landowners or farm managers, farmers engaged in the new "business" of agriculture. These progressive farmers chose a traditional one-room plan widely used by the rural population of central Delaware. Considering this simple and inexpensive form as the appropriate level of housing for their laborers, landowners adapted it to fit the prescriptions of agricultural reformers and adopted the name "house and garden" for the building type. Typically, a house and garden dwelling contained a main room on the first floor with an enclosed winding stair leading to a single open room above, and a rough one-story shed extending from either the gable end or the rear elevation (fig. 9.2). Rectangular in shape and covered by a gable roof, average dimensions for the main block ranged from 16 by 16 feet to 18 by 20 feet with a door and one or two windows across the front elevation (figs. 9.1 and 9.5). The dwellings might be constructed of log or frame (either braced-frame or balloon-frame, depending upon the date of construction). Interior finishes characteristically consisted of whitewash on rafters, joists, and wooden walls, with early upgrades in finish marked by the use of lath and plaster. Almost invariably these dwellings rested on pier foundations (of wood, brick, or stone) to protect them from ground moisture and make them easily portable. The houses sat on small par-

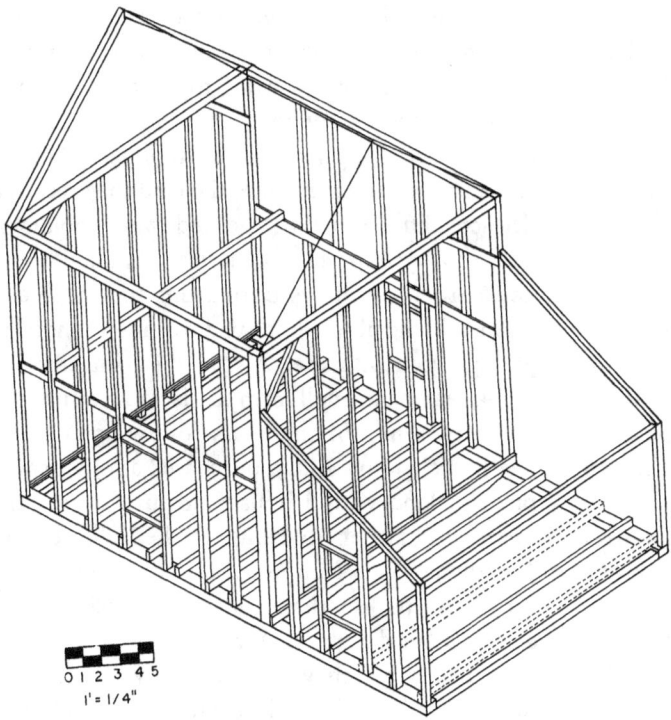

Fig. 9.2. Moody-Clayton House, St. Georges Hundred, New Castle County, Delaware. This axonometric drawing of the Moody-Clayton House shows the typical house and garden dwelling configuration of a single room and gable-end shed room on the ground floor. Deidre McCarthy, CHAE, 1995.

cels of land, usually between one and five acres. Sometimes this land was simply part of a larger farm, with no clear boundary other than the edges of the planted fields; at other times, the parcel occupied a legally defined area. Occasionally, fences marked the outline of the property, but more often they enclosed the garden itself. In either case, the tenants secured the right to plant small gardens, pasture a cow, and raise a few pigs and some chickens. Construction of this form for the purpose of housing agricultural laborers continued from the early 1800s through the first quarter of the twentieth century.

Before its adoption as the building type most appropriate for housing agricultural laborers, the idea of a small house and a garden served as a solution for housing individuals who held only tenuous economic claims on neighboring farm households and rural communities. Between 1780 and 1820, landowners used these simple dwellings to house itinerant artisans, single women, elderly relatives, former slaves or servants, and laborers of all sorts.[8] Landowners who felt some responsibility toward these individuals might rent or give to them small dwellings with a few acres of land. In many cases, this action served as an expression of the paternalism expected from a male head of household toward certain family members, slaves, and other servants. John Dickinson, for example, owned more than thirty-five hundred acres along the St. Jones Creek in the 1790s. Divided into six large holdings run by individual farm managers, the property also included numerous additional small dwellings. Dickinson leased these small houses to a variety of tenants, such as Samuel Bennett, an itinerant carpenter. Under his agreement with Dickinson, Bennett received a small house with several acres of ground and a yearly wage of one hundred dollars in return for carrying out any carpentry work needed on the St. Jones Neck farms. Dickinson executed more than ten similar arrangements that provided housing in exchange for the services of ditch diggers, masons, and farm laborers between 1785 and 1808.[9]

Many farmers in central Delaware freed their slaves between 1790 and 1820. Newly freed blacks often inhabited these early house and garden dwellings. Sometimes part of the act of manumission included the gift of a small piece of land with a house, marked in documentary records by references such as "an acre set aside for negro Priscilla" or "the house and one acre now occupied by black Nathan."[10] Orphans Court plats for the region illustrate the presence of these dwellings in small pockets of marginal land (fig. 9.3). Typically these pieces of land existed in locations that created no major incursions on the former master's prime agricultural land. Sometimes the parcels were at the edge of a larger tract, often next to a road; in other cases, they contained land considered unsuitable or unusable for agriculture, such as marsh or swamp. Thomas Denney, for example, gave land to his former slave Priscilla at the edge of a coppiced field in Duck Creek Hundred.[11] Coppiced land was previously wooded land where the trees had been girdled or felled, leaving large stumps in the ground and new shoots just starting to grow, so that the land was not yet suitable for tillage. Thus, while the new occupants of these dwellings achieved some level of independence, the land they received detracted little from the large landowner's holdings.

A third group that commonly inhabited house and garden dwellings during this time included women living alone, both widows and unmarried young women. Israel Alston died intestate in 1794, leaving a small farm to his widow and several children.[12] In the years following Alston's death, his widow, Mary, purchased another small piece of land with a house and turned over the farm and larger dwelling to her eldest son, Jonathan. When Mary died in 1803, she left the farm land to Jonathan and made special provisions for her daughters. While any of the five girls remained single, they "shall have my House, Garden and full privilege of the lane . . . for a Home

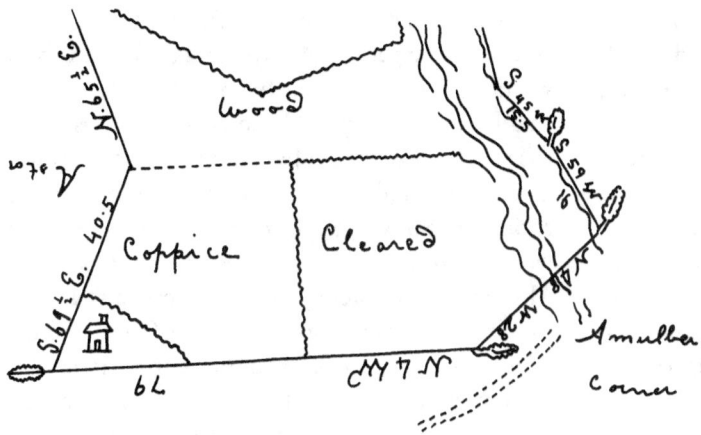

Fig. 9.3. A Kent County Orphans Court Plot. This plot shows the division of land among the heirs of Thomas Denney. Land is clearly set aside for Denney's former slave, Priscilla. Central Delaware landowners commonly set aside land for former slaves during the early nineteenth century, typically in marginal areas like the coppiced land surrounding Priscilla's small house. Kent County Orphans Court Plot Book 1, 31, lands of Thomas Denney, 1819–23. Courtesy of the Kent County Register in Chancery and the Delaware State Archives.

for them." After marriage, Mary Alston expected their husbands to provide for her daughters, but so long as they stayed single, she guaranteed them a home of their own.[13]

The room-by-room inventory of Mary Alston's estate allows us to visualize her small dwelling. It contained two rooms on the ground floor, along with a shed kitchen, and a half-story workroom on the second floor. The "inner room" contained the bulk of the large furniture, including five beds, two tables, eight chairs, and a corner cupboard. By contrast, the "outer room" held a desk, two tables, and five chairs. The single room upstairs apparently served as a workroom for textile production, containing only a spinning wheel, table, and a quantity of thread on spools.[14]

This configuration also represents a common dwelling form for many farmers in the area in the late eighteenth and early nineteenth centuries. In fact, the greatest distinction between the dwellings inhabited by different segments of the population lay in the level of interior finishes used, the type of construction material, and the number of stories, with significant increases in dwelling size and the use of brick construction occurring only among the wealthy.[15] Despite the construction of increasing numbers of larger and more elaborate houses between 1780 and 1850, the bulk of dwellings continued to fall within this category of small frame or log buildings containing between one and three rooms on the ground floor.

Persistence of this building tradition as one acceptable for either tenants or owners of middling or lower economic status can be seen in the case of James Hurlock's log dwelling, constructed about 1820. Built by Hurlock to house his young family, this dwelling held a minimal amount of furniture. Two beds, two tables, one desk, a corner cupboard, and four chairs, along with some cooking utensils, a gun, and a "Yankee clock," constituted the family's belongings.[16] After Hurlock's death in 1832, a tenant named John Jackson occupied the fifty-acre farm. Jackson tenanted the house for two years before purchasing another log dwelling and thirty acres of land nearby.[17] While he continued to farm the Hurlock property, Jackson lived in this new dwelling, which probably resembled Hurlock's closely. It contained one main room of nineteen by sixteen feet and possibly a one-story shed kitchen on the ground floor; the winder stair led to a single room upstairs open to the rafters. Simple whitewash covered the log walls, joists, and rafters. Jackson presumably considered either dwelling acceptable for himself and his family, regardless of his change in status from tenant to owner.

From the 1820s through the mid-1860s, farmers systematically adapted the earlier idea of the house and garden dwelling as a building type suitable to shelter agricultural laborers. But this was not the only option used for laborers; in fact, landowners and farm managers employed a variety of methods for housing their agricultural laborers during the nineteenth century. Some farm owners and farm managers found space for their laborers within their own homes, usually in a common sleeping room above a kitchen or workroom. Often there was no access to the second floor of the main house from these rooms. In these cases farmers provided laborers with room and board, and often some arrangement for washing and mending their clothes, as part of their wages. Farmers also hired the young sons of neighbors; these men lived at home and incurred no charges for room and board or washing and mending at the home of their employer. As a final alternative, employers might locate a family willing to board laborers for a fee.[18]

The Forkner House and its inhabitants illustrate one common solution for handling a household full of laborers. In 1857 Andrew Jackson Forkner purchased a frame dwelling on twenty acres. Forkner lived in this dwelling, and managed the adjoining 320-acre farm with the assistance of nearly a dozen servants and laborers. Forkner's house existed as a hall-parlor plan measuring roughly thirty by sixteen feet, with varying roof heights over the two ground-floor rooms. Above the larger of the two rooms, accessed by a winder staircase, lay an open stair hall and two smaller rooms of roughly equal size. This section rose two full stories in height with an attic above. Over the smaller first-floor room lay a single room, probably open to the rafters and separated from the rest of the second floor by a solid wall. This area most likely provided sleeping space for the ten single men who worked for Forkner, most of whom were recent immigrants from Ireland.[19] This method functioned efficiently so long as the laborers were men without wives and children.

But for married laborers and their families, large landowners made other arrangements, leasing them a property called variously a house, house and lot, tenement, tenant house, tenement and garden, or house and garden. Under formal arrangements like the one between John Alston and James Ryan or more informal ledger accounts, farm-laborer families acquired a separate dwelling in which to maintain their own households, as well as sufficient land to raise a garden, a cow, and a few pigs or chickens. These situations granted laboring families some measure of autonomy, perhaps in recognition of the yeoman ideal that sought to place independent householders on their own land. The dwellings built for these laborers closely matched the prescriptions for worker housing made by agricultural reform writers like J. B. Bordley, an American farmer heavily influenced by English reform writings.[20]

In 1801, Bordley described his version of a cottage suitable for laborers, stating that a farmer would find it to his advantage to provide his laborers with housing in the form of "a small very confined house called a cottage." He described the cottage as follows:

> It is recommended by an experienced farmer, that for a man, wife, and children, it be in the clear 12 by 16 feet area for the ground floor, of which 12 feet square is for the family to sit in,

dine, &c. The rest of the area of the ground floor, 12 by 4 feet, is divided for the stairs and closet or pantry. The steps are 7½ inches rise, 9 inches tread. Over the ground floor are two rooms for beds, partly in the roof, and 3 feet from the eaves down to the second floor; that is the pitch or height of the wall or side is 11 feet from the ground floor up to the eaves, of which 3 feet are in the second story or floor of room upstairs; the other 8 feet are the pitch of the room on the first or ground floor.[21]

Bordley's proposed design showed both the dwelling and the garden area, which he claimed "gives employment and comfort to the wife and children" (fig. 9.4). He specified that the garden plot attached to the house should not be so large as to tempt the cottager to put his effort into his own crops and livestock at the expense of his employer's. This, Bordley felt, could only result in the laborer becoming "uneasy in himself" instead of remaining a "decent, independent and contented laborer." While farmers in central Delaware may or may not have been influenced directly by writers like Bordley, the dwellings they constructed for their agricultural laborers bore a strong resemblance to the writers' recommendations but their garden plots were characteristically larger.[22]

The Ridgely Tenant House, built about 1850 near a small rural crossroads community called Cowgill's Corner, might almost have been built using Bordley's specifications (figs. 9.1 and 9.4). Standing one and a half stories high with a main block of roughly sixteen by eighteen feet, the house originally contained a single finished room and a shed addition on the ground floor and two rooms of equal size on the second floor. The front elevation, which faced the road, displayed only a single door and window on the ground floor. Small windows in the gable ends illuminated the second-floor rooms. The west gable end of the house held a chimney stack, most likely fitted for a stove rather

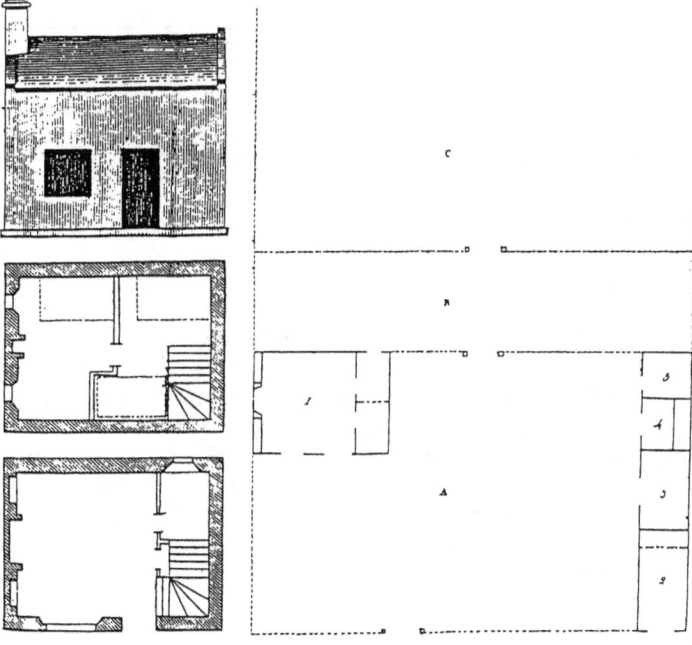

Fig. 9.4. J. B. Bordley's Plan of a Cottage and Garden for Agricultural Laborers. This plan included most of the features typical of house and gardens in Delaware. It showed not only the two-bay elevation and the one-room floor plan with a winder stair in one corner, but also the fenced-in garden and a series of small support buildings along the rear edge of the property. From J. B. Bordley, *Essays and Notes on Husbandry and Rural Affairs* (Philadelphia: Budd and Bartram, 1801). Courtesy of Morris Library Special Collections, University of Delaware, Newark, Delaware.

than a fireplace, and a narrow winder stair leading to the second floor. Built of braced-frame construction, the main block of the building displayed very plain finishes on both floors—simple whitewash-covered joists and rafters while lath and plaster insulated the walls. When first built, this dwelling sat on a wooded lot of twenty-five acres next to a second house of similar proportions, possibly following advice from reformers who advocated building laborers' cottages in pairs. Renting from Dr. Henry Ridgely, who possessed several farms in the Dover area, the tenants of this house likely worked for Ridgely's farm manager, who lived on the larger farm across the road. The two small dwellings existed as part of a row of ten similar dwellings located along both sides of the road over a distance of approximately one mile. The ten houses were owned by four multiple property owners who controlled large farms near Cowgill's Corner.

The Wharton Tenant House, also built about 1850, exemplifies a slightly more elaborate version of a house and garden dwelling. Standing a full two stories in height with a main block of roughly sixteen by eighteen feet, the house originally consisted of a single room on the ground floor and two rooms on the second floor (figs. 9.5, 9.6). In this case, the front of the dwelling is located in the gable end rather than on one of the long elevations. An early one-story shed addition projects from the rear gable. Like the Ridgely Tenant House, the gable wall of the main block contains a chimney stack with stove-pipe access and a winder stair leading to the second floor. While the basic characteristics of the house are almost identical to the Ridgely Tenant House, the Wharton Tenant House is slightly larger, better lit, and displays a higher level of finish in the form of lath and plaster on all walls and ceilings and more elaborate woodwork on doors and windows. This house and garden dwelling sat at the edge of a larger tenant farm owned by a wealthy landowner who lived about two miles away. A white farm manager rented the tenant farm, while

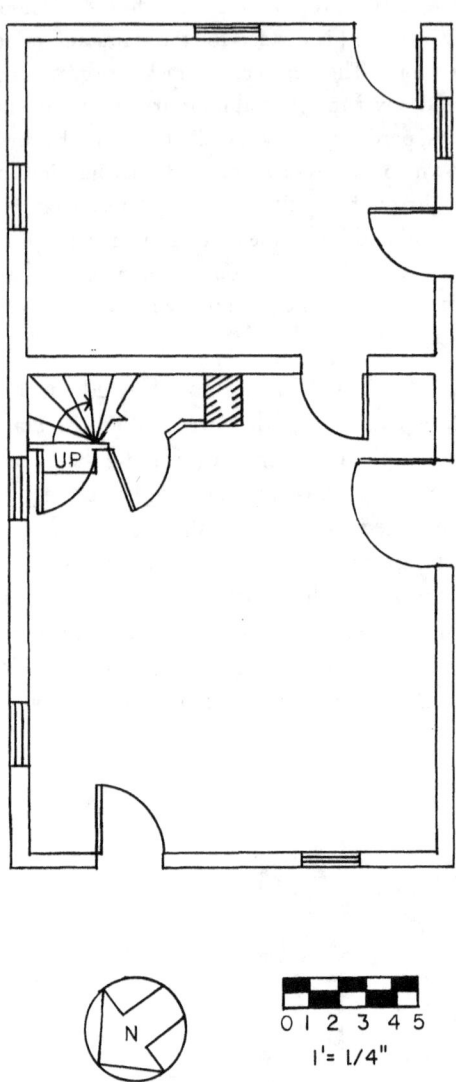

Fig. 9.5. Wharton Tenant House, Murderkill Hundred, Kent County, Delaware. Typical of many house and garden dwellings, the main room of the first-floor plan of the Wharton Tenant House measures roughly sixteen by eighteen feet, with an early shed room extending off the rear gable elevation. Deidre McCarthy, CHAE, 1995.

Fig. 9.6. Wharton Tenant House, Murderkill Hundred, Kent County, Delaware. This view of the front elevation of the Wharton Tenant House shows a variation on the typical house and garden dwelling. While most of these dwellings contained a door in the long elevation, in this case the door was placed in the gable end. Anna Andrzejewski, CHAE, 1995.

a free black man, Andrew Brown, occupied the house and garden. Brown's household included his wife and several young children, a typical family configuration of house and garden tenants. The house and garden lot contained roughly three acres, enough land for a house, small garden, a few pigs, and pasture for Brown's cow.[23]

In addition to the physical characteristics of the dwelling itself, other features of the house and garden demonstrate the influence of the changing agricultural practices and attitudes toward labor. The siting of the house and garden dwelling on the agricultural landscape of central Delaware differs significantly from the larger agricultural complexes in the area. Farm complexes, whether tenant- or owner-occupied, tended to be set back from the road. Often a tree-lined lane led up to the front of the house, and a garden with ornamental plantings spread across the front yard. These dwellings and their complexes of outbuildings occupied several acres of space in the middle of prime agricultural land. Field survey, oral histories, and documentary evidence strongly suggest that farmers in central Delaware followed very different patterns in choosing sites for house and garden dwellings. In most cases they placed the dwellings on land considered marginal in terms of agricultural value. Farmers tucked some dwellings against the trees at the edge of a planted field. In other locations, groups of two to five house and garden dwellings clustered along the road. A third alternative for placement of a house and garden dwelling called for location in or near a complex of agricultural outbuildings, sometimes even in the middle of a planted field.

While the house and garden clearly separated the laborer and his family from the farmer's household, farmers usually placed the house and garden dwelling within visual range of the main farm dwelling.[24] The farm at Barker's Landing exemplifies this practice (fig. 9.7). The main house, home to the owner of a wharf, general store, and extensive farm holdings in the late eighteenth and early nineteenth centuries, lies set back from the road along a lane and is surrounded by fields planted in wheat and corn. The farm also contained at least four house and garden dwellings. Three still stand today, forming a row along the main road from the river to the town of Magnolia, sheltered by a line of trees but still visually linked to the main house. A fourth building sat on the edge of a planted field, near a stream and a line of trees that formed a boundary for the property. Thus, while the laborers achieved some level of independence in the form of individual homes, they still carried out their

Fig. 9.7. Barker's Landing Tenant House, Murderkill Hundred, Kent County, Delaware. This is one of four house and garden dwellings associated with the main farm at Barker's Landing. Three of the dwellings formed a line along the road between the landing and the nearby town of Magnolia, while the fourth rested against the tree line of the agricultural fields. The main farm dwelling is clearly visible across the fields separating it from the row of house and garden dwellings. Rebecca J. Siders, CHAE, 1994.

activities within range of the surveilling gaze of their employer.

The location of house and garden dwellings was often affected by their portability. Depending upon their needs, farmers moved house and garden dwellings about the landscape on a regular basis.[25] The owner of the Ridgely Tenant House, for example, moved two house and garden dwellings from their original location to a site nearly a mile away; subsequent owners moved this building back to its earlier position.[26] In fact, farmers constructed the dwellings in a fashion that made them easy to move, resting them on simple pier foundations made of tree stumps, bricks, concrete blocks, and even granite slabs. The tradition of moving many types of buildings, including houses, has a long history in central and southern Delaware, and the houses built for agricultural laborers appear to be one of the few building types intentionally constructed to allow easy movement. This practice reflects the farmers' desire to maximize the amount of land available for crop rotation, but it may also be connected to the transient nature of house and garden tenants.

House and garden tenant-laborers maintained a high level of geographic mobility. They moved frequently, shifting from one landlord to another, and were sometimes so mobile that the census missed them completely. This transience generally occurred within a circumscribed region; most movement took place within an area of twelve to sixteen square miles.[27] Between 1828 and 1870, for example, John Jackson lived in at least five different locations in Little Creek, Duck Creek, and Dover hundreds, and possibly in Maryland for a short period.[28] Timothy Collins's movements document an extreme case of mobility. Between 1838 and 1850, Collins and his wife (recent immigrants from Ireland) rented a house and garden from Daniel Corbit for thirty-two dollars. Over the next decade they explored the possibilities for advancement in the Ohio Valley, living for some time in Illinois and Pennsylvania before returning to central Delaware in 1850 with their four young children.[29] Within this predominant pattern of mobility, there existed some long-term commitments between tenant and landlord. Some of Daniel Corbit's laborers remained in his tenant houses for as many as eight or nine years, sometimes consecutively, sometimes in shorter periods broken by intervals of a year or more.[30]

The construction of dwellings specifically intended to separate some laborers from the households of their employers represented only one of two key aspects of the house and garden as it emerged in the nineteenth century. The house and garden dwellings, with their distinctive physical appearance and siting, provided a visible marker on the landscape of the changing relationship between laborers and employers. One part of that changing relationship was the creation of a more business-like arrangement between tenant-laborer and landlord-employer, specifically as it appeared in lease agreements and farmers' account books. The agricultural reform movement, with its emphasis on efficiency and scientific management of farms, and the growing population of free blacks in the region played significant roles in this shift in labor relationships.

The agricultural reform movement exerted a powerful influence on the landscape of central Delaware and on the behavior of its inhabitants. While the motivation for employing these innovations varied greatly from one region to another, the effects on the landscape and on labor relationships in Delaware were very specific.[31] In their attempt to maximize crop yields and streamline the agricultural system, reformers introduced new crops, new designs for dwellings and agricultural complexes, new types of outbuildings, and fostered a new attitude toward the "business" of agriculture.[32] Through the middle decades of the nineteenth century, central Delaware was the scene of intensive improvements in farming and architectural design. Social organization, images of domestic order, and the structure of regional economic systems were reconsidered and reformed. The most visible result was a landscape transformed by new and rebuilt farm dwellings and outbuildings and the reorganization of farm complexes to separate work functions from domestic activities.

Demographic forces present in the early nineteenth century also fostered the development of the house and garden dwelling and the specific arrangements that governed its use in central Delaware. In this period, many property owners migrated out of the region, often heading to urban areas or the newly opened western frontier.[33] The farmers who stayed behind purchased the vacant properties, and a rising level of inequity in property holding developed. A small minority of wealthy landowners controlled multiple pieces of property, prompting an increased need on their part for farm tenants and laborers.[34] The new concentration of land in the hands of large property owners left many young families searching for homes.[35] This shift in population and land ownership also prompted a need to more clearly define the relationships between these different groups.

The agreements that described lease-labor and

hired-labor contracts contributed to the definition of those relationships. Opportunities for power and control existed on both sides of the house and garden lease agreement. The farmer needed the tenant's labor at crucial points in the agricultural season. In order to keep that labor available, he had to provide housing in a form agreeable to the tenant. The tenant, on the other hand, wanted a place for his family to live. He also sought a way to produce the food and other items needed to guarantee his family's survival. So he promised his labor in return for a house and garden. Both parties possessed something the other needed, giving them each some level of power and authority in the relationship. Account books and ledgers suggest that the relationships between tenant-laborer and employer-landlord retained a great deal of flexibility while still clearly defining the authority of the landowner.

Comparison of lease-labor arrangements with simple hired-labor contracts help describe the growing gap between economic groups in the region. A key difference between the lease-labor agreement and a contract for hired labor lay in the length of the contracts, which followed patterns established by the agricultural year.[36] While leases invariably lasted for a twelve-month period starting in March, the hired-labor agreements contracted for only seven or eight months, usually beginning in March or April and ending in November or December. House and garden leases covered a full year to allow for housing needs and to assure the ongoing presence of a laborer. Hired laborers, on the other hand, were only required by the employer during periods of intensive agricultural activity. Most often single men, hired laborers could maintain a higher degree of mobility, often leaving a job in the middle of the season simply because they did not like their employer.[37] Tenant-laborers, on the other hand, felt a greater obligation to the employer-landlord; if they refused to work for him, he could break the lease and evict the family.

The account book statements kept by farmers for tenant-laborers and hired hands reveal significant differences in the relationships between these individuals and their employers. Lease-labor agreements could be executed formally, like the one between John Alston and James Ryan, but in many cases the only record of the contract existed in the form of the account book kept by the farm owner or manager to document the conditions of the agreement and any debits or credits built up over the lease year. Rental payments could be made on either a yearly or quarterly basis and sometimes included firewood as part of the rental agreement. Charges for food, and other basic supplies such as seed, counterbalanced specific days worked and the particular tasks accomplished. By the end of the lease year, the account generally balanced very closely, requiring a minimal exchange of cash between employer and employee, or tenant and landlord. In contrast, on the premise of constant employment for a set period, hired hands received a monthly wage that varied greatly, depending upon whether it included room and board or washing and mending. Charges incurred against labor accounts included clothing, liquor, and other personal items, but rarely food or agricultural supplies; credits included simply the month's wages without indication of specific tasks. At the end of the contract, the employer tallied the final account by deducting any days missed for reasons ranging from illness to attendance at funerals. Hired laborers usually netted some amount of cash at the end of their contract period.

Unlike hired laborers, whose time during their contract was fully obligated to the employer, tenant-laborers were free to market their labor to other farmers in the area. They did so with great frequency, often applying their wages directly to rental payments or store accounts. Census records for 1850 and 1860, which specify occupations of the inhabitants, demonstrate the connections between house and garden households and their neighbors, both farmers and other house and garden tenants. As one follows the census taker from one household to another, a clear pattern emerges—clusters of two to four tenant-laborer households sandwiched between the households of farm owners or farm managers who provided their housing and employment opportunities.[38] House and garden tenants offered their services to many of these neighbors; most of the time they did not, in fact, work exclusively for one employer during the term of their lease contract, regardless of his primary claim on the tenant's labor at peak periods.

Many farmers became increasingly methodical about recording their expenses and obligations for labor in standardized formats such as ledgers and account books. In the late eighteenth and early nineteenth centuries, they operated on an intricate local web of exchange. Between 1830 and 1860, account book statements reveal a shift in the method of payment.[39] While early accounts documented extensive charges for both hired laborers and tenant-laborers in the form of goods and services, by the end of this period the majority of transactions took place in the form of cash. Debts and credits on both sides of the accounts appeared as cash payments rather than an exchange of services. This shift in the neighborhood economic structure may have prompted many farmers to decide that they no longer needed to maintain house and garden dwellings for laborers on their farms.

Between 1820 and 1860, a definite shift occurred in the ownership of properties that fit the house and garden framework. While in 1820, at least one-third of the dwellings were listed on a tax assessment as part of a larger farm complex, very few were described that way by 1860. Secondly, while owners occupied less than one-quarter of the dwellings in 1820, they occupied roughly half of them by 1860.[40] Beginning in the late 1850s, some farmers partitioned and sold the plots of land that held the house and garden dwellings to their tenant-laborers. Sometimes the transaction took the form of a gift in return for years of service, but most often some money changed hands.[41] The Robert Grose House, near the town of Port Penn, is situated close to a crossroads with a cluster of four other house and garden dwellings and provides a good example of this pattern. The dwelling was built about 1850 by a farmer who used it to house his tenant-laborers. Within a few years, he sold the house with its one-acre parcel of land to a free African American who continued to work for local farmers. Succeeding owners of the property, also free African Americans, maintained this practice into the early twentieth century.

While increasing numbers of house and garden properties were owned by individual laborers after 1850, not all late-nineteenth-century farm owners abandoned the house and garden as an effective method of housing agricultural laborers. Some maintained ownership of the tenant houses well into the twentieth century; in fact, some continued to build new dwellings in the same form. The White-Warren Tenant House stands on a farm occupied by the same family since the late eighteenth century. When John White died in 1825, he left a widowed mother, his own widow, and two small daughters. During the time his children remained minors, the Kent County Orphans Court oversaw the rental of the farm to generate income for their care.[42] The administration accounts document the presence of at least one house and garden dwelling on the farm in this period. When the daughters came into their inheritance they continued to operate the farm with their husbands in much the same manner. The family built new house and garden dwellings when the older ones deteriorated, following the same pattern of hall-chamber plans with second-floor spaces finished only with whitewash on rafters and studs. In the early twentieth century, three or four of the small dwellings still sat along the tree line across the field from the farmhouse.[43]

The Warren family chose not to sell off these dwellings, preferring to retain control over their laborers' housing as well as responsibility for the dwellings. By the 1930s, however, the practice of housing laborers in house and garden dwellings ceased in all but a few instances. Increased mechanization of farming and changes in crops and livestock lessened the need for laborers on many farms. The dwellings became owner-occupied homes for families whose employment came from a variety of sources other than farming, and the earlier ties of dependency between employer-landlord and tenant-laborer virtually disappeared.

The nineteenth century witnessed a multifaceted transformation of the agricultural landscape in central Delaware; the house and garden is just one element in a series of changes that reflected an increasingly hierarchical rural society. These changes affected not just large landowners like Daniel Corbit, who invested in excess of $100,000 in real estate and employed dozens of tenant farmers and tenant laborers, but also the middling landowners like John Alston. In his lifetime Alston possessed one farm of 153 acres inherited from his father. After his marriage in 1856, he controlled a second farm inherited by his wife. On a smaller scale, Alston heeded the same recommendations of agricultural reform writers followed by large landowners. He farmed his lands intensively, leaving none unimproved. He produced a range of crops including wheat, Indian corn, oats, Irish potatoes, and hay, along with butter and a small number of livestock raised for slaughter. He used horses rather than oxen to plow his fields, valuing their speed over the low-maintenance cost of oxen. Before he married in his late fifties, Alston had no wife and children to help work the farm. Instead, he relied on a combination of live-in housekeepers, hired men, and house and garden tenant-laborers to accomplish the work of farming his land.[44]

With growing levels of inequity in the ownership of property and a new orientation to markets and agriculture for profit, farmers reorganized their landholdings, buildings, and labor arrangements. In response to demographic pressures, changing agricultural practices, and the influence of agricultural reform writers, central Delaware farmers adopted the earlier idea of the house and garden as a strategy for housing their married agricultural laborers, and created a specific building form to meet their needs. The house and garden—as a housing form and as a characteristic contractual relationship—helped bring order and stratification to the agricultural landscape by making a clear statement about the physical and social place of laborers in the business of agriculture. Farmers recognized the need to create an environment that would keep good laborers in the community, but insisted that the form and appearance of the buildings reinforce the economic and social distinction between farm owners or managers and their employees. Laborers and their families valued the greater independence provided by the house and garden and the flexible leases that allowed them to seek work with several employers at once. Likewise, this form of housing represented a significant improvement for former slaves over the quarters and attic spaces they once occupied. The pronounced differences between the homes of both wealthy and middling farmers and the house and garden dwellings inhabited by their laborers served to reinforce the social and economic separations between them.

Notes

This chapter is based on the results of research conducted for the preparation of a National Register of Historic Places nomination. Funding for the nomination was provided by a matching funds grant from the Delaware State Historic Preservation Office's Historic Preservation Fund. Unless otherwise indicated, all documentary sources cited in this paper are located at the Delaware State Archives, Dover, Delaware.

The authors are grateful to many people for their help with this project. Deidre McCarthy provided invaluable assistance with fieldwork and documentary research; she also produced most of the architectural drawings for the study. Other graduate students at the Center for Historic Architecture and Engineering (hereafter cited as CHAE) also helped with fieldwork and commented on early drafts: Kirk Ranzetta, Connie Anderton, Mark Parker-Miller, and Louis Nelson. Bernard L. Herman, David L. Ames, Gabrielle M. Lanier, and Dell Upton provided valuable insights and comment on early drafts of the paper. Last, but certainly not least, we are grateful for the willing, though often bemused, cooperation of the many property owners who allowed us to prowl through their house and garden dwellings.

1. Lease from John Alston to James Ryan, Apr. 1847; John Alston Papers, Folder 2, Friends Historical Library, Swarthmore College.
2. The study area for this project encompassed the central portion of the state of Delaware, stretching roughly from the Chesapeake and Delaware Canal to a line approximately ten miles south of Dover. These dwellings tend to be identified in formal documents (such as tax assessments, property deeds, probate and court records) under a variety of names, and numbers are thus hard to quantify. Yet, informed examination of tax assessments for central Delaware between 1820 and 1860 indicates that the number of dwellings fitting the framework of the house and garden building type nearly doubled in this period. The increase in farm dwellings for the same period, in comparison, was only 51 percent. Furthermore, field surveys of the study area identified nearly one hundred surviving house and garden dwellings. Kent County Tax Assessments (hereafter cited as KCTA), 1820–22 and 1860–61.
3. See, for example, the records of Daniel Corbit and John White; nineteenth-century tax assessments and property deeds also reference these arrangements. Daniel Corbit, account books and ledgers, Historical Society of Delaware (hereafter cited as HSD); Kent County Probate Records (hereafter cited as KCPR), John White, guardianship accounts, 1825–1838; New Castle and Kent County tax assessments, 1797–1896.
4. See Sharon Clark, paper presented at 1992 Annual Meeting of Vernacular Architecture Forum, on slave spaces in Maryland. John Dickinson Papers, maps and leases, Delaware State Museums, Dover, Delaware.
5. Between 1800 and 1860 the slave population in Kent County declined from 26 percent of the African American population to only 3 percent. This proportional drop was matched by a decline in real numbers, indicating that slavery no longer formed a major force in the labor pool by the time of the Civil War. Delawareans employed both legislative action and strategic manumission (freeing adult males in a family but not women and children) to keep free African American laborers in the region. Elizabeth Homsey, "Free Blacks in Kent County, Delaware, 1790–1900," *Working Papers from the Regional Economic History Research Center,* 1979; Rebecca Siders, with Bernard L. Herman, Andrea L. Marth, Gabrielle M. Lanier, Margaret Watson, Elizabeth Bellingrath, Nancy I. Van Dolsen, Leslie D. Bashman, and Susan M. Chase, *Agricultural Tenancy in Central Delaware, 1770–1900+/−: An Historic Context* (Newark, Del.: Center for Historic Architecture and Engineering, 1991), 73.

6. Barbara Fields's examination of slave and free labor in Maryland after the Revolution links the transition from tobacco to wheat with changing labor needs that reveal similar issues to those faced in central Delaware. Barbara Fields, *Slavery and Freedom on the Middle Ground: Maryland During the Nineteenth Century* (New Haven: Yale Univ. Press, 1985).

7. The process of reform and rebuilding in central Delaware has been well-documented by Bernard L. Herman, *Architecture and Rural Life in Central Delaware, 1700–1900* (Knoxville, Tenn.: Univ. of Tennessee Press, 1987). See also Siders et al, *Agricultural Tenancy*, 96–109.

8. Lucy Simler discovered similar patterns of tenancy among the farmers of colonial Chester County, where the dwellings were known as "Garden Tenements" and cottages. Simler, "The Landless Laborer in Perspective: Part II. Inmates and Freemen: A Landless Labor Force in Colonial Chester County," paper presented to the Philadelphia Center for Early American Studies, Apr. 1986. Simler's work, particularly that in collaboration with Paul Clemens, focuses primarily on the economic and social relationships between farmers and laborers between 1750 and 1820. See Clemens and Simler, "Rural Labor and the Farm Household in Chester County, Pennsylvania, 1750–1820," in *Work and Labor in Early America*, ed. Stephen Innes (Chapel Hill and London: Univ. of North Carolina Press for the Institute of Early American History and Culture, 1988), 106–43.

9. Rebecca Siders and Pamela Edwards, *The Changing Landscape of the St. Jones Neck Under the Influence of the Dickinson Family, 1680–1850: An Exhibit Script* (Newark, Del.: Center for Historic Architecture and Engineering, 1994), 26–27.

10. These types of references appear in many property deeds and Orphans Court records for Kent County between 1780 and 1820.

11. Lands of Thomas Denney, Kent County Orphans Court Plot Book 1, 1819–23, p. 31.

12. KCPR, Israel Alston, 1794–1803.

13. KCPR, Mary Alston, will, 1803.

14. KCPR, Mary Alston, inventory of goods, 1804.

15. Bernard L. Herman, "Ordinary Mansions," in *After Ratification: Material Life in Delaware, 1789–1820*, ed. J. Ritchie Garrison, Bernard L. Herman, and Barbara McLean Ward (Newark, Del.: Museum Studies Program, Univ. of Delaware, 1988).

16. KCPR, James Hurlock, inventory of goods, 1838.

17. KCTA, Duck Creek Hundred, 1820–45; Kent County Recorder of Deeds, Book N, vol. 3: 157.

18. While these findings are specific to central Delaware, other scholars report similar patterns for housing agricultural laborers in other regions. For example, in his study of Essex County, Massachusetts, Daniel Vickers found a localized pattern of hired labor, particularly of single young men, in the eighteenth century. These men lived at home while working for a neighboring farmer, or boarded with the farmer's family. By the nineteenth century, Essex County witnessed the emergence of a system for hiring laborers on a monthly basis; these were still largely single young men living in the local community. Vickers also found an increasing number of laborers with families renting houses in the neighborhood during the first half of the nineteenth century. These patterns of hiring and housing laborers, particularly single men, in New England are also evident in the work of Richard Lyman Jr. and Jack Larkin, who stress the transient and businesslike nature of hiring agricultural laborers in nineteenth-century Massachusetts. Daniel Vickers, *Farmers and Fishermen: Two Centuries of Work in Essex County, Massachusetts, 1630–1850* (Chapel Hill and London: Univ. of North Carolina Press for the Institute of Early American History and Culture, 1994), 232–37, 298–309. Richard D. Brown, Ross W. Beales Jr., Richard B. Lyman Jr., and Jack Larkin, *Farm Labor in Southern New England During the Agricultural-Industrial Transition* (Worcester: American Antiquarian Society, 1989).

19. United States Population Census (hereafter cited as

USPC), manuscript returns for the state of Delaware, Appoquinimink Hundred, 1860, listing for Andrew Forkner.

20. John Beale Bordley (1727–1804) lived in Maryland all of his life, the child of English immigrants. After the American Revolution, he began experimenting with new systems of crop rotation and different strains of crops. Instrumental in the formation of the Philadelphia Society for the Improvement of Agriculture in 1785, Bordley served as its vice-president until his death in 1804. He published several books on farming and husbandry during the late eighteenth century, focusing on a scientific approach to agriculture and often comparing American and English farms. *Dictionary of American Biography* (New York: C. Scribner's Sons, 1958–64), 1: 460–61.

21. John B. Bordley, *Essays and Notes on Husbandry and Rural Affairs* (Philadelphia: Budd and Bartram, 1801), 389–91.

22. William Chapman's work on slave housing in the West Indies discovered similar adaptations of reform writings to local needs. William Chapman, "Slave Villages in the Danish West Indies: Changes of the Late Eighteenth and Early Nineteenth Centuries," in *Perspectives in Vernacular Architecture, IV*, ed. Thomas Carter and Bernard L. Herman (Columbia and London: Univ. of Missouri Press, 1991), 115–17.

23. KCTA, Murderkill Hundred, 1845–72.

24. This statement is based on observations of location and position during windshield survey of the study area, as well as historic maps and property deeds.

25. On the tradition of moving many different types of buildings in central and southern Delaware, see Bernard L. Herman, *The Stolen House* (Charlottesville: Univ. Press of Virginia, 1992.)

26. *Beers' Atlas of the State of Delaware, 1868* (Philadelphia: Pomeroy and Beers, 1868); interview with John Clendaniel by CHAE staff, Jan. 1995.

27. While these findings regarding mobility pertain primarily to house and garden tenants, there are indications that they apply more generally to the landless population of central Delaware as well. Both farm tenants and live-in hired laborers demonstrate some of the same patterns of mobility.

28. KCTA, Little Creek, Duck Creek, and Dover hundreds, 1822–72.

29. KCPR; Daniel Corbit, Account Books and Ledgers, 1835–60 (HSD); USPC, St. Georges and Appoquinimink hundreds, 1840 and 1850.

30. KCPR; Daniel Corbit, Account Books and Ledgers, 1835–60 (HSD).

31. Historians have been debating the issue of capitalist and anticapitalist motivations for the market revolution in general, and the agricultural reform movement in particular, in the United States for some time. Their findings vary depending upon both region and sources. Regardless of motive, these forces or events resulted in very specific consequences for the agricultural landscape of Delaware. Key sources for this debate include: Steven Hahn, *The Roots of Southern Populism: Yeomen Farmers and the Transformation of the Georgia Upcountry, 1850–1890* (New York: Oxford Univ. Press, 1983); Barbara Fields, *Slavery and Freedom on the Middle Ground: Maryland During the Nineteenth Century* (New Haven: Yale Univ. Press, 1985); Tamara Plakins Thornton, *Cultivating Gentlemen: The Meaning of Country life among the Boston Elite, 1785–1860* (New Haven: Yale Univ. Press, 1989); Christopher Clark, *The Roots of Rural Capitalism: Western Massachusetts, 1780–1860* (Ithaca: Cornell Univ. Press, 1990); Winifred Barr Rothenberg, *From Market-Places to a Market Economy: The Transformation of Rural Massachusetts, 1750–1850* (Chicago: Univ. of Chicago Press, 1992); Michael Merrill, "Cash Is Good to Eat: Self-Sufficiency and Exchange in the Rural Economy of the United States," *Radical History Review* 3 (1977): 42–71; James Henretta, "Families and Farms: *Mentalité* in Pre-Industrial America," *William and Mary Quarterly* 3d ser., 35 (1978): 2–32; and Allan Kulikoff, "The Transition to Capitalism in Rural America," *William and Mary Quarterly* 3d ser., 46 (1989): 120–44.

32. Bernard L. Herman, *Architecture and Rural Life*; Siders et al., *Agricultural Tenancy,* 96–109.
33. A study of Quaker migration from central Delaware between 1770 and 1830 reveals that in 124 out of 302 instances of migration, the immediate destination was an urban location such as Philadelphia or Wilmington. In addition, two-thirds of the families who migrated between 1790 and 1830 headed for rural destinations such as western Pennsylvania, Virginia, or the Ohio Valley. Rebecca J. Siders, "The Outmigration of Quakers from Central Delaware, 1775–1830," unpublished manuscript, 1993.
34. Siders et al, *Agricultural Tenancy,* 58–63.
35. Census data for the region between 1800 and 1860 indicates that, while the population size remained remarkably stable, average household size declined steadily from approximately nine people to six in the same period. At the same time the number of households increased roughly 45 percent in that time frame, and the single largest age group throughout the period was men and women between the age of twenty and twenty-nine. These figures suggest the presence of an increased number of young families seeking independent households—specifically the population that the house and garden system was designed to serve.
36. Tenant farm leases ran for blocks of time based on March to March years, only the number of years in the lease varied. The start and end dates for the leases were tied to the timing of planting and harvesting of crops used for rental payments. Siders et al, *Agricultural Tenancy,* 85–92.
37. John Alston's accounts, for example, show that either employer or laborer might break the contract at any point for a variety of reasons, ranging from personality conflicts to poor work. John Alston Papers, account book.
38. USPC, St. Georges and Little Creek hundreds, 1850 and 1860; see also *Beers' Atlas of the State of Delaware, 1868.*
39. The account books of Daniel Corbit, for example, clearly demonstrate this shift from the exchange of goods and services to one based on cash between 1830 and 1850. KCPR; Daniel Corbit, account books and ledgers (HSD).
40. KCTA, 1820–22 and 1860–61.
41. This information is difficult to substantiate as the documentation is buried in records other than conventional property deeds. Often it is a matter of piecing together scraps of information about an individual's employment history and changes in the tax assessment listings for his employer.
42. KCPR, guardianship accounts for the minor children of John White, 1825–40.
43. Interview with Albert Warren by CHAE staff, Jan. 1995.
44. John Alston Papers, account books and journals; United States Agricultural Census, manuscript returns for the state of Delaware, Appoquinimink Hundred, 1850 and 1860.

CHAPTER 10

Susan W. Fair

Story, Storage, and Symbol: Functional Cache Architecture, Cache Narratives, and Roadside Attractions

A house rarely stands alone in rural Alaska and other northern regions, but must be accompanied by subsidiary buildings including various types of food and gear-storage structures referred to as caches. Although these unique buildings are being replaced by modern freezers in many areas, they remain necessary and practical structures.[1] Caches are used to store a variety of goods including subsistence gear, furs, and foods.

Storage caches include two basic types still in use in most regions—elevated and underground. The cache type so familiar and endearing to most Alaskans looks like a small cabin elevated on logs or posts of various heights. The storage structure itself may be made of logs, planks, milled lumber, or even canvas or strips of birchbark over a two-by-four frame. Vertical planked caches are boxed or set on end on a platform without framing, while log caches have joined corners typical of log cabins, including dovetails, pig troughs, and other methods. The average high cache is roughly seven to nine feet square and tall enough at the gable for an adult to stoop inside. In the past, the protected area under the floor of elevated caches was often used to dry fish (fig. 10.1). After drying, the fish were generally stacked and stored in the enclosed part of the cache. Moose meat is often still cached above ground after hanging, while among northern Native peoples, marine mammal meats, oils, and berries are usually stored in underground caches. When cached, these foods remain frozen for the entire winter. Underground caches—set in permafrost—maintain a constant temperature and do not thaw.

Elevated cache types include the log or plank cache, open racks, platform caches, and tree caches.[2] The high cabin-on-post cache was probably not an indigenous form among either Eskimos or Athabaskans, who originally used racks

Fig. 10.1. A Bering Sea Eskimo Man Hangs His Nets. These nets are being placed under a hewn driftwood plank cache, c. 1900. The roof of the cache is also driftwood overlaid with scrap metal stripping and sod. Courtesy of the Thwaites Collection, Alaska State Library.

or opportunistic above-ground storage, although only further research will confirm when the transition from elevated racks to cabin-on-post caches occurred, among which groups at what times. Underground caches include semisubterranean, completely underground,[3] natural ice caves, cut block-ice caches placed near water, and the storage caches of small rodents, from which emergency foods are sometimes gathered by Native peoples.

Elevation above the ground was an important feature of the structure among many Native groups. Yup'ik and Inupiat Eskimos constructed caches of both horizontal and vertical hewn driftwood planks and logs. Elevated caches might be either very high, well above the height of the average man, or fairly low, two to three feet off the ground, depending upon local preferences and the kind of vermin or intruders the cache was designed to obstruct, which might include sled dogs, rodents, polar bears, or other humans. Among coastal Inupiat, caches were usually fairly high, and it is likely that the structures were also used at times for spotting migrating marine mammals, as driftwood towers are frequently constructed for doing so today.

Caches are built, or have been built in the past, by nearly all Alaska Native peoples and by non-Native pioneer and rural Alaskans. Among non-Natives, high-caches were generally used for the storage of tools, camping, and trapline equipment, with some spill-off storage from the main dwelling and other storage sheds. Caches in this context are purely utilitarian and are becoming obsolete. An elevated cache built and owned by pioneer trapper Kenneth Condit of Moose Pass, who came to Alaska with his wife Margaret in the 1930s when there "were no people in the country,"[4] houses dozens of different categories of items ranging from traps and snares to pots and pans, "stinkum" (rotted meat for trapping various kinds of animals), handmade signs that say "Wolf Traps Ahead" to warn snowmachiners of snares, and several packages of horsehair stuffing for a couch which was never reupholstered (fig. 10.2).

Caches are built near permanent settlements as well as at campsites. Solitary caches were frequently constructed to serve trappers, miners, and Natives who plied out-of-the-way routes; such journeys might be years apart. The building of elevated storehouses in isolated locations sometimes preceded or completely superseded construction of a cabin. Solitary caches were somewhat ephemeral in that their builders occasionally forgot where they were, making them, presumably, one of the few types of buildings misplaced on a fairly regular basis. Moses Cruikshank, a Gwich'in Athabaskan elder, once contracted with a prospector who grubstaked his gold-mining ventures by cutting firewood for steamboats which plied the Yukon. On a trip up the Chandalar River with his partner, Cruikshank discovered that Ambro had forgotten the location of one of his caches. Cruikshank recalls building their cabin, putting up wood, and hunting caribou before winter set in; then Ambro searched for his cache to no avail while his partner thawed out claims. Finally, Cruikshank went to look for the well-hidden building himself:

Story, Storage, and Symbol

Fig. 10.2. The Kenneth Condit Cache, Moose Pass, Alaska. This cache is constructed of log poles nailed to a corner "pig trough." It has swallow houses under the eaves and characteristic metal banding on the logs to keep predators away. This building is one of nine distinct structures on Condit's intensively used half-acre lot. Drawing by Hai On, Livingston Slone, Inc., Anchorage.

I took off and went up, I forget how many miles . . . upriver from there, where there's a creek come in. You look in there, why it's just a dead end. But you go in a ways, and it makes a right angle. . . . So, I follow that creek and here it open up into a wide valley, and then I see a big cache standing up there. . . . By golly, here was an old-fashioned boiler underneath that cache, and all kinds of stuff on top. . . . Well, I look in this cache, there's all kinds of stuff grub from 'way back. He cached it there years ago, you know. The tobacco was still good, it was in tin cans—"Edgeworth."[5]

Cache Types

Various types of caches were constructed throughout the north.[6] The structures are an important reflection of the cultures, past history, and region of their makers, but they are more than that. As Henry Glassie has elegantly phrased it: "Buildings, like poems and rituals, realize culture. . . . One will say he designs and builds as he does because that is the way of his people, and to do otherwise would be wrong. . . ."[7]

As an integral part of the northern cultural and natural landscape, caches also provide a backdrop for tales of thievery and murder, personal narratives like Cruikshank's, survival narratives, stories of the magical increase of food and furs among Native tellers, and speak of symbolic connections with gender. The cache symbol has also been adopted by non-Native "wannabees"—nouveau-Alaskans—on the "last frontier."[8] In this context, caches function as minor tourist attractions; what author Tom Robbins might refer to as a "roadside attraction" and what John Margolies would call commercial vernacular or, in some cases, a "ticky-tacky roadside stand."[9]

The caches discussed and illustrated here are built by Eskimo peoples including the Yup'ik, Inupiat, and Alutiiq, several Athabaskan tribes of Alaska, neighboring Athabaskans in the Canadian subarctic, and non-Natives of European extraction. In regions where the cabin-on-post cache is present, the existence, history, and meaning of this particular type attracts the imagination of residents and visitors alike (fig. 10.3).

Cabin-on-post caches are thought to have appeared in the 1870s, but the date may have been earlier, especially on the Kenai Peninsula near present-day Anchorage, deep in the interior at Fort Yukon, and on the Seward Peninsula—all of which were frequented by traders from various nations.[10]

In the subarctic, high caches may not have been constructed until the arrival of the Western Union Telegraph Expedition in the mid-1860s, after which the structures were first portrayed in carved ivory, particularly on pipes made for sale. An earlier Eskimo tool made ex-

Fig. 10.3. A Goodpaster-Big Delta Athabaskan Plank Cache. This cache is located at Goodpaster Village near the Tanana River, c. 1898. It is painted with a symbol which probably signifies ownership. Such marks were also seen frequently on tools and household goods in Eskimo communities, where they are thought to represent the track of Raven, the creator. The structure at left is a drying rack. Courtesy of the A. H. Brooks Collection (125), U.S. Geological Survey, Denver.

clusively for Native use, the drill-bow, commonly featured engravings of elevated racks and village scenes, but does not depict cabin-on-post caches.[11] The cabin-on-post form may thus have been introduced by early traders, miners, or missionaries, who would have brought with them memories of the domestic and storage structures constructed in their homelands.

Log buildings and elevated caches were popular and necessary in Scandinavia, Switzerland, and other European countries. Lapp examples from Finland include elevated racks, low caches with four legs, high caches mounted on single stumps, and semisubterranean types,[12] and it was Lapp herders who were brought to northwest Alaska by the Rev. Sheldon Jackson from Norway in 1894 to instruct Alaska Natives in reindeer husbandry. In Alaska, cache types similar to the Scandinavian forms occur. Other variations include caches with five or six legs, three posts, and caches with sprawling underpinnings for drying fish and nets.[13]

Architectural diffusion is sometimes relatively swift—new forms may simply be considered better than old ones and adopted readily.[14] It is likely, then, that before European contact, elevated racks, tree caches, and underground storage would have been pervasive among Alaska Natives and that because log cabins were not a Native house form, the high cabin-on-post cache was only introduced in the mid-1800s.[15]

Among Native peoples during traditional times, the function of the cache could be secular or sacred, or a combination of both. Tree caches and cabin-on-post caches might both contain sacred or ceremonial objects, and they sometimes held intangible intellectual property—luck in particular. Among the Holikachuk and Ingalik, the "lucky animal fur cache" housed dried lucky animal amulets which were used to predict success or failure in the coming trapping season, as well as furs which were thought to increase magically.[16] A belief in the concept of sympathetic magic influenced the contents of this type of cache. If like produced like—rich and sensuous pelts produced more furs—then the structure and its industrious owner would become even luckier.

The construction, use, and meaning of the cache and its contents were often gender-related among Native peoples. These are general statements, because I speak of many cultures and enormous areas (there are eleven Athabaskan groups and corresponding languages alone in Alaska) but if a cache or rack was owned by a man, it typically held tools or supported boats and sleds. A cache owned by a woman might house only fish (and sometimes furs). Members of one sex were sometimes not allowed to touch the cache, rack, or contents which belonged to a member of the opposite sex, presumably because of possible contamination, particularly by females.

The materials themselves used by men in cache construction and decoration were often signifiers of good fortune. Among Koyukon Athabaskans, for example, white spruce is regarded as a tree with a special inner spirit, a protector which dominates both built and natural environments—this includes the construction of caches.[17] Symbolic reference to female-owned caches or feminine contents was sometimes made through the use of red ochre trim (as among the Holikachuk and Ingalik), which in nearly all Alaska Native regions depicted fertility, renewal, and creation.[18]

Symbols of ownership, sometimes referred to as totems, were sometimes painted on cache doors, as described by Edward W. Nelson at Sabotnisky, a Yup'ik Eskimo community on the lower Yukon, in the 1870s: "I saw an oval door of hewn boards in a storehouse, one which was marked with red ochre the outline of an extended wolf skin with the rude figure of a wolf outlined on the skin and surrounded by a circle." In response to his queries about the symbol, Nelson was told that it was a "family mark . . . handed down by our fathers from very long ago."[19] Buildings often pose as metaphors for the human body and, in the case of the Native cache, for well-defined gender roles. Male energy thus dominated the construction of a cache and its exterior—the built form and mark of patrilineal ownership—just as a man might support and maintain his family, yet he was dependent upon the female, who processed, nurtured, and increased contents for the inner cache, just as she carried children within herself.

Cache Narratives and Tales

In addition to their importance as an architectural form, cache narratives and stories comprise a popular, common, and revealing type of northern oral and literary genre. These may take the form of a personal narrative, a newspaper article, a tale of mythic or didactic proportions, an instructive segment of Native family history, a non-Native fictional work, or a pictographic Eskimo engraving on ivory. When cache tales are conveyed through oral history, they vary dramatically between Native and non-Native tellers. Cache stories written down or told as anecdotes (like tales about airplane crashes and bear encounters) by non-Natives seem to be as popular today as they were when the cache was a necessity.

Native cache narratives tend to emphasize traditional rules for living, like sharing food or treating one's spouse kindly. Often, they are cautionary tales that dictate appropriate and inappropriate behaviors. These stories are still told today, especially when a family is together at a particularly important site. Many Native toponyms are thus associated literally and metaphorically with caching. Hattie Ningeulook of Shishmaref, for example, told a tale about *Sigluaq* ("storage place") hill, a bountiful locality used by former *Inaagzruk* residents. There, a powerful father and son resided; both were Inupiat shamans who could readily transform themselves into other creatures. *Anizugaksraak* and *Tizisriq* stored their game at the site and did not share it freely. Once, when a war raged outside, they transformed themselves into dogs and, another time, into vicious worms so they would not only survive the fray but preserve their stores. The tale, told on-site during berry picking to Edgar Ningeulook by his mother, illustrates well the important connections between local family history and place. It is a story about power and ingenuity, for the shamans mentioned were ancestors of her family.[20]

Caches and racks were also depicted by Yup'ik and Inupiat carvers in historical narratives engraved on ivory tusks and souvenir pipes. These village histories meticulously illustrate architecture, hunt scenes, counts of animals taken, feasts and festivals, and, often, brutal battles between Eskimo nations. They frequently show a resident escaping up a ladder into hiding in a high cache—sometimes falling to an enemy's bow and arrow. If he or she survived while others fought, this person could not have been particularly popular among remaining villagers (fig. 10.4). The detail in these engravings is significant. It is possible to tell, for example, whether the cache construction is horizontal log or vertical planks and whether the ladders are notched logs with steps or fitted with driftwood rungs.

Personal narratives collected from Native speakers often reflect on the society- and community-wide security associated with stores of food, as well as the joy tied to the hunt. Gwich'in Athabaskan elder Eunice Carney remembered with great pleasure her experiences as a girl, traveling with her people to follow great herds of migrating caribou, helping her mother cut and dry the meat, then driving dogs with her brother into Old Crow, Yukon Territory, where the family wintered: "I'm sittin' way up on top there, and we get back to Old Crow, and they put [the meat] in this cache, they call it. . . . They have four stilts that hold the thing up . . . and then they build a little house and a door there. . . . And they just take the sacks in there, and lock it up."[21]

Among Native peoples, a cache fully stocked with dry fish, various foods, or furs symbolized wealth and the talent it took to obtain it. It brought attention to the astute leader of an extended family and to his wife, who processed these goods. This family would live well during the winter.[22] Further, abundant cached food usually implied this person's ability and willingness to share, and sharing and reciprocity are among the most important aspects of Native world view. Native belief requires that captured animals be treated with ritual respect so that more will give themselves to the hunter. One Yup'ik tale tells of a starving hunter who cleans a walrus head in a specified manner, then places the head in his food cache. Five days later, the skull is covered with meat and, presumably, continues to renew itself.[23] This man and his family will thus be able to survive and—gratefully—to share. When women take similar actions, the theme is usually one of renewal, preserving a marriage or increasing a family's status.

But while some of these tales point to the historical (and traditional) success of particular individuals, others tell of failure, and many stress the

Fig. 10.4. An Ivory Pipe, c. 1870–1900. This pipe is engraved with scenes of Inupiat Eskimo village life. The structure at left is a dance house (*qazgri*) with a semi-subterranean entryway. A battle is raging outside while dancers remain unaware, although enemy warriors have invaded the entryway and one villager is escaping into an elevated cache. Chris Arend.
Courtesy of the Anchorage Museum of History and Art and Chris Arend.

dangers associated for Natives caught after European contact in a liminal social and economic position—those who straddle the line between gift and market economies. If these people did not store or share traditional foods, they risked becoming completely disenfranchised from their kin. By Alaska Native standards, to be without kin is to be completely impoverished, no matter how much cash one might earn. Dena'ina Athabaskan Jack Tyone noted such an example when discussing a local man named Talkeetna Nicolie, the last chief of his group and final Native resident of his ancestral locality. Nicolie is known to have maintained a large cache of subsistence goods and to have had so much gold that he had to "pack it around. He can't leave it home. Somebody would steal 'em." Regardless of his cache of food and his access to non-Native wealth, Nicolie was said "to have had 'no power' because he had no relatives."[24] And he had no relatives because he did not share food from his cache.

Among non-Natives, the cache tale forms a popular literary genre of both fiction and nonfiction as well as a common anecdote. Popular writers like Jack London used the cache, along with dog mushers, tamed wolves, and gritty gold miners, to make their points about the spirit of the north. And while a fully stocked cache and well-husbanded gear assure seasons of attending successfully to other pursuits, there are many tales of poorly prepared non-Native travelers (fig. 10.5).

Consequently, non-Native cache tales almost always center around two themes: heroic individualism or tragedy. The first type focuses on an isolated loner who survives because he discovers the storage cache of another individual and feeds from it. He is usually not prepared to share anything in return and may not realize that sharing is required. A symbolic sidebar to this tale type is that individual survival of this kind signifies not only that the interloper lived to tell the story but gained intimacy with the wilderness and, in isolation, became less a stranger to himself. These tales

Fig. 10.5. Non-Natives Often Built Their Caches Opportunistically. The cache pictured here on Nob Hill, Dawson City, Yukon Territory, in 1897 (right front) was constructed from a Lake Lindeman boat sawn in half and stacked together with a large door added. Courtesy of the Anchorage Museum of History and Art.

are specifically about manly rites of passage in an unforgiving environment.[25]

Three cache tales form an important core of John McPhee's nonfiction essay "Coming into the Country." In one, the copilot of a B-24 bomber survives a crash over the isolated Fortymile country in winter. Wandering about in temperatures ranging from -30 to -50 below, Leon Crane stumbles onto an abandoned, fully provisioned trapper's cabin and cache. He survives the winter on the man's stash of tools, food, and reading materials, then walks out before spring thaw, feeding from another cache along the way.²⁶ When he expresses his gratitude to the man who built the cache and saved his life, Phil Berail replies with understatement that "he was pleased that it had been useful." Thus, the act of provisioning and subsequent "sharing" was not necessarily directed toward any greater good and certainly not toward the particular survivor. Leaving a cabin comfortable and cache stocked is simply what one does in the north.²⁷

"In a Far Country," Jack London's fictional cache tale, equates the inappropriate use of cached goods with a foolish and romantic misinterpretation of the dangers of the wilderness. The story focuses on the need for northern adventurers to leave "civilized habits" behind. London contrasts the primary value of Outsiders—which might be distilled simply to "look out for yourself"—with the intrinsic agenda of Native societies, which insures that everyone will be cared for. In the tale, Percy Cuthfert sets out for the Klondike longing for adventure. Cuthfert and his partner convince their leader, son of a Chippewa mother and a French voyageur, to take an alternative route north. The two cheechakos,²⁸ chronic complainers who shirk camp chores, slow the group to a pace that leaves them far south of their goal at freezeup. When the party votes to move on, the pair stay behind in an abandoned cabin with an appended cache full of pancake flour and sugar.

The area is rich enough to support the pair through the winter, but they rely entirely on the cache contents and do not hunt. Their ill-gotten fare represents the toils of other men, and, for lack of incentive and fresh food, the men develop scurvy and begin to loathe each other.²⁹ The sugar in the cache becomes the focus of greed and paranoia, and as it is consumed each man separately hoards what remains. Ultimately, Cuthfert mistakes Weatherbee's sugar sack for his own, and the delirious partners murder each other. The failure to hunt combined with the misuse of cached goods compose an allegory underscoring the code of the north. Plunder of cached goods is permissible only if one reciprocates with a fair share of generosity and labor. Men, especially, must accept the rules of the game and the power of the land with clear thinking and congeniality. Sugar becomes a metaphor for civilization, ill-will, and bad judgment: addictive and unnecessary. London's contempt for the decadence of Western civilization and his reverence for the practicality of the Noble Savage (the guide Baptiste) are clear.

There are many northern nonfiction accounts of caches abandoned and caches robbed. Turn-of-the-century newspapers and magazines often dramatized the punishment of miners and trappers who robbed the caches of others. Alice Christoe's "A Sympathetic Journey to the Klondike" discusses a realm where "villains and heroes mingle." One photograph is entitled "Flogging a Cache Thief on the Dyea Trail." Another article, this one from Juneau's *The Alaska Transcript* (1908) proclaims: "Miners Will Lynch Cache Robber." According to the news release, the roughly 250 miners in the Innoko River district were so plagued by a cache thief known locally as "Five-Finger Jimmy," who was thought to be Athabaskan, that they were forced to cease prospecting entirely in order to protect their subsistence goods.³⁰

Although caches were sometimes abandoned for practical reasons, an abandoned cache portrayed in northern literature often stands as a symbol of desolation or a passing way of life. More pointedly, it can mean potential starvation, the failure of a family to stay together, a mining claim that produces, or even a murder. Pioneer naturalist Margaret Murie recorded in her 1956 journal at Lobo Lake that her party had stumbled onto an abandoned tree cache. Murie recorded the cache contents, then learned later that its elderly owner, Daniel Christian, had frozen to death in his cabin after falling ill and failing to keep his fire lit.³¹

The Cache as Roadside Attraction

Robert Venturi, Denise Scott Brown, and Steven Izenour, in their classic *Learning from Las Vegas,* have stated that "architecture depends in its perception and creation of past experience and emotional association . . . these symbolic and representational elements may often be contradictory to the form, structure, and program with which they combine."[32] The northern cache is an unusual structure in that it functions both as a sign, as the genuine storage cache does, and a symbol—the roadside attraction cache.

As a semiotic form, the cabin-on-post cache is repeated over and over in Alaska, even in regions where it never belonged. The functional cache is the original symbol of security, but it has also been adopted by many recently arrived Alaskans to express their embrace of an invented frontier and of Alaska Native cultures. Nonfunctional caches serve as tourist attractions, as artifacts for purchase by new residents in Alaska, and, in miniature form, for sale to visitors who take them back to the lower forty-eight. Caches, nevertheless, retain a sacred quality for many non-Native Alaskans, who remember when the cache was a necessity. Tourist attractions, as John Sears points out, "often become the sacred places of a nation or people."[33]

Roadside-attraction caches are made in a number of forms, including small yard-art caches, cache models, and cache souvenirs (cache and cabin salt-and-pepper shakers, commemorative ceramic cache plates, cache clocks, ivory carvings, and painted goldpans). More sophisticated versions of the symbol include the many cache images created by generations of Alaskan painters as one of their most romantic and salable themes. Tonalist painter Sydney Laurence rendered the cache dozens of times, just as he did Denali (formerly Mt. McKinley).[34] More recently, Anchorage artist Byron Birdsall has combined a view of Denali with a cache and fireweed, all three immensely popular representational Alaskan motifs (fig. 10.6).

On the long-distance roadside landscape, caches tend to be larger than life. Cabins and caches often serve as information centers on northern highways, for example. When used as signage, the cabin-on-post cache, the graphic symbol for the cache, or simply the term itself implies an "authentic" Alaskan experience or a connection to particular and abundant goods or services: art objects, food, or liquor (fig. 10.7). In this context, the cache functions as a link with the great frontier. Even strangers recognize this attraction, as one visiting architect-lecturer noted when he said: "I think if you're a visitor to Alaska, you think of the log cabin—not these neoclassical forms."[35] Cache signage attempts to convey to the consumer a sense of belonging, while signifying for the owner that "cache" means "cash." It also encourages Alaska residents, already xenophobic, to buy from Alaskan

Fig. 10.6. "The Great Alaskan Cliche." Anchorage artist Byron Birdsall once vowed never to paint a cache. Several years ago, tongue-in-cheek, Birdsall produced this watercolor and gave it its ironic name. It conveys everything Alaskan: blossoming fireweed flanking Denali (formerly Mt. McKinley) under a harvest moon—and the quintessential log cache. Copyright Byron Birdsall 1991, courtesy of Artique, Ltd., Anchorage.

Fig. 10.7. "The Mail Cache." This is one of many commercial ventures in Anchorage which use the cache as a name or logo. The practice implies the security of dealing with an Alaskan-owned and -operated business.

desire for the cache/cabin combination, no longer needed in heavily populated areas but a part of northern city landscapes as recently as the 1950s. Near Anchorage, many of these small caches are made in the Dena'ina Athabaskan village of Eklutna, and their owners proudly point out a connection, however disingenuous, to that community—thus demonstrating what they claim to be a "genuine" tie to Native culture.

Some of the yard-art caches are elaborate; many homeowners who move to the state build them as a first Alaskan project. And while sophis-

Fig. 10.8. Yard-Art Caches Are Common in Urban Alaskan Subdivisions. Many are made in the nearby Dena'ina Athabaskan village of Eklutna or are constructed by new Alaskan residents as their first Alaskan project.

businesses or those who pose as such. The results are often inexplicable, however, resulting in diverse commercial offerings like the Bridal Cache, the Keyboard Cache, the Book Cache, Greatland Christian Cache, the Burger Cache, and scores more.

Probably the most common roadside cache type is the miniature yard-art cache displayed on the lawns of urban and suburban Anchorage, Fairbanks, and Whitehorse, Yukon Territory (fig. 10.8). While the functioning cache is oriented to the scale of the human body, the urban cache is usually tiny: engulfed and dominated by the city but not forgotten. This form appears to reflect a ticated urban residents are often openly derisive of caches and cache motifs, regarding them as ridiculous comments on an authentic but outdated way of life, many tiny derelict caches occupy a place of stature, if not semi-sacred space in urban yards, remaining even when the houses which flank them are sold, renovated, and constructed anew. The new owners take their role seriously. They don't tear the small caches down, and they speak of the adopted structures fondly: "I feel terrible that I've let it get so run down" or "It was left here by the owner, who had a Native friend who made it." In a self-conscious way, urban Alaskans attempt to merge both with the past and the healing, rejuvenating power of the frontier, our "last great place," by placing a miniature cache at their doorstep.

Attachment to what the cache represents runs deep in Alaska. In the community of Talkeetna, a local town character places the cache models he makes outdoors near streams and marshes. He regards them as ephemeral, and he knows they will eventually be swept away into the nearby Talkeetna River.[36] A neighbor says of this man that he suffers from post-traumatic stress disorder—a result of his service in Vietnam—and that a stranger might be assaulted for removing the models from their natural home. The man himself says that he originally imagined local children might find the caches and play with them. The cache has become, for this maker in his very personal and ideal world, an untainted object.

Caches, whether functional or ornamental, reflect not only the desires, needs, and histories of their makers and users (whether Native or non-Native), but varied building preferences and cultural traditions as well. They also tell us something about who we are—as northerners—through verbal and material associations with Alaska Native peoples and non-Natives who settled the territory. The working cache in Native society, the sign, could be said, following Marcel Mauss, to embody joint functions of security, preservation, and generosity, calling forth a series of "rights and duties" including the obligation to share, the obligation formally to accept, and, finally, the necessity to reciprocate.[37] At the roadside, the cache image does not "work" in this manner, but is intended to function metaphorically.

The cache refers to the romanticized past of the last frontier, informing us not only who we are, but who we might have wanted to be. Cache stories, in whatever form they take, are an important part of the literature of the north. Not only do they tell us that Alaskans and other northern residents are survivors in a bountiful but risky place, but they often define for us the rules for living there. Thus, to categorize these humble satellite structures as unimportant, or to denigrate made-for-sale caches and cache signage spawned from the once indispensable buildings—as many Alaskans do—misses several important points. The first is worth repeating: neither a house nor a community in rural Alaska can stand alone. Its inhabitants must have appropriate survival and subsistence gear; they must have adequate food. These items will be cached in either modern or traditional manner. Cache miniatures, models, and images serve as mediators between nature—the Alaskan wilderness—and culture; they stand between the contemporary architecture of the houses, corporations, and commercial structures upon which they comment and the tiny logs from which they are constructed. There is no doubt that they are at once sign, symbol, and sentiment.

Notes

Amy Craver, Tim Cochrane, R. Duncan Kerst, and Craig Mishler commented with insight on various drafts of this essay. Dorothy Jean Ray graciously discussed with me the etching of caches and their relative dates on ivory drill bows and pipes made by Yup'ik and Inupiat Eskimos in the nineteenth century. Eileen DeVinney helped unload (and load) Kenneth Condit's cache, while Jimmie Froelich photographed. Later, Hai On did masterful drawings of the Condit homesite. DeVinney and Angela Demma contributed research assistance, photo support, and enthusiasm, as did Michael Burwell and Steve Levi. Funding for two phases of this research was obtained from the Alaska Humanities Forum and research in the Shishmaref area was supported by the National Park Service, Division of Cultural Resources, Shared Beringian Heritage Project. Craig Gerlach, Aron Crowell, Diane Brenner, and Robert Blair St. George gave support on my behalf in obtaining the AHF grant. Thank you all.

1. Most rural residents will tell you that village power plants are unreliable, and many simply keep freezers out in the cold entryway to the house if there is space. Other people, especially elders, prefer to cache their food in the traditional way because they like the taste better. Interestingly, as present-day refrigerators and small freezers wear out, they are frequently being buried in the permafrost for use as pit caches.

2. The term "tree caches" refers to several types of storage. Some solitary tree caches used mainly by Native travelers held items which were simply bagged and stowed up out of the way of predators until the trail was used again. The term also refers to tree caches in which ceremonial items are placed in an out-of-the-way location (in a tree or on a tree trunk) so contamination of persons or community will not occur or until they are used again. Among Holikachuk and Ingalik Athabaskans, for example, tree caches are used for the storage of various ceremonial and shamanistic objects: lucky animal sticks, masks, fish traps, and fortune-telling dolls. This cache location is known only to shamans and to discover it will invite ill-fortune. See Cornelius Osgood, Ingalik Material Culture, *Yale University Publications in Anthropology* 22 (1940; reprint, New Haven, Conn.: Human Relations Area Files Press, 1970), 423–29. Non-natives also use tree caches. Pioneer Alaskan trapper Kenneth Condit stores many traps and snares up the hill on a tree from his built cache. The exposure of these tools to the natural world keeps them from smelling so strongly of human contact; the contrast of their storage to the items in the main cache, which are predominantly "civilized," is significant.

3. Semisubterranean caches are usually supported with driftwood or whalebone members and faced with sod blocks among northern Eskimos, as were their homes in the past. Caches built completely underground are referred to by different terms among all groups but are usually called "pit caches" in the ethnographic literature. Both are usually lined with driftwood.

4. See John McPhee's classic northern essay "Coming Into the Country," in *Coming into the Country* (New York: Farrar, Straus and Giroux, 1976), 179–438. When I first moved to Alaska twenty years ago, this book was being discussed—almost always with hostility—everywhere, because it drew attention to government meddling in Alaskan wilderness affairs. Before this interview with Condit, I had never heard any sourdough actually say it. It sent chills down my spine and bolstered my attachment to the north. Condit's comments are from an audiotaped interview with him and with his wife, Margaret, at his home in Moose Pass, Alaska, on June 28, 1992, Tape 1, Side A, transcript p. 3.

5. Cruikshank's birthdate is thought to have been either 1902 or 1906. This life history was recorded and compiled by William Schneider, Oral History Department, Univ. of Alaska Fairbanks. Cruikshank gives no date for his work with Ambro. He took the precious tobacco back to camp to his partner; the

pair used the old boiler to sink claims for the rest of the winter. See Moses Cruikshank, *The Life I've Been Living* (Fairbanks: Univ. of Alaska Press, 1986), 70.

6. What constitutes "north" is always subject to debate in Alaska. My examination of caches is not confined to the arctic and subarctic, but addresses structures on the Kenai Peninsula south of Anchorage (just north of the Fifty-ninth parallel). Northwest Coast Indian groups, in fact, extend much farther south than that, but I have confined my studies in general to caches west, north, and in the vicinity of Anchorage, including some examples in the Yukon Territory. This is essentially a practical matter. I have done more research, both field and archival, in these regions than in others.

7. Henry Glassie, "Architects, Vernacular Traditions, and Society," in *Traditional Dwellings and Settlements Review* (1) 6 (Spring 1990): 9–21, ed. Nezar Alsayyad and Jean-Paul Bourdier. An elegant example of Glassie's premise is the Ingalik tree cache, which does not bear a name that can be translated into English. The root of the term, *tox*, however, is from *xotox*, "in the forest." See Osgood, *Ingalik Material Culture*, 337.

8. Alaskans are both proud and xenophobic. They refer to the lower forty-eight states as "Outside" with a capital O, a practice sanctioned even in the newspaper, proclaiming: "We don't care how they do it Outside."

9. See Margolies's *The End of the Road: Vanishing Highway Architecture in America* (exhibition catalogue) (New York: Penguin Books/The Hudson River Museum, 1981), 13, for discussions of professional architects versus roadside vernacular and the assertion that what "we [as Americans] are really best at is being tacky and commercial." Also, a cache is at first appearance not much like John Paul Ziller's thirty-foot-long roadside hot dog created by Tom Robbins for his *Another Roadside Attraction* (New York: Ballantine Books, 1971): "The sausage itself possesses a kind of peasant-folk serenity. . . ." (63). On the other hand, all of these objects can tell us something about ourselves, and both, as structures, function as both sign and symbol. See also Keith A. Sculle's "Oral History: A Key to Writing the History of American Roadside Architecture," *Journal of American Culture* 3 (13) (Fall 1990): 79–88.

10. Anyone researching Native Americans should consult the Smithsonian's *Handbook of North American Indians*, a major series still being compiled (general ed., William C. Sturtevant). See Edward H. Hosley, "Intercultural Relations and Cultural Change in the Alaska Plateau," in *Subarctic*, vol. 6 of *Handbook of North American Indians*, ed. June Helm (Washington, D.C.: Smithsonian Institution, 1981), 546–55.

11. Dorothy Jean Ray, who has made an intensive study of drill-bows, ivory pipes, and northern Eskimo material culture in general, informs me that in her detailed inventory of pictographs and symbols inscribed on the drill-bows, no cabin-on-post caches appear; only elevated racks occur (personal communication, Mar. 3, 1995). The earliest drill-bow collected was by the Cook expedition in 1778. See Ray, "Reflections in Ivory," in *Inua: Spirit World of the Bering Sea Eskimo* (Washington, D.C.: Smithsonian Institution Press, published for the American Museum of Natural History, 1982), 255–67. Establishing a firm origin or transition date for the covered cache may be next to impossible, as the gap between racks engraved on drill-bows, cabin-on-post caches portrayed on ivory pipes, the time and locality in which an object was actually collected (assuming that they are even known), and the photographic and ethnographic records which refer to or portray caches are all inconsistent.

12. See T. I. Itkonen, *Suomen Lappalaiset* (Helsinki: Vouteen, 1948).

13. The caption of an illustration in *Bits and Pieces of Alaskan History*, vol. 1, 1935–59 (no author, Anchorage: Alaska Northwest Publishing Co, 1981, excerpted from *Alaska Magazine's* monthly column "From Ketchikan to Barrow,") notes: "Tradition to the contrary, a one-legged cache is better and lasts

longer than the standard four-leg model, according to Sonny Holmberg. William Woolard of Medfra provided this photo of Holmberg's one-poler on the Nixon River near McGrath" (142). Caption aside, the cache looks very rickety. Also see Drew and Louise Langsner, *Handmade: Vanishing Cultures of Europe and the Middle East* (New York: Harmony Books, 1974), 127, for a beautiful photograph of a single-post Lapp cache.

14. Michael Ann Williams discusses this in *Homeplace: The Social Use and Meaning of the Folk Dwelling in Southwestern North Carolina* (Athens: Univ. of Georgia Press, 1991), 24, 26. She says that the Cherokee "abandoned traditional techniques in the building of dwellings in favor of horizontal log construction," completing the transition in about fifty years.

15. It has been suggested to me that because the log cache was not a Native building, it must have occurred only when paired with log cabins. This is not the case. Driftwood log caches of varying elevations were built by many Eskimo groups in conjunction with traditional semisubterranean sod houses; now they are constructed along with HUD housing and other modern houses.

16. See Osgood, *Ingalik Material Culture,* 333–39. He goes into detail about architecture, recording seven cache types among this group. Of the lucky cache, Osgood notes that the structure was placed "well back from a village" so other residents would not stumble across it, else they would go blind (332).

17. See Richard K. Nelson, *Make Prayers to the Raven: A Koyukon View of the Northern Forest* (Chicago: Univ. of Chicago Press, 1983), 51, and his *The Athabaskans: People of the Boreal Forest,* ed. Terry B. Dickey and Mary Beth Smetzer (Fairbanks: Univ. of Alaska Museum), especially the chart "Athabaskan Utilization of the White Spruce," reprinted from Eliza Jones, comp. Priscilla Kari, *Dena'ina K'et'una: Tanaina Plantlore* (Fairbanks: Adult Literacy Laboratory, Univ. of Alaska, 1977), 16.

18. See Osgood, *Ingalik Material Culture,* 329, and Ann Fienup-Riordan, *The Living Tradition of Yup'ik Masks* (Seattle: Univ. of Washington Press in association with the Anchorage Museum of History and the Anchorage Museum Association, Anchorage, 1996), 156–58.

19. Edward William Nelson was a field naturalist and meticulous ethnographic observer who collected more than ten thousand objects among the Yup'ik and Inupiat in the late nineteenth century. He devotes considerable attention to "villages and houses," as well as caches and to "house-life and social customs," in his Smithsonian classic *The Eskimo About Bering Strait* (1893; reprint, Washington, D.C.: Smithsonian Institution, 1983; originally published as pp. 3–518 in the eighteenth annual report of the Bureau of American Ethnology, 1896–97, part 1). See also William W. Fitzhugh and Susan Kaplan, *Inua: Spirit World of the Bering Sea Eskimo* (Washington, D.C.: Smithsonian Institution Press, published for the American Museum of Natural History, 1982), a major catalogue for the display of Nelson's acquisitions. Eskimo kinship systems are bilateral, but dominant patriarchs exist in the form of boat captains, strong men, and exceptional providers. It is thus likely that a "family mark" represents a clan or kinship group which has strong patriarchal affiliations but does not exclude female lineage.

20. Hattie Ningeulook told this story to her son Edgar at the family campsite on August 25, 1981. He taped it later, and I retell it here with his permission. See also Kathryn Koutsky, "Early Days on Norton Sound and Bering Strait: An Overview of Historic Sites in the BSNC Region," vol. 1, The Shishmaref Area, Occasional Paper No. 29, Fairbanks: Univ. of Alaska, Cooperative Park Studies Unit, 1981, for another version of the *Sigluaq* tale, told by a different Shishmaref family. Instead of emphasizing the ingenuity of the two shamans, it points up the not-sharing motif, which is not an enviable Inupiat trait.

21. I tape recorded this interview with Eunice Carney on Jan. 9, 1992, at the Institute of Alaska Native

Art offices (IANA) in Fairbanks. I thank IANA staff for their gracious assistance and for their long-standing commitment to Alaska Native art and Native artists. This audiotape was produced for the Alaska State Council on the Arts (Anchorage) *Tradition, Innovation, Continuity* project and exhibition, and will be deposited at Alaska and Polar Regions, Oral History Department, Elmer E. Rasmuson Library, Univ. of Alaska Fairbanks.

22. See Linda J. Ellanna and Andrew Balluta, *Nuvendaltin Quht'ana: The People of Nondalton* (Washington, D.C.: Smithsonian Institution Press, 1992), regarding *qeshqa* status among the Inland Dena'ina, which was aligned with "power derived from and authenticated by extensive knowledge, personal skills in acquiring wealth and organizing the productive and redistributive behavior of others, and [who] demonstrated concern and generosity for the overall well-being of those in [the chief's] charge" (268).

23. Ann Fienup-Riordan quotes here from a tale told by Tim Agartak of Nightmute, Alaska, on July 17, 1985 (NI71), retold in her *Boundaries and Passages* (Norman: Univ. of Oklahoma Press, 1994). Also see Mauss's *The Gift: Form and Functions of Exchange in Archaic Societies,* trans. by Ian Cunnison (New York: W. W. Norton, 1967).

24. See James M. Kari and James A. Fall, *Shem Pete's Alaska: The Territory of the Upper Cook Inlet Dena'ina* (Fairbanks: Alaska Native Language Center, Univ. of Alaska Fairbanks), 203.

25. In non-Native cache stories, the protagonist is never a she, while in Native tales, the main character is often an ingenious female nurturer or mediator.

26. Northern residents call this period breakup. River and shore ice break up at this time and the ground is very soft. This season and freezeup are the two most difficult travel times in the north. In the arctic, travel from island locations to the mainland cannot occur until freezeup is complete, sometimes leaving residents stranded for weeks. Winter, while it seems harsh to outsiders, is the most congenial time for travel by foot, snowshoe, dogteam, or snowmachine.

27. See McPhee, "Coming into the Country," 257.

28. A cheechako is a newcomer to the north, effectively the same as a greenhorn.

29. Jack London, "In a Far Country," in *Tales of the North* (Seacaucus, N.J.: Castle Books, 1979), 137–48.

30. See Alice Christoe, "A Sympathetic Journey to the Klondike," in *Alaska-Yukon Magazine* 7 (2) (1909): 83–97, and "Miners Will Lynch Cache Robber," in *The* (Juneau) *Alaska Transcript,* Feb. 15, 1908. The assumption that "Jimmy" is Athabaskan is based, apparently, on the fact that a miner named Fiedler had 2,200 pounds of provisions stored on Little Creek in a tent while building a cabin (and probably a cache). Fiedler went on an overnight trip and returned to find only a few beans. Only moccasin tracks led away from the scene. During this era, there was only rare acknowledgment of the fact that miners were unwelcome on many Native lands. Despite the fact that they brought low-paying cash wage labor, they trammeled the landscape and decimated the game. They also commonly purchased Native footgear, as it was much more efficient and comfortable than their own, so Jimmy might just as easily have been a white man.

31. Margaret E. Murie, *Two in the Far North* (1957; Anchorage: Alaska Northwest Publishing Company, 1978), 286.

32. The utilitarian cache is both sign and symbol of successful food gathering and potential (and required) generosity. It is a traditional necessity in rural Alaska. The roadside cache associates its keepers with frontier Alaska only symbolically. Very often, commercial cache signs do exactly what Venturi, Scott Brown, and Izenour say: "The sign at the front is a vulgar extravaganza, the building at the back, a modest necessity." See Robert Venturi, Denise Scott Brown, and Steven Izenour, *Learning from Las Vegas* (Cambridge: MIT Press, 1972), 13.

33. John F. Sears, *Sacred Places* (New York: Oxford Univ. Press, 1989), 7.
34. Kesler E. Woodward, *Sydney Laurence, Painter of the North* (Seattle: Univ. of Washington Press in association with the Anchorage Museum of History and Art, 1990).
35. This discussion, "Architects Look at Anchorage," was aired by Mike Zohatski on Mar. 10, 1993, on National Public Radio, *Morning Edition,* Anchorage, KSKA Radio.
36. See Kari and Fall, *Shem Pete's Alaska,* for the Dena'ina Athabaskan name for the Talkeetna River. The term itself provides a powerful illustration of the importance of the cache; it translates "Food is Stored River." According to Dena'ina elder Shem Pete, the river and locality "got just like a cache there—that's what the name means."
37. See Mauss, *The Gift.*

CHAPTER 11

Carolyn Torma

The Spatial Order of Work

Work is central to the study of people and culture. Work "is like the spine which structures the way people live, how they make contact with material and social reality, and how they achieve status and self esteem" writes anthropologist Herbert Applebaum.[1] What an architectural analysis provides to the discourse on work is insight into the spatial dimensions of the workplace. These spatial dimensions can be examined at many scales, or as anthropologist Sandra Wallman writes, work "can be analyzed in terms of physical transformations, social transactions, economic activities or personal identities."[2] The social status and personal aspects of work and space form the center of this study.

Architectural studies of work are quite limited. There are numerous architectural studies of the buildings that house work, the vast majority dealing with commercial structures. Architectural historians most often discuss architectural imagery, engineering features, and the public's experience of the architecture. One recent example is Daniel Bluestone's chapter on skyscrapers in *Constructing Chicago* in which he examines the phenomenon of tall buildings and their common features, including mixed-use retailing and light wells.[3] Few of these architectural studies look at the workplace as it is experienced by workers in the multiple dimensions laid out by Applebaum and Wallman. Two recent notable exceptions are Angel Kwolek-Folland's *Engendering Business: Men and Women in the Corporate Office, 1870–1930* and Susan Porter Benson's *Counter Cultures: Saleswomen, Managers, and Customers in American Department Stores, 1890–1940*. Although neither can be classified as strictly architectural history, both incorporate architectural analysis. Both also examine the workplace through the filter of gender over a historic period.

In contrast, this essay is much smaller in scope

and focuses on a single, white-collar workplace. The principal method of research is participatory observation. Indeed, this study is an exercise in how to observe architectural usage. Therefore, more attention is given to how workers use and modify space today than to how the space was initially designed to be used.

While the architectural literature is slim, other scholarly fields have an extensive literature on work ranging from anthropology and sociology to industrial psychology.[4] While this literature provides rich and interesting insights into the nature of work, the most illuminating studies for this essay—those that look closely at how people actually perform work and interact within a work environment—are hard to come by. Sociologist Arthur Stinchcombe, writing in 1990, observes, "[One] thing I want to complain about . . . is that too few people are doing field observation of work institutions."[5] He concludes later in the article, "[Our] general inclination nowadays is to summarize all a person's activity at work in an occupational name, sum up occupational names in four or five dimensions of social standing, work with things, people and data, or core versus periphery, and so miss the normative complexity that interaction at work involves."[6]

Because the work environment is such a complex world, this essay considers only several key questions: What is the nature of the work taking place? How is the work performed in spatial terms? How is space perceived and used by contemporary workers, organizational officers, and managers to play out the drama of work definition, social interaction, and status?

Background

The workplace at hand is known by its street address, "1313." In 1994, 1313 E. 60th Street, Chicago, was home to two institutions, the American Planning Association and the Center for the Study of Urban Inequality. Located on the southernmost edge of the University of Chicago campus on Chicago's south side, the building was erected in 1938 to house a new institution of social change. It was built "to bring together a group of national public administration organizations. In part because of the vision of its founders—particularly Louis Brownlow and Charles Merriam. . . ."[7] In bringing these groups together, Brownlow and Merriam aimed to develop "national associations to support the various professions working in the emerging field of public administration."[8] Indeed, the building served as the catalyst for creating new professions. One of APA's antecedents, the American Society of Planning Officials, was founded in 1938 to help give credence to the emerging field of city planning. Simultaneously, other groups, such as the American Association for Municipal Improvements, founded in 1894, grew slowly into modern professions—in this case, the American Public Works Association—complete with self-regulating professional programs.

The associations had their roots in the urban development of the late nineteenth century; many were born out of the Progressive-era impulse for professionalization and local political reform. Brownlow and Merriam wished to create a cadre of professional public administrators who, independent of the whims of local politics, would bring important civic change at the local government level while adhering to the standards set by their own professions. These professions buttressed themselves and their independent standards through the production for information, certification of members, codes of ethics, and professional loyalty.

Both men had long and distinguished political careers, as well as excellent political contacts. Merriam, a professor at the University of Chicago, and Brownlow, the first city manager of the master-planned community of Radburn, New Jersey, both held appointments in Franklin Roosevelt's administration. Financial support for the building came from the Spelman Fund created by John D. Rockefeller, who was the principal benefactor of the University of Chicago. The site chosen for the building was the south edge of the midway, which had been the entertainment district of the 1893 Columbian Exhibition. The location of 1313 was enhanced in many members' minds by its physical association with the World's Fair, an event that brought carefully planned, grand civic spaces to the attention of the American public.

By 1938 when the building opened, seventeen associations had assembled at 1313, including the American Legislators' Association (now the National Association of Housing and Rehabilitation Officials). The building was designed in an Art Deco version of the Gothic Revival style. The Gothic Revival was the official style used throughout the University of Chicago campus for many years. University tours point out that it was the last building on campus to be built in the Gothic style. Originally designed as an L-shaped building, a second ell was added in later years. Four stories in height, the building also had a spacious basement containing the lower level of the library, a lunchroom, storage and work areas. The building was clad in gray limestone (fig. 11.1). Among the building's unusual amenities was its clublike atmosphere, complete with large, paneled conference rooms, fireplaces, a complete set of china and silver, and elegant Gothic Deco trim. The rather luxurious appointments were meant to "'set an example and to give officials a sense of self-respect and dignity when they visited their association headquarters'" (fig. 11.2).[9]

Both Porter Benson and Kwolek-Folland describe the emergence of these clublike amenities in the commercial and corporate environments. Kwolek-Folland ascribes the origin of these furnishings to domestic architecture. "The initial prototypes for office fixtures probably came from the 'gentleman's study.'"[10] However, she demonstrates that the home and office influenced one another. She writes, "[thus] business fixtures reappeared transformed in middle-class kitchens and dining rooms, and the furnishings of men's domestic rooms transferred to the office."[11] Porter Benson attributes the inspiration to two sources. She points out, "department-store managers modeled the store along two complementary lines: as a home and as a downtown club."[12] But what was behind the desire for a clublike atmosphere at 1313 and, more broadly, in corpo-

Fig. 11.1. 1313 East 60th St., Chicago, Illinois, 1938.

Fig. 11.2. 1313 East 60th St., Large Meeting Room. Courtesy of Ruth Knack.

rate offices and downtown department stores? For the founders of 1313, the atmosphere mimicked the social status and exaggerated comfort of the wealthy class. Porter Benson writes that "men's clubs eased the burdens of paid employment for men."[13] So, too, the toil of public employment was dignified through the architectural amenities of a private men's club atmosphere.

Location

Within this short history lie the first spatial dimensions of the case study. First, 1313 was deliberately sited in Chicago as opposed to Washington, D.C., the home of the largest number of associations. Brownlow wrote in his autobiography: "I strongly opposed Washington . . . it would be impossible for the staff of such an organization in Washington to think in terms of state and local government, that whatever was the original purpose, the overshadowing presence of the federal government would almost compel the staff to think federally."[14]

It is important that 1313 is located not just *in* Chicago, but *on* the University of Chicago campus. Throughout the early and mid-twentieth century, the university became a center for sociology and social science research, much of it funded by Rockefeller's Spelman Fund. In 1933, for example, the Spelman Fund helped establish the Social Science Research Council, which focused on political science research and training.[15] The founders placed 1313 in proximity to this center to allow for the feeding of the professions with the best and most up-to-date social science research.

But, since its bright inception, 1313 has lost all of its original occupants except the Chicago office of the American Planning Association. The dream of social science research–based public administration also disappeared as the split between the academic and the practitioners' worlds widened. Prior to the departure of the other associations, 1313's occupants had already developed their research departments that focused on best-case practice, rather than on social science. Today APA, for example, publishes a variety of books, a magazine, an academic journal, a law digest, and several newsletters devoted to the practice of planning.

Despite Brownlow's conception, in 1991 the APA Board of Directors attempted to move the Chicago office to Washington, D.C. While Brownlow wanted independence, the board had other concerns. Sandra Wallman, the anthropologist of work, illuminates this impulse to move the office. She writes, "[I]t often matters very much *where* work is done. In some cases the work is so closely identified with a particular place that the place becomes its means of performance."[16] APA actually has two offices—the headquarters are in Washington, D.C., and the production office is in Chicago. The organization developed from the merger in 1978 between two planning organizations located in different cities. The 1991 move discussion revealed that many board members thought a unified office in Washington, D.C., would give the organization a higher profile and stronger national presence. Further, board members believed that Washington was the site for making serious social policy.

When a consultant's study revealed the move to be very costly, the board abandoned the idea. However, a disappointed board member commented that the Chicago office, in his eyes, did not have the appropriate image and appeared too academic and informal. Location as well as appearance presented problems for many members, indicating APA and 1313 had grown far from its roots.

What is the work of APA and why did the board believe that the appearance and performance of that work in Washington was so significant? APA exists to promote urban planning as an important endeavor, a legitimate profession, and as work that is the domain of planners. APA's tangible products are publications, educational events, and research. Its intangible products are threefold: service, influence, and status. These are delivered through administration, legislative and judicial planning advocacy, media promotion of planners and planning, awards, and the certification of planners.

Work, as it is defined at APA, is not simply about production; as Wallman states, it also "implies control over the values ascribed" to the work and its products.[17] This, then, is APA's central task—to increase the value ascribed to planning and to increase the social status of planners. Industrial psychologist Andrew Abbot writes that "on the basis of their successful construction of problems, professions claim certain rights from others in the work place., from the public, clients and the state."[18] Brownlow and Merriam originally constructed the problem—corrupt, mismanaged local government—their solution: a professional cadre. Today, APA continues to make claims on behalf of its planner members for such things as the right to influence legislation, the right to more public recognition, and so forth.

These ideas were implicit in the deliberation about moving the office. However, the board did not make the decision in isolation, for the decision not to merge was also influenced by a debate that developed within the organization. Since there was some logic to merging the two offices, the resistance to the merger expressed by highly vocal members must be understood from another perspective.

Consider the study by geographer Sherry Olson. Writing in "Occupational and Residential Spaces in 19th Century Montreal," she observes, "[A]s hypothesized in sociological and ecological studies . . . geographical position may specify social position, spatial distance may translate into social distance. . . ."[19] The board undoubtedly feared that APA's Chicago office suffered from its social distance from Washington, implying an inferior political and social standing. As Wallman sums up this point of view: "the true measure of peripherality [is] . . . a measure of distance from the centre of power."[20]

Further, Olson found that certain occupations clustered near the commercial and political heart of Montreal, much the same way that political consultants, the media, lobbying groups, and associations cluster around the political heart of America. Olson writes, "[M]any households [near the center of town] were associated with a high information content and a high rate of innovation, including the fickle novelties of fashion, art and luxury markets."[21] It can be suggested that APA is an organization/business with a high information content. Therefore, having both access to valued information and the perception that information has more value if it originates from Washington may have contributed to the board's deliberation. In contrast, dissenting members may have perceived the move as being a bow to mere fashion and, like Brownlow, believed that distance still gave the organization some political and intellectual independence.

The Formal and the Restricted Codes of the Work Place

Workplaces are social organizations and cultural environments. Social organization is ostensibly the mechanism that manages the production of work. The social organization is expressed formally in management hierarchies, architectural floor plans, and official graphics. Yet, within every workplace, observes sociologist Arthur Stinchcombe, are two codes of behavior—the formal and restricted (also called the informal) codes. The formal code governs through formal expressions such as job descriptions, salaries, performance evaluations, administrative procedures, and work plans, while the restricted code is both learned and governed by observed behavior and has no or very little official written life. The formal code determines the shape, size, and location of space, as well its expressed use. The restricted code determines how space is modified and much of how it is actually used. In this sense, the restricted code is the vernacular use of architecture. The formal code is intended to apply to everyone and in all situations; however, the restricted code is limited to certain circumstances and to certain people. All employees participate in the restricted code, yet only in certain circumstances.

For Stinchcombe, the study of the workplace is the study of "the ancient problem of the relations between formal and informal organization in work life. . . ."[22] An important part of understanding the relations between the two codes, writes Stinchcombe, is that the restricted code is often mistakenly "conceived to be a matter of social organization, while in reality it is cultural."[23]

Wallman elaborates further on the role of power and control in these two codes. She claims that much of "the social-cultural embroidery of work tends to be concerned with the control of one person or category of people over another—whether direct control by means of command over the actions of others, or indirect control achieved either by limiting their access to resources and benefits or by devaluing the resources and the benefits they have."[24] Theoretically, the social organization and its controls should be enough to govern the conduct of work. Wallman clearly suggests that they are not. The restricted code both reinforces and subverts the authority structure of the social organization. Porter Benson comments on the restricted code, or what she calls "work culture." "More than simply reactive, work culture embodies workers' own definition of a good day's work, their own sense of satisfying and useful labor."[25] The restricted code, therefore, plays a vital role in negotiating how work will be conducted.

If not all norms for behavior are expressed formally, how does the worker learn to perform adequately within both sets of codes? James Spradley points out: "[P]eople learn the rules for appropriate behavior. They acquire cognitive maps which enable them to interpret the behavior and events they observe."[26] All of us, then, construct maps and mental plans that allow us to function in a wide variety of circumstances, from family holiday dinners to negotiating the treacherous waters of the workplace.

Let us begin to look at the spatial manifestations of the formal code of 1313's space. The social construction of space at APA consists of three categories: the worker's private space, communal work space, and public space. The private spaces are the offices and other worksites. As designed, writing, researching, and all other tasks have the office as their primary place of work, with the department serving as the organizing framework. Located primarily on the upper floors, these workrooms are quite conventional. Each floor is organized in a U-shape, with individual rooms leading off the central corridor (fig. 11.3). There is little exceptional about the office space designs in this plan; indeed, the second-floor plan, with its characteristic double-loaded corridors, closely resembles Chicago office tower floor plans, such as the 1891–92 Ashland Block and the 1891–92 Unity Building.[27]

Among the most interesting features in the original plans for 1313 are several types of communal spaces. The first type includes the formal meeting rooms. Designed to hold meetings for officers, members, and their staff, they were used from the first for purely staff events as well. Located on the first floor, these communal areas included the clublike board room, a large meeting room with attached kitchen, and the library. At one time the staff of all the organizations—some 130 people—met in the large room for regular monthly teas. However, there is a second type of communal space that the public never entered. This space includes the showers in the basement restrooms, a ladies' lounge, and a lunchroom.

Porter Benson and Kwolek-Folland offer insight into this latter category of communal spaces. Both chronicle the rise of what Porter Benson refers to as "welfare work" in business. She describes programs originated by the managers in the first decades of the twentieth century that were intended to create a better work environment and more productive workers by providing welfare services. These included gymnasiums, self-improvement courses, lounges, and recreational activities. A small remnant of this management approach to workers is found at 1313 in the form of the showers and lounge. Designed to be used after lunch-hour exercise or bicycle rides to work, the showers by 1994 had not been used for many years. The ladies' lounge was only used occasionally.

It is useful to compare the work culture at 1313 to the workplaces that Porter Benson and Kwolek-Folland examine. While both the insurance company and department store cultures of the pre–World War II era included company-organized social and recreational events, by the 1960s, in many work environments, including APA, these had fallen out of favor. Even the staff softball team eventually disbanded. Employee habits changed, and APA employees, like workers elsewhere, may have resented what Porter Benson describes as "[department] store facilities and social programs for workers' activities that were implicitly rather than directly didactic."[28] In short, APA employees

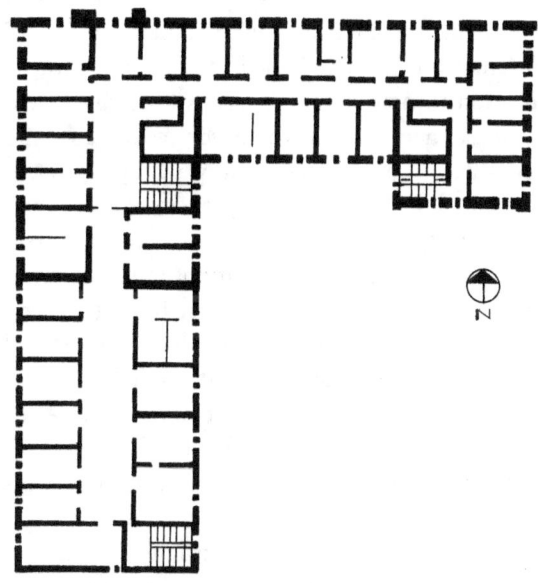

Fig. 11.3. 1313 East 60th St., Sketch of Second-Floor Plan.

did not need these types of social activities to make them into productive workers or to encourage their sense of personal value to the organization. While 1313 staff members socialize today, they often prefer to initiate their own social arrangements. This was summed up neatly by the receptionist, who said, "[N]ext week is the official lunch, today is our event." The "official" lunch was organized by management to celebrate a landmark event, "our" event was an outdoor picnic organized in an impromptu fashion over computer network mail by staff.

While communal space underwent major changes in use, the third type of space—public space—remained constant. Public spaces include the entry, hallways, elevators, stairs, and restrooms. The public areas serve to connect all three spaces. The only change over time in these spaces had to do with the declining safety of the neighborhood. The receptionist controls access through the front door with a security system that requires the public to ask for permission to enter.

What are the other spatial dimensions of the APA formal code? One formal cognitive map is the organizational chart found in the "APA Board Orientation Manual," used to explain the organization to newcomers. There is little that is exceptional here. APA has an executive director and his office, significantly, is in Washington, D.C. Beneath him are the deputy executive director, who manages the Chicago office, and the director of finance and administration. In the next tier are the departmental managers; beneath them, their professional staffs. Beneath the professional staff are the administrative and support staff. Finally, at the very bottom are the homeless of APA, the interns, who have no fixed office space of their own nor any formal recognition in the organizational chart.

This cognitive structure translates into a spatial plan where hierarchy is expressed in terms of high-, mid-, and low-status space. Specific considerations have spatial configurations, such as large versus small, and open (multi-use) versus closed (private office with door), open access versus restricted access, and assigned parking space versus no parking space.

The size of office is the first obvious status marker. Managers have the largest offices. In addition to size, location expresses high status; the boss (the deputy executive director) has the corner office and the best furniture. The next most powerful person has the office adjacent. However, while assignment of quality office space is determined along hierarchical lines, in some cases space is also allocated along longevity or seniority lines. Seniority also serves as a form of status. Parking spaces are assigned purely by seniority. Sometimes seniority and hierarchical position are merged, as in the case of managers with seniority, who have the most appealing offices.

Barriers, such as anterooms, enhance the status of space as well. They are used to distinguish public and private space and privileged space from communal space. In the corner offices of 1313, one must walk through the secretary's space to enter the director's or finance director's office.

In the formal as well as the restricted code, the control of space signifies status and power. As expected, higher-status people have control over their space and how visitors behave in that space. In some cases, the informal code will reinforce the formal code. So, while nothing is explicitly said about how to behave with a manager, it is understood. For example, managers control who enters their office by nodding, smiling, or waving a hand to signal the approved entry of the visitor. Staff members of higher or equal social status to the manager readily take a seat; staff members of lower status most often stand to conduct their business, even though the manager may make no overt sign that they are not welcome to sit down. In contrast, the receptionist must allow everyone into her space, and she is never asked for her permission to enter her space. In fact, her space contains communal equipment and materials, such as the FAX machine, the message boxes, and messenger service order forms.

Working within the social organization and its formal code is the informal code. Significantly, not all work is conducted in private offices. Many discussions resolving problems or sharing information are conducted in the public space of the hallways. Many conversations take place in the hallway outside the mail-coffee room, the receptionist's office, or the director's office, and midway between the men's and women's restrooms. Lengthy and more private conversations most often end up in the private space of an office, some with the door closed. Many of these private discussions revolve around information control, threatened status, and power. In the hallways and other public and communal areas, the interaction freely mixes social and work topics and plays a large role in the work life of APA. Collaborative work is highly valued among many managers at APA, and collaboration requires a high degree of coordination and continual "pulse talking" through verbal interaction.

Communal and public spaces are fluid and flexible. So, while first-floor conference rooms are used for staff meetings, they also host purely social events, such as farewell parties. Likewise, spaces designed as private may have communal functions. Three offices function routinely as the sites of managers' meetings and collaborative work. While collaboration is not written into the formal codes of the APA social organization, collaborative space is clearly provided.

Other dimensions to spatial use are governed almost exclusively by the restricted code—in particular, ritualized social events. In the restricted code of 1313, scheduling an event in the first-floor board room or large meeting room signals that all staff are to join in the event. The executive managers hold organizationwide staff meetings in the first-floor large meeting room. Some events, although social, are considered mandatory. For example, farewell parties or lunches with the visiting executive director are events that everyone is both invited to and expected to attend.

Not all social events occur in the large communal spaces, nor are they open to all staff. Participation and location are determined by the restricted code. For events such as birthdays judged to be more private and less monumental, a restricted work group or department celebrates the birthday. Each department develops its own "sub" code. For example, one department celebrates birthdays by throwing a little event in the office to which only fellow department members are invited. For events such as these, the celebration takes place in second-floor spaces that are converted from work to social spaces. These may be offices or the open work areas, such as the reference library in the research department.

In planning these events, a member of one department does not appropriate space in another department's territory, even if it is more convenient. So, ambiguous social events demand inventive uses of space. One example was the dual work anniversary two staff members chose to celebrate. The two staff members baked all the desserts themselves, appropriated the hallway between their two departments, and invited all staff into this public area.

Some social events are daily occurrences, such as socializing around the coffee machine. Coffee schmoozing takes place in a recognized communal space, and, no matter what the topic of conversation, everyone is welcome to join in the conversation. While standing in the coffee queue (in this case, access to the resource of coffee is determined by who gets there first), all staff greet and chat with one another (fig. 11.4). The restricted code of queue standing, which takes place in communal areas, is patterned on the coffee line. So, whether waiting to FAX a document or photocopy a bill, staff of all levels join in free-floating and often humorous or mildly complaining discussions. Other events include a regular breakfast work group. This event takes place in a somewhat secluded work area and is open to only the work group.

Breaking the Codes

Codes are never one neat set of rules by which everyone behaves. Instead, they are a jumble of different rules in which a core set of principles are agreed upon. One of the agreed-upon rules is that the rules may be inverted or flouted, as long as they do not substantially undermine the formal code and the authorized power structure.

To return to the example of the corner boss's office, a staff member must walk through the secretary's office to enter the boss's office. However, no secretary in the Chicago office considers the role of gatekeeper as part of her job, and so movement through the space is unconstrained. The restricted, rather than the formal code, governs how this space is "read" and used.

Decoration is one of the most common means of breaking with or challenging the formal code. Cartoons on office doors are a kind of genial anarchy, signaling the occupant's individuality and resistance to the seriousness of work that assigns value and status. Other decoration may indicate a personal taste that is at odds (or at least in a different arena) with the assigned role—for example, the member services' director displays calendars and other items related to fine cooking rather than membership recruitment (fig. 11.5).

Communication between staff and upper-level managers, which most often reinforces the authority of the manager, may also be subverted. While one would expect that the lower-status person must go to the high-status person's space to interact, at APA one is as likely to find the executive deputy director going to a staff member's office to talk as vice versa. Similarly, one administrative assistant, who is lower in formal social standing than her managers, cannot shut them out of her space, but she has arranged her open work space to provide a reasonably secluded work area that is difficult to penetrate. So, too, the receptionist with the least amount of control over her space is very adept at keeping staff members away from her desk and her supplies.

Some exclusivity based on professional alliances or work group cadres is readily tolerated, as in the instance of lunch-eating rituals. One cadre in a department has a series of tables where work is cleared aside for daily lunching. While other department members are tolerated at the lunch tables, no nondepartment staff are ever actually invited or openly welcomed.

Significantly, social events are used to invert the formal code and, to some degree, to mock it. Both Porter Benson and Kwolek-Folland discuss the use of social events by managers to create rap-

Fig. 11.4. Morning Coffee Line, 1313 East 60th St.

port. Like "welfare work," social events as management techniques have to tread a fine line between transparent manipulation and impulsive fun. At APA, brown bag lunches serve both a continuing education (didactic) role and a social role. Staff feel free to regard attendance as voluntary. In the social context of the brown bag lunch, the deputy executive director attends regularly and often makes self-deprecating jokes. Other staff members assert their opinions in open opposition to managers, and everyone teases, jokes, and laughs. The director attempts to assert no authority, and staff treat him as they would a colleague or friend in this setting.

What does all of this ritualized cake eating and kibitzing in hallways mean? What is the discourse? Collaboration is one key. The workspace at 1313 was designed to encourage collaboration, whether among the associations housed there or between the university and the public administration associations. While much of that original intent failed, the work style developed by APA did not. Collaborative work requires certain things.

One is a laying aside of certain hierarchical frameworks and certain status issues. Control of a collaborative project may flow through many hands and credit is claimed by the group as a whole. Collaboration, in a very real sense, defies the hierarchy of the social organization and, for that matter, defies much contemporary management practice. Yet, APA has seldom openly admitted this. Collaboration is not written into job descriptions or other formal codes. It is neither explicitly rewarded nor condemned. Rather, it relies on the informal, restricted code to allow it to take place.

Yet, if the restricted code supports collegiality, why are there so many elaborate subrules? First, the subrules help to create team loyalty. A worker cannot be loyal to everyone and both function effectively and accrue status. In the treacherous environment of work, a worker must be loyal strategically to people within the work group and often that loyalty is to department members. Porter Benson discusses the role of department-based loyalty and workplace friction in her study of department stores as well. While one-on-one of-

Fig. 11.5. Office Bulletin Board, 1313 East 60th St.

fice politics is one way of building bonds in private, ritualized social events are a more open and organizationally acceptable means of creating bonds of loyalty and work group trust.

Second, because the formal code can never fully describe or control work, the restricted code helps an employee both understand and define the work. As Porter Benson suggests, the restricted code helps the worker define the work on his or her terms. Importantly, the restricted code takes over where the formal code leaves gaps. It is the restricted code that determines how the work will get done without explicit rules governing its production.

Third, the restricted code allows for variety, creativity, and a pleasurable work environment. It also provides alternatives for status and merit, based not simply on position within the hierarchy, but also on the role assumed in the restricted code—such as holding the honor of best cook, funniest partygoer, most skillful cake decorator. It can become a means by which alternate claims to status, resources, and attention are asserted without an all-out challenge to the formal code.

Finally, the restricted code can, if not always successfully, allow resistance, anger, and other code breaking to be absorbed. Regular face-to-face social events serve to keep dissatisfaction in check.

The restricted code, Stinchcombe observes, serves as the "code of loyalty, of helpfulness, of judgments of individuals . . . (and its very) informality, then, is a matter of the character of discourse."[29] Further, he writes, "informal organization [is] . . . not social organization at all but rather a mode of discourse within all organizations."[30] The discourse allows the rules of power to be suspended at times in favor of something else. At APA that something else is collaborative work, the constantly negotiated means of work, and the value ascribed to work. Socializing allows co-workers to break down barriers and form relationships across formal boundaries. While some subgroups are departmental, not all are formed along those lines. Many subgroups are created around mutual interests. So not only is space used flexibly, but social relations are flexible, and many staff members shift almost effortlessly from one role to another as the work demands.

What is most interesting about 1313 is that, although it lost much of its original purpose and with it the status that an academic underpinning might have provided, the architecture of the building permitted spatial relationships that fostered the spirit of collaboration and sharing. This spirit persisted long after 1313's original mission was transformed.

Coda

Since this chapter was written, APA has had two new executive directors and the Chicago office moved out of 1313. While the office culture of 1313 survived the change in directors largely intact, the office move had a different impact. In December 1994 the deputy executive director announced to staff that APA would be leaving 1313 for an office in downtown Chicago in the area called the Loop. The University of Chicago would take over the building in June 1995. Vigorous debate broke out immediately among staff over how that new space should be designed.

The new office space is located on the sixteenth floor of a 1910 office building designed by Daniel Burnham. Although many communal spaces were designed into the new office, the dynamic of the office has changed dramatically. After the first twelve months of residency, the staff is still trying to develop a comfortable restricted code in a new and more formal environment.

Notes

1. Herbert Applebaum, *The Concept of Work: Ancient, Medieval, Modern* (Albany: State Univ. of New York Press, 1992), ix.
2. Sandra Wallman, "Introduction," in *Social Anthropology of Work,* ed. Sandra Wallman (London and New York: Academic Press, 1979), 1.
3. Daniel Bluestone, "A City Under One Roof: Skyscrapers, 1880–1895," in *Constructing Chicago* (New Haven and London: Yale University Press, 1991), 104–51.
4. For current thinking on the anthropology of work, see Applebaum's *The Concept of Work.* An older but excellent anthropology anthology is Wallman's *Social Anthropology of Work.* For current sociological perspectives on work, see Kai Erickson and Steven Peter Vallas, ed., *The Nature of Work: Sociological Perspectives* (New Haven: Yale Univ. Press, 1990).

    The term "industrial psychology" is somewhat outdated and refers to psychologists who study the workplace, often on behalf of management. A somewhat older publication which summarizes industrial psychology literature is Anant R. Negandhi, ed., *Work Organization Research: American and European Perspectives* (Kent, Ohio: The Comparative Administration Research Institute, distributed by Kent State Univ. Press, 1978).
5. Arthur L. Stinchcombe, "Work Institutions and the Sociology of Everyday Life," in *The Nature of Work: Sociological Perspectives,* 100.
6. Ibid., 114.
7. Ruth Eckdish Knack and Howard Rosen, "Terrible 1313 Turns 50: The Golden Anniversary of the Merriam Center," *Working Paper Series 1990, The Society for American City and Regional Planning History,* 2.
8. Ibid.
9. Ibid., 4.
10. Angel Kwolek-Folland, *Engendering Business: Men and Women in the Corporate Office, 1870–1930* (Baltimore and London: Johns Hopkins Univ. Press, 1994), 117–18.
11. Ibid., 118.
12. Susan Porter Benson, *Counter Cultures: Saleswomen, Managers, and Customers in American Department Stores, 1890–1940* (Urbana: Univ. of Illinois Press, 1988), 83.
13. Ibid., 83.
14. Knack and Rosen, "Terrible 1313 Turns 50," 6, and Louis Brownlow, *A Passion for Anonymity: The Autobiography of Louis Brownlow* (Chicago: Univ. of Chicago Press, 1958), 38.
15. Knack and Rosen, "Terrible 1313 Turns 50," 5.
16. Wallman, *Social Anthropology of Work,* 12.
17. Ibid., 2.
18. Andrew Abbott, "The New Occupational Structure," *Work and Occupations* 16 (3) (Aug. 1989): 278.
19. Sherry Olson, "Occupations and Residential Spaces in 19th Century Montreal," *Historical Methods* 22 (3) (Summer 1989): 82.
20. Wallman, "Introduction," 12.
21. Olson, "Occupations and Residential Spaces," 89.
22. Stinchcombe, "Work Institutions," 99.
23. Ibid., 100.
24. Wallman, "Introduction," 1.
25. Porter Benson, *Counter Cultures,* 228.
26. James P. Spradley, "Foundations of Cultural Knowledge," in *Culture and Cognition: Rules, Maps, and Plans,* ed. James P. Spradley (New York: Harper and Row, reissue 1987): 4.
27. Bluestone, *Constructing Chicago,* 122, 133.
28. Porter Benson, *Counter Cultures,* 143.
29. Stinchcombe, "Work Institutions," 100.
30. Ibid., 104.

PART IV

BEYOND RELIGIOUS INSTITUTIONS

CHAPTER 12

Geoffrey M. Gyrisco

East Slav Identity and Church Architecture in Minneapolis, Minnesota

Anyone who has closely observed onion-dome churches in places as disparate as Pennsylvania coal towns, Midwestern industrial cities, and Alaskan villages has found the forms intriguing. But the sources of this architecture are complex and poorly understood. While the Ukrainian churches of the Canadian plains have been well-studied and organized into basic typologies, research on similar Orthodox and Eastern church architecture in the United States has only begun.[1] The topic offers many challenges. Group identity was complex and fluid as immigrants of the Orthodox and Eastern churches often changed religious jurisdiction and even redefined their European ethnic identity shortly after arriving in America. Concurrently, they often stated that they were preserving their valued traditions as they were consciously and selectively adopting American practices.

Benedict Anderson in *Imagined Communities: Reflections on the Origin and Spread of Nationalism* presents modern nations as "imagined communities," not in the sense that they are fabricated or false, rather that the "members of even the smallest nation will never know of most of their fellow-members, meet them, or even hear of them, yet in the minds of each lives the image of their communion."[2] The development of such imagined communities is often linked with the development of a common written language and vernacular literature or the emergence of nation-states in the nineteenth century.

In *The Invention of Tradition*, Eric Hobsbawm and Terence Ranger surveyed the modern history of western Europe and the United States, showing that many cherished national symbols to which great antiquity is ascribed are recent developments. They demonstrate that the modern nation involves a constructed component that includes "fairly recent symbols or suitably tailored discourse (such as 'national history').">[3] We should expect the "invention of tradition," as Hobsbawm describes it, "to occur more frequently when a rapid transformation of society weakens or destroys the social patterns for which 'old' traditions has been designed . . . or when such old traditions and their institutional carriers and promulgators no longer prove sufficiently adaptable."[4] The peasants of the Austro-Hungarian Empire who immigrated to the industrial cities of the American Midwest underwent a rapid transformation of their social patterns. Some institutions were dropped or transformed while others were renewed or acquired.

Just as national identity is a construct subject to redefinition with new symbols, ethnic identity is also highly malleable. As the anthropologists Akhil Gupta and James Ferguson note, "people undoubtedly always have been more mobile and identities less fixed than the static typologizing approaches of classical anthropology would suggest."[5] Mary C. Waters states in *Ethnic Options: Choosing Identities in America* that "the idea that ethnic self-identification is not biological or primordial and that it involves a great deal of choice may be startling to some people, because it is counterintuitive when viewed from the popular conception of ethnicity."[6] Recognizing that ethnic or national identity is created suggests that it is a powerful force that can be molded or re-created in changed circumstances. Architecture can serve as a medium for the conscious public expression of this identity.

A striking example of this in the upper Midwest is the case of the East Slav immigrants from the Carpathian Mountains of the Austro-Hungarian Empire, from the provinces of Hungarian Subcarpathia, and Austrian Galicia and Bukovina (now falling within southeast Poland, Slovakia, eastern Hungary, western Ukraine, and northern Romania).[7] By World War I, these people became identified as Slovaks, Ukrainians, Rusyns (also known as Ruthenians), and Russians, although they were not of Russian ancestry, nor were the Carpathians controlled by Russia up to that time.

Coming from the polyglot Austro-Hungarian Empire, their church, with its traditional liturgy and customs, was a major source of immigrant community identity. When these immigrants from the Carpathians arrived in America, they were primarily of the Greek Catholic rite as it was then called (though it is now referred to as Byzantine Catholic and Ukrainian Catholic). Greek Catholicism had its roots in Orthodox Christianity. The ancient Kievian Rus' state had officially adopted the Orthodox Christianity of Byzantium in 988 A.D. In the sixteenth and seventeenth centuries, when the Carpathians were under the rule of the Roman Catholic Polish-Lithuanian Kingdom, much of the Carpathians' clergy changed allegiance to the Catholic pope, but were allowed to maintain their Orthodox religious practices. Over the centuries, depending on the place and time, Roman Catholic practices were added or deleted from what became a synthesis of Eastern and Western Christianity. Referred to as Greek Catholics (or Uniates) to distinguish them from Roman Catholics, many of the laity may never have comprehended the change in jurisdiction.[8]

For many Greek Catholics, it was not the ultimate ecclesiastical authority that mattered, but the forms of worship and customs. These included the ancient liturgies, generally chanted in Slavonic without musical instruments. Parish priests were usually married, and bishops were drawn from the ranks of monks and widowers. Painted icons played a central role in devotional life. Three-dimensional images were almost entirely absent.

By the nineteenth century, a typical form for an Orthodox or Greek Catholic church in rural Central Europe consisted of a three-part plan with a narthex or entry at the west, a compact nave often covered by a dome, and the sanctuary at the east set apart from the nave by an iconostas or icon screen. There were many variations of this basic plan. Worshippers traditionally stood or knelt without pews, although seats for the infirm were arranged along the perimeter of the nave.

Typically, the choir stood to one side of the iconostas or in the west over the entrance. Other traditional features included the *soleas,* or platform in front of the iconostas, icon stands, candle stands, a large central chandelier, and icon banners. The elaborate vestments of the clergy, clouds of incense, and the a cappella chanting involved the senses in the worship and created an impression of holy awe and mystery.

In the period from the 1880s through World War I, during the great migration of people from southern and eastern Europe, more than nine hundred thousand Greek Catholics settled in the United States, primarily in the coal towns of Pennsylvania and in the belt of great industrial cities from New York, around the Great Lakes, to Minneapolis. The first to arrive in Minneapolis in 1878 were some of the poorest peasants of western Subcarpathia. Their holdings had become too small to provide enough food for their families; laws favored the wealthy landlords; taxes were heavy; and military service was lengthy.[9] Being largely illiterate, these immigrants had not participated in the emerging national identities of Central Europe. Centuries of rule by the Poles, Lithuanians, and the Hungarians had subjected the Carpathian peasants to Roman Catholic Polish and Hungarian gentry. Speaking a dialect of Ukrainian closely related to Slovak—often confusingly referred to as Russian—further separated these peasants from their Polish and Hungarian-speaking landlords' national identities. As a consequence, Carpathian immigrants arrived in America with little sense of national or geographical identity that extended beyond the native *"okolica"* (the surrounding countryside).[10] Their sense of larger group identity came from the Greek Catholic Church. Their membership in the Greek Catholic Church defined them as *Rusyns,* or *Ruthenians,* the latinized term used by government and church officials, terms derived from the ancient *Rus'*.[11]

This church-centered ethnic identity is revealed in the immigrants' religious architecture. In 1887, a small group of Rusyns in Minneapolis, desiring to worship in their traditional way, organized themselves as a congregation. Without a priest or the permission of any ecclesiastical authority, the congregation constructed St. Mary's Church (fig. 12.1). The work was supervised by two members—Peter Dzubay Sr. and Stephen Reshetar—who were carpenters, and the rest of the parish assisted physically or financially.[12] This small, wooden church was traditional in its rectangular yet compact plan with a small narthex and choir loft at the west end and a sanctuary in the apse at the east end. The western tower has a steeple rather than a dome and

Fig. 12.1. St. Mary's Church, Minneapolis, Built 1887. Courtesy of St. Mary's Cathedral.

may reflect the tradition of church building in the Carpathians, where many churches have western towers without domes. On the other hand, it may represent an intent to make St. Mary's look more like a typical small American church. Certainly, the Gothic Revival windows, perhaps ready-made from a sash-and-door factory, are standard features of American churches; the Greek Catholic and Orthodox churches of Europe almost never employed the pointed arch.[13]

The simplicity of the church is probably the result of the congregation's meager financial resources and possibly also reflects the limited skills of Dzubay and Reshetar. Variously listed in city directories and census records as house carpenters and day laborers, they were twenty-three and eighteen years old respectively when they supervised the construction of the church. As they were only twenty and seventeen years old when they immigrated, they could not have been highly skilled in the tradition of finely crafted log building of the Carpathians and may have been more familiar with simple American balloon-frame construction. The congregation may also have preferred American balloon-frame construction over European log construction. Only after World War II was the exquisite log-building tradition of the Carpathians expressed in the lower forty-eight states.[14]

Many of the Greek Catholic and Orthodox churches built in the next forty years in Minnesota and northwest Wisconsin followed the form of St. Mary's. Each was erected by a different builder, who probably only constructed a single Greek Catholic or Orthodox church. For example, St. Mary's in Two Rivers, Minnesota, built in 1900, employs a short western tower with a long nave.[15] St. John the Baptist, built in Huron, Wisconsin, in 1907 has massing and composition similar to St. Mary's, Minneapolis, with a simplified onion dome.[16] Holy Assumption in Lublin, Wisconsin, built in 1926 has the characteristic three unevenly spaced Gothic Revival windows on each side of the compact nave.[17] Holy Trinity, built in 1921 outside Thorp, Wisconsin, has the same basic form with similar though evenly spaced fenestration and a modified Gothic Revival steeple similar to St. Mary's, Minneapolis.

After constructing their church, the parishioners of St. Mary's wrote the bishop of Presov, in Saris county, in Transcarpathian Hungary (now Slovakia) requesting a priest. Eventually the bishop sent Father Alexis Toth, a seminary faculty member at Presov and a widower. When Father Toth presented his credentials to the Roman Catholic archbishop of St. Paul, John Ireland, the archbishop, rejected the validity of the Greek Catholic rite, refused to recognize Toth's standing as a priest, and ordered St. Mary's parishioners to attend the Polish Roman Catholic Church though they understood neither the language nor the Latin rite.[18] As the parishioners owned the church property, Father Toth continued to serve. Father Toth and his congregation sought out the Russian Orthodox bishop for North America in San Francisco, who ultimately accepted this new parish of immigrant Slavs into his diocese, which then consisted primarily of native Alaskans, along with a few Russians, Greeks, and Syrians. Matters of religious jurisdiction were of less importance for this immigrant congregation than its objective of preserving its traditional form of worship. As Keith Dyrud noted in his book, *The Quest for the Rusyn Soul*, the congregation sought a church that "had the 'look and feel' of the church back home."[19]

While the congregation maintained its traditional liturgy, the church architecture was soon remodeled reflecting Orthodox practices and Russian influence. The Orthodox bishop ordered the replacement of the existing altar with a free-standing, square Orthodox-type altar. Fourteen statues representing the stations of the cross were removed. A multi-tiered iconostas reaching to the ceiling in the manner of Orthodox churches of Russia and Ukraine was added. The congregation purchased the four large icons for the first tier in

L'viv, in Austrian Galicia, reflecting continuing ties to Central Europe. The Holy Synod of Russia gave two series of small icons for the second and third tiers, confirming new ties to Russia (fig. 12.2).[20]

Father Toth left Minneapolis in 1893 for the Anthracite region of Pennsylvania, leading a growing movement from the Greek Catholic Church to the Russian Orthodox Church. Archbishop Ireland's response to the establishment of a Greek Catholic parish was typical of the responses of the Irish-dominated American Roman Catholic hierarchy, which vigorously opposed the establishment of the Greek Catholic rite in America. Facing such opposition by Roman Catholic bishops, in the ensuing decades more than 300,000 persons in more than 125 parishes likewise changed jurisdiction from the Greek Catholic Church to the Russian Orthodox Church. When these congregations joined the Russian Orthodox Church, they generally did so without their Greek Catholic priests. Most of the priests remained Greek Catholic or ultimately returned to the Greek Catholic Church. Father Toth was the leading exception.[21] The Orthodox Church in America confirmed Toth's central role by canonizing him in 1994 as St. Alexis, "Confessor and Defender of Orthodoxy in America."

While the immigrants clearly initiated the movement to Russian Orthodox jurisdiction, the Russian Orthodox Church and the Tsarist government quickly supported it with financial aid and talented priests from leading Russian seminaries. They also sent Rusyn immigrants to Russia for seminary training. As one of the most prominent parishes of the Russian Orthodox Church in America, St. Mary's was assisted by an annual subsidy from the Tsarist government as well as by the Holy Synod. The churches in America were affected by geopolitical circumstances in Europe. At the time, Russia aimed to seize the Carpathians from Austria-Hungary; the Russian government's support for the growth of the Russian Orthodox jurisdiction in America was part of an attempt to obtain the loyalty of the Rusyns in both America and in Europe.[22]

By the time St. Mary's, Minneapolis, burned in 1904 and was to be rebuilt, the congregation had not only changed religious jurisdiction, but also had adopted the overlay of a new Russian cultural identity and political orientation. As Father Toth proclaimed in his sermon when the congregation was accepted into the Russian Orthodox Church,

Fig. 12.2. Iconostas, St. Mary's Church, Minneapolis, 1892. Courtesy of St. Mary's Cathedral.

"we are uniting spiritually with our own brothers—not only in faith, but by nationality—with the great, mighty, glorious, pious-Russian Nation!"[23] Though there were few if any Russians in the congregation, Father Toth's successor was a priest from Russia. As St. Mary's parishioners became literate, most became part of the Russian and American "imagined" communities. Evidence of this appears in church-sponsored activities. The parish provided a reading room stocked with books and newspapers published in Russia or in America with a Russophile perspective and classes in Russian. In 1910 the priest reported thirty-five reading classes in Russian with more than eighty persons participating.[24] Large majorities of first- and second-generation families sent their children to church school where they were taught Russian, "which the parents themselves did not understand."[25] Seemingly only a minority of members of later generations were of the opinion that the congregation was "inclined too slavishly to emphasize purely Great-Russian customs, dances, music and ignore our real Rusyn ethnic heritage."[26] The majority of the congregation adopted this Russian overlay. The foremost scholar of the Minnesota Rusyns, Keith Dyrud, states that "many third-generation descendants of Rusyn immigrants know only that they are Russian. Yet they are curious when they discover that their grand-parents' home village is in eastern Czechoslovakia."[27]

Seventeen years after the construction of the original church, the congregation was better established. There were far more members, and they had greater outside assistance. The congregation had the resources to construct a monumental and highly symbolic building. To express the newly adopted Russian association, the parish built a Russian church designed by Victor Cordella (fig. 12.3).[28] Cordella was a master of creating church buildings to symbolize the chosen identities of their Slavic immigrant congregations. Cordella was born in 1872 in Krakow, a university town and the leading Polish intellectual center. His mother was Polish; his father was an Italian sculptor. Cordella acquired a professional foundation in an outstanding education that exposed him to multiple Central European architectural traditions, cultures, and national identities. He attended graded schools in Austrian Poland; then the Royal Art Academy in Krakow; and finally studied technology under Prof. Michael Kowalczuk in L'viv. L'viv was a Polish-language university town, with a thriving artistic community, and the center of Ukrainian national consciousness. After coming to the United States in 1893, Cordella began his architectural training in the office of the still little-known Cass Gilbert, in St. Paul, Minnesota.[29]

Fig. 12.3. St. Mary's Church, Minneapolis, Built 1904. Courtesy of St. Mary's Cathedral.

For St. Mary's, Cordella designed a Russian-type church, based on a photograph of Omsk Cathedral, though Omsk is located in Russian Siberia, more than one thousand miles from the region of origin of St. Mary's parishioners.[30] Given the priest's role in the parish, the Russian priest Constantine Popoff may have played a major role in the selection of the design. The plan is an elongated Greek cross, the longer western arm accommodating the choir loft and narthex. A large cupola and dome cover the nave. Set beyond the west arm of the cross is a tower rising taller than the central dome, topped with an onion dome drawn up into a great flame or *flèche*. The basic plan and form was one favored for larger Russian Orthodox churches of the second half of the nineteenth century and early twentieth century from eastern Ukraine to Siberia, Alaska, and the United States. On the interior of the new St. Mary's Church, a large multi-tiered iconostas held a set of icons painted at the Russian monastery of Sergievsky, evidence of the new and close connection with Russia (fig. 12.4).

At the same time St. Mary's was becoming a Russian church, it intentionally was becoming an American church in selected ways. Pews filled much of the nave. Pictorial stained glass was one of the outstanding artistic features of the new church. While designs incorporate elements of Orthodox iconography, the use of stained glass, common in America, was foreign to European Orthodox practice. In historic photographs of St. Mary's, the American flag was proudly displayed along with the traditional icon church banners. Further evidence of the Americanization of the Russian Orthodox Church was the translation of the liturgy into English in 1906, and the use of the English liturgy at the first Orthodox seminary in America, operated at Minneapolis from 1905 to 1912.[31] Initially organizing a church to preserve their familiar Slavonic liturgy and church customs and to worship with those whose language they understood, St. Mary's parishioners adopted an overlay of a new Russian cultural identity while selectively becoming American.

In the early twentieth century, Greek Catholic Rusyns from Subcarpathia continued to arrive in Minneapolis. Some did not feel comfortable with St. Mary's new Russian identity nor with the traditional Orthodox practices that the Russian priests had substituted for Greek Catholic practices. In 1907 these Rusyns obtained the support of Arch-

Fig. 12.4. Iconostas. St. Mary's Church, 1907. Courtesy of St. Mary's Cathedral.

bishop John Ireland and founded St. John the Baptist Greek Catholic Church to preserve their Rusyn identity and Greek Catholic practices. The congregation initially occupied a small wooden former Polish Roman Catholic church a few blocks from St. Mary's. In 1926 the congregation had grown and prospered sufficiently that it could afford to make an architectural statement of its identity. The congregation hired Victor Cordella, who designed a building that reflected the Greek Catholic blend of Orthodox and Roman Catholic practices characteristic of the time. This Romanesque-style structure with a central western tower differed little from the designs of Roman Catholic churches for western European congregations. The design included Roman Catholic style confessionals and no iconostas. Architectural references to Eastern Christian traditions were primarily limited to the fine Byzantine-style mosaics on the interior of the apse and the faceted dome on the tower, a detail favored by Slavic congregations.[32]

Political developments in Europe and migration patterns resulted in additional East Slav churches in Minneapolis. Another group of East Slav immigrants to Minneapolis arrived a little later. This group, including some intellectuals, came from Austrian Galicia following the rise of a renewed Ukrainian national identity. The Ukrainian national revival, a movement confined to intellectuals until the mid-1890s, became a popular movement after the turn of the century. Austria encouraged the movement in Galicia. Russia, which controlled much of Ukraine, attempted to suppress the movement as part of a centuries-old policy of forced integration of all its subjects into Russian culture. Thus, the Galicians newly arrived in America were unsympathetic to the new Russian identity of St. Mary's parishioners and initially joined St. John's Greek Catholic Church with Rusyns from Subcarpathia. But they soon realized that they differed from the Subcarpathian Rusyns in dialect, cultural and political experiences, and in the way they sang the services. These differences were not apparent until they lived together in the United States. The differences perceived in Minneapolis existed at the national level and ultimately resulted in the establishment of separate ecclesiastical administrations for Rusyn Greek Catholics and Ukrainian Greek Catholics. In 1912 the Minneapolis Galicians organized St. Constantine's Parish, desiring to maintain a Ukrainian identity and remain Greek Catholic.[33]

Victor Cordella in 1913 designed a church which was an expression of their ethnic identity and faith (fig. 12.5). The design was based on elements of churches with rich historical and symbolic meaning that the congregation wished to be identified with. It did not nor was it intended to re-create the modest rural churches attended by many of the

Fig. 12.5. St. Constantine's Church, Minneapolis, Built 1913. From *St. Constantine's Ukrainian Catholic Church, Minneapolis, Minnesota*, Dedication Souvenir Book (1972).

parishioners or their parents in Galicia. The church was built on an elongated Greek cross plan. It had a central dome with a pair of smaller domed towers embracing the gabled front facade and portico. The lower portions of the church are in the Romanesque and Classical Revival styles; the squat, angular onion domes set on low cupolas are readily identifiable as Ukrainian Baroque Revival. Tellingly referred to in some Ukrainian sources as "Cossack Baroque," these domes refer to the great monuments of Ukrainian Baroque architecture, built in the sixteenth through the eighteenth centuries. In a nation that was repeatedly invaded and subject to foreign rule, this last great period of independence under the democratic warrior Cossack state remains one of the most powerful images of Ukrainian identity. The interior of St. Constantine's reflected the congregation's Greek Catholic heritage, with a fusion of Roman Catholic and Orthodox elements. It had an altar rail not an iconostas. Yet, it had a wide central aisle leading to an icon stand and some icons.

The composition of Greek cross plan, central dome, and towers set into the front corners, often with a pedimented portico, was common for Ukrainian churches throughout the United States and Canada. Generally, the style is predominantly Romanesque or Classical Revival and usually the domes are set on low cupolas. Examples contemporary with Cordella's design for St. Constantine's include St. John the Baptist Ukrainian Catholic Church in Pittsburgh (1894) and Saints Cyril and Methodius Ukrainian Catholic Church in Olyphant, Pennsylvania (1908).[34] Numerous churches of generally similar design are found across the Ukrainian-settled belt of Manitoba, Saskatchewan, and Alberta, built throughout much of the twentieth century by Ukrainian architects and builders.[35]

In 1970, when the original St. Constantine's Church was demolished, the design of the new structure by Hills, Gilbertson, Fisher, and Born again employed the Greek cross plan with a central dome and inset corner towers topped with smaller domes (fig. 12.6). This version of the design is more Byzantine in style, with half-round domes. Again, the dome is used as a symbol of national identity, this time the central dome displaying the Ukrainian national colors, blue and yellow, and Ukrainian national symbol, the trident.[36] The new church, built following the decree of Vatican II that the members of Eastern Rite churches should "preserve their lawful liturgical rites" and "take pains to return to their ancestral ways," contains an iconostas based on ancient models.[37]

While St. Mary's, St. John's, and St. Constantine's are striking examples of the use of architecture by Minneapolis East Slavs to symbolize religious and ethnic identity, they were not the only choices for churchgoing East Slavs. Another group of East Slavs left St. Constantine's in 1925 to establish St. Michael's Ukrainian Orthodox Church. As a parish in the new Ukrainian Autocephalous Orthodox Church, it was both Ukrainian and Orthodox. The parishioners could be Orthodox without adopting the Russian overlay as St. Mary's Church had. They could be Ukrainian without accepting the increasingly latinized Greek Catholic practices at St. Constantine's Church. The exterior architecture of the church does not show this identity but may have been intended to express other aspects of the congregation's identity. The church has a basilican plan with a single western tower resembling a Roman Catholic church more than an Orthodox church. The exterior is not distinctly Ukrainian in design. Yet, this form was favored for new Ukrainian Orthodox churches constructed in Chicago, the Anthracite region of Pennsylvania, and Australia.[38] The form of the building may reflect the Ukrainian Orthodox Church's emphasis on reform, which replaced Slavonic with Ukrainian in the liturgy, modernized the style of clerical dress, and established democratic self-governance.[39]

Religious and political developments of the

Fig. 12.6. St. Constantine's Church, Minneapolis, Built 1970.

mid-twentieth century produced new definitions of identity, resulting in new congregations and new options. In 1942, changes in the Greek Catholic rite led a group of St. John's parishioners to form a new independent parish, St. Michael's Greek Catholic Carpathian Orthodox Church. Yet another option emerged in 1956, when a group of Ukrainian and Russian post–World War II exiles established St. Panteleimon Russian Orthodox Church. These exiles did not feel comfortable with the Americanized members of St. Mary's Church. The Bolshevik Revolution and Communist interference in the Russian Orthodox Church had led a group of exiled bishops to establish the Synod of the Russian Orthodox Church Outside Russia independent of the patriarch of Moscow.[40] The post–World War II exiles who fled communism placed themselves under this staunchly anticommunist synod. They remodeled a former Protestant church as an Orthodox church with the addition of onion domes and a bell tower. The East Slavs of Minneapolis were not compelled to attend a particular church with a particular cultural or political orientation because there was no alternative. In Minneapolis (unlike Europe) they had many choices, and they selected a parish with a particular definition of their ethnic identity, religious practices, language or dialect, and political orientation. Their selection, however, was often influenced by their European experiences or by those of their parents.

In conclusion, if national and ethnic identities are imagined and created through language, literature, symbols, and material culture, individuals or groups can choose to maintain or change their national or ethnic identity. The complexity of the Orthodox and Eastern church building forms reflects the complexity of this history as some immigrants maintained their European identities while hundreds of thousands of other immigrants changed religious jurisdiction and adopted new ethnic identities soon after their arrival in America. Newly adopted traditions were combined with traditions that genuinely extended back a thousand years in Central Europe. In the process the immigrants maintained some traditional customs and building forms, but adopted some new ones associated with new European identities and others of American origin as they adapted to life in the United States. Thus, in the process of church building, we can see the construction—and reconstruction—of ethnic identity.

Notes

The author would like to acknowledge the assistance of Roman Stepchuk and the other members of the staff of the Immigration History Research Center and Northwest Architectural Archives at the University of Minnesota; John Barns, Orthodox iconographer and iconologist, in Harrisburg, Pennsylvania; Wendy Harris, archaeologist; John Radzilowski, historian; Thomas Hubka, professor of architecture; the anonymous reviewer of this article; Myron Stachiw and the Ukrainian hosts on the VAF tour of Ukraine; and the many clergy and laity who kindly opened their churches for study and photography.

1. Anna Maria Baran, *Ukrains'ki Katolyts'ki Tserky Saskachevanu/Ukrainian Catholic Churches of Saskatchewan* (Saskatoon, Saskatchewan: Ukrainian Catholic Church Council of Saskatchewan, 1977); Basil Rotoff, Roman Yereniuk, and Stella Hryniuk, *Monuments to Faith: Ukrainian Churches in Manitoba* (Winnipeg, Manitoba: Univ. of Manitoba Press, 1990); Walter Daschko, "Ukrainians in Ontario," *Polyphony: The Bulletin of the Multicultural History Society of Ontario* 10 (1988): 191–201.
2. Benedict Anderson, *Imagined Communities: Reflections on the Origin and Spread of Nationalism* (London: Verso, 1983), 15.
3. Eric Hobsbawm, "Introduction: Inventing Traditions," in *The Invention of Tradition,* ed. Eric Hobsbawm and Terence Ranger (New York: Cambridge Univ. Press, 1983), 14.
4. Ibid., 4.
5. Akhil Gupta and James Ferguson, "Beyond 'Culture': Space, Identity, and the Politics of Difference," *Cultural Anthropology* 7 (1992): 9; Werner Sollors, ed., *The Invention of Ethnicity* (New York: Oxford Univ. Press, 1989).
6. Mary C. Waters, *Ethnic Options: Choosing Identities in America* (Berkeley: Univ. of California Press, 1990), 16–17.
7. Paul Robert Magocsi, *Ukraine: A Historical Atlas* (Toronto: Univ. of Toronto Press, 1985).
8. James S. Dutko, "The Uniate Question Revisited," *Your Diocese Alive in Christ: The Magazine of the Diocese of Eastern Pennsylvania, Orthodox Church in America* 10 (2) (Summer 1994): 55–62; Keith S. Russin, "The Very Reverend Mitred Archpriest Alexis G. Toth," *Your Diocese Alive in Christ* 9 (3) (Winter 1993): 50–51.
9. Keith P. Dyrud, "The East Slavs—Rusins, Ukrainians, Russians, and Belorussians," in *They Chose Minnesota: A Survey of the State's Ethnic Groups,* ed. June Drenning Holmquist (St. Paul, Minn.: Minnesota Historical Society Press, 1981), 408; John Bodnar, *The Transplanted: A History of Immigrants in Urban America* (Bloomington: Indiana Univ. Press, 1985), 10; Walter C. Warzeski, "The Rusin Community in Pennsylvania," in *The Ethnic Experience in Pennsylvania,* ed. John E. Bodnar (Lewisburg, Pa.: Bucknell Univ. Press, 1973), 175–77.
10. Kathleen Neils Conzen, David A. Gerber, Ewa Morawska, George E. Pozzetta, and Rudolf J. Vecoli, "The Invention of Ethnicity: A Perspective from the U.S.A.," *Journal of American Ethnic History* 12 (1992): 22.
11. Constantin Simon, "Before the Birth of Ecumenism: The Background Relating to the Mass 'Conversion' of Oriental Rite Catholics to Russian Orthodoxy in the United States," *Diakona* 20 (1986): 131.
12. St. Mary's Russian Orthodox Greek Catholic Church, Minneapolis, Minnesota, *Golden Jubilee Album of the St. Mary's Russian Orthodox Greek Catholic Church, Minneapolis, Minnesota* (1937); *75th Anniversary Diamond Jubilee 1887–1962, October 12, St. Mary's Russian Orthodox Greek Catholic Church, Minneapolis, Minnesota* (1962); Constance J. Tarasar, ed. *Orthodox America 1794–1976: Development of the Orthodox Church in America* (Syosset, N.Y.: The Orthodox Church in America, 1975), 48.
13. Rotoff, Yereniuk, and Hryniuk, *Monuments to*

Faith, 16; David Buxton, *The Wooden Churches of Eastern Europe: An Introductory Survey* (Cambridge: Cambridge Univ. Press, 1981); Titus D. Hewryk, *Masterpieces in Wood: Houses of Worship in Ukraine* (New York: The Ukrainian Museum, 1987).

14. Twelfth Census of the U.S. Schedule No. 1—Population, Hennepin County Enumeration District 6, Sheet 5 and Enumeration District 8, Sheet 5 (1900); *Davison's Minneapolis City Directory for 1892-93* (Minneapolis, Minn.: Minneapolis Directory Company), 419; ibid., *1895-96*, 864; ibid., *1897*, 991; ibid., *1896*, 925; ibid., *1899*, 399, 1084; Hewryk, *Masterpieces in Wood*, 98–104.

15. Dyrud, "East Slavs," 408–9.

16. Built under direction of carpenter Joseph Burnette or Bennett. "Site Files," Division of Historic Preservation, State Historical Society of Wisconsin, Madison.

17. Built under direction of carpenters Simeon and Feodor Dubiak. Holy Assumption Orthodox Church, Lublin, Wisconsin, *Holy Assumption Orthodox Church, Lublin, Wisconsin, Seventy Fifth Anniversary 1908-1983* (1983).

18. St. Mary's Russian Orthodox Greek Catholic Church, *Golden Jubilee*; St. Mary's Russian Orthodox Greek Catholic Church, *Diamond Jubilee*; Tarasar, *Orthodox America*, 49–53; Keith P. Dyrud, *The Quest for the Rusyn Soul: The Politics of Religion and Culture in Eastern Europe and America, 1890–World War I* (Philadelphia: Balch Institute Press, 1992), 65–66.

19. Dyrud, *Quest for the Rusyn Soul*, 105.

20. Tarasar, *Orthodox America*, 53; St. Mary's Russian Orthodox Greek Catholic Church, *Diamond Jubilee*, 23.

21. Dyrud, *Quest for the Rusyn Soul*, 71–73.

22. Ibid., 66–73; Tarasar, *Orthodox America*, 177.

23. George Soldatow, trans. and ed., *The Writings of St. Alexis Toth, Confessor and Defender of Orthodoxy in America*, vol. 3 (Minneapolis: Archives of Americans of Russian Descent in Minnesota Press, 1994), 75.

24. Dyrud, "East Slavs," 407–8; Dyrud, "The Rusin Question in Eastern Europe and in America, 1890–World War I," (Ph.D. diss., Univ. of Minnesota, Minneapolis, 1976), 174.

25. Alex Simirenko, *Pilgrims, Colonists, and Frontiersmen: An Ethnic Community in Transition* (London: Free Press of Glencoe, Collier-Macmillan Limited, 1964), 171.

26. Dyrud, "East Slavs," 407–8.

27. Dyrud, *Quest for the Rusyn Soul*, 86.

28. Horace B. Hudson, ed., *A Half Century of Minneapolis* (Minneapolis: Hudson Publishing Company, 1908), 128; Fourteenth Census of the U.S. Schedule No. 1—Population, Hennepin County Enumeration District 73, Sheet 20 (1920); *Davison's Minneapolis Directory 1905*, 453–54. The U.S. Census of 1900 records that both of Victor Cordella's parents were born in Austrian Poland; however, the U.S. Censuses of 1910 and 1920 record that his father was born in Italy and his mother in Poland.

29. Subsequently, Cordella was associated with several other architects in St. Paul: W. H. Dennis, W. B. Dunnell, Charles R. Aldrich, and then joined in partnership with Christopher A. Boehme, according to Hudson in *A Half Century of Minneapolis*. Later, Cordella was in partnership with Edwin E. Olson, according to Minneapolis Directory Co., *Minneapolis City Directory 1925*.

30. St. Mary's Russian Orthodox Greek Catholic Church, *Diamond Jubilee*, 27.

31. St. Mary's Russian Orthodox Greek Catholic Church, *Golden Jubilee*; St. Mary's Russian Orthodox Greek Catholic Church, *Diamond Jubilee*; Tarasar, *Orthodox America*, 52, 109–10; Dyrud, "East Slavs," 409.

32. Dyrud, "East Slavs," 409–10; St. John the Baptist Eastern Rite Catholic Church, Minneapolis, Minnesota, *Golden Jubilee: Catholic Church of St. John the Baptist, Eastern Rite, 1907-1957, Minneapolis, Minnesota* (1957). St. John the Baptist Church can be attributed to Cordella based on similarities with documented works.

33. Dyrud, *Quest for the Rusyn Soul,* 59, 87–118; Dyrud, "East Slavs," 410; Bohdan P. Procko, "Soter Ortinsky: First Ruthenian Bishop in the United States, 1907–1916," in *The Other Catholics,* ed. Keith P. Dyrud, Michael Novak, and Rudolph J. Vecoli (New York: Arno Press, 1978); Simon, "Before the Birth of Ecumenism," 136–38; on liturgical differences, see Paul Robert Magocsi, "Made or Remade in America?: Nationality and Identity Formation Among Carpatho-Rusyn Immigrants and their Descendants," in *The Persistence of Regional Cultures: Rusyn and Ukrainians in their Carpathian Homeland and Abroad,* ed. Paul Robert Magocsi (New York: Eastern European Monographs, Columbia Univ. Press, 1993), 166.
34. Julian K. Jastremsky, "Ukrainian Architecture in America," in *The Ukrainian Heritage in America,* ed. Walter Dushnyck and Nicholas L. Fr.-Chirovsky (New York: Ukrainian Congress Committee of America), 273–74, 286. Sts. Cyril and Methodius Church, Olyphant, Pennsylvania, was designed by Lester Davis.
35. In Manitoba, examples include Ukrainian Catholic Church of St. Andrew, Winnipeg, and Ukrainian Orthodox Cathedral of St. Mary Protectress, Winnipeg, 1925. In Saskatchewan, examples include the following Ukrainian Catholic churches: St. Nicholas, Bedfordville, 1951; Transfiguration, Beckenham, 1940–44; Ascension, Swan Plain, 1938; St. George, Melville, 1939; St. John the Baptist, Arran, 1925; St. Michael, Gronlid, 1949–51; St. George, Prince Albert, 1957–60; St. Basil, Regina, 1928; Saints Peter and Paul, Canora, 1960–64; Sacred Heart, Wynyard, 1953–54; Nativity of the Blessed Virgin Mary, Whitebeech, 1949. In Alberta, there is one example, the Ukrainian Orthodox Cathedral of St. John, Edmonton. For photos and descriptions of the churches in Saskatchewan, see Barran, *Ukrainian Catholic Churches of Saskatchewan,* for photos of the other churches, see Peter Kardash, *Ukraine and Ukrainians* (Melbourne, Australia: Fortuna Company, 1988). Perhaps the church most similar to St. Constantine's is the Ukrainian Orthodox Church of the Holy Virgin's Protection in Melbourne, Australia, built in 1961 by architect Ivan Slynko. The striking similarity suggests a common and currently unknown source of inspiration for both designs. See illustration in Kardash, *Ukraine and Ukrainians,* 194.
36. St. Constantine's Ukrainian Catholic Church, Minneapolis, *St. Constantine's Ukrainian Catholic Church, Minneapolis, Minnesota, Dedication Souvenir Book* (1972).
37. Dutko, "The Uniate Question Revisited," 60–61.
38. St. Michael's Ukrainian Orthodox Church, Minneapolis, *St. Michael's Ukrainian Orthodox Church, Minneapolis, Minnesota, 1925–1975* (1975), 37; Dyrud, "East Slavs," 414–17; Myron B. Kuropas, *The Ukrainian Americans: Roots and Aspirations 1884–1954* (Toronto: Univ. of Toronto Press, 1991), 306–13; in George Korbyn, *Ukrainian Style in Church Architecture* (Arcadia, Calif.: George Korbyn: 1983), 116–19, see, for example, St. Michael's Ukrainian Orthodox Church, Scranton, Pennsylvania, Orthodox Church of the Holy Spirit, Coatesville, Pennsylvania, 1924, Saints Peter and Paul Orthodox Church, Chicago, Illinois, and St. Mary Protectress Orthodox Church, Sydney, Australia, 1962.
39. Orest Subtelny, *Ukraine: A History,* 2d ed. (Toronto: Univ. of Toronto Press, 1994), 401.
40. Dyrud, "East Slavs," 414, 416–17.

CHAPTER 13

Tania Martin

Housing the Grey Nuns: Power, Religion, and Women in fin-de-siècle Montréal

Marie-Anne Falardeau, like many women in turn-of-the-century Montréal, chose an option other than "marriage, motherhood and spinsterhood": the convent.[1] A member of *les Soeurs de la Charité de l'Hôpital-Général de Montréal*, more commonly known as *les Soeurs Grises*, or the Grey Nuns, Marie-Anne came from a modest background. She was born to French-Canadian parents and baptized in St-Henri Parish, a largely working-class district of Montréal, on March 25, 1854.[2] As an adolescent, she dreamed of becoming a Sister of Charity and entered the religious community at age sixteen. Here, Marie-Anne Falardeau assumed the name Soeur Saint Jean de la Croix. Despite weak health, Soeur Saint Jean de la Croix's career followed a typical path for nineteenth-century women religious.[3] She seems to have been particularly gifted in art and architecture, however, a trait for which she was remembered in her obituary when she died on November 17, 1921.

Convents were among the most prominent religious buildings in nineteenth-century Montréal. Today, these sophisticated buildings dot Montréal's urban landscape. As a legacy of the power of the Roman Catholic Church in Québec, they form a part of our cultural and architectural heritage.[4] Broadly defined as a form of collective housing for a religious community of women, convents were not solely residential in function, but accommodated hospitals, schools, orphanages, hospices, and workshops of various sorts, under the same roof. In Québec, religious orders of women operated many important institutions in the fields of health, education, and welfare, until the 1960s wave of secularization.[5]

The Mother House of the Grey Nuns belongs to a long-established tradition, a veritable typology of conventual buildings. A brief survey of Montréal's convents reveals their common architectural traits. Generally made of local building materials, these four- to five-story gray limestone structures comprised an H- or E-shaped plan bisected by a central chapel, recalling the institutional architecture of the French Ancien Régime. Their mansards or gable roofs were pierced with dormer windows, and tripartite windows punctuated the ends facing the street. In addition, most convents featured stark, unornamented facades, symmetrically composed with aligned bays of uniformly sized openings.

The Mother House was designed by prominent Montréal architect Victor Bourgeau (1809–1888). This essay, however, focuses on the users, rather than on the intentions of the building's famous designer; with this approach we can explore how large women's institutions operated. The division of the plans, among other aspects, communicates the nuns' distinct way of life, one that questioned the traditional boundaries between public and private imposed by society in turn-of-the-century Montréal. Construction of the Mother House began in December 1868 and stretched over a period of thirty years. Each wing or phase of the complex was initiated as funds became available or as the need for space dictated. Soeur Saint Jean de la Croix's meticulously recorded accounts of the changes in the physical fabric and the organization of the convent permit us to reconstruct the evolution of this collective dwelling arrangement.

Soeur Saint Jean de la Croix's chronicles and drawings trace the history of the building from its initial construction to c. 1909.[6] Her immense (approximately 7 by 8 feet) ink-and-gouache drawings convey not only the plan about 1900, but also represent the technology and indicate demolition and renovation work with impressive technical clarity. Water, steam, and sewage systems were carefully indicated and color coded. Note, for example, the *privées disparues*; these toilets served the dormitories of the orphan boys when the community first occupied the building in 1871 (fig. 13.1).

The Mother House of the Grey Nuns is situated in what was the English-speaking, middle-class, residential quarter of St-Antoine. As rendered in an engraving signed by Eugène Haberer that appeared in the December 1875 issue of the *Canadian Illustrated News*, the convent is centered on its own block, approximately 200 feet from Dorchester Boulevard (now Blvd. René Lévesque), a major east-west thoroughfare in downtown Montréal (fig. 13.2).[7] The overall dimensions of this monumental, five-story building were impressive. Generous floor-to-floor heights were 14 and 15 feet in the first and second stories

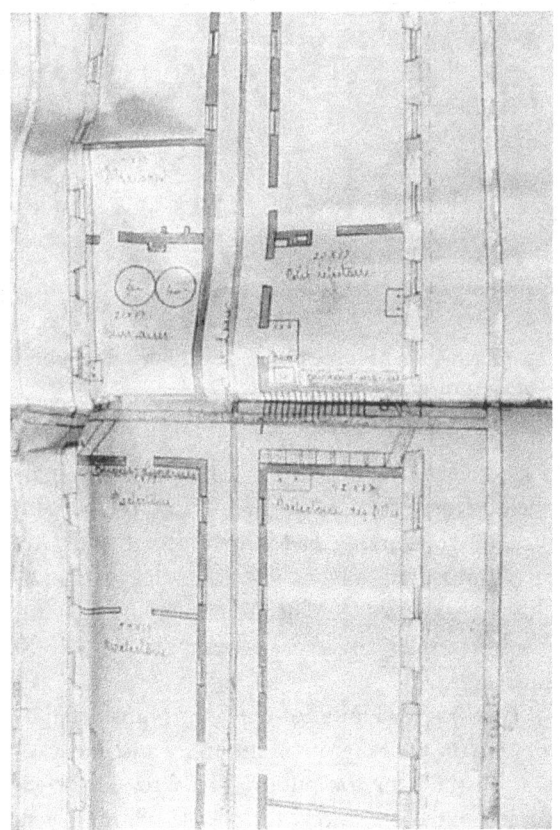

Fig. 13.1. Mother House of the Grey Nuns, Montréal, Canada. Drawing by Soeur Saint Jean de la Croix, c. 1900. Courtesy of ASGM MM 1190 rue Guy Plans Doc. 76A, *Relevé des Plans de l'Hôpital Général de Montréal, soubassement, divisions en 1900*.

Fig. 13.2. Mother House of the Grey Nuns. Engraving by Eugène Haberer, 1875. From *Canadian Illustrated News*, April 12, 1875.

respectively. The convent's east-west facade parallel to Dorchester measured 573 feet; the perpendicular wings along St-Mathieu Street and Guy Street measured 308 and 436 feet respectively (including galleries).[8] When completed, this immense complex covered an area of some 84,000 square feet.[9]

The Mother House of the Grey Nuns acted as a home for the religious community and as a general hospital for the public. The Grey Nuns accommodated and cared for people whom others in Montréal society could not: the alienated, the elderly, the blind, the orphaned, the mentally ill, the infirm, abandoned infants, and other persons in need. In 1905, for example, Soeur Saint Jean de la Croix recorded 324 women making up the religious community. She also noted 185 elderly persons, 60 girls, 340 orphans, 52 abandoned infants, 26 paying boarders, and 33 male employees as residents of the convent.[10] In all, over 1,000 people lived in the Mother House at the turn of the century.

Such a large and diverse population required an effective form of organization. Located at the center of the complex, the *chapelle de l'Invention de la Sainte-Croix* functioned as the primary organizational device. It essentially divided the H-shaped convent into two blocks. The sisters, along with their employees, inhabited the eastern block along Guy Street, whereas the destitute inmates occupied the western block, along St-Mathieu Street.[11] Further analysis of the plans reveals that each block was subdivided into wings, organized by levels, into what the nuns termed apartments. Each residential apartment comprised dormitories, a communal recreation space, a small kitchen, a refectory, an infirmary, a parlor, an oratory, a storage room for clothes and linens *(décharge)*, exterior galleries, toilets, and baths (fig. 13.3).

By analyzing the plans of the Guy Street block, we can discern the hierarchical ordering of the religious community. There were two distinct ranks of nuns within the community by the turn of the century, despite the fact that 80 percent of the nuns in the social services sector (like the Grey Nuns) came from rural, working-class backgrounds.[12] Called choir nuns *(soeurs vocales)* and auxiliary nuns *(soeurs auxiliaires)* respectively,

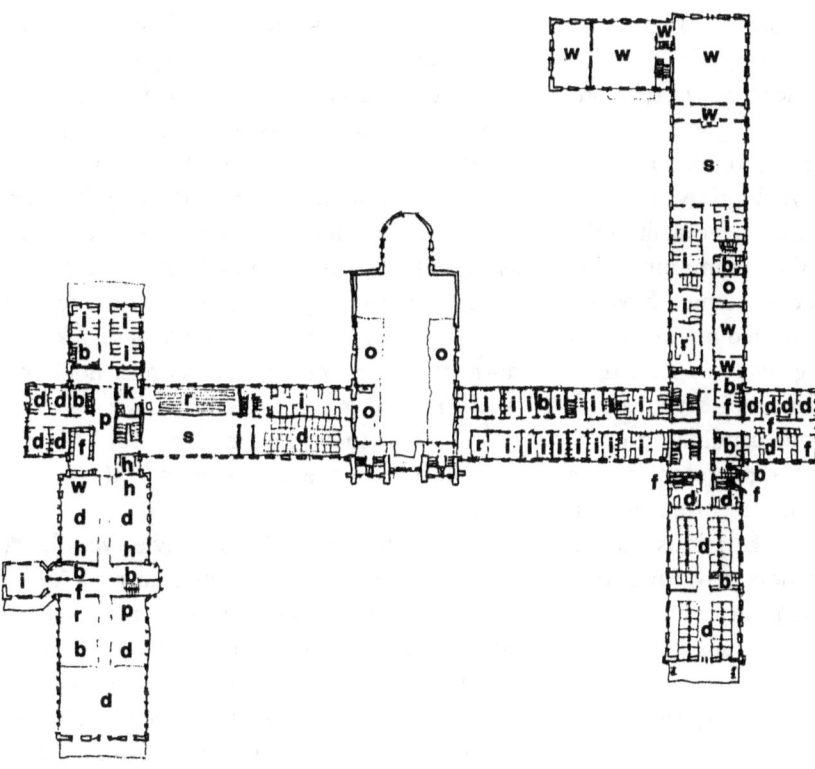

Fig. 13.3. Mother House of the Grey Nuns. Diagram showing room types.

a	administration	k	kitchen
b	bathroom / toilet	m	laundry
c	chapel	o	oratory
d	dormitory	p	parlour
f	décharge (storage)	r	refectory
h	hospitalière	s	salle / classroom
i	infirmary	w	workspace

each category was divided into three vocational stages—postulant, novice, and professed. This duality, as well as differences in status within each rank, are clearly expressed in the buildings' plans.

Admission to the order as a professed nun, regardless of rank, involved an initiatory process. Progress in one's vocation was marked not only by religious ceremonies and minor variations in religious costume, but also through the allocation of spaces to the different vocational stages in which the initiates were furthest removed from the public realm.[13] A greater degree of seclusion theoretically offered the initiate a quiet space to convert from a secular lifestyle to one of religious devotion.

Soeur Saint Jean de la Croix, for example, entered the Grey Nuns' convent on August 15, 1870. As a postulant, she would have slept in the fourth-floor dormitory of the community wing *(aile de la communauté)*, and she would have received instruction in rooms located on the second floor of the workshop wing *(aile des ateliers)*.[14] Upon the successful completion of a probationary period of six months, the candidate to religious life graduated from the postulant to the novice stage. Novices learned catechism, the history of the order, and the regulations among other subjects in the second-floor novitiate, comprising classrooms and recreation spaces, in the workshop wing, adjacent to the space reserved for the postulants (fig. 13.4).

According to a member of the Congregation of Notre Dame: "In those days at the novitiate, you learned all kinds of jobs from the classroom to the kitchen, from the sacristy to the laundry room ... every older sister had a postulant or a novice to help her in her duties and she in turn looked after her professional training."[15] The Grey Nuns, too, used the apprenticeship system. Because apprenticeships were carried out in different areas of the convent, the sequestering of novices, then, remained at a symbolic level with the Grey Nuns.

The novices' dormitories, located on the third floor of the community wing, were vertically sandwiched between the postulants above and the professed nuns below. Soeur Saint Jean de la Croix completed her postulancy and novitiate within two years of her admission; she probably carried out only half of her training in the Mother House.[16] She took her vows as a professed choir nun on August 15, 1872. The community room *(salle de la communauté)* on the first floor was reserved for the professed choir nuns as a recreation space, whereas all choir nuns—postulants, novices, and professed—dined in the ground-floor refectory immediately below this space.

The community wing, conceived as its own independent wing, separated the choir nuns (of all vocational stages) from all other members of the convent community. In effect, the wing defined an exclusive space for what was considered in 1871 as the religious community proper. Spaces allotted to the auxiliary nuns, by contrast, were dispersed throughout the Guy Street block. Their dormitories occupied the uppermost floor of the workshop wing and the infirmary wing *(aile de l'infirmerie)*, their novitiate the third floor and their refectory the basement of the workshop wing, respectively.[17]

The late historian Marta Danylewycz observed that "in making the distinction in rank and status between *les soeurs converses* and *les soeurs de choeurs,* the Congregation [of Notre Dame] assured middle-class lay women who took the veil after 1888 that in the convent they would live as middle-class nuns."[18] The attribution of higher status to choir nuns, at least conceptually, likely appealed to middle-class women's notions of social standing, especially since auxiliary status was traditionally associated with manual labor. With the Grey Nuns, the distinction between hierarchical ranks occurred partly by historical accident.

For approximately the first hundred years of existence, their order was not permitted to expand beyond twelve professed nuns who acted as administrators of the general hospital, as outlined

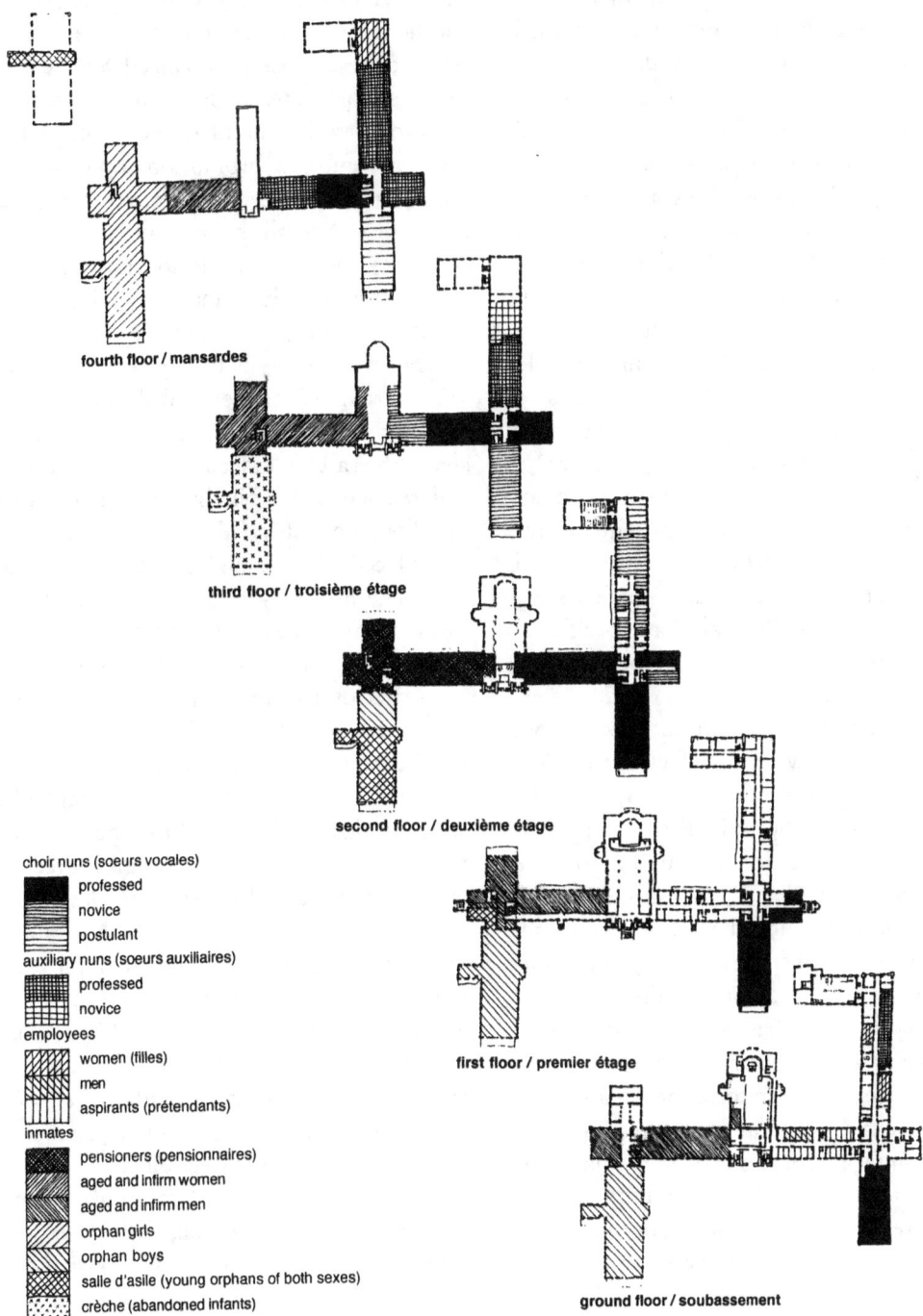

Fig. 13.4. Mother House of the Grey Nuns. Diagram of the five different floor plans showing spatial distribution of occupant groups.

in their original patent letters.[19] Nonetheless, the Grey Nuns attracted many women who attached themselves to the community and devoted their lives to the service of the poor. They lived like women religious without having taken formal vows.[20] Initially called *les filles données,* these women were "good persons who wanted to serve God and the other without, however, committing themselves irrevocably . . . undertaking the humbler tasks . . . serving without any other remuneration than their daily bread and the guarantee of being assisted and provided for in their old age."[21] The auxiliary nuns, then, as entrusted helpmates in the daily routines and in undertaking housekeeping chores—cooking, cleaning, ironing—liberated time for the choir nuns to engage in more professional and administrative tasks such as nursing, accounting, or personnel management. This division of labor made collective living possible; each worker had specific responsibilities, which ensured the smooth operation of the institution.

In 1889, prior to their canonical recognition, the auxiliary nuns may have in fact shared dormitories with the female employees *(filles).* Although relegation to the attic also extended to choir nuns of lower vocational status and to those sisters suffering from illness, the especial allocation of the attic to the subordinate, auxiliary rank recalls the hierarchy of spaces in the typical bourgeois home; the attic was traditionally associated with the servant class, female domestics in particular. Even in their former abode, the Maison Mère d'Youville, the dormitories of the auxiliary nuns were located in the indigent persons' wing *(aile des pauvres),* with those of the female employees, rather than in the community wing.[22] The 1894 creation of a new dormitory in the attic above the novices' infirmary in the Mother House of the Grey Nuns, then, essentially reintroduced the physical separation of this newly organized class of nuns from secular women employees. The auxiliaries were also outfitted with their own novitiate at this time.[23] The plans of the Mother House retain remnants of the transformation of these loosely organized female workers into a subordinate, yet in many respects parallel, vocational rank of auxiliary nuns, one that possibly represented a promotion for those women who yearned for a canonically recognized religious life.[24] Not all the indentured women, however, took the habit. Their dormitories, located at the other end of the community wing attic, are a holdover of this previous condition.

The distinctions between rank and status of women religious also extended to the location of infirmaries; they, too, respected the established spatial hierarchy. Indeed, sick choir nuns had an isolated wing, diagonally across from their second-floor dormitory; the novices' infirmary was also placed at right angles to the novices' dormitory. The auxiliary nuns, instead, had an infirmary outfitted beside their third-floor novitiate and below their dormitory. This distinction indicates that though the quarters reserved for choir nuns were pre-planned, those for the auxiliary nuns consisted of post-occupancy adaptations. Though this condition may have implied lower status, it not only reflected the changing attitude toward and the impending canonical recognition of auxiliary nuns, but also articulated spatially the official distinctions between choir nuns, auxiliary nuns, and secular women employees committed to the community. Some of the spaces given over to the auxiliaries had been inhabited by inmates before construction of the St-Mathieu Street block. Thus, the boundaries between the secular and the religious (public/private) shifted over time in the Guy Street block.

Soeur Saint Jean de la Croix's plans show that the Grey Nuns accommodated another group of aspirants to religious life, called *prétendants,* in the preparatory novitiate on the ground floor. Perhaps at this early stage one was perceived as pursuing an occupation rather than a vocation, so their quarters were placed closest to the secular world. While some secular women lived as part of the community, others came in daily as hired help. Male employees lodged in a separate building, the *maison des engagés,* located behind the Mother House.[25]

Within the Guy Street block, the divisions between religious members, clustered according to rank and vocational stage, and secular workers, segregated according to gender, reflected the hierarchical structure of the community. Women religious who were required to perform regular religious duties needed special training and careful initiation into the rites of collective living, a mode of life perhaps unfamiliar to young, lay women who chose to pursue a vocation. Secular workers, although they contributed immensely to the work of the religious community in accomplishing the more menial chores and as hired nurses in the crèche, did not observe the same rules and therefore lived separately from the religious community. Together, these two groups served the inmates housed in the St-Mathieu Street block.

Transience characterized the destitute population of the Mother House. Inmates generally stayed anywhere from a few months to a few years, although some may have resided at the convent for decades. For the elderly and the infirm, the convent acted as a hospice, a safe Christian place to live out their final days.[26] For the orphans, it served as a temporary home where the nuns schooled them until they reached twelve to fourteen years of age, after which the nuns placed them in an apprenticeship, unless a family adopted them.[27] In any case, there was a higher turnover within the inmate population than in the religious community. Even if some nuns rotated between missions, they remained lifelong members of the community. The tremendous and unpredictable fluctuation of the rather large destitute population affected the organization of the Mother House. Plans of the St-Mathieu block show the classification of the inmates according to age, gender, and class.

Within the orphans' wing, boys occupied the lower floors and girls the uppermost. The nuns classed orphans of both sexes into similar age groups. The crèche for the abandoned infants occupied the third floor, thus underlining this segregation along gender lines, although boy and girl infants under two years of age shared apartments. Preschool boys and girls also shared a recreation space *(salle d'asile)* on the second floor, although they had separate classrooms and other rooms *(salles).* Similarly, within the indigent persons' wing *(aile des vieillards),* aged and infirm men and women inhabited different apartments, men in the ground floors, women in the garret. The more affluent pensioners could afford their own private bed-sitting rooms in the *bel étage* (fig. 13.4). The nuns' classification system reproduced divisions prevalent within middle-class, turn-of-the-century urban society; the nuns placed the men closer to the public outdoor realm while removing women, especially girls, from it.

Soeur Saint Jean de la Croix's drawings also show six grand staircases (three pairs) in the Mother House, notably at the intersections of the main axes of the structure. These became important circulation and transportation nodes as two sets of stairs occupied the large, well-defined space. The dumbwaiters (and later elevators) were also installed in these areas of the building. Located at the juncture or outside of particular apartments, these stairs acted as collectors for different population groups within a given wing. The one nearest the community wing, however, was probably used exclusively by the choir nuns. In some areas, the large stair landings acted as social spaces—as a parlor for the elderly people, for instance. Another landing outside the choir nuns' dormitory served as an oratory; one side of the landing was fitted with an altar, a religious statue, and *prie-dieu.*

In addition, secondary sets of stairs, located at the midway point of each wing, connected different floors within a wing, especially related apartments: the orphan boys' sleeping and eating areas on the ground floor to their classrooms above, for instance. This stair continued upward into the younger orphan boys' apartment and the recreation room farther up into the crèche and then up into the orphan girls' wing. Another set of stairs in the laundry connected washing and drying facilities to the ironing department. Some of these stairs were installed by the nuns for convenience only, such as the mid-wing set, which effectively shortened the distance between the infirmaries of the novice and professed choir nuns.[28] Smaller, hidden, narrow stairs led up into the upper attic proper (above the *mansardes*) used for storage. Within this system of vertically interconnected apartments, resident groups in the Mother House overlapped and possibilities existed for encounters between them.

The convent featured double-loaded corridors with unusual interior windows between the corridor and adjacent spaces (fig. 13.5). At first this would suggest that the convent embodied an architectural language of discipline and surveillance. The internal fenestration, however, allowed for cross-ventilation and for the borrowing of daylight in an era that preceded the widespread use of electric light and air-conditioning systems. Furthermore, the lower sections of these windows contained translucent glass panes which obscured views into work spaces from the corridors.[29] This situation undermined the building's panoptic qualities. Moreover, many rooms not only opened into the corridor, but were themselves interconnected *en suite* (fig. 13.6). Perhaps visual contact between different spaces permitted the nuns to be aware of what each was doing, reinforcing the cooperative and communal aspects of their work, largely conducted in silence. This multivalent reading of the plan attenuates popular assumptions that emphasize the architecture of the convent as an apparatus of authoritarian power.[30]

One particular nine-foot-wide corridor, offset to the south side of the indigent persons' wing, acted like an enclosed gallery. It effectively kept all other destitute inmates from traveling directly through the elderly men's apartments on their way to church, provided a processional space, and ensured that the elderly men enjoyed a view to the south, in addition to filling their rooms with light and air. Together, the different stair types and corridors created multiple paths, both horizontally and vertically, through the building and gave the occupants a choice of routes. Indeed, on special feast days, all the inhabitants of

Fig. 13.5. Mother House of the Grey Nuns, Corridor Saint-Joseph, 1910. Courtesy of ASGM, *Hôpital General des Soeurs Grises, 390 Rue Guy, Montréal,* Librarie Beauchemin Limitée, 1910.

Fig. 13.6. Mother House of the Grey Nuns. "Imprimerie," early twentieth century. Courtesy of ASGM "Photos Maison Mère—Guy 13D Intérieur."

the Mother House participated in commemorative processions that wound their way through one end of the building to another, through various corridors and up and down stairs.[31] If fully mobile, the inmates were expected to attend mass in the Church.[32] They also descended into the gardens and yards that the nuns put at their disposal. Thus, contact between resident groups of different classes, ages, and genders must have occurred regularly in the Mother House, lending a degree of liveliness to its halls.[33]

Running a residential institution of this size and complexity called for a substantial work force, skilled in many different areas. The community's annual *Statistiques* show the variety of jobs, ranging from the most menial *(couture, buanderie, Dépensaire)* through the administrative *(Econome, Première Sous-Maîtresse, Supérieure Local)*.[34] Some offices drew on the traditionally female dominated professions of nursing and education *(pharmacie, Hospitalière de la crèche)*. Other jobs within the institution were less traditional, like the nuns' productive labor in the workshops, located on the first floor along Guy Street. The printing press and the bookbinding shop, for example, took in commissions for catechism and hymn books. In these *ateliers*, women handled large mechanical equipment and supervised their employees, re-creating a miniature factory of sorts within the institution. The manufacturing of religious relics, candles, and wax figurines also generated income for the community. As dentists and pharmacists, the Grey Nuns provided important professional services for the poor. In 1902, for instance, they distributed 24,094 prescriptions to inmates and to the needy.[35]

Many of the occupations that these women pursued within their *ateliers* (and even in administration) were traditionally male-associated activities. They were not the only examples of gender reversals within the convent. Ironically, male employees helped out in food preparation in the Grey Nuns' kitchens—a task traditionally relegated to the private sphere (fig. 13.7). In this way, convents were "[a]s self-managed institutions . . . immune to the sexual division of labor that determined status and rank of secular society."[36]

Although a distinct hierarchy did exist within the organization of the convent, the powers associated with different positions were limited spatially

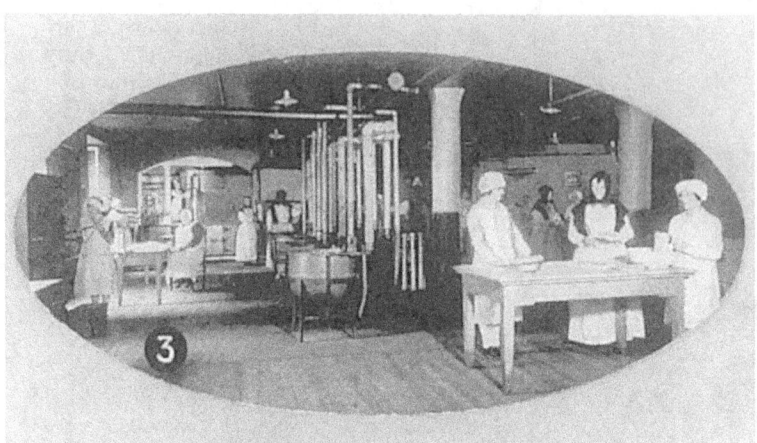

Fig. 13.7. Mother House of the Grey Nuns. "Cuisine," early twentieth century Courtesy of ASGM "Photos Maison Mère-Guy 11B Intérieur."

and temporally. Any authority a nun exercised over other people was limited to the confines of her own office; under all other circumstances, she was considered equal to her peers. The *Constitutions particulières* outlined the tasks and responsibilities of all office holders, the position of mother superior included. A sister appointed in charge of an office had specific obligations: to supervise, train (if work was unfamiliar), and otherwise set an example for her associates, novices, and employees assigned to work *with* her. Because no work was considered extraneous or unnecessary, each individual was esteemed as contributing to the smooth operation of the institution.

In principle, work was delegated according to individual capabilities and periodically rotated so that individuals acquired a variety of experiences.[37] Even if the type of work assigned remained the same, the location and team of co-workers could change as offices not only rotated within the Mother House, but between missions throughout the Institute of the Grey Nuns. For example, in the fifty-one years Soeur Saint Jean de la Croix lived as member of the community: "I have been employed," she wrote, "in 44 offices, that is to say except for the crèche and the laundry, I have passed just about everywhere."[38] She taught catechism at *l'Hospice Saint-Joseph,* comforted and cared for smallpox victims, acted as *Sacristine de l'infirmerie,* and later as *Réfectorière de l'infirmerie.* She also served as an *Hospitalière* at *l'Hôpital St-Camille, l'Asile Ste-Brigitte,* and *l'Asile St-Patrice* on different occasions for various lengths of time. In addition, Soeur Saint Jean de la Croix worked in the *atelier des divers ouvrages* and held several other positions throughout her career. Few middle-class housewives had opportunities to exercise such professional skills or to work among their peers in supportive environments.[39]

The 1888 introduction of steam-power and gas appliances revolutionized the convent. Modern industrial appliances were first introduced to the work spaces traditionally associated with women's domestic work—the laundry and the kitchens. "Let us enter the kitchen" the annalist invited her readers, "this is where we prepare the food of the pensioners and the poor; everything is powered with steam; nothing seems so convenient as the gas ovens and stoves, just as all these drawers that are placed around the room within easy reach of the cook and that contain all the implements necessary to the culinary arts."[40] Gas stoves also equipped the kitchenettes in the various apartments, ateliers, and ironing rooms (to heat the irons) as well as the crèche (for the provision of additional heat and to warm bottles, etc.).[41]

Steam-powered rotating tumbling vats, wringers, and mangles equipped the Mother House laundry. It compared with contemporary, commercial steam laundries in Montréal, some of which "employed up to one hundred women to wash, iron and fold" using the latest machinery.[42] Most individual households could not afford the costs associated with these technological developments which facilitated collective work. In addition to the huge, industrial laundry appliances, the nuns outfitted *ateliers* and other work spaces with steam-powered sewing machines and knitting machines. The work spaces in the laundry wing were vertically interconnected with the installation of a steam-powered elevator in 1888. An addition just off of the laundry wing housed the steam engines.[43] These industrialized and modernized facilities efficiently served the large population in this building and permitted the religious community to take on extra paid work.

In some respects, the convent approached the collective housing models heralded in the late nineteenth century, although it necessarily followed a different organizational structure. The mechanization and centralization of domestic household labor marked an essential tenet of nineteenth-century "material feminists," who made significant efforts to reorganize their lives and work through design, actively seeking to better not only their own situation, but that of the larger community.[44] Proposals for kitchenless houses and cooperative housekeeping questioned traditional gender constructions as they raised possibilities for different household organizations and a revised division of labor: domestic work was to be shared and even remunerated, if not taken on by male members of the household. Collectivized services included electricity, running hot water, sanitary plumbing, building maintenance, housekeeping, laundry, food preparation in central kitchens, and public dining rooms. Apartment living afforded women many advantages—access to the city with its social and cultural events and work opportunities, an alleviation from domestic chores (except childrearing), and contact with a wider social community. Utopian communities offered similar conditions; women no longer needed to live in the isolation of the single family home.[45]

Other nineteenth-century, non-conventual, purpose-built structures for women also reached beyond the realm of domesticity by providing women with an institutional, professional framework.[46] Two Montréal buildings, the Royal Victoria College (1899), a women's college at McGill University, and the nurses' residence at the Royal Victoria Hospital (1906) provide a useful comparison to the convent. The RVC women's college was originally planned by American architect Bruce Price as a self-sufficient structure. It integrated academic spaces, such as classrooms and an auditorium, with bed-sitting rooms, parlors, and a dining hall, exclusively for the use of women students.[47] Incorporation of institutional and domestic functions occurred later in the nurses' residence with the 1930s introduction of laboratories and classrooms. Designed by Montréal architects Edward and William Sutherland Maxwell, the RVH nurses' residence was constructed to the west of the main hospital structure on the slopes of Mount-Royal. The building, outfitted with bedrooms, sitting rooms, a dining room, a library, a living room, as well as an assembly hall, re-created a decidedly homelike environment for its nurse residents.[48] The strategy of hybridization followed in the two buildings, combined with architectural allusions to the private domestic sphere, validated women's choice to live outside the family context.

Although the convent is an institution as paternalistic as the home, it blurred the distinctions between the private and public realms of late-nineteenth-century Montréal: nuns lived and worked under the same roof, and people of all classes could be found within its walls. The convent gathered individual women's efforts, integrating their social work, religious rituals, and domestic and industrial activities into a cooperative enterprise. The nuns' access to modern technologies at an industrial scale liberated their time and energy to pursue productive, professional, and religious work. Clearly, the Grey Nuns did not fit into the neat construction of the "separate spheres," a nineteenth-century notion that relegated women to family situations and middle-class houses.[49] Their own work and physical environment breached the clear divisions of male and female, public and private, active and passive, rich and poor. The convent, then, offered women like Soeur Saint Jean de la Croix an alternative urban "space," one in which they could realize themselves individually and collectively.

Notes

The author would like to acknowledge the assistance of Annmarie Adams, Deborah Miller, and Andres Musta. Deborah Weiner read an earlier version of this paper and provided valuable commentary, as did two anonymous readers. This chapter is drawn from my M.Arch. thesis, "Housing the Grey Nuns: Power, Religion and Women in fin-de-siècle Montréal" (School of Architecture, McGill Univ., 1995). I am grateful for the support of a Canada Mortgage and Housing Corporation Graduate Scholarship, a McGill Humanities Research Grant, and a McGill Center for Research and Teaching on Women Graduate Research Award.

1. Marta Danylewycz, *Taking the Veil: An Alternative to Marriage, Motherhood and Spinsterhood in Québec, 1840–1920* (Toronto: McClelland and Stewart, 1987); Nicole Laurin, Danielle Juteau, and Lorraine Duchesne, *À la recherche d'un monde oublié: Les communautés religieuses de femmes au Québec de 1900 à 1970* (Montréal: Le Jour, Éditeur, 1991), 241–73, observed that conventual life was a definite, first choice (over marriage and celibacy) for those who entered religious communities of women. Further, the authors calculated that 2 percent of the female population over fifteen years of age in Québec in 1901 belonged to communities of women religious (223–25).
2. All personal information on Soeur Saint Jean de la Croix is taken from *Archives des Soeurs Grises de Montréal* (hereafter cited as ASGM) *Notice Biographique Soeur Saint Jean de la Croix* or from mentions of her in ASGM *Annales*.
3. "Women religious" is a current term for nuns, in contrast to the phrase "religious women," which has a different connotation. The term has a counterpart in "male religious" where "religious" is used as a noun to indicate a member of a religious community.
4. Communauté Urbaine de Montréal (CUM), Service de la Planification du Territoire, *Architecture Religieuses II: les Couvents Montréal* Répertoire d'Architecture Traditionelle sur le Territoire de la CUM (Montréal: CUM, 1984), documents a significant number of convents on the island of Montréal. Robert Caron, *Un Couvent du XIXe siècle: La Maison des Soeurs de la Charité de Québec* (Montréal: Libre Expression, 1980), and Robert Lahaise, *Les Edifices Conventuels du Vieux Montréal: Aspects Ethno-historiques* (Québec: Hurtubise HMH, 1980), explore the architecture of convents, but only from the perspective of their design and construction.
5. For a historical survey of religious communities of women in Québec see Marguerite Jean, *Évolution des Communautés Religieuses de Femmes du Québec de 1639 à nos jours* (Montréal: Fides, 1977). Literature on institutions operated by nuns includes the following: Peter Gossage, "Les enfants abandonées à Montréal au 19e siècle: la Crèche d'Youville des Soeurs Grises 1820–1871," *Revue d'histoire de l'amérique*

française (hereafter cited as *RHAF*) 40 (4) (printemps 1987): 537–59; see also his "Abandoned Children in Nineteenth Century Montréal" (M.A. thesis, dept. of history, McGill Univ., 1983); Micheline Dumont-Johnson, "Des garderies au XIXe siècle: Les salles d'asile des Soeurs Grises à Montréal," *RHAF* (34) 1 (juin 1980): 27–56; Micheline Dumont and Nadia Fahmy-Eid, *Les Couventines L'éducation des filles au Québec dans les congrégations religieuses enseignantes 1840–1960* (Montréal: Boréal, 1986); Huguette Lapointe-Roy, *Charité Bien Ordonné: Le Premier Réseau de Lutte Contre la Pauvreté à Montréal au 19e Siècle* (Montréal: Boréal Express, 1987); Andrée Lévesque, *La Norme et les déviantes: Des femmes au Québec pendant l'entre-deux-guerres* (Montréal: Les Éditions du remue-ménage, 1989).

6. ASGM MM 1190 rue Guy Plans 1900 Doc. 76 A–E (Soeur Saint Jean de la Croix) *Relevé des Plans de l'Hôpital Général de Montréal* contains five plans, one of each story of the Mother House drawn in gouache on *toile ciré* at a scale of 1 inch equals 8 feet. The *soubassement* plan, the largest in the set, measures approximately 8 by 12 feet; it shows the whole site, including ancillary buildings. The other plans are somewhat smaller, approximately 7 by 8 feet, and depict only the Mother House. One other set of sketches, perhaps her working copy, seems to have preceded this set (also dated *vers* 1900), as the St-Mathieu wing is shown as uncompleted. It is titled *Plan—à-terre et divisions de la Maison Mère*. ASGM *Détails Historiques concernant les plans de la maison mère primitive et de l'actuelle, Cahier A; Relève des plans 1ère maison mère (1765–1871) maison mère actuelle (1871–1909), Cahier B; Maison Mère rue Guy constructions etc. 1861–1909 3e volume; Maison Mère rue Guy—eau, gaz etc. Volume iv; Maison Mère rue Guy—constructions et services 1871–1909, historique, vol. iii et iv, Mont Ste-Croix* ("blue" books); and ASGM MM 1190 rue Guy Plans Doc. 11 *Diverses notes pour servir d'historique et de pièces justificatives au relevé des plans et des terrains 1900* ("red" book) comprise all of the documents produced by Soeur Saint Jean de la Croix that I consulted. Analysis of the Mother House is based on these unless otherwise noted.

It is difficult to ascertain in what order Soeur Saint Jean de la Croix produced her chronicles of the Mother House. Draft prints in Doc. 5, which document the location of *canaux* and other pipes, are dated 1906. They were annotated with a message that reads *"à vérifier et à corriger avant tirer au propre."* The homemade "blue" and "red" books, conserved in the archive are dated 1907. Since the information contained in the books overlap, together they may have consisted of working editions. Perhaps Soeur Saint Jean de la Croix worked backwards in time in order to reconstitute drawings of the Mother House based on the memories of other older nuns (since she compiled similar information on the Maison Mère d'Youville) and other miscellaneous sources. Or perhaps these documents did indeed chart changes in the convent since her first set of drawings.

Soeur Saint Jean de la Croix produced complete sets of as-built plans some thirty years before women were accepted to schools of architecture in Québec. Blanche Lemco van Ginkel, "Slowly and Surely (and Somewhat Painfully): More or Less the History of Women in Architecture in Canada," *Society for the Study of Architecture in Canada Bulletin* (Mar. 1991): 5–11; and Annmarie Adams, "Building Barriers: Images of Women in Canada's Architectural Press, 1924–73," *Resources for Feminist Research* 23 (3) (Fall 1994): 11–23, note that a woman first registered with the Québec architectural profession only in 1942. According to the 1906 and 1907 *Statistiques,* Soeur Saint Jean de la Croix was listed as *Sacristine de l'infirmerie* and not until 1919 was she given the title of "architect" as an obedience, hence official recognition. See ASGM *Annales* 1904–6, 693, *Annales* 1906–8, 151, and *Annales* 1919–20, 8, 367.

Soeur Saint Jean de la Croix is not unique among Canadian nuns. Sister St-Joseph (1856–1910) acted as architect for les Soeurs de la Providence in British Columbia and in the northwestern United States, designing and supervising the construction of several buildings. The architecture of West Coast religious communities and Sister St-Joseph, in particular, form the subject of Deborah Rink's ongoing research. See her "Convents as Planned Communities" (Master's thesis, dept. of landscape architecture and planning, Univ. of Oregon, 1990). Sister St-Joseph was included in the exhibition, "Constructing Careers: A Contemporary View of Women Architects in British Columbia Since 1850," Vancouver, Apr. 18–May 12, 1995.

7. "Our Public Institutions" *Canadian Illustrated News* 12 (23) (Dec. 4 1875): 355–56. Five days later, the engraving appeared in *CIN*'s French counterpart, *L'Opinion Publique* 6 (Dec. 9 1875): 580, 582. It is also reproduced in Barbara Salomon de Friedberg, *Le Domaine des Soeurs Grises, Boulevard Dorchester* (Montréal: Ministère des Affaires Culturelles, Direction générale du Patrimoine, Service de l'Inventaire des Biens Culturels, Division Reconnaissance et Classement, 1975), 15.

8. ASGM *Détails Historiques Cahier A* and *Relève des plans Cahier B*, both by Soeur Saint Jean de la Croix. Guy Pinard, *Montréal: Son Histoire, Son Architecture* (Ottawa: Les Éditions La Presse, 1989), 287, gives slightly different dimensions.

9. Pinard, 284; CUM, however, gives the historic building area as 13,512 square meters (101,676 square feet), which includes ancillary buildings.

10. These numbers vary slightly from those of the annals, probably because Soeur Saint Jean de la Croix grouped people into different categories and possibly because she noted her statistics mid-year rather than at the end of the year.

11. Inmate here is used according to its obsolete definition "a person who lives with others in a house."

12. Laurin, Juteau, and Duchesne, *À la recherche d'un monde oublié*, 317–37.

13. The play of power as read in the plans has methodological precedent in Dell Upton, *Holy Things and Profane: Anglican Parish Churches in Colonial Virginia* (Cambridge, Mass.: MIT Press for the Architectural History Foundation, 1986); Anthony Vidler, *The Writing of the Walls: Architectural Theory in the Late Enlightenment* (Princeton: Princeton Architectural Press, 1987); and David J. T. Vanderburgh, "Cultures of Public Architecture in Nineteenth-Century France: Re-forming the Provincial Prison" (Ph.D. diss., dept. of architecture, Univ. of California, Berkeley, 1993). For a discussion on the importance of costume, see Elizabeth McGahan, "Inside the Hallowed Walls: Convent Life through Material History," *Material History Bulletin* [now known as *Material History Review*] 25 (spring 1987): 1–9.

14. Although the nuns' designations for various parts of the convent changed with the accretion of the building, in this chapter the term "Guy Street block" describes the part of the convent east of the chapel, while "St-Mathieu block" describes the part west of chapel. Similarly, "community wing" refers to the particular portion within the Guy Street block, south of the main Dorchester transversal, and "workshop wing" refers to the particular portion to the north.

15. Even for the women who left the community, the novitiate imparted valuable and marketable skills. Danylewycz, *Taking the Veil*, 105–6.

16. Soeur Saint Jean de la Croix probably spent her first year at the Maison Mère d'Youville, since the Mother House was still under construction at the time of her admission.

17. The infirmary wing was located between the chapel and the wings along Guy Street.

18. Danylewycz, *Taking the Veil*, 93. The labels *"converses"* and *"choeurs"* correspond to the designations "auxiliary" and "choir" as used by the Grey Nuns.

19. Jean, *Évolution des Communautés Religieuses de Femmes*, 65; [Soeur Albina Fauteux], *L'Hôpital Général des Soeurs de la Charité (Soeurs Grises)*

depuis sa fondation jusqu'à nos jours, vol. 1 (Montréal: Imprimerie des Soeurs Grises de Montréal, 1915), 598–600.

20. Many foundresses of Montréal orders, like Marie-Marguerite Du Frost de Lajemmerais d'Youville (Mère d'Youville of the Grey Nuns), began their missions this way (technically called "pious associations"), only after living fully secular lives as mothers and widows. See, for example, Denise Robillard, *Émilie Tavernier Gamelin* (Montréal: Éditions du Méridien, 1988). Like the early founding members of the Grey Nuns, these religious women simply worked without a canonically recognized rule. See Jean, *Évolution des Communautés Religieuses de Femmes*, 132–38, for the establishment of "third" orders.

21. Estelle Mitchell s.g.m., *L'essor apostolique: Soeurs de la Charité de Montréal, "Soeurs Grises", 1877–1910* (Montréal, 1981), 14 n. 11, continues: "These *filles données* would be successively called *les Maries, les Soeurs Franciscaines* and *les Soeurs de Ste-Marthe*. In 1889, *l'association des Petites Soeurs auxiliaires* was created; two years later, in 1891, the name *Petites Soeurs auxiliaires* was chosen. In 1905, the association was canonically established; *les Soeurs auxiliaires* fused with the *Soeurs vocales* on December 3, 1946," thus formally ending the distinction between the two ranks. Translated from French by the author.

22. Predecessor to the Mother House of the Grey Nuns, Maison Mère d'Youville, originally built 1694, still stands in the old city of Montréal. See plans of Maison Mère d'Youville reproduced in Lahaise, *Les Edifices Conventuels*, 475–96.

23. ASGM *Annales* 1892–95, 406. The 1894 annal entry makes reference to the provision of a larger space, a *salle de reunion*, for the *Petites Soeurs Auxiliaries* as their previous one became too small. It was turned into an oratory. On Soeur Saint Jean de la Croix's drawings, the *salle* is labeled novitiate.

24. Even when the auxiliary nuns obtained canonical recognition, their religious responsibilities—*obédiances*—differed than those of the choir nuns. The auxiliary nuns were exempt from certain religious functions and did not have an active nor passive role in governing. Despite this apparent subordination, they were entitled to the same care and subsistence. See *Constitutions*. The annual *statistiques* also retained these distinctions as only the professed choir nuns were named with their office, but after 1907 the postings for the auxiliary nuns are given.

25. According to 1880 constitutions, male employees were to help out in the destitute men's sections, but photos c. 1930 show them in laundry and kitchen as well. The language of the 1880 constitutions, however, refers to workers in laundry and kitchen as female.

26. Bettina Bradbury, "Mourir Chrétiennement: La Vie et la Mort dans les Établissements Catholiques pour Personnes Agées à Montréal au XIXe siècle," *RHAF* 46 (1) (été 1992): 143–75, underscores the importance the elderly and infirm women attached to the preparation for a Christian death.

27. Due to lack of space in the Maison Mère d'Youville, the nuns rarely kept the children beyond the age of ten to eleven years old. See Lapointe-Roy, *Charité Bien Ordonné*, 156.

28. ASGM *Annales* 1877–80, 260–61.

29. As far as is known, semiopaque glass was used in the lower lights of interior windows in the initial construction. Photographs show that some rooms had curtains, thus ensuring privacy when desired. See, for example, ASGM "Photos Maison Mère—Guy 16D Intérieur."

30. The ultimate model for an architecture of discipline and surveillance is Jeremy Bentham's Panopticon. It featured, in its purest form, a circular plan. Isolated cells lined the exterior perimeter and opened onto a gallery. Inspectors could thus see into every cell, monitoring the inmates activities. For a more detailed discussion, see Paul Rabinow, ed. *The Foucault Reader* (New York: Pantheon Books, 1984); Michel Foucault, *Discipline and Punish: The Birth of the Prison*, trans.

Alan M. Sheridan (London: Penguin, 1977), discusses the uses of architecture as an apparatus of power.

31. See ASGM *Annales* 1902–3, 109, for example.
32. Bradbury, *Mourir Chrétiennement*, 161–62.
33. The following provide comparative studies on contemporary workhouses, hospitals, and asylums: Felix Driver, *Power and Pauperism: The Workhouse System, 1834–1884* (Cambridge: Cambridge Univ. Press, 1993); Adrian Forty, "The Modern Hospital in England and France: The Social and Medical Uses of Architecture," in *Buildings and Society: Essays on the Social Development of the Built Environment*, ed. Anthony King (London: Routledge and Kegan Paul, 1980), 61–93; Lindsay Prior, "The Architecture of the Hospital: A Study of Spatial Organization and Medical Knowledge," *British Journal of Sociology* 39 (1) (1988); David J. Rothman, *The Discovery of the Asylum: Social Order and Disorder in the New Republic* (Boston: Little, Brown and Company, 1971); Jeremy Taylor, *Hospital and Asylum Architecture in England 1840–1914: Building for Health Care* (London: Mansell Publishing Limited, 1991).
34. A survey of the *Statistiques* in the annals evinces the range of offices and their periodic rotation between members of the community, both within the Mother House and throughout the different missions. These statistics also kept track of the number of inmates in each category housed in the Mother House.
35. ASGM MM 1190 rue Guy Plans Doc. 11 Soeur Saint Jean de la Croix.
36. Danylewycz, *Taking the Veil*, 95.
37. Danylewycz also found this to be the case in her study of the Congrégation de Notre Dame. See ibid., 100–8.
38. Translated from French by the author.
39. Bettina Bradbury, *Working Families: Age, Gender and Daily Survival in Industrializing Montreal* (Toronto: McClelland and Stewart, 1993), 137, notes that the "putting out" system was advantageous to employers precisely because women (in addition to providing their own machines and work spaces) worked isolated in their own homes so posed no threat—"there was no danger in their organizing or knowing what other employees earned." For general sources on housekeeping, see Denyse Baillargeon, *Ménagères au temps de la Crise* (Montréal: Les Éditions du remue-ménage, 1991); Meg Luxton, *More Than a Labor of Love: Three Generations of Women's Work in the Home* (Toronto: Women's Press, 1980); Ruth Schwartz Cowan, *More Work for Mother: The Ironies of Household Technologies from the Hearth to the Microwave* (New York: Basic, 1983).
40. ASGM *Annales* 1888–92, 172–75. Translated from French by the author.
41. ASGM *Maison Mère rue Guy—constructions, vol. iii et iv*, 25.
42. Bradbury, "Women's Workplaces: The Impact of Technological Change on Working-class Women in the Home and in the Workplace in Nineteenth-Century Montreal," in *Women, Work, and Place*, ed. Audrey Kobayashi (Montreal: McGill-Queen's Univ. Press, 1994), 41.
43. ASGM *Détails Historiques Cahier A*; *Relève des plans Cahier B*; and *Annales* 1902–3, 161–62.
44. Dolores Hayden, *The Grand Domestic Revolution: A History of Feminist Designs for American Homes, Neighborhoods and Cities* (Cambridge, Mass.: MIT Press, 1981), 3.
45. Dolores Hayden, *Seven American Utopias: the Architecture of Communitarian Socialism, 1790–1975* (Cambridge: MIT Press, 1976); Lynn Pearson, *The Architectural and Social History of Cooperative Living* (London: Macmillan, 1988); Elizabeth Cromley, *Alone Together: A History of New York's Early Apartments* (Ithaca and London: Cornell Univ. Press, 1990).
46. On the image of the "big house" see: Martha Vicinus, *Independent Women: Work and Community for Single Women 1850–1920* (Chicago: Univ. of Chicago Press, 1985), 129; and Annmarie Adams, "Architecture in the Family Way: Health Reform, Feminism, and the Middle-Class House in England, 1870–1900" (Ph.D. diss., dept. of archi-

tecture, Univ. of California, Berkeley, 1992), 208–67. For the metaphor of the home as a tool of social reform, see Deborah E. B. Weiner, *Architecture and Social Reform in Late-Victorian London* (Manchester: Manchester Univ. Press, 1994), 57–86; and Abigail A. Van Slyck, "'The Utmost Amount of Effctiv[sic] Accommodation': Andrew Carnegie and the Reform of the American Library" *Journal of the Society of Architectural Historians* 4 (Dec. 1991): 359–83.

47. Deborah Miller, "The Three R's: Residence, Resistance and Redesign, Royal Victoria College and the Architecture of Feminism" (M.Arch. thesis, School of Architecture, McGill Univ., in progress).

48. Annmarie Adams, "Rooms of Their Own: The Nurses' Residence at Montreal's Royal Victoria Hospital," *Material History Review* 40 (Fall 1994): 29–41.

49. On women and domesticity, see Clifford Clark, "Domestic Architecture as an index to Social History: The Romantic Revival and the Cult of Domesticity in America, 1840–1890," *Journal of Interdisciplinary History* 7 (Summer 1976): 33–56; Colleen McDannell, *The Christian Home in Victorian America, 1840–1900* (Bloomington: Indiana Univ. Press, 1988); Gwendolyn Wright, *Moralism and the Model Home: Domestic Architecture and Cultural Conflict in Chicago, 1873–1913* (Chicago: Univ. of Chicago Press, 1980). Linda Kerber, "Separate Spheres, Female Worlds, Woman's Place: The Rhetoric of Women's History," *Journal of American History* 75 (1) (June 1988): 9–39, is a succinct review of the literature on the theory of separate spheres. Some scholars have counterargued this construct: see Leonore Davidoff and Catherine Hall, *Family Fortunes: Men and Women of the English Middle Class, 1780–1850* (London: Hutchinson, 1987); Mary P. Ryan, *Women in Public: Between Banners and Ballots, 1825–1880* (Baltimore: Johns Hopkins Univ. Press, 1990). Joan Landes, *Women and the Public Sphere in the Age of the French Revolution* (Ithaca: Cornell Univ. Press, 1988), brings into question the category of "public" in relation to women and feminism.

CHAPTER 14

William D. Moore

"To Hold Communion with Nature and the Spirit-World": New England's Spiritualist Camp Meetings, 1865–1910

The *Annals of Psychical Science* reported in 1907 that forty-three Spiritualist camp meetings had been held the previous summer in the United States.[1] New England was both the birthplace of the Spiritualist camp meeting movement, and the region in which such camps were located most densely. During the 1880s, ten significant annual Spiritualist camp meetings took place over the summer months in New England. Three camps were located in each of the states of Maine and Massachusetts. Two camps were held in New Hampshire, while one each was established in Connecticut and Vermont.[2] With the success of these gatherings in New England, others were founded across the country, in states including New York, Iowa, Indiana, Michigan, Ohio, Oregon, Illinois, Florida, California, Wisconsin, and Tennessee.[3]

Protestant camp meetings first appeared in rural America during the final decades of the eighteenth century as a means for itinerant preachers to bring religion to the unchurched on the frontier. Following the success of a meeting at Cane Ridge, Kentucky, in August of 1801, which drew twenty thousand Presbyterian, Methodist, and Baptist worshippers, camp meeting groves became omnipresent in the American landscape. Throughout the nineteenth century, these seasonal communities prospered and assumed increasingly complex material forms surrounding the sites of evangelical revival meetings both in newly settled territories and in rural areas just outside of Eastern cities. Described by Henry David Thoreau as "a singular combination of a prayer-meeting and a picnic," mainstream Protestant camp meetings reached their greatest popularity between the Civil War and the First World War.[4]

Like those organized by the Baptists and Methodists, Spiritualist camp meetings were annual seasonal communities formed by individuals who spent the majority of the year in other locations. Confining their sacred spaces to wooded areas near water, initially Spiritualists gathered outdoors beneath the trees, in informal settings that utilized the natural landscape to inform their discourse about religion. Over time, as the temporary communities of Spiritualists became formalized, permanent structures enabled members to demarcate the forest as their own institutional property. Cottages, tents, and hotels provided lodging, while auditoriums, bandstands, dancing pavilions, roller-skating rinks, and other buildings were erected to house both sacred and secular pastimes.

Baptist and Methodist camps have been described and analyzed by historians and architectural historians such as Ellen Weiss, Kenneth Brown, and Charles A. Parker. Scholarly discourse, however, largely has ignored Spiritualist camp meetings.[5] Although these camps, in their heyday, drew tens of thousands of Americans, they have yet to be adequately recognized and explicated as part of the North American vernacular landscape. This essay draws upon the fields of religious, architectural and landscape history, and gender studies to analyze the Spiritualist camps located in New England between 1865 and 1910. Lake Pleasant and Onset Bay Grove in Montague and Wareham, Massachusetts, respectively, are addressed in detail as they were, by all criteria, the most successful of New England's Spiritualist camp meetings.[6] New England's camps, however, must be considered as an analytical unit because, beyond their stylistic and formal similarities, they shared patronage and functioned as a circuit for enthusiasts and mediums who passed the summer by spending time at each location.

Connections between the camps' built form and Spiritualist theology will be employed to interpret the camps' function as liminal zones in which late-Victorian middle-class Anglo-Americans redefined their cultural identities and experimented with reconciling concepts perceived as binary opposites by American society. Further, by exploring the relations among the groups who interacted to shape the camp grounds, this essay argues that the camps assumed form through the interaction of Spiritualist associations, professional mediums, recreational campers, railroad developers, dance-hall operators, and hotel managers. The intercourse among these disparate groups produced environments mediating earlier, primarily sacred, Protestant revival meetings and later secular commercial resorts such as Coney Island.

Spiritualism, a religious movement based upon faith in the immortality of the human soul and the belief that communication occurs between the living and the dead, attracted many advocates in nineteenth-century America. While the movement coalesced following the famous mysterious rappings surrounding the Fox Sisters of Hydesville, New York, in 1848, it was the logical culmination of the early-nineteenth-century liberal transformation of American Christianity. By positing that spirits on the other side of the great divide could communicate with the living, Spiritualism rejected received patriarchy, religious dogma, and other constructs of cultural authority. All human sources of knowledge and power were of secondary importance when compared with insight gained through communication with supernatural forces. Passive, unschooled mediums, serving as conduits for disembodied spirits, replaced patriarchal, educated ministers as sources of religious authority.

Denigrated for more than a century as eccentrics and charlatans, Spiritualists—like Millerites, Shakers, and Christian Scientists—generally were earnest Americans seeking religious revelation. Although some frauds profited by duping the credulous, the vast majority of the Spiritualist community was composed of believers who sincerely accepted the immortality of the soul and their departed loved ones' ability to communicate from the other side of the grave. Much of the discourse surrounding Spiritualism has focused on the exposure of fakes, but, as historian Ann Braude has argued, "the historical significance of Spiritualism lies . . . in the masses of faithful followers who made it a popular movement."[7]

Spiritualist camp meetings first appeared following the Civil War and grew in popularity throughout the last decades of the nineteenth century. In Melrose, Massachusetts, approximately ten miles north of Boston, Spiritualists first met outdoors during the summer of 1866.[8] Throughout the late 1860s, meetings continued to be held in this town's Pierpont Grove, drawing participants from New York, Pennsylvania, Connecticut, and as far away as Texas and Kansas. Although participants' tents were available within the grove, individuals also commuted to the event from Boston by horse and steam car to hear nationally recognized mediums such as Mrs. Hattie Wilson, an African American who spoke at the 1867 meeting.[9]

The Spiritualist camp meeting at Pierpont Grove met annually for only a few years and involved little construction beyond the erection of a speaker's stand. These successful meetings, however, set a precedent for other Spiritualist "grove meetings" subsequently held elsewhere in Massachusetts. For example, in 1869, Island Grove, in Abington, Massachusetts, was the site of a meeting held over three days in August. As reported at the time, the activities of the first two days, Friday and Saturday, included speeches, but also consisted of "the usual amusements at picnics, such as Dancing, Swinging, Bowling, and Boating, etc." On Sunday, time was devoted to "speaking, and such other exercises as [were] consistent to the day and occasion."[10] The grove itself, which the promoters described as being "the best in the state for holding Camp or Grove Meetings," consisted of "about fifty acres of fine trees, set at convenient distances."[11] Around this time, Thoreau's Walden Pond in Concord, Massachusetts, served as the site of meetings organized by A. H. Richardson.[12] These gatherings, described in William Dean Howells's 1880 Spiritualist novel, *The Undiscovered Country,* apparently grew out of a series of picnics organized by Boston's Spiritualists and a fraternal organization known as the Sons of Joshua.[13]

Similarly, in 1869 an annual Spiritualist camp meeting was inaugurated on Cape Cod at Nickerson's Grove in Harwich, Massachusetts. Writing for the *Banner of Light,* the nation's most prominent Spiritualist newspaper, a correspondent described this initial meeting. "We soon found on one of the small hills," he wrote, "thickly studded with oaks of about ten years' growth, the underbrushed spot, with a speakers' stand, plenty of benches, and several tents for feeding and lodging visitors, a well of pure water, a few little knick-knacks, a[nd] plenty of good substantial food. . . . The accommodations on the ground for visitors were rude and new, and not entirely satisfactory; but this being the first season of holding it here, they will no doubt be better in coming years."[14]

While the Melrose, Abington, Concord, and Harwich gatherings set the pattern, they all were greatly overshadowed in the 1870s with the founding of Massachusetts's two most successful and formally organized Spiritualist camp meetings: Lake Pleasant and Onset Bay Grove. These two communities were the anchors of New England's Spiritualist camp circuit. Mediums, Spiritualists, and curiosity seekers traveled this circuit by train and ferry, spending time at each of the camps.[15]

The Fitchburg Railroad Company originally developed Lake Pleasant in 1872 as a resort to promote travel over its lines. Having placed picnic tables near the lake and constructed the depot, bandstand, and dancing pavilion, the railroad advertised Lake Pleasant as a resort destination (fig. 14.1). For the next two years, the site was used for Masonic picnics, Fourth of July celebrations, Grange parties, and temperance conventions.[16] The Spiritualists first appropriated this property during

Fig. 14.1. Lake Pleasant, Massachusetts. *Hoosac Tunnel Route, A Popular Summer Resort*. Published by the Bufford Sons Lith. Co., Boston. Courtesy of the Boston Athenaeum, Boston, Massachusetts.

the summer of 1874 when H. A. Budington, the editor of the *Franklin County Times* of Greenfield, Massachusetts, and a group of local Spiritualists, in consultation with Mr. Comee, the superintendent of the Fitchburg Railroad, sponsored a meeting that lasted from August 13 to August 27. Over this two-week period, the Fitchburg Band performed twice a day and received half its wages from the railroad. Seventy-five tents were pitched on the grounds, similar to one visible in a photographic portrait of the founders of the camp (fig. 14.2). The tents were supplied by Gardner and Richardson of Boston, presumably the same H. F. Gardner and A. H. Richardson who organized the meeting at Walden Pond and had promoted the camp in Abington, Massachusetts.[17] Throughout the meeting, "street speaking was frequent; many of the speakers and mediums holding forth in front of their tents to a gaping and astonished crowd. The enthusiasm was catching and the grove resounded with harangues."

Following the success of the meeting in 1874, Lake Pleasant became the site of annual gatherings.[18] Under the direction of Harvey Lyman, the next year a committee laid out the grounds and plotted locations for tents. The camp meeting attendees assumed a legal identity in 1879 when they incorporated as the New England Spiritualist Campmeeting Association.[19] Many of the organization's charter members were from the

Fig. 14.2. Founders of the Spiritualist Camp at Lake Pleasant, Massachusetts. From H. A. Budington, *History of the New England Spiritualist Campmeeting Association at Lake Pleasant, Mass.* (Springfield, Mass.: Star Publishing Company, 1907). Courtesy of the Pocumtuck Valley Memorial Association Library, Deerfield, Massachusetts.

surrounding communities of central Massachusetts, but others hailed from Boston, Brooklyn, New York, Hartford, Connecticut, and even as far away as Lombard and Stafford, Illinois.

In the summer of 1880, the *Springfield Republican* reported that the grove had grown to include more than 90 cottages, 175 tents, 8 restaurants, and a hotel built at a cost of $10,000 (fig. 14.3). The earliest cottages in the grove were built on land originally demarcated for tents and assumed a form similar to those in the Methodist's Wesleyan Grove on Martha's Vineyard described by Ellen Weiss in her seminal study, *City in the Woods*. The cabins were story-and-a-half structures with bilaterally symmetrical facades centered on a front entrance and gabled roofs facing the paths on which they were located. With the front facade pierced by windows and the main door, and the interior spaces thus largely open to the public thoroughfare, these structures, like the tents they replaced, provided shelter but little privacy. In describing Lake Pleasant, a correspondent for the *New York Times* found these cottages to be the community's outstanding feature. The journalist reported:

Lake Pleasant counts its cottages by the scores and the cottages are its essence. They are all alike in general plan and all different in little details. They resemble wall tents in shape, and like tents the front is almost all door. Each has its narrow porch in front. . . . The parlor, sitting room, and sometimes bedroom combined, which takes up the front of the cottage, is easily inspected from the outside, and it is clear that everybody must have a pretty accurate idea of what his neighbors are doing—that is unless he is near-sighted. A dining room and kitchen take up the rear of the little house, and up stairs are a couple of little bedrooms. Bright paint may vary the exteriors, but the interiors are all alike in general arrangements.[20]

In 1880 a new plot of ground was opened and divided into fifty-foot-square building lots, allowing for the construction of larger cabins. Separated from the camp's center by a ravine, these houselots were accessible by a bridge connecting the two areas of the grove.[21] Within a Spiritualist context, crossing over this structure, referred to as the "Bridge of Souls," represented more than a passage to one's cottage. The bridge, linking two localities divided by a chasm, became a physical metaphor for the transition from this life to the "summeland" on the other side of death.

In 1884, H. L. Barnard built a roller-skating rink, and the next year he erected a new bandstand. Previously having leased the property on which the camp was built, the Campmeeting Association finally purchased this land in 1887 from the Fitchburg Railroad. The camp prospered continually until 1907, when a blaze swept the closely settled grounds. Within three hours, 112 buildings were destroyed, with damage to the property estimated at one hundred thousand dollars. Although some rebuilding followed the fire and the Spiritualist association exists into the present, the Spiritualist moment had passed its peak, and the grove never regained its former vitality.[22]

During the summer meeting at Lake Pleasant in 1876, a small group composed of Dr. H. B. Storer, who had been active in the organization of the Pierpont Grove meeting, E. Gerry Brown, the crusading editor of the *Spiritual Scientist,* and H. S. Williams of Boston initiated a movement to institute a new camp on the Massachusetts shore. By January of 1877 the Onset Bay Grove Association had been formally chartered by the State of Massachusetts with a board of directors that included a number of individuals, like Storer and Brown, who simultaneously served as officers of Lake Pleasant's New England Spiritualist Camp-

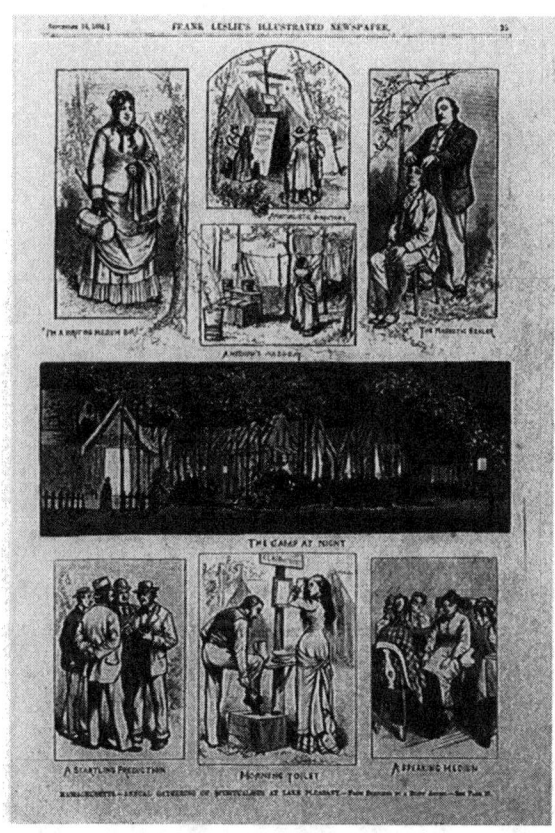

Fig. 14.3. Annual Gathering of Spiritualists at Lake Pleasant, Massachusetts, 1881. From *Frank Leslie's Illustrated Newspaper* (Sept. 10, 1881), 25. Courtesy of Richard Candee, Boston University, Boston, Massachusetts.

meeting Association.[23] The newly chartered association purchased a 125-acre waterfront plot on Buzzard's Bay in the town of Wareham, Massachusetts, and laid out streets, parks, and more than 700 building lots. The grove was opened officially on June 14, 1877 (fig. 14.4).[24] Elvira S. Loring of Fitchburg, Massachusetts, erected the first cottage almost immediately (fig. 14.5), and others quickly followed suit, building houses, a number of hotels, and an auditorium, which contemporaries referred to as a "temple." Onset's peak season was scheduled for July 8–22 of that year so it would not conflict with Lake Pleasant's announced activity period between August 6 and August 28. Brown, in an editorial for the *Spiritual Scientist,* prophesied that the two camps would work together "for the good of the general movement."[25]

Assuming forms similar to those at both the Methodists' Wesleyan Grove and the Spiritualists' Lake Pleasant, Onset Bay Grove's cottages were identified by appellations referring both to the natural world and to the fact that the grove supposedly had been a Native American religious site. With names such as "Wamsutta," "Forest Flower," "Weetamoe," "Sagamore Cottage," "Sunset," and "Forest Lodge," these structures became the standard residences within the grove,

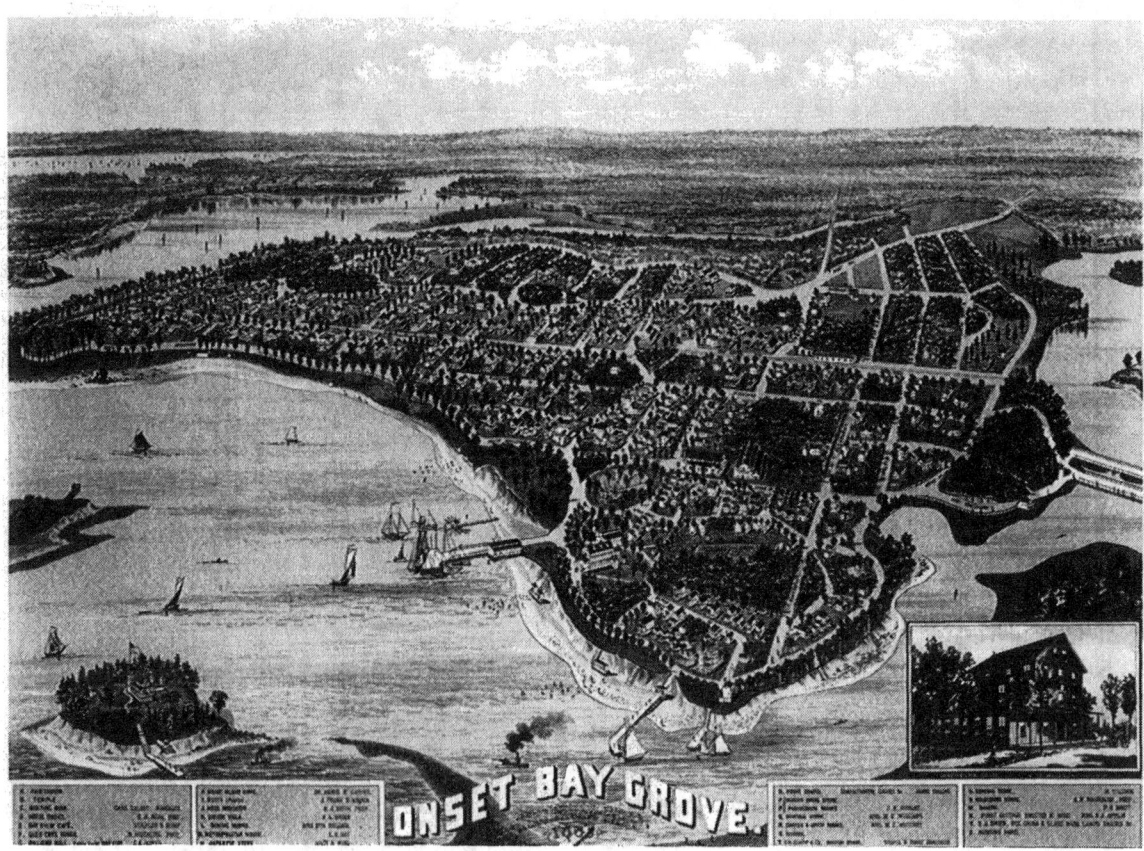

Fig. 14.4. Onset Bay Grove, Wareham, Massachusetts. Published by Oscar W. Walker, Boston, 1885. Courtesy of the Library of Congress.

Fig. 14.5. First House Built at Onset Bay Grove, Onset, Massachusetts. Postcard, author's collection.

but some individuals continued to pass their visit in tents.[26]

New England's other camps developed similarly. In 1881, Connecticut Spiritualists purchased thirty acres of land on a pine-covered knoll surrounded on three sides by Long Island Sound. Near the village of Niantic, the property was divided into lots and sold to buyers from throughout the state. By 1883, approximately seventy-five cottages had been erected, and a similar number of tents provided more temporary housing.[27] Maine's Camp Aetna, near the town of Carmel, was formally organized in 1879 with the first cottage built the same year. An auditorium seating one thousand people was opened during the summer of 1882.[28] Similarly, in describing the Verona Park Camp Meeting outside Bucksport, Maine, in 1885, H. H. Brown reported, "The camp is only two years old, but there are many cottages; an eating-house, a wharf, etc., are already builded [sic]."[29]

Spiritualist activities at the camps included both spirit-inspired public lectures and private seances. In the 1880s, *Facts* magazine, published in Boston, reported a wide range of spirit manifestations occurring at Onset and featured advertisements placed by professional mediums who attended the meetings.[30] While spiritual in content, the activities of the mediums were also commercial in nature. As professionals who charged for their supposed ability to breach the barrier between the visible and the invisible worlds, these individuals trafficked in both the powers of the unseen territory and in the hard currency of this material realm.

Although the camps were nominally Spiritualist, a wide range of secular activities also drew people. Leisure pastimes such as dancing, roller skating, and boating, frowned upon or banned at Methodist camps as inappropriate within a sacred context, were supported at these Spiritualist gatherings.[31] Concessionaires received franchises to build dance halls, roller-skating rinks, photographic studios, and other entertainment structures. In an article about Lake Pleasant, the *New York Times* reported:

> On a bulletin board near the hotel is an announcement that there is "Dancing from 3 to 5 and 8 to 10 every week day; tickets 50 cents" . . . and right beside it are the notices of the mediums and the hours at which their seances are to be held. Business and pleasure go hand in hand at Lake Pleasant. A shooting gallery, a place where one can throw a baseball at an image's head, and one or two other places where the visitor can dispose of his spare time and change flourish under the hill not far from the outdoor amphitheatre.

This correspondent reinforced the representation of the settlement's carnivalesque atmosphere later in the article by noting, "[l]ung testers and muscle testers do a brisk business, and the card writer, who could make a fortune by indorsing [sic] hair tonics, is surrounded by wondering crowds. Proprietors of refreshment stands are busy from morning to night and see a steady stream of silver pour into their tills."[32] At the camp in Niantic, Connecticut, the sacred and secular were so fully merged that the lecture pavilion also served as a dance hall and roller-skating rink.[33]

The mix of commercial and sacred pastimes at the camps provoked discussion within the community about how a suitable dignity could be maintained while simultaneously accommodating recreation. Correspondence in contemporary Spiritualist periodicals indicate that some individuals saw entertainment and spectacle as beneficial to the environment within the camps, while others believed that entrepreneurship required regulation. The former position is epitomized by an 1876 report in the *Spiritual Scientist*. "The sound of the music from the dance-hall," a contributor wrote, "was just sufficiently subdued by distance to add an inexpressible charm, and cause the ear to drink it in with pleasure, without interfering with the attention due to the excellence of the discourses from the speaker's stand."[34] A correspondent in the same periodical a year earlier had argued an opposing position. This unidentified writer—probably the editor E. Gerry Brown—held that organizational restrictions were necessary to ensure "the good of the greatest number." "Individual enterprise," he claimed, "estimates success by the number of dollars coined. The interest of the pockets is consulted rather than the interest of spiritualism. A performing elephant, a raging lion, or a tame jackass would be put on the platform as a spiritual medium or speaker, providing these celebrities would draw large audiences."[35] While individuals disagreed upon the extent to which commercialism should intrude upon religious pursuits, everyone agreed that commercial interests had a place within the groves.

These activities appealed to Spiritualists, but also were employed consciously to draw the general public to the camps. In 1879, Nettie Pease Fox, the editor of the Rochester, New York, *Spiritual Offering*, wrote, "Much of the success attending the spreading of Methodism, in its earlier and purer days, may be attributed to the effect of their camp meetings, held on almost every 'circuit.' The Spiritualists of Massachusetts years ago became convinced of their efficacy. . . . Through this instrumentality, our teachings may be scattered broadcast, thousands attend who would not otherwise hear the Gospel of Spiritualism."[36]

The efforts to draw audiences proved successful; the Spiritualist groves were tremendously popular. Camp Aetna had five thousand people on the grounds during the last day of its season in 1883.[37] The Onset Bay Grove Association claimed that an audience of ten thousand heard A. B. French speak in August of 1885.[38] The *New*

York Times, which had no apparent motive for overestimating crowds, even testified to the camps' popularity. "Sunday sees half the population of the neighboring towns" visiting Lake Pleasant, the paper reported. "Long excursion trains come in from all directions, and the country roads are black with vehicles of all descriptions bound toward the camp."[39]

While the camps attracted outsiders and exposed them to the teachings of Spiritualism, they also served as communication centers for a movement that rejected hierarchy and institutionalization. The Spiritualists were suspicious of any attempts to organize or regulate their religious experiences, yet they also craved fellowship and group support for their beliefs.[40] The seasonal, temporary communities of the camps proved to be nonthreatening forums for the solidification of support for the Spiritualist movement.[41] As Nettie Pease Fox wrote in 1879, the camps provided "opportunity . . . for social intercourse. Spiritualists and liberalists from different parts of the country are brought together, become acquainted, and plans can be matured for the spread of spiritual teachings."[42]

Participants in these meetings simultaneously fled the artifice of the cities and consciously immersed themselves in the natural world. "Coming as most of us now here do, from the heat and dust of city life," Flora B. Cabell wrote to the *Banner of Light* in 1885, "every one seems to have left all care behind, and to enter heartily into the semi-gypsy life of Onset, to hold communion with nature and the spirit-world."[43] Spiritualist camp meetings were a physical expression of the nineteenth-century concept of nature as both healing and sacred.[44] A promotional article for Onset Bay Grove, appearing in the secular *New England Magazine* of 1905, claimed that "[t]hose who seek renewed health can find, regardless of creed, no better place than Onset for a summer vacation, for the air is lifegiving, being impregnated with the healing balm of the pine forests of Plymouth."[45] Fox, the Spiritualist editor, had expressed this sentiment nearly thirty years earlier when she wrote that at camp meetings "our wearied bodies get rest by drawing nearer to Nature in her beautiful, leafy temple."[46] Similarly, in 1876 the *Spiritual Scientist* described one of the camps as "the healthy grove of Lake Pleasant."[47] The Spiritualists' religious motivation for gathering in groves in the woods was made explicit by a correspondent for the *Banner of Light* in 1869. "The groves were God's first temples," this author, identified only as "S," wrote,

> and in no place can the soul of man approach so near to or come so perfectly *en rapport* with the soul of all things, as when surrounded only by the manifestations in nature which spontaneously clothe it in beauty and majesty. . . . The nearer we get to Nature, the nearer we are to God. . . . The ground alone as pavement is a better 'conductor' of the soul reforming influences than mosaic marbles: and an open shed with an entrance all around, has witnessed many an outpouring of the spirit which painted windows and gilded organs would have failed to call down.[48]

As this correspondent makes clear, in embracing nature the campers were simultaneously rejecting artifice and what were perceived as the constraints of culture.

Because they rejected human contrivance and instead embraced nature, Spiritualists included in their camps' designs curvilinear forms which could be construed as organic. The plans of these camps stand in stark contrast to those of the roughly contemporaneous Methodist camps which are rational, rectilinear, and rigidly hierarchical. The Methodist camp at Pitman Grove outside Philadelphia in southern New Jersey, for example, is ordered around a series of spokes radiating out from a center defined by the tabernacle, a ritually charged location where the realm of the spirit symbolically intersects with the material world. Ocean Grove on the New Jersey

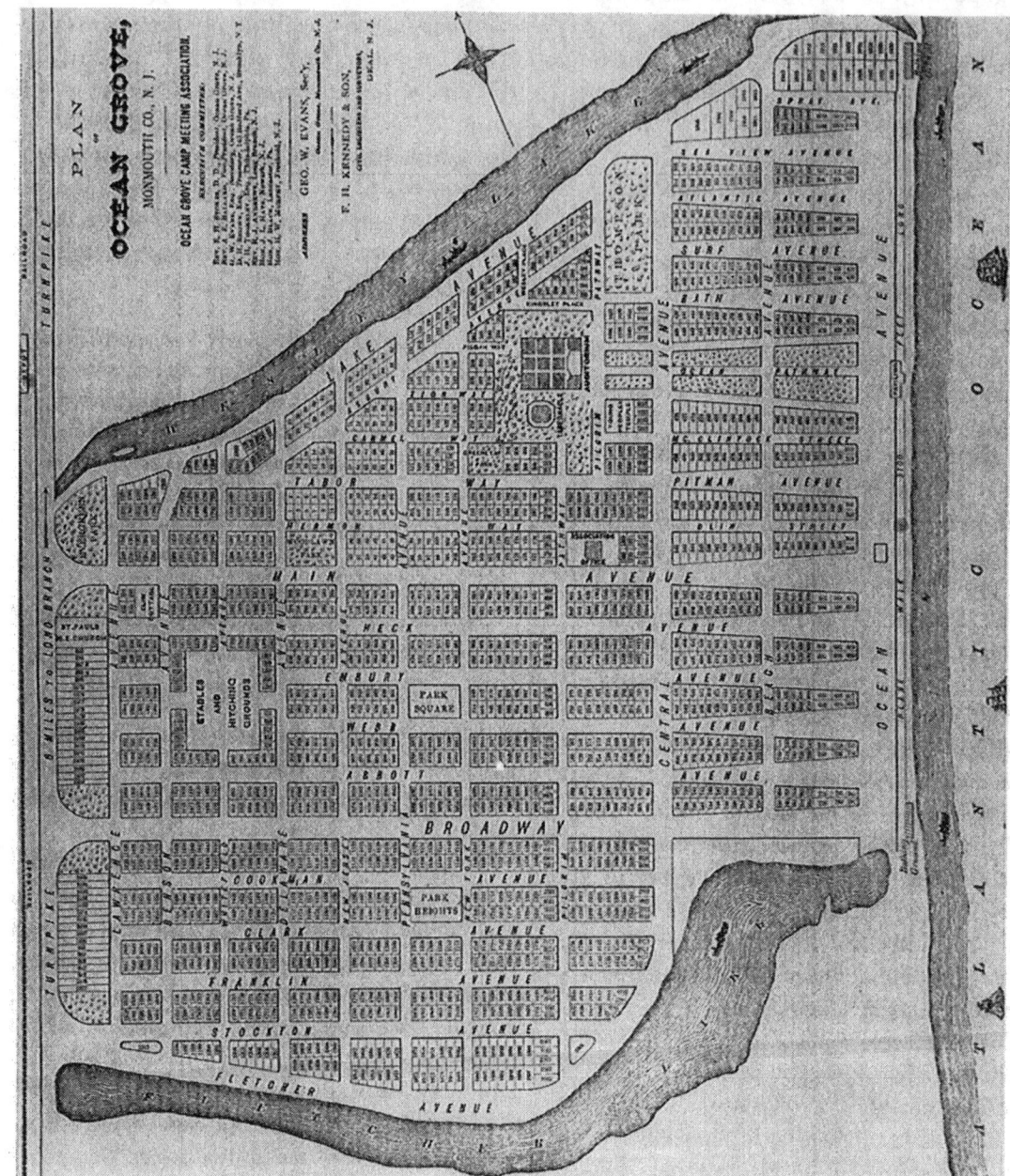

Fig. 14.6. Plan of Ocean Grove, Monmouth Co., N.J. Published by Fisk & Co., New York. Courtesy of Special Collections and University Archives, Rutgers University Libraries, New Brunswick, New Jersey.

Shore, the "Queen of the Victorian Methodist Camp Meeting Resorts," has a rigid plan, similar to urban, nineteenth-century grids, with straight streets meeting at right angles and a grand ceremonial plaza with an auditorium as its focal point (fig. 14.6). These designs placed individuals within the grove in specific spatial relationships to the institutional identity of the church as manifested in the physical presence of the tabernacle.

Conversely, Onset Bay Grove features curvilinear streets arranged around a series of irregularly shaped parks. Lake Pleasant, although it was platted in 1879, has no overarching imposed plan; the interaction of the natural landscape and the railroad determined the form of the community. New Hampshire's Blodgett's Landing is organized around the curving shoreline of Lake Sunapee. None of the Spiritualist camps is dominated by a single structure. The landscape is more egalitarian; no one space or structure is privileged as the source of enlightenment. The barrier between the visible and the invisible worlds could be pierced at any point within the grove.

Like American rural cemeteries of the mid-nineteenth century, the Spiritualist camps drew upon concepts of landscape design which had gained prominence in eighteenth-century England. Influenced by writers such as John Evelyn, Francis Hutcheson, and Alexander Pope, English elites adorned their estates with gardens designed to celebrate nature and inspire melancholy contemplation.[49] These aristocratic pastoral retreats, typified by Sir Richard Temple's Stowe in Buckinghamshire, England, featured curving paths, vistas overlooking bodies of water, and architectural confections designed to help visitors reflect on their relationship to history and to the universe.

In the United States, these ideas first were implemented at Mount Auburn cemetery in Cambridge, Massachusetts, consecrated in 1831 (fig. 14.7). This burial ground, a product of Boston's liberal Unitarianism, in many ways was a precursor to the Spiritualist camp meetings. Designed to assist individuals in contemplating death and memorializing their deceased relations, the cemetery also served as a pleasure park in which Bostonians could enjoy a pastoral landscape. In his consecration address, United States Supreme Court Justice Joseph Story declared that in Mount Auburn, "We stand, as it were, upon the borders of two worlds."[50] The cemetery connected the living with the dead and the city with the country.[51]

Both rural cemeteries and Spiritualism were products of American religious liberalism.[52] The winding paths and wooded parks of these pastoral landscapes provided a fitting forum for the Spiritualists' romantic reunions with the dead. In 1856, John Shoebridge Williams, who had been converted to Spiritualism by the Fox sisters five years earlier, designed Urbana, Ohio's Oak Dale Cemetery, to be a place of spiritual uplift.[53] The cemeteries, with their benches, glades, and grottoes, provided spaces for individuals to personally come to terms with the hereafter with minimal institutional mediation. Although Methodist camps served as models for Spiritualist summer communities, the rationality and hierarchy of Methodist designs were rejected in favor of a landscape architecture emphasizing the emotionalism and egalitarianism of Spiritualist belief systems. America's pastoral cemeteries, with their consciously designed naturalistic contours, provided prototypes for this desired form.

In the Spiritualist view, cultural constructs, including religious institutions, interfered with human freedom and hampered the actions of the spirits. As historian Ann Braude has argued, gender and racial roles were included in the cultural constrictions Spiritualists questioned.[54] The camps served as seemingly unstructured arenas in which participants put their beliefs into action and experimented with expanding the boundaries of behavior prescribed by Victorian American society. Women actively participated within Spiritualist organizations, in some instances assuming

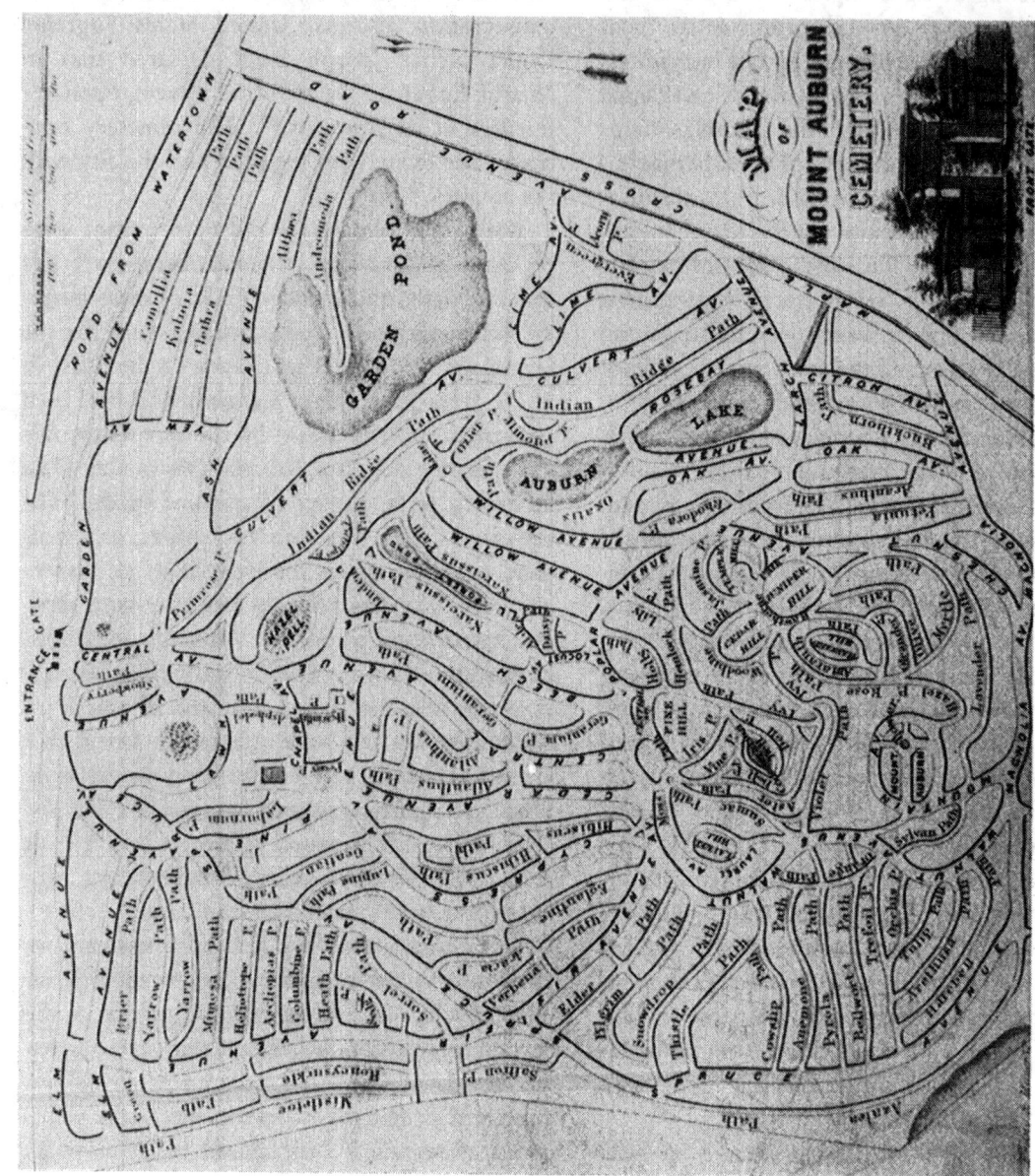

Fig. 14.7. Mt. Auburn Cemetery, Cambridge, Massachusetts, landscape design by Henry A. S. Dearborn, photography by Thomas Denenberg, 1831. Courtesy of the Cambridge Historical Society, Cambridge, Massachusetts.

leadership capacities that would have been denied them in other contexts. They played such central roles in the affairs of the Spiritualists that the groups came to be described as "petticoat oligarchies."[55] Furthermore, because of the opportunity for expanded gender definitions within the Spiritualist camps, these groves became centers for suffragist activism. Days were set aside for discussion of political emancipation of women, and women's rights advocates such as Mary A. Livermore and Susan B. Anthony spoke before enthusiastic audiences.[56]

The loosening of Victorian cultural boundaries also worked along racial and ethnic lines. As noted previously, Mrs. Hattie Wilson, an African American woman, spoke at one of the earliest Spiritualist meetings, and many of the Spiritualists had been active in abolitionism before the Civil War. At Onset Bay Grove in 1894, one group of believers experimented with transcending racial denominations and assumed the identity of a cultural other by building and inhabiting a supposedly Native American "wig-wam" (fig. 14.8). Erected by William J. Cairns, a contractor and builder from Cochesett, Massachusetts, this structure was reserved for the use of predominantly Anglo-American mediums who channeled the spirits and were believed to speak with the voices of deceased Native Americans.[57] Similarly, Connecticut's Niantic camp featured a tent identified as the "Red Fire Wig Wam."[58] In these wigwams, a cultural group which was marginalized, disenfranchised, and massacred by mainstream America supposedly was given a voice by the Spiritualists. The mediums spoke as Native Americans who, they claimed, could no longer speak for themselves.

The stretching of cultural preconceptions also may have allowed New England's Spiritualist camps to serve as a beachhead for the entrance of Eastern mysticism into American thought. Between 1874 and 1876, Spiritualist newspaper editor E. Gerry Brown, an officer of both the Onset Bay Grove Association and Lake Pleasant's New England Spiritualist Campmeeting Association, actively promoted his weekly *Spiritual Scientist* at Lake Pleasant by distributing sample issues and selling subscriptions. During this period, he also published a number of esoteric articles written by Helena Petrovna Blavatsky and Henry Steel Olcott, just as these two hierophants were founding the Theosophical Society.[59] In the 1870s, Blavatsky's

Fig. 14.8. The Wig-Wam, Built in 1894 by William J. Cairns, Onset Bay Grove, Massachusetts. Postcard, author's collection.

occult knowledge was purported to be grounded in ancient Egyptian mysteries. By the early 1880s, her Theosophical Society was acting as a conduit through which esoteric ideas from the Indian subcontinent were introduced to the West.[60] While neither Blavatsky nor Olcott presently can be documented as having attended New England's Spiritualist camps, by publishing their work Brown likely brought the Theosophists' explorations of Middle Eastern mystic fraternities and interactions with unseen Himalayan masters to the attention of his fellow summer campers.

While the Spiritualists' acceptance of exotic ideas and seemingly bizarre claims may be ridiculed as gullibility or categorized as a commodified antimodernist desire for intense experience, these camps must be recognized for providing environments in which progressive ideas could be received and developed.[61] Such diverse phenomena as the mystical propensities of early-twentieth-century Arts and Crafts ideology, the introduction of Zen Buddhism to America, and the growth of the suffragist movement may be linked, directly or indirectly, to the camps' fertile religious and intellectual environments.[62]

In conclusion, Spiritualist camp meetings developed in New England in the decade following the Civil War and reached their fullest manifestations in New England in the camps at Lake Pleasant and Onset Bay Grove. By incorporating secular activities into the resort camp meeting environment developed earlier by mainstream Protestant denominations, the Spiritualists both exposed the public to their beliefs and presaged later fully commercial resorts such as Coney Island. Although the Spiritualist camps resembled evangelical Protestant camps, the overall design of the environment drew upon the garden cemeteries popular in mid-nineteenth-century America, de-emphasized structure and hierarchy, and offered instead a built form based upon emotional egalitarianism.

Spiritualist camps were liminal zones removed from the work-a-day world of their inhabitants. Their fecund cultural environments fostered alternative religious and ethical thought, influencing later twentieth-century American culture. Brought into being by the interaction of railroad promoters, true believers, holiday travelers, professional mediums, and speculators in recreational activities, these camps situated betwixt and between served as forums in which Americans, in the final decades of the nineteenth century and first decades of the twentieth, worked to construct new identities by breaking down barriers separating cultural conceptions constructed by society as binary opposites. While in these camps where land met water and nature mingled with artifice, the Spiritualists inhabited a world neither enclosed nor exposed to the elements and brought into unity the worlds of the living and the dead, the sacred and the secular, the spiritual and the commercial, the male and the female, and the middle-class American and groups perceived as the cultural other.

Notes

The author thanks Patricia Hills and Kate and Peter Diamond for introducing him to Ocean Grove and Blodgett's Landing, respectively, thus inspiring this research. Keith Morgan, Richard Candee, Edward S. Cooke, and Ellen Weiss read drafts of this essay and provided valuable comments and encouragement. Particular thanks go to Charlotte Emans Moore for the thousand and one ways that she has added to this undertaking.

1. Lilian Whiting, "The Spiritualistic Camp Meetings in the United States," *Annals of Psychical Science* 5 (25) (Jan. 1907): 17. For an overview of the history of American Spiritualism, see Joseph McCabe, *Spiritualism: A Popular History from 1847* (New York: Dodd, Mead and Company, 1920). For the best recent work on Spiritualism in America, see Ann Braude, *Radical Spirits: Spiritualism and Women's Rights in Nineteenth-Century America* (Boston: Beacon Press, 1989).
2. In Maine, Spiritualists gathered at the Aetna Camp-Meeting outside Bangor, at Temple Heights Camp in Northport, and at Verona Park near Bucksport. In Massachusetts, Spiritualists attended meetings across the state, from Lake Pleasant in Montague, to Onset Bay Grove, in Wareham, and Ocean Grove, in Harwich. New Hampshire hosted two camps, Blodgett's Landing on Lake Sunapee and the Medium's Camp Meeting of the Two Worlds in Rindge. The Queen City Park Association of Spiritualists met outside of Burlington, Vermont, while the Niantic meeting was located near New London, Connecticut. See H. D. Barrett and A. W. McCoy, *Cassadaga; Its History and Teachings* (Meadville, Pa.: The Gazette Printing Company, 1891), 14–35.
3. Victoria Barnes, comp., *Centennial Book of Modern Spiritualism* (Chicago: National Spiritualist Association, 1948), 107–242; "Spiritual Conventions and Camp-Meetings," *Spiritual Scientist* 4 (14) (June 8, 1876): 163; "Spiritualist Meetings," *Spiritual Scientist* 4 (21) (July 27, 1876): 242; "Spiritualist Camp and Grove Meetings," *Spiritual Scientist* 4 (25) (Aug. 24, 1876): 294. I am indebted to John Patrick Deveney for making the *Spiritual Scientist* accessible to me.
4. John R. Stilgoe, *Common Landscape of America, 1580–1845* (New Haven and London: Yale Univ. Press, 1982), 231–38; Charles A. Parker, *Pitman Grove: Through a Tiffany Window, 1870–1900* (Woodbury, N.J.: Gloucester County Historical Society, 1984), 1–15.
5. Kenneth O. Brown, *Holy Ground: A Study of the American Camp Meeting* (New York: Garland, 1992); Charles A. Parker, "The Camp Meeting on the Frontier and the Methodist Religious Resort in the East—Before 1900," *Methodist History* 18 (3) (Apr. 1980); Parker, "Ocean Grove, New Jersey: Queen of the Victorian Methodist Camp Meeting Resorts," *Nineteenth Century* 9 (1–2) (Spring 1984): 19–25; Ellen Weiss, *City in the Woods: The Life and Design of an American Camp Meeting on Martha's Vineyard* (New York: Oxford Univ. Press, 1987); Weiss, "The Wesleyan Grove Campground," *Architecture Plus* 1 (Nov. 1973): 44–49. For a brief overview of the Spiritualist camp meeting movement, see Braude, *Radical Spirits*, 173–76.
6. Lake Pleasant and Onset Bay Grove were the largest, most prosperous, well-attended, and famous of New England's Spiritualist camp meetings.
7. Braude, *Radical Spirits*, 31.
8. Barrett and McCoy, *Cassadaga*, 14.
9. "Fourth Annual Spiritualist Camp-Meeting, at Pierpont Grove, Melrose, Mass," *Banner of Light* 25 (20) (July 31, 1869): 5; "Camp Meeting at Melrose," *Banner of Light* 25 (25) (Sept. 4, 1869): 8; "Spiritualists' Camp Meeting at Pierpont Grove," *Boston Journal*, Sept. 2, 1867.
10. "Spiritualists' Grand Mass Grove Meeting," *Banner of Light* 25 (21) (Aug. 7, 1869): 5.
11. H. E. Gardner, "Spiritualists' Grand Mass Grove Meeting," *Banner of Light* 25 (22) (Aug. 14, 1869): 5.
12. Barrett and McCoy, *Cassadaga*, 15.
13. "Picnic at Walden Pond," *Banner of Light* 25 (14)

(June 19, 1869): 8; William Dean Howells, *The Undiscovered Country* (Boston: Houghton, Mifflin and Co., 1880), 254–56.

14. W. C., "Camp Meeting at Harwich, Mass," *Banner of Light* 25 (21) (Aug. 7, 1869): 8.
15. "A Camp-Meeting Trip," *Facts* 6 (6) (May/June 1887): 154–57.
16. H. A. Budington, *History of the New England Spiritualist Campmeeting Association at Lake Pleasant, Mass.* (Springfield, Mass.: Star Publishing Company, 1907), 1–2.
17. Ibid., 4–5; Barrett and McCoy, *Cassadaga*, 15. In 1876, Gardner and Richardson also promoted a Spiritualist camp meeting in Highland Lake Grove outside of Norfolk, Massachusetts. "Spiritualists' Picnic," *Spiritual Scientist* 4 (15) (June 15, 1876): 175; "Highland Lake Grove," *Spiritual Scientist* 4 (16) (June 22, 1876): 183; "Highland Lake Camp-Meeting," *Spiritual Scientist* 4 (21) (July 27, 1876): 241, 243.
18. For directories of individuals renting space at the Lake Pleasant camp meeting, see "Lake Pleasant Camp Meeting," *Spiritual Scientist* 2 (24) (Aug. 19, 1875): 278–79; and "Lake Pleasant Camp-Meeting," *Spiritual Scientist* 4 (25) (Aug. 24, 1876): 291–92.
19. For a preliminary set of constitution and bylaws of the New England Spiritualists' Camp-Meeting Association [*sic*], see *Spiritual Scientist* 5 (5) (Oct. 5, 1876): 52–53. For a discussion of the importance of camp meeting organizations, see "Camp-Meetings and the Necessity of Organization," *Spiritual Scientist* 4 (24) (Aug. 17, 1876): 282. This article argues that organizations protect the camps from "the whims and caprices of railroads and other corporations."
20. "Seances and Dancing: How Spiritualists Enjoy Themselves in Camp at Lake Pleasant," *New York Times*, Aug. 27, 1886.
21. Budington, *History of the New England Spiritualist Campmeeting Association*, 24–26.
22. Robert B. Begg, "Lake Pleasant—The Village Comes of Age Today," *Greenfield Recorder*, Aug. 14, 1974.
23. "Onset Bay Grove Association," *Spiritual Scientist* 5 (20) (Jan. 18, 1877): 234–35; "N. E. Spiritualists' Camp-Meeting Association," *Spiritual Scientist* 6 (5) (Apr. 5, 1877): 54–55.
24. "Onset Bay Grove Association," *Spiritual Scientist* 6 (10) (May 10, 1877): 114–15.
25. "Camp-Meetings," *Spiritual Scientist* 6 (10) (May 10, 1877): 114.
26. Barrett and McCoy, *Cassadaga*, 17–19; C. B. Vaughn, "Onset, a Famous Camping Ground," *New England Magazine* 32 (6) (Aug. 1905): 617–25. Further research is required in sources as yet unlocated to isolate the factors determining who built cottages and who camped in tents.
27. "Spirits in Cozy Places: Charming Retreat of the Connecticut Spiritualists," *New York Times*, Aug. 17, 1883.
28. Barnes, *Centennial Book of Modern Spiritualism*, 143.
29. H. H. Brown, "Verona Park Camp-Meeting," *Banner of Light* 57 (24) (Aug. 29, 1885): 8.
30. See, for example, "The Facts Seance at Onset," *Facts* 6 (7) (July 1887): 176–81; *Facts* 4 (8) (Aug. 1885): 134.
31. For Methodist camp meeting rules, see Parker, *Pitman Grove*, 63–74, 101–7.
32. "Seances and Dancing: How Spiritualists Enjoy Themselves in Camp at Lake Pleasant," *New York Times*, Aug. 27, 1886.
33. "Spirits in Cozy Places: Charming Retreat of the Connecticut Spiritualists," *New York Times*, Aug. 17, 1883.
34. "Highland Lake Campmeeting," *Spiritual Scientist* 4 (21) (July 27, 1876): 243.
35. "Lake Pleasant Camp Meeting," *Spiritual Scientist* 2 (23) (Aug. 12, 1875): 271.
36. Nettie Pease Fox, "Camp Meetings," *Spiritual Offering* (Apr. 1879): 375–76. Little is known currently about Nettie Pease Fox. She was not one of the famous Fox sisters and apparently gained the

Fox surname through marriage to Col. D. M. Fox. She seems to have arrived in Rochester in 1878, having previously resided in Missouri. See *Spiritual Offering* (Apr. 1879): 378; *Spiritual Offering* (Nov. 1878): 60.

37. Charles M. Brown, "About Aetna (Me.) Camp-Meeting," *Banner of Light* 57 (22) (Aug. 15, 1885): 8.
38. "Onset Bay Grove," *Banner of Light* 57 (22) (Aug. 15, 1885): 8.
39. "Seances and Dancing: How Spiritualists Enjoy Themselves in Camp at Lake Pleasant," *New York Times,* Aug. 27, 1886.
40. There are many dogmatic and institutional similarities between nineteenth-century Spiritualists and the Gnostic Christian communities of the second and third centuries A.D. Among these are a belief in communication with unembodied forces, a lack of hierarchies, and a rejection of reified patriarchy. See Elaine Pagels, *The Gnostic Gospels* (New York: Random House, 1979).
41. In 1876, E. Gerry Brown, the editor of the *Spiritual Scientist,* attempted to parlay the success of the Lake Pleasant camp meeting into a statewide Spiritualist association. See "An Opportunity That Should Be Improved," *Spiritual Scientist* 4 (25) (Aug. 24, 1876): 294; "Organization," *Spiritual Scientist* 4 (26) (Aug. 31, 1876): 306.
42. Fox, "Camp Meetings," 376.
43. Flora B. Cabell, "To the Editor of the Banner of Light," *Banner of Light* 57 (21) (Aug. 8, 1885): 8.
44. Braude, *Radical Spirits,* 36. For a discussion of American visions of nature in this period, see Peter J. Schmitt, *Back to Nature: The Arcadian Myth in Urban America* (New York: Oxford Univ. Press, 1969). For a discussion of the concepts of health and nature in relation to the development of resorts in New York State during this period, see W. Douglas McCombs, "Therapeutic Rusticity: Antimodernism, Health and the Wilderness Vacation, 1870–1915," *New York History* 76 (4) (Oct. 1995): 409–28.
45. Vaughn, "Onset, a Famous Camping Ground," 625.
46. Fox, "Camp Meetings," 375–76.
47. "Lake Pleasant Camp-Meeting," *Spiritual Scientist* 4 (18) (July 6, 1876), 207.
48. "S," "Places for Spiritual Meetings, and How to Build Them," *Banner of Light* 25 (15) (June 26, 1869): 3. The quotation, "The groves were God's first temples," is from William Cullen Bryant's poem "A Forest Hymn." See William Cullen Bryant, "A Forest Hymn," in *Poems* (Philadelphia: A. Hart, 1851), 130–34.
49. For a discussion of the origins of the English landscape tradition, see Blanche Linden-Ward, *Silent City on a Hill: Landscapes of Memory and Boston's Mount Auburn Cemetery* (Columbus: Ohio State Univ. Press, 1989), 35–63.
50. William Wetmore Story, ed., *Life and Letters of Joseph Story* (Boston: Little, Brown, 1851), 2: 65–67.
51. Linden-Ward, *Silent City on a Hill,* 167–96. See also Stanley French, "The Cemetery as Cultural Institution: The Establishment of Mount Auburn and the 'Rural Cemetery' Movement," in *Death in America,* ed. David E. Stannard (Philadelphia: Univ. of Pennsylvania Press, 1975), 69–91.
52. See Ann Douglas, "Heaven Our Home: Consolation Literature in the Northern United States, 1830–1880," in *Death in America,* 49–68.
53. Braude, *Radical Spirits,* 53.
54. Ibid., 78, 116–61.
55. C. E. B., "A Ride With the Spiritualists," *New York Daily Tribune,* Aug. 25, 1861, 3.
56. Whiting, "The Spiritualistic Camp Meetings," 19.
57. Russ H. Gilbert, *The Story of a Wigwam* (Onset: n.p., 1904).
58. "Spirits in Cozy Places: Charming Retreat of the Connecticut Spiritualists," *New York Times,* Aug. 17, 1883.
59. For references to the relations between Brown and both Blavatsky and Olcott, see Michael Gomes, *The Dawning of the Theosophical Movement*

(Wheaton, Ill: The Theosophical Publishing House, 1987), 68–71. See also Joscelyn Godwin, "The Haunting of E. Gerry Brown: A Contemporary Document," *Theosophical History* 4 (4–5) (Oct. 1992–Jan. 1993): 115–20. I am indebted to John Patrick Deveney for bringing this relationship to my attention.

60. Joscelyn Godwin, *The Theosophical Enlightenment* (Albany: State Univ. of New York Press, 1994), 277–331.

61. T. J. Jackson Lears, *No Place of Grace: Antimodernism and the Transformation of American Culture, 1880–1920* (New York: Pantheon, 1981), 142–81.

62. Godwin, *Theosophical Enlightenment*, 187–379; Richard Guy Wilson, "'Divine Excellence': The Arts and Crafts Life in California," in *The Arts and Crafts Movement in California: Living the Good Life*, ed. Kenneth R. Trapp (New York: Abbeville Press, 1993), 26–33. For a history of Theosophy and its wide influence, see Peter Washington, *Madame Blavatsky's Baboon* (New York: Schocken Books, 1995).

PART V

HOUSE AND HOME

CHAPTER 15

Richard Harris

Reading Sanborns for the Spoor of the Owner-Builder, 1890s–1950s

Here, from some supernal height,
is visible the universal grid of urban living,
as delicate a tracery as the lace on a christening gown.
—Verlyn Klinkenborg, *The Last Fine Time*

[W]herever similar patterns of self-building [on] small parcels of land predominated, mixed and irregular patterns, with houses of different ages and styles set back varying distances from the curb were likely to result.
—Graeme Wynn, "The Rise of Vancouver"

In North America many families have housed themselves by building homes, literally, with their own hands.[1] This practice was common until the 1920s, declined, and then rebounded after World War II. By 1949 one-quarter of all new single-family homes in the United States were owner built.[2] (The situation in Canada was probably quite similar.) This proportion rose for a year or two, dropped to about 10 percent by 1955, and has fluctuated a little below that level ever since.[3] Over the decades, then, owner-builders have played a substantial role in the making of North American cities, but how substantial, and where have their activities been concentrated? We have no satisfactory answers, and in this chapter I outline a method for addressing them.

The method that I propose assumes that owner-builders created a distinctive type of urban landscape and that key elements were captured in fire insurance atlases, such as those produced by the Sanborn Company. In effect, I argue that we can track the owner-builder by reading the spoor he left on the ground, and hence in the Sanborns. (Most owner-builders are men.[4]) To make this argument it is necessary to link specific features recorded in the Sanborns with the building processes typical of owner-construction. This I do in general terms (in the first section), before interpreting the development of specific blocks in two cities, Milwaukee and Flint (in the second section). I have chosen these from the few documented cases of owner-building, so that it is possible to interpret with some authority the atlas evidence.

Using only two case studies, it is impossible to do justice to the local and regional variation in owner-built landscapes. This is especially true since, as the constraints faced by owner-builders changed over time, so too did the most typical built forms. Between about 1910 and the 1950s the advent of the automobile made it possible to build at steadily lower residential densities. By contrasting portions of Milwaukee developed around the turn of the century with fringe development around Flint from the 1920s onwards, I merely illustrate the broad pattern of historical development. Sanborns document other places and times, however, and in the conclusion I assess their broader limitations and potentialities.

Building Process and Form

If Sanborns are useful as sources of information about owner building then this is partly by default. Prior to 1949 there is no national source which documents owner building, while local evidence is sparse. Many suburbs did not require building permits as late as the 1940s, and this was especially true in rural and urban fringe areas where owner-builders were most active.[5] Alternatively, property assessment records can be used to infer the extent of owner-building.[6] To be useful, of course, assessments must have survived, and often they have not. Moreover, to obtain useful information from this source one must invest scores of hours of work.

A more practicable way of determining the extent and location of owner building is to infer the process from its product. Most of those men who built their own homes did so from necessity, not choice. Although some were employed in the building trades, the majority were untutored in construction and used the simplest available technology, the balloon frame. As a result, they began by building modest, one-story, frame structures. An exception emerged with the development of cement and cinder blocks, which were easier and cheaper to use than brick. Recognizing this, several authors wrote manuals explaining how to lay concrete blocks, even to the extent of making one's own.[7] Amateurs could use this newer technology, and in the late 1940s the presence of occasional block homes in fringe areas is a clue to the presence of owner-builders. In general, however, frame construction was the rule.

Some owners could call upon the help of immediate family or friends, and many hired contractors to perform specific tasks. Even so, in North America as opposed to Western Europe, each owner-builder family usually acted independently and produced a dwelling that was unique in terms of its size and placement on the lot, and often in plan and style too.[8] Aggregated at the scale of the block or subdivision, owner-builders usually produced a distinctive landscape, gap-toothed in the early years, of small, single-storied, frame dwellings with varied setbacks and styles. The scene in a Toronto suburb in 1916 shows each of these elements (fig. 15.1). The architectural historian Alan Gowans, who grew up in this area, has pointed out that one or two of the dwellings in this photograph, including that with a porch in the very center, might have been kits.[9] It is true that many of the kits sold by mail-order companies were erected by their owners. The Sears home catalog for 1926, for example, included testimonials from at least two owner-builders.[10] More important, much larger numbers of kits (and near-kits) were sold by local lumber dealers. Wahlfeld Mfg. Co. in Peoria, Illinois, is a case in point. In 1940–41 Wahlfeld mounted and advertised an "Owner Built" program under which the company provided materials and technical assistance, including on-site supervision.[11] It attracted scores of customers. Judging from surviving photographs that Wahlfeld took for promotional purposes, all were modest frame structures.¹²

As dealers involved themselves more closely, dwellings became more standardized. Wahlfeld encouraged customers to work from standard plans, and many homes pictured in its album looked somewhat similar. Those built by Pittinger and Williams in Sunnyland illustrate the point. One of the more substantial homes was built by LaVern Schwab in Robein. Schwab's daughter recalls that her father made the blocks for the basement, and that the family moved in as soon as the basement was enclosed.¹³ The process was typical of earlier generations of owner-builders. The result, however, was not as easily distinguishable from the handiwork of other owner-builders, nor indeed from the work of commercial operators.

In such situations, the best remaining clue is scattered development with varied street setbacks.

Even in the late 1940s, however, most owners assembled their homes in a more piecemeal fashion, buying materials bit by bit from dealers or scavenging them from other building sites. Geno Reck worked this way, saving from week to week to build a small, three-bedroom home in El Vista, a suburb of Peoria, in the late 1930s.¹⁴ On Reck's income as an unskilled laborer, a basement was at first an unaffordable luxury. He added one later, after wartime wages enabled him to acquire a cement mixer—from Sears, as he recalls. He then used the same mixer to help build the basement of a second home. On slightly larger lots, then, families like the Schwabs and the Recks produced a landscape around Peoria in the 1930s and 1940s which shared a family resemblance

Fig. 15.1. Earlscourt, a Suburb of Toronto, in 1916. Scattered development of modest frame dwellings is indicative of owner building. John Boyd, courtesy of National Archives of Canada.

with that of Toronto's suburbs a generation earlier. Anarchic and unpretentious, this landscape is the spoor of the owner-builder.

This landscape has survived in many parts of some cities, and in some parts of just about all. In and around Peoria, it is everywhere. In larger cities, circumstances rarely favored owner building to the same degree: suburban land was likely to be more expensive, and more tightly regulated. Moreover, market pressures have often led to the demolition of owner-built dwellings, either on a piecemeal basis or through wholesale renewal. The landscape of today is not always a reliable guide to the way an area was originally developed. In this context, insurance atlases, such as those made for U.S. cities by the Sanborn Company, and for Canadian cities by Charles Goad, are an invaluable source.[15] Urban and architectural historians are fairly familiar with these atlases and have used them to identify past land use. Indeed, for this purpose they were once heavily used, and endorsed, by the U.S. census.[16] Several geographers have used them to document the character of residential development, including areas where owner building was quite common.[17] These writers hint at the ways in which Sanborns might be used to make inferences about the manner in which sites and districts were developed, but they do not make explicit such a method.[18] In the present context, atlases are useful because they record several items of information which are critical in forming a judgment as to how dwellings were developed.[19] They show the footprint of the dwelling, its placement on the lot, the number of stories, and materials of construction. Small, one-story, frame dwellings are readily identified. Moreover, it is easy to assess the uniqueness of individual structures by comparing their dimensions and lot placement with that of neighbors. Indeed, the large-page atlas format makes it possible to scan and assess whole districts of the city at once. They let the researcher's fingers do the walking, albeit under the archivist's watchful eye, encased in white cotton gloves.

Two Studies in Historical Evolution

One problem in identifying owner-built dwellings is that their characteristic form has changed over time. In the late nineteenth century, most workers walked to work, while some used the streetcar. By the 1950s many were using automobiles. In general this shift made it possible for families to acquire homes on larger lots and encouraged the construction of suburban bungalows instead of two- and three-story dwellings. This affected everyone, but it had a particular significance for owner-builders. Single-story dwellings were easier to build, and any increase in lot size made them more viable, enlarging the opportunities for owner building. At the same time, automobiles enabled workers to live in unregulated exurban settings where land was cheap. Since amateur builders often lacked skills, freedom from regulation was a powerful incentive to relocate and build.[20] For these reasons, the social diffusion of the automobile not only changed the form of the owner-built dwelling but also helps account for its temporary resurgence, reaching a flood in the immediate postwar years.

Streetcar Development: Polish Flats in Milwaukee from the 1890s

Milwaukee and Flint illustrate the changing form of owner-built dwellings. As an industrial city, Milwaukee attracted immigrants in the late 1800s. The second-largest of these groups were the Poles, who adopted a solution to their housing problem which elsewhere was known as the raised cottage, but which in Milwaukee was soon referred to as the Polish flat; this practice was an up-and-down duplex arrangement where the owner typically lived in one unit and rented out the other. Commonly, these dwellings were erected in stages, with the owner building and occupying a cottage built more or less at ground level and then raising it to accommodate a live-in basement when finances allowed.

This process is discussed for the south side of the city by Roger Simon and Judith Kenny, and for north side areas by Craig Reisser.[21] Reisser used oral histories, building permits, and photographs to document specific dwellings in a manner which illuminates and is enriched by the insurance atlas. I have chosen two facing blocks on North Weil to illustrate the process and pattern of growth. Lying over four miles from the center of the city, toward the northern limits, this area was subdivided before electric streetcars had been introduced (fig. 15.2). Lots were narrow: thirty-three feet was the norm on Weil, while thirty-foot and even twenty-five-foot lots were known in Polish areas on the south side (fig. 15.3). A streetcar line running parallel to Weil was opened in about 1891.[22] The route lay five blocks to the east, and by 1899 it offered direct service downtown at ten-minute intervals from 5:35 A.M. to 12:55 A.M.[23] The 1894 Sanborn atlas shows that in that year most of the lots on Weil between Hadley and Chambers were still vacant, but the next atlas shows that most were developed by 1910 (fig. 15.3). Although lying within city limits, the area was, in effect, a streetcar suburb.

Reisser indicates that many buildings on North Weil were owner built. For example, in 1892 Stanislaus Sterczinski received a permit to erect a cottage at 2932 N. Weil.[24] Noting that the estimated cost was only $150, Reisser argues that the owner must have done the work himself.[25] This cottage is shown on the Sanborn map of 1894 where, even lacking other information, one might infer the activity of owner-builders (fig. 15.3). In that year, the cottage at 2932 was one of half a dozen small frame dwellings scattered along N. Weil between Locust and Chambers. No two were identical, and several (no. 2923 and two at no. 2939) sat at the back of their lots. Rear placement was common in areas of owner-building: an owner would put up a modest home on the back of the lot, intending to erect something more substantial in due course.[26] In fact, this seems to be what often happened. At both no. 2923 and no. 2939, larger dwellings were built on the front of the lot. It is likely that the original structures were simply moved and expanded. Sometimes the pattern was reversed, as at no. 2920, and then again front and rear structures might be built within a short period of time so that one cannot tell from the Sanborns which came first. The two cramped structures at no. 2875 N. Weil, both built between 1894 and 1910, are a case in point. In general, however, the existence of front and rear dwellings suggests that an owner-builder has been active.

Owners also often added to their existing houses.[27] At no. 2932, minor additions were made to Sterczinski's modest dwelling between 1894 and 1910, one of which was also removed. Additions were more common on the adjacent block between Hadley and Locust, where more homes had been built before 1894 (fig. 15.3). Some additions were minor. At no. 2852 the owner added a small room at the back, probably a shed. His neighbor did likewise. Other additions were more substantial. At no. 2863 the owner doubled the size of his small frame dwelling by extending it forward on the lot, and so too did a neighbor (fig. 15.3). Similarly, the atlas shows that a frame building at no. 2812 was doubled in size with a rear extension. According to Reisser, the original structure had been built elsewhere and subsequently moved to the site on N. Weil.[28] Such removals were apparently common, and at least two contractors within the Polish community in the 1900s specialized in house moving.[29] In extreme cases, various additions were made. Between 1894 and 1910, a dwelling was added as an extension to the store at no. 1000 Locust, while a house was built separately on the rear of the lot, fronting onto Weil (fig.

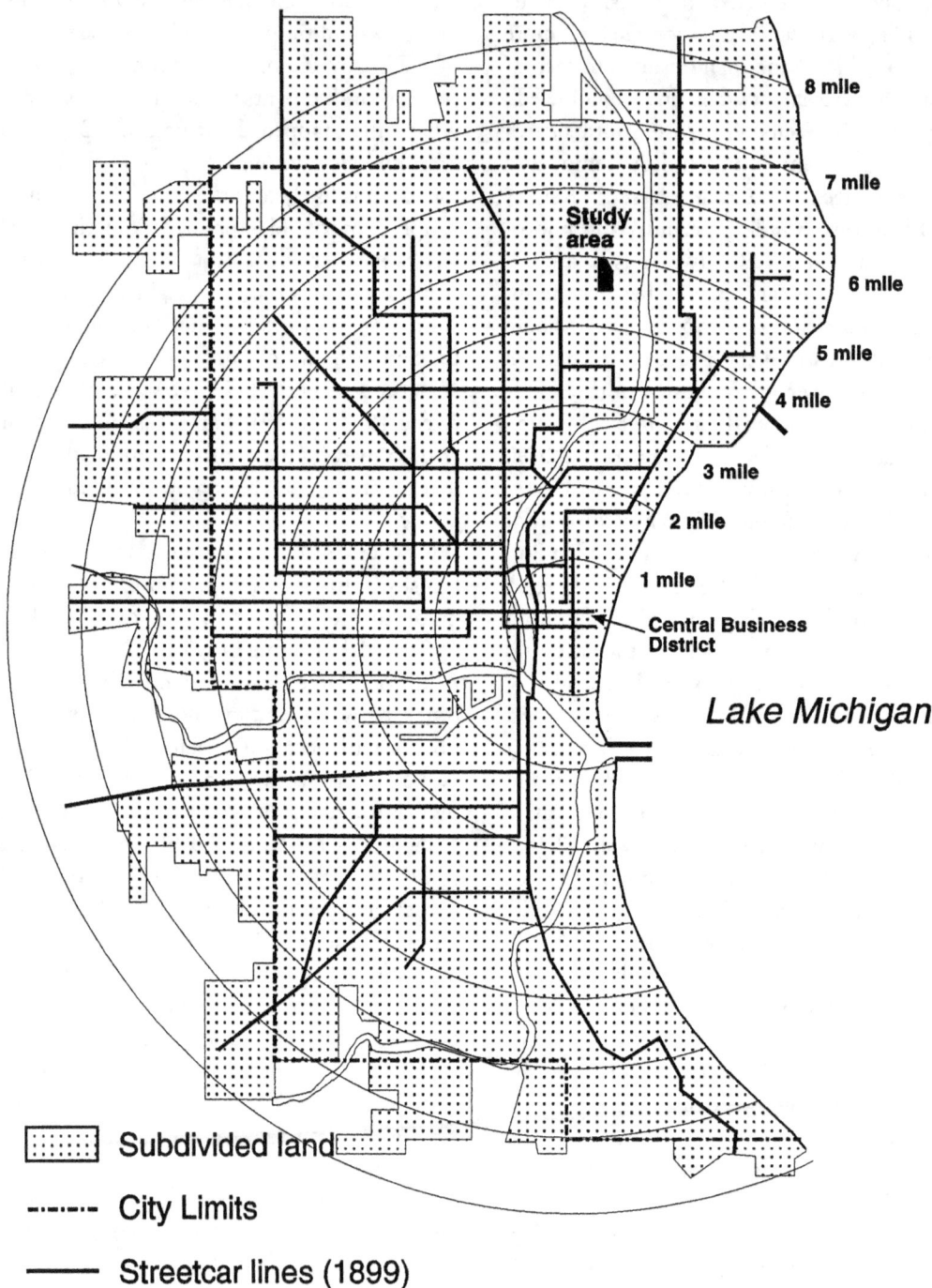

Fig. 15.2. Milwaukee in 1899. Although lying within city limits, the area that included North Weil developed as a streetcar suburb. From Evan Evans, *Street Railway Map of the City of Milwaukee*, 1899.

15.3). In time, further additions created an imposing structure.

Many extensions were vertical. Room could be created below the original house. For example, John Stipinski built the dwelling at no. 2953 N. Weil with a wooden foundation. In 1905 Reisser reports that a John Stephanski obtained a permit to add a brick basement with a separate entrance.[30] Like so many others, Stephanski presumably intended to rent out this new space. It is not clear how soon he was able to do so. The 1910 Sanborn shows this single-story frame building as unaltered. It was only later, according to the 1951 revision to the 1910 atlas, that a company surveyor added a "B" to indicate the presence of a basement.[31] Occasionally, the ground-floor basement was built first, and a vertical addition was made by adding a second floor. Where such additions had not been planned, the ground-floor structure sometimes had to be strengthened.[32]

A comparison of the Sanborn of 1910 with the revised version for 1951 might suggest that vertical additions were common. Within this period many dwellings ("D") seem to have become flats ("F"), especially on the west side of Weil between Hadley and Locust (figs. 15.3, 15.4). In fact, this evidence is spurious. Sanborn did not identify flats in 1910, and most of the structures so labeled in 1950 contained more than one dwelling unit in 1910. Indeed, even when instructed to do so it seems that Sanborn's surveyors were not sure how to categorize the Polish flats. "Flat" supposedly referred to single-family occupancy of each floor of a building with more than two floors.[33] In many cases, however, the Sanborn atlas in 1950 records the presence of flats with no more than two floors. Nos. 2829 and 2855 were shown

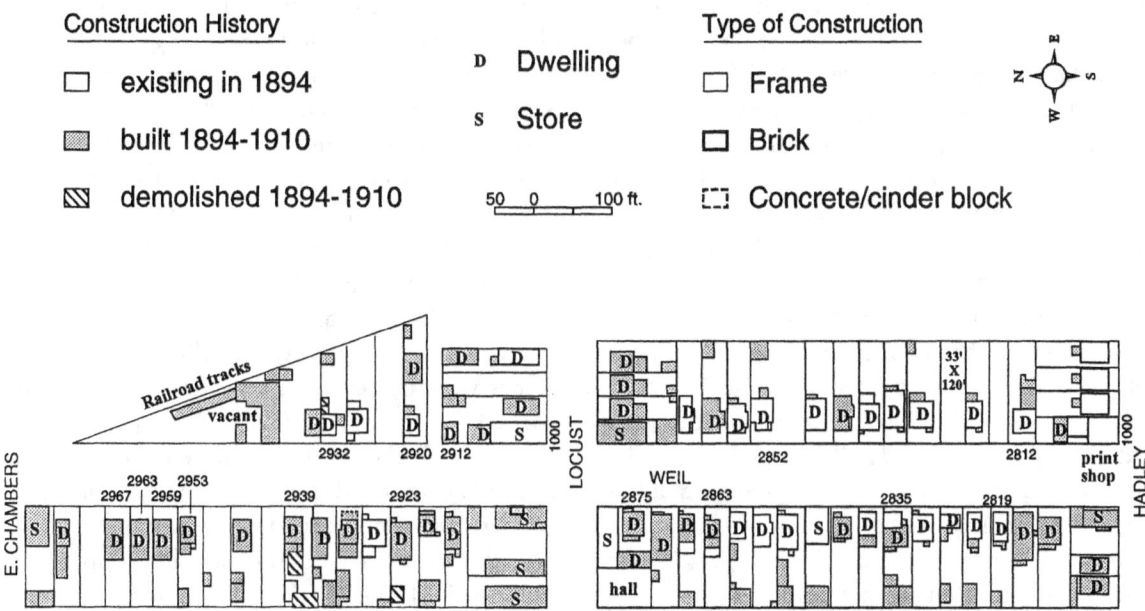

Fig. 15.3. Polish Flats, Milwaukee, 1894–1910. Many homes were moved, replaced, or extended by their owners. From Sanborn Company, *Milwaukee, Wisconsin*, 1894 and 1910, vol. 2, pl. 133, 134.

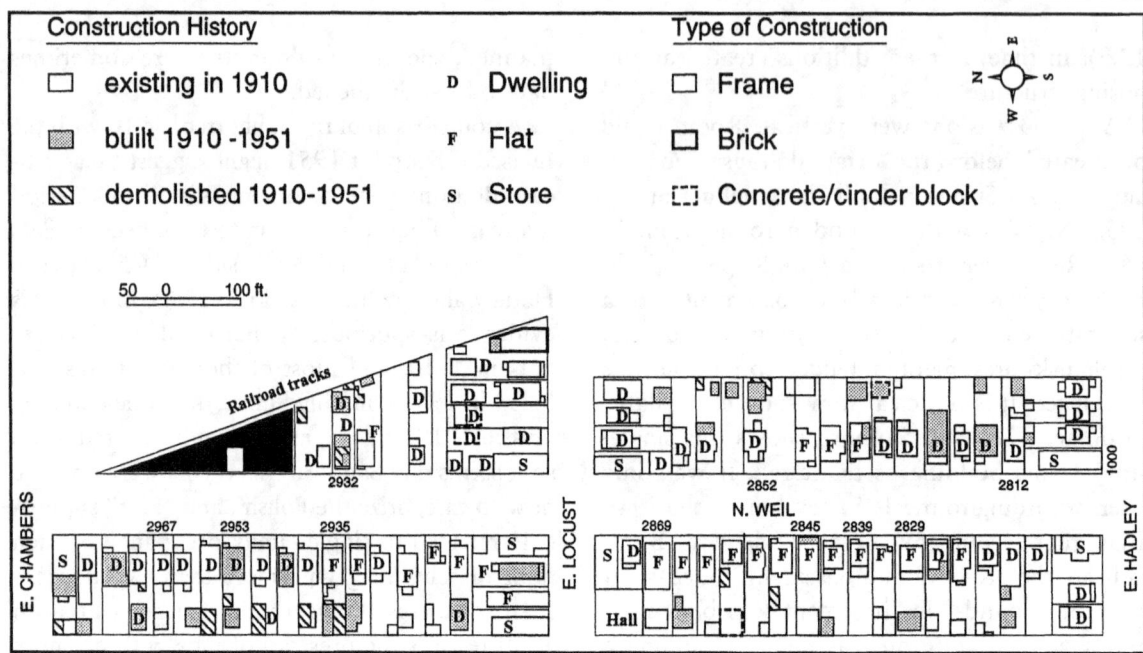

Fig. 15.4. Polish Flats, Milwaukee, 1910–51. From Sanborn Company, *Milwaukee, Wisconsin*, 1910 and 1910 (revised to 1951), vol. 2, pl. 133, 134.

as having two, while 2839 had only one and a half. None of these had basements, the latter being defined as a living space with a floor below ground level and a ceiling at least four feet above.[34] Other flats, for example, no. 2845, were shown with a basement and only one other story (fig. 15.5). Apparently, in practice "flat" could refer to a two-story structure occupied by two families, one on each floor.

A more meaningful analysis of vertical additions employs the reported data on the number of stories (not shown on figs. 15.3 and 15.4). Of the seventeen residential structures on the west side of Weil between Hadley and Locust, the Sanborn suggests that six received vertical additions between 1910 and 1950. No. 2845 acquired a basement, while nos. 2809, 2823, and 2839 each acquired half a story, and the owners of no. 2829 added a full story. More substantially, the flat at no. 2827 was given a rear extension as well as a half-story addition. (It might have been torn down and replaced.) Across the road, the owner of the store at no. 1000 East Hadley continued a process of extension that had begun before 1910 with the construction of a dwelling addition. According to Reisser, in that year the owner employed a carpenter to add a second floor in the form of two apartments.[35] This addition is apparent in the Sanborn revision of 1951. By this time, however, the whole of the main structure was apparently being used as a store (fig. 15.4).

As this case suggests, not all additions and homes were owner-built. The three dwellings at nos. 2959, 2963, and 2967 N. Weil appear identical in the Sanborn atlas as, indeed, they still do. They indicate the activity of a small commercial builder, and Reisser confirms that these were "standardized tract houses built by Louis Auer and Son in 1903."[36] The owners soon adapted them to family needs. In 1911 the owner of no. 2967, John Hamerski, built a rear dwelling for his son. It is not clear whether he employed a con-

Fig. 15.5. No. 2845 North Weil, Milwaukee. Unique duplex homes with raised basements were a typical form of owner construction in Milwaukee. Jason Nyberg.

tractor, but evidently in this case the existence of a front and rear dwelling does not indicate a pure history of owner building. The built environment, and in particular the Sanborns, offer only suggestive clues to the process of development, an issue to which I will return later.

Automobile Suburbs: Flint, Michigan, from the 1920s

The raised cottage was one form of owner building in the streetcar era. In other cases, even before they had cars, families were able to build single-family homes on small suburban lots. This was most common in towns and small cities, but, as we saw earlier, it was possible in a city the size of Toronto. The lots, however, were small: frontages in cheaper subdivisions ranged from twenty to thirty-three feet. It is not clear whether owner-builders in other cities were as able, or as willing, to accept such small lots as the price of fringe living. At any rate, larger lots, and single-detached houses, only became widespread with the diffusion of the automobile after World War I.

Flint, Michigan, exemplifies the possibilities faced by owner-builders in the automobile era. Flint and the automobile industry prospered together. During the 1920s the city's population grew from 91,599 to 156,492.[37] In a local report, A. C. Findlay noted in 1938 that many of families had housed themselves, often with the help of friends on a "work exchange" basis.[38] As in Milwaukee, they used an additive building strategy, although in Flint the basement usually came first. A new arrangement was for a family to occupy a garage and then erect a dwelling later, in the interim making do without piped water, sewers, or electricity. This was made legal by an amendment to the Michigan housing law in 1925, and in Flint the building inspector created a category for garage dwellings. His records show that in the late 1920s garages accounted for more than one in ten new dwellings in Flint, and probably a much higher proportion of new homes beyond city limits.[39]

The results are exemplified by the block along Cotharin Boulevard between Pasadena and Dartmouth, at the western city limits (fig. 15.6). During the 1920s, this block saw owner building of the sort described by Findlay. The Sanborn shows that in 1931 every dwelling (fourteen in all) was one story in height, small, and of frame construction (fig. 15.7). Except for no. 3301 and its neighbor, no two were alike. Many sat on the rear of the lot, and were small enough to serve eventually as garages (for instance, no. 3110). Several dwellings possessed garages, perhaps vestiges of the earliest

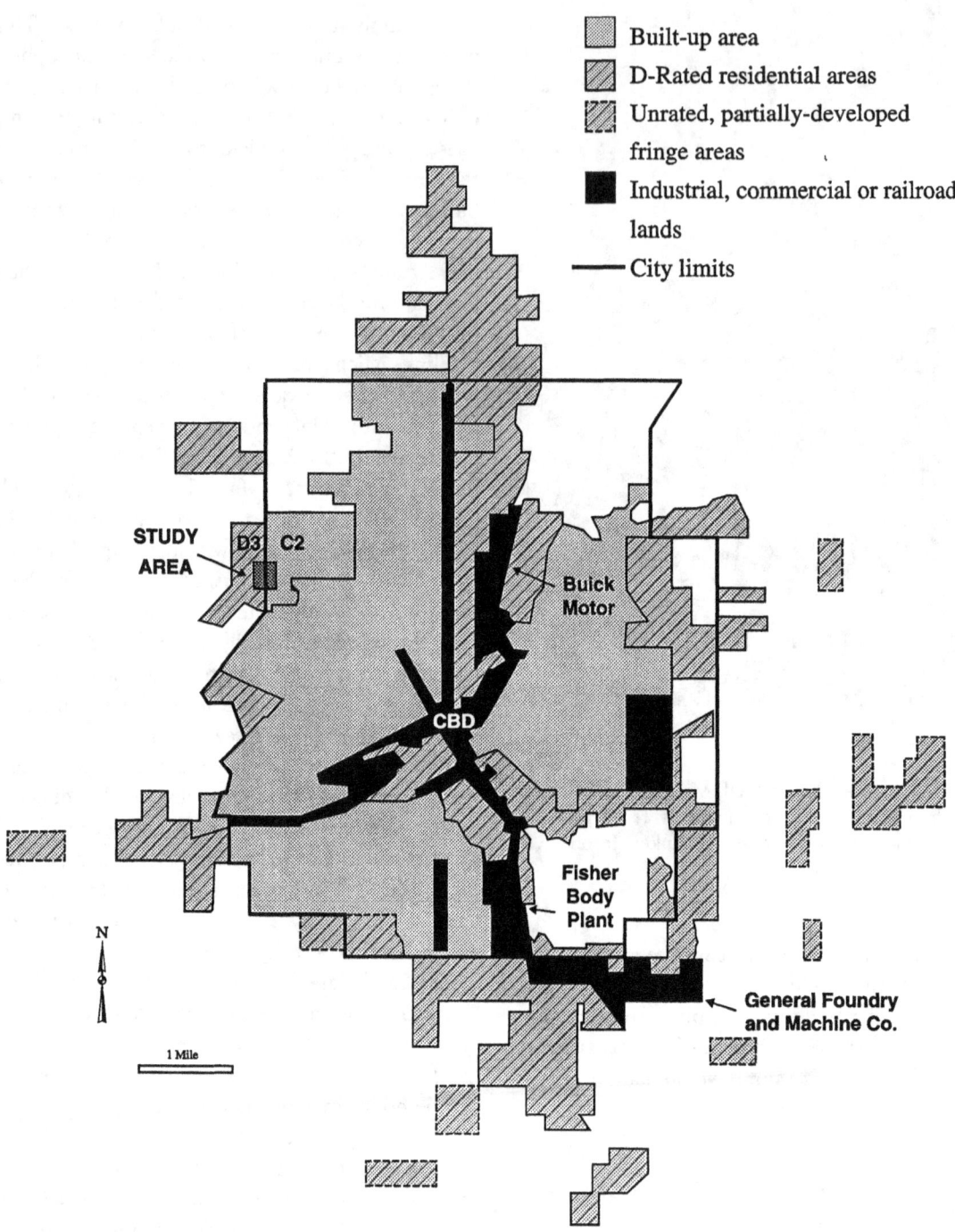

Fig. 15.6. Flint, Michigan, in 1937. Most of the areas that were low-rated by the Home Owners Loan Corporation were owner-built districts at or beyond city limits. From Home Owners' Loan Corporation, *Residential Security Map*, Flint, July 1937.

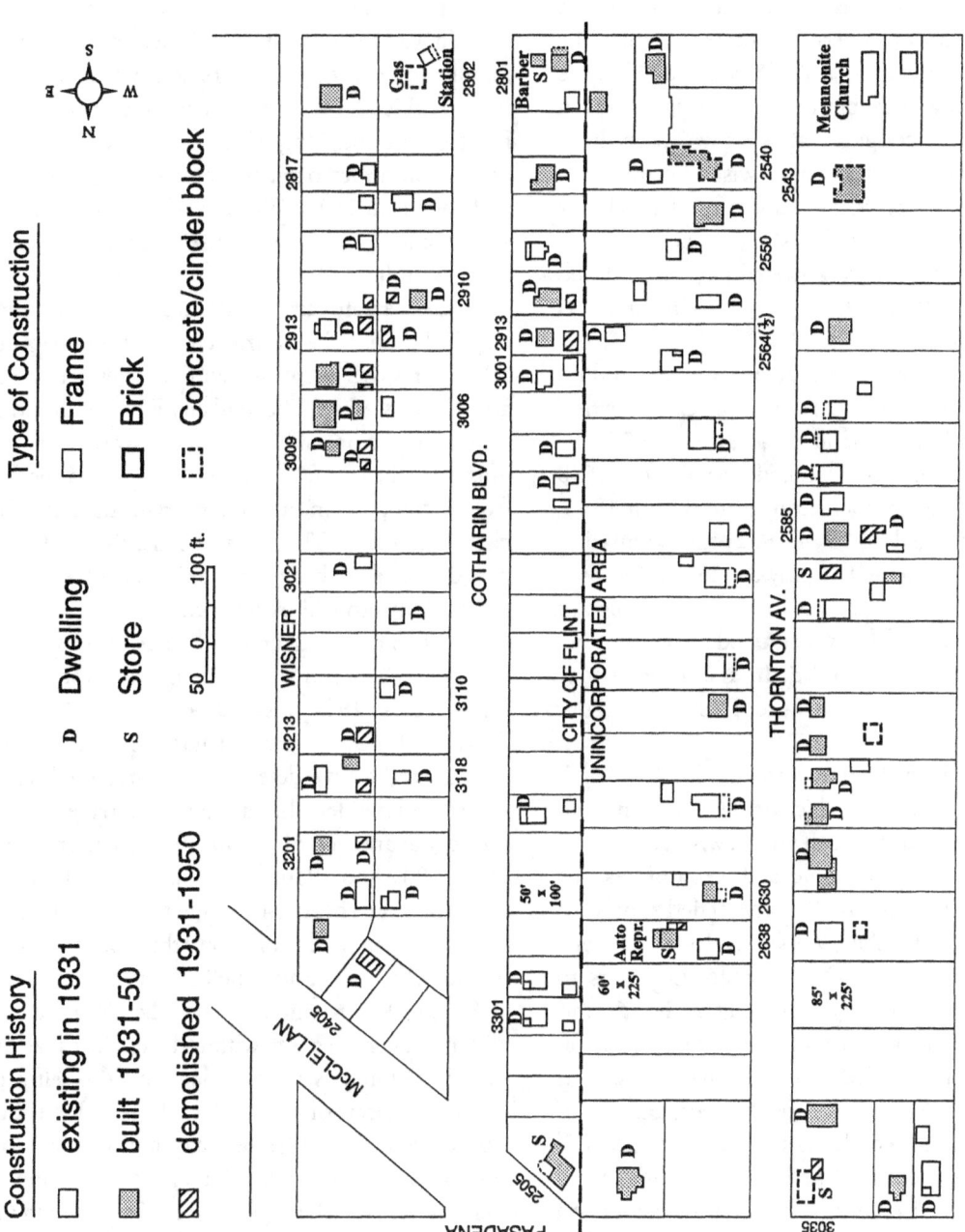

Fig. 15.7. Vicinity of Thornton (Flint, Michigan), 1931–50. Owner building was rife within the city limits, but even more common beyond them. From Sanborn Company, *Flint, Michigan*, 1928 and 1928 (revised to 1950), pl. 278 (1931).

phase of development. The large garage behind no. 3001, for example, might readily have served as temporary accommodation for a small family. Other structures are perhaps indicative too. The solitary structure at no. 3006 was identified in the Sanborn as a garage, but the fact that it was given a street address, coupled with what we know about garage homes, suggests otherwise. Overall, the character and placement of structures on this block indicates that owner-builders had been active. So, too, does the randomly scattered pattern of development: overall, in 1931 barely one in three lots were built upon.

The Depression created unemployment and reduced migration to the Flint area. Construction within city limits ground to a halt. In 1927, the city's building inspector issued permits for 3,538 dwellings. This number dropped to 375 in 1930, and then to a paltry 13 in 1932; the population of the city actually fell slightly during the 1930s.[40] Beyond the city limits homebuilding continued at a modest rate. If the city stagnated, it was not because it was fully occupied. In a study of fringe development in the area, Walter Firey pointed out that even in 1946 the city still contained a great deal of subdivided but vacant land. Much of it was serviced and available for development, but most builders preferred to go elsewhere.[41]

Again, Cotharin Boulevard exemplifies the larger picture. Here, infilling proceeded slowly after 1931. During the 1930s the Home Owners' Loan Corporation (HOLC) employed agents to identify fairly homogeneous neighborhoods and to assess each for mortgage risk. The block on Cotharin was included in area C2 where, according to the judgment of a field agent, only one-third of all lots were developed in March 1937.[42] The building boom of the late 1940s did not fill in the gaps. In 1950 more than half of the lots on Cotharin were still vacant. Indeed, between 1931 and 1950 new construction was partially counterbalanced by attrition. Three dwellings on Cotharin were demolished, only two replaced (nos. 2910 and 2913). Attrition was even more apparent on nearby Wisner. On the west side of Wisner alone, five of the eleven dwellings that existed in 1931 had been demolished by 1950. In a manner typical of owner-construction, four had been replaced by larger structures toward the front of the lot. Only three new dwellings were erected on hitherto vacant lots, leaving seven lots still vacant in 1951. Within such areas, then, the 1930s and 1940s saw consolidation, but only modest infill.

Areas beyond city limits grew more rapidly, largely because they attracted owner-builders. In 1937, a HOLC agent judged that sales activity in area C2 was "slow." Beyond city limits in the adjacent subdivision of Thornton, however, it was judged to be "fair."[43] The net effect is apparent from a comparison of Cotharin with the adjacent, parallel block on Thornton Avenue. By 1931 both blocks were equally developed. The absence of zoning in Thornton allowed some intermingling of homes with nonresidential land uses. In 1931 there had been a store in the center of the west side of the street. By 1951 this had been demolished, but the east side now boasted an auto repair shop. Such mixing might have deterred some potential home buyers and builders, but it did not override the perceived advantages of a suburban location.[44] Between 1931 and 1950, there was less attrition and more infill on Thornton Avenue than on Cotharin, and by the latter year only one-third of the lots on the suburban block remained vacant.

Blocks like Thornton Avenue filled in more rapidly than nearby streets within the city because the suburbs favored owner building, and also self-provisioning. Firey observes that during the 1930s workers had moved beyond city limits to buy lots and build modest homes. He explains this movement in terms of the higher costs of housing in the city, coupled with the availability of cheap land, low taxes, and lax regulation in the suburbs.[45] Certainly, such contrasts did exist. Taxes were higher in the city because most land was serviced. Lots at the fringe were widely available for a dollar down and a dollar a week, while, in Thornton, a deed restriction which defined a minimum building cost of $600 was widely ignored.[46] As a result, in 1937 the HOLC agent judged that few dwellings in area C2 were worth less than $1,500, but in Thornton the range extended down to $1,000.[47] This price included the land, and suburban lots were larger. Those on Cotharin were of moderate dimensions (50 feet by 100 feet), but the suburban parcels onto which they backed were almost three times as large (60 feet by 225 feet). Those on the other side of Thornton Avenue were almost half as large again (85 feet by 225 feet), while farther out, acreages were available. A few of the large lots on Thornton Avenue were subdivided and by 1951 accommodated two dwellings side by side. This was not typical, however, and in general Firey emphasizes that to people who had weathered the Depression, large lots were preferred because they enabled families to provide much of their own food. Of course, working people, including Milwaukee's Polish population, had long used their yards for growing produce, but larger lots meant greater self-sufficiency. Firey quotes one resident: "We couldn't live without the vegetables we grow" and asserts that in this area two ideas were "pervasive . . . the fear of 'the layoff' and the idea of security-on-the-land."[48] Vegetables, chickens, and, farther out, even cows were raised, often on a cooperative basis. Suburban land was cheaper to buy and provided a resource for partial subsistence.

As had happened earlier around Toronto, unserviced land discouraged speculative builders.[49] In 1947, an agent of the Federal Office of the Housing Expediter prepared a report on housing in the Flint area. He observed that commercial builders operated only within the city, leaving the unserviced suburbs to "individuals."[50] A year earlier, Firey had described the ways in which individuals were building homes and the varied results. In Thornton, among the more prosperous and well-respected settlers was family B, who had moved out of the city in 1941. They lived in four tents until they had completed the basement and then in the basement for another two years while finishing the upstairs. By 1946 they had a "neat, solid, and well-painted home." Less fortunate were the X's, who in 1946 had lived for two years "in a makeshift board and tar paper shack set on the rear of the lot which is littered with piles of old rotting lumber."[51] This family was in the process of laying the foundation for a replacement cement-block

Fig. 15.8. No. 2540 Thornton Avenue, Flint. Superficially similar to owner-built frame homes in the 1940s, the rear extensions made this concrete-block home quite substantial. Isolated block homes are a clue to owner construction in this era. Jordan Herron.

home. The Sanborn atlas indicates that there was a similar diversity of structures on Thornton Avenue. At one extreme was no. 2630. Lying next to an auto repair shop, it was one of the smallest frame structures on the street. A still smaller garage, perhaps once used as a dwelling, sat farther back on the lot. At the other extreme were more substantial houses at nos. 2540 and 2543 (fig. 15.8). Symptomatic of a minority of owner-built homes in this period, both of the latter were block-built.[52]

Discussion and Conclusions

There are obvious differences between Milwaukee's Polish flats and Flint's fringe in the 1950s. The narrow buildings on N. Weil crowded the front of the lot and extended backward. Eventually rising two or three stories (counting the basement), they give an urban feel to the block. In contrast, smaller frame bungalows on Thornton Avenue sat back on wider lots. Behind these differences, however, are fundamental similarities in the manner of development and in built form. Owners built homes in stages, adding extensions and structures as their finances allowed. They did so as individual families, and the resultant landscapes are distinctively haphazard, even anarchic.

Sanborns do not fully capture the form or process involved in this type of construction. They abstract from architectural style. Infrequent revisions, and our inability to date with precision the revisions that were made, mean that such atlases do not show us much of the live-in basements and other makeshifts that amateur builders employed. More important, the built environment itself does not speak unambiguously of the building process. Some of the scattered frame buildings on Cotharin Boulevard might have been put there by commercial builders. Conversely, a dwelling that is identical to its neighbor might have been owner-built. This was especially true after World War II, when dealers like Wahlfeld in Peoria offered help in building from stock plans or sold standardized kits. The owner-builder did not always leave a telltale spoor.

Given their limitations, how can the insurance atlases be used? I would suggest two answers. First, as I hope the examples of Milwaukee and Flint demonstrate, atlases enrich our understanding of situations where owner building has already been documented. In particular, they provide systematic evidence on the character of the housing stock and residential additions. Second, they are valuable when used for a preliminary survey. Here they provide clues as to which blocks or neighborhoods within a metropolitan area saw an appreciable amount of owner building. At this scale, errors of inference with respect to specific dwellings tend to cancel each other out. Thus, although one might debate exactly who built any particular home on Cotharin Boulevard, at Flint's fringe, in looking at the block as a whole it is apparent that owners were responsible for a good many.[53] Following such clues, we can narrow down our inquiries to particular areas, where surviving evidence can be consulted directly, on foot. City directories can then tell us when specific dwellings were first occupied (and by whom), while long-term residents might recall details of the building process.[54] It is of course true, as Verlyn Klinkenborg has observed, that Sanborns do not speak directly of the "private life [that] is a grave of incident—once lived, soon forgotten." They do not capture the owner-builder himself, or his wife "whose hands smelled different every day of the week—lye soup one morning, the next morning flour."[55] But, far better than any other source, they give us a sense of where and in what numbers owner-builders dwelt.

Sanborns speak only in general terms of the way in which North Americans made their way into the suburbs. Some of the broad and varied paths which suburbanites blazed have since become overgrown, but none of their trails are completely cold. On maps, and on the ground, the spoor of the owner-builder can still be found.

Notes

The research reported here was supported by a Fulbright Scholar Award and a grant (no. 410-93-0488) from the Social Sciences and Humanities Research Council of Canada. I would like to thank the librarians of the cartographic division of the Library of Congress for assistance; Ric Hamilton for drawing maps. Deryck Holdsworth, Robert Lewis, Cathy Moulder, Paula Oeler, Matthew Sendbuehler, and two reviewers made helpful comments on earlier drafts.

1. This statement is valid for Mexico, but I confine my argument to the United States and Canada. The term "owner building" is sometimes used to refer to situations where owners initiated the construction process but hired contractors to do the work. I use the term more narrowly to denote situations where the owners themselves invested a substantial amount of sweat equity.
2. United States, Housing and Home Finance Agency, *Housing in the United States* (Washington, D.C.: H.H.F.A., 1956), 54–55.
3. Kathryn Murphy, "Builders of New One-Family Houses, 1955–56," *Construction Review* 4 (8–9) (Aug.–Sept. 1958): 7; Jack McLaughlin, *The House-Building Experience* (New York: Van Nostrand, 1981), 2.
4. This generalization is based on my own oral history research in Toronto (1900–50), Peoria, Illinois (1935–55), and Hamilton, Ontario (1945–55). See Richard Harris, *Unplanned Suburbs: Toronto's American Tragedy, 1900–1950* (Baltimore: Johns Hopkins Univ. Press, 1996), 200–32. It is also consistent with the contemporary studies of various U.S. and Canadian cities that are listed in *Unplanned Suburbs*; see p. 335n. 33. In many cases women did a good deal of manual work, too, and typically influenced the design of the house. The notion of common homes as cultural spoor is developed by Pierce Lewis in "Common Houses, Cultural Spoor," in *Re-reading Cultural Geography*, ed. Kenneth Foote, Peter Hugill, Kent Mathewson, and Jonathan M. Smith (Austin: Univ. of Texas Press, 1994), 82–110.
5. Richard Harris, "The Impact of Building Controls on Residential Development in Toronto, 1900–40," *Planning Perspectives* 6 (1991): 271–74.
6. Richard Harris, "Self-Building in the Urban Housing Market," *Economic Geography* 67 (1) (1991): 1–21. The use of assessment assumes that there was a threshold price/value below which speculative builders would not operate.
7. Frazier F. Peters, *Pour Yourself a House: Low Cost Building with Concrete and Stone* (New York: Whittlesey House, 1949); James R. Ward, *Popular Mechanics' Famous Concrete Block House* (Chicago: Popular Mechanics Press, 1949).
8. For a detailed case study, see Harris, *Unplanned Suburbs*.
9. Alan Gowans, letter to the author, Dec. 9, 1992.
10. Sears, Roebuck and Co., *Sears, Roebuck Catalog of Houses* (1926; reprint, New York: Dover, 1991), 6–7. In my judgment, although scholars have recently paid them a good deal of attention, kits made up only a small minority of all owner-built homes.
11. See, for example, "No Matter What You Earn You Can Own a Wahlfeld 'Owner-Built' Home," *Peoria Journal-Transcript,* Apr. 28, 1940. Wahlfeld was atypical in that it began as a manufacturer of millwork and only entered the retail lumber business in 1935. Almost certainly, it was the "wide-awake building materials dealer" referred to in an article about Peoria published in a national magazine several years later. See "How 4,000 Peoria Families Built Their Own Homes," *House Beautiful* 88 (3) (Mar. 1946): 112. The company's "owner-built" scheme, however, was not unique. Reinhard Lumber, a dealer in the neighboring town of Pekin, Ill., mounted an even more ambitious program in the late 1940s and 1950s. Conversation with Dick Bolam, Pekin, Ill., Mar. 20, 1995. Bolam worked for Reinhard as a salesman and site consultant for owner-builder customers.
12. I would like to thank John Wahlfeld, vice-president,

Wahlfeld Mfg. Co., for allowing me to consult the company's business records and to borrow the photograph album in which the achievements of the "owner built" program were recorded. Some of the images were published in the local newspaper. See, for example, "Norwood Park Subdivision Growing Rapidly," *Peoria Journal-Transcript,* May 26, 1940.

13. Conversation with Sally Davis, Peoria, Ill., Mar. 20, 1995.
14. Conversations with Geno Reck and Carole Hoffman, Peoria, Ill., Mar. 21, 1995.
15. For recent discussions, see William B. Keller, "Collecting and Using Fire Insurance and Real Estate Atlases: An Individual Perspective," *Arts Reference Services Quarterly* 1 (3) (1993): 31–48; Cathy Moulder, "Fire Insurance Plans as a Data Source in Urban Research: An Annotated Bibliography of Examples," *Arts Reference Services Quarterly* 1 (3) (1993): 49–62; Kim Keister, "Charts of Change," *Historic Preservation* 45 (3) (May/June 1993): 42–49, 91–92.
16. Robert L. Wrigley, "The Sanborn Map as a Source of Land Use Information for City Planning," *Land Economics* 25 (2) (1949): 216–19. The core collection of Sanborns at the Library of Congress was donated by the U.S. Bureau of the Census after being used extensively for the 1950 census.
17. Anne E. Mosher and Deryck W. Holdsworth, "The Meaning of Alley Housing in Industrial Towns: Examples from Late Nineteenth and Early-Twentieth Century Pennsylvania," *Journal of Historical Geography* 18 (2) (1992): 176–77, 183; Graeme Wynn, "The Rise of Vancouver," in *Vancouver and Its Region,* ed. Graeme Wynn and Timothy Oke (Vancouver: UBC Press, 1992), 94–101. For an interesting early example, see Arthur G. Dalzell, *To the Citizens of St. John's: Is all Well?* (Toronto: Ryerson, 1929), 19.
18. Moulder, "Fire Insurance Plans."
19. For a glossary of the recorded information on residential areas, see Sanborn Map Company, *Description and Utilization of the Sanborn Map* (New York: Sanborn Map Company, 1953), 11–13. Most of the critical information is reproduced in the redrawn maps that I present here. The exception concerns the reported information on number of stories.
20. Harris, "The Impact of Building Controls."
21. Roger Simon, "Housing and Services in an Immigrant Neighborhood," *Journal of Urban History* 2 (4) (1976): 435–58; and "City-Building Process: Housing and Services in New Milwaukee Neighborhoods 1880–1910," *Transactions of the American Philosophical Society* 65 (1978): 39–40; Judith Kenny, "Polish Routes to Americanization: House Form and Landscape on Milwaukee's Polish South Side," in *Wisconsin Land and Life,* ed. R. Ostergren and T. Vale (Madison: Univ. of Wisconsin Press, forthcoming); Craig Thomas Reisser, "Immigrants and House Form in Northeast Milwaukee" (M.A. thesis, Univ. of Wisconsin—Milwaukee, 1977). See also Landscape Research, *Built in Milwaukee: An Architectural View of the City* (Milwaukee: City of Milwaukee, 1980), 64–65, 68–69.
22. This date is inferred by comparing information reported on maps for 1890 and 1891. See the following maps: A. N. Marquis, *Official Map of Milwaukee,* 1890; Silas Chapman, *City of Milwaukee and Suburbs,* 1891.
23. Evan Evans, *Milwaukee and Racine Street Railway Directory* (Milwaukee: Evan Evans, 1899), 27.
24. Street numbers were changed after initial development took place. To save confusion, I use those numbers that are employed today.
25. Reisser, "Immigrants and House Form," 40.
26. For example, see Harris, *Unplanned Suburbs,* chap. 8; Mosher and Holdsworth, "The Meaning of Alley Housing."
27. For three-dimensional illustrations, see Kenny, "Polish Routes to Americanization."
28. Reisser, "Immigrants and House Form," 43. According to Reisser, the move was made only in 1899. If this date is correct, the house that was moved must have replaced the structure that is shown in the 1894 atlas.
29. Waclaw Kruska, *A History of Poles in America to*

29. *1908*, trans. Krystyna Jankowski (1908; reprint, Washington, D.C.: Catholic Univ. of America Press, 1993), 185–86. I am indebted to Paula Oeler for this fact.
30. Reisser, "Immigrants and House Form," 59.
31. Revisions to published atlases were made more or less continuously in the form of paste-ons. Revised atlases accumulated paste-ons until they were retired. I have used those atlases that are available at the Library of Congress. Many of these were inherited from the Bureau of the Census and include revisions to 1950 or 1951. Revisions to 1926 are available for Milwaukee in the Milwaukee Public Library.
32. Reisser, "Immigrants and House Form," 48, 53.
33. Sanborn Map Company, *Description and Utilization*, 13.
34. Ibid., 11. Although the Sanborns usually indicated construction materials by colors, in the case of brick basements in this area they apparently used the letters "BB." This, too, seems to indicate that surveyors were uncertain how to treat Polish flats. I am indebted to Paula Oeler for this suggestion.
35. Reisser, "Immigrants and House Form," 48.
36. Ibid., 138.
37. Walter Firey, *Social Aspects to Land Use Planning in the Country-City Fringe: The Case of Flint, Michigan,* East Lansing, Mich.: Special Bulletin 339, Agricultural Experiment Station, Michigan State College, 1946, 9.
38. A. C. Findlay, "The Housing Situation in Flint, Michigan," typescript, Flint Institute of Research and Planning, Flint, Michigan, Feb. 1938, 8.
39. Ibid., 26.
40. Ibid.
41. Firey, *Social Aspects,* 22–23.
42. Home Owners' Loan Corporation, *City Survey: Flint,* Area Description C2, Flint, 1937, typescript, Records of Federal Home Loan Bank Board, Home Owners' Loan Corporation, Records of the City Survey File, 1935–1940, National Archives and Records Administration, Record Group 195, Washington, D.C.
43. Ibid., Area Descriptions C2, D3. Because of the absence of services and regulations, the HOLC agent judged the suburban area to have a higher mortgage risk than the neighboring area within the city, even though the market in the former area was more active.
44. There were commercial businesses at the ends of both Cotharin Boulevard and Thornton Avenue.
45. Firey, *Social Aspects,* 9.
46. Ibid., 19–20, 27.
47. Home Owners' Loan Corporation, *City Survey: Flint,* Area Descriptions C2, D3.
48. Firey, *Social Aspects,* 30, 47.
49. Harris, *Unplanned Suburbs,* chap. 7; Harris, "The Impact of Building Controls."
50. Frank W. Brewer, "Special Monthly Report on Land and Public Services. Flint, Michigan," in "Supplement to January Monthly Report on Land and Public Services, Region VIII, Cleveland, Ohio," Feb. 7, 1947, p. 2, Office of the Housing Expediter Land and Public Utilities Advisory Service, Box 13, Monthly Reg. Reports of Land and Public Services, Region VIII, National Archives and Records Administration, Record Group 252, Washington, D.C.
51. Firey, *Social Aspects,* 43–44.
52. The Sanborn does not distinguish between cement and cinder block.
53. The use of Sanborns to infer general patterns of development is advocated by Eric Mumford, who is one of the few people to have raised questions about the accuracy of this source. Eric Mumford, "Re: Sanborns," H-Urban (e-mail bulletin board), Aug. 3, 1993, "Listserv@uicvm.edu."
54. In principle, it is possible to use oral accounts to confirm the accuracy of inferences about the building process that are made from the insurance atlas. In practice, at a distance of half a century or more, it is likely to be too difficult to identify original occupants for such a procedure to be practicable.
55. Verlyn Klinkenborg, *The Last Fine Time* (New York: Knopf, 1991), 11.

CHAPTER 16

M. Ruth Little

The Other Side of the Tracks: The Middle-Class Neighborhoods That Jim Crow Built in Early-Twentieth-Century North Carolina

During the past ten years, thematic surveys have been conducted of African American communities in a number of North Carolina cities.[1] Surveyors have been sensitive to cultural differences that might be reflected in building form and design. One of the often unacknowledged lures of African American material culture is the promise of Africanisms, features which form a link back to African customs. These range from a concrete gravestone decorated with children's marbles in an African American cemetery to the name of a beauty shop, "Doing Da Doos," seen in a black neighborhood. Architectural historians generally assume that African American buildings exhibit ethnic traditions. John Vlach's well-known tracing of the shotgun house as a form that African immigrants created in Haiti and carried to Louisiana raises the possibility of discoveries of other African-linked house forms in America.[2]

The Afrocentric interpretation of material culture holds that numerous examples of African-inspired material culture forms survive in America if we know where to look for them. Some African Americans claim African derivation for certain elements of American architecture, such as the porch.[3] But do we operate under a black and white double standard? We would certainly never expect the architecture of European immigrant groups such as Germans or Scotch-Irish to exhibit cultural retention by the twentieth century, yet we look for it in the twentieth-century architecture of African immigrants. Many African Americans would be surprised to learn that their architecture is sometimes considered ethnic. Most probably assume that their buildings represent an architectural vocabulary that is shared with whites.

Enough research has now been done to ask our central question: Is the surviving African American housing in North Carolina different from white housing, and if so, how? I submit that we cannot answer this question with existing surveys because we are not comparing apples with apples—that is, black neighborhoods to white neighborhoods created through the same forces, or agency. Agency is usually not an issue in analyzing the dominant building traditions in white communities since the surveyor subconsciously assumes that all of the agents—the developer, the builder, and the buyer—are white and are acting out of free choice. This is certainly not always valid in white communities, such as in institutional and worker housing. In African American sectors, however, an understanding of the degree of control blacks possessed over the location of their community, the physical structure of the streets, and the forms of their buildings is crucial to interpreting this architecture as a reflection of African American history. Many African American building surveys do not recognize distinctions among rental housing, owner-built housing, or "hand-me-down" housing (my term for white housing that went black) because inadequate historical research has been done to make these important distinctions. Can a rental neighborhood built by white landlords for African American tenants be considered an example of African American architecture? Can a neighborhood built for white residents but now occupied by black residents be considered African American architecture? We cannot compare white housing reflecting freedom of choice with black housing in which blacks had no choice. If a neighborhood was not created by African Americans for themselves, how can it represent them aesthetically?

To answer the central question—whether African American architecture is different—let us look at the history of building and agency in the black community. Only isolated African American buildings survive from before 1900, when black and white housing was not rigidly segregated, but followed a salt-and-pepper pattern in North Carolina towns. After emancipation, mutual dependency of whites and blacks continued, and many blacks lived "on the alleys" in former slave quarters or newer tenements.[4] Urban blacks often established small communities in the least desirable, most affordable corners of cities.

The earliest surviving African American communities in the state were built during the Jim Crow era of segregation, beginning about 1900. Jim Crow was a minstrel show character whose name has become synonymous with segregation laws. The Jim Crow laws and social codes that legalized segregation throughout the South began in the late nineteenth century and coalesced in North Carolina in 1900, when the Disfranchisement Amendment essentially stripped blacks of their right to vote. In the early years of Jim Crow, attempts were made to impose rigid apartheid in North Carolina. In 1913 North Carolinian Clarence Poe, well-known editor of the *Progressive Farmer*, launched a two-year crusade to establish rural segregation throughout the South, modeling his plans on the apartheid policies being enacted at that time in South Africa.[5] In 1913 the city of Winston-Salem was one of the earliest cities in the South to follow the method invented in Richmond, Virginia, of designating blocks throughout the city black or white according to the majority of the residents of the block, forbidding any person to live in any block where the majority were of another race.[6] None of these schemes was fully realized, but during the Jim Crow years from 1900 to the Civil Rights era and the abolition of segregation laws in the 1960s, segregated urban landscapes evolved in North Carolina towns through the forces of restrictive covenants, economics, and social codes, and they exist to this day.

In each city, the African American sectors that took shape from the late 1800s to the 1960s consist of streets of middle- and working-class housing, brick churches, schools, and institutional buildings. Yet, there were and are black shantytowns in hollows and urban edges, and block after block of shotgun rental housing generally associated with African American occupancy; most have been demolished by urban renewal programs.

The four basic types of black urban clusters—shantytowns, private rental ghettos, public-housing projects, and owner-occupied neighborhoods—rarely stand alone, and nearly all African American sectors have pockets of each. Shantytowns represent free agency, but because of their temporary squatter status few have survived to be studied. Fig. 16.1 shows the edge of the white section of the town of New Bern, in coastal North Carolina, about 1912, with small, dilapidated frame houses of African Americans crammed against one another and the sidewalk. Rather than being relegated to a separate section of town, these New Bern blacks were still living in cramped quarters among the larger dwellings of white residents. Government projects represent clear government agency. But rental housing was never a simple arrangement between white landlords and black tenants. One of the largest developers and builders of African American rental housing in the state was the North Carolina Mutual Life Insurance Company, a black-owned business in Durham, North Carolina (fig. 16.2). The company entered the real estate business in 1903, and built hundreds of rental units in Hayti and other southeast Durham black neighborhoods to satisfy the demand for housing caused by the influx of black laborers employed in Durham's tobacco factories.

The rental housing and the projects reflect the agency of domination—either by private investors of both races or by the government, and there is no doubt that the majority of urban blacks lived in such housing. In 1940 80 percent of urban black families in North Carolina lived in substandard housing that was probably largely rented.[7] This history of domination may be reflected in black speech. In common African American parlance, "stay" is used instead of "live." Blacks ask each other "Where do you stay?" rather than "Where do you live?" as whites would say.[8] Does this semantic practice reflect a deeply embedded

Fig. 16.1. 600 Block of New Street, New Bern, North Carolina, c. 1912. Romulus A. Nunn Papers, Courtesy of Special Collections Library, Duke University.

Fig. 16.2. Hayti Neighborhood, Durham, c. 1920. This row of five two-story, front-hipped rental houses was built in Durham by the North Carolina Mutual Life Insurance Company, a black-owned business.

sense of impermanence of residence and the absence of a tradition of home ownership in the African American community, or are other factors at work?

Owner Neighborhoods

In order to determine whether Jim Crow housing is aesthetically different from white housing of the era, this chapter will focus on the only segment of segregated black communities that clearly reflects a degree of free agency—the owner-occupied housing—in three North Carolina towns: New Bern, Raleigh, and Durham (fig. 16.3).

An educated and property-owning black elite created its own "separate but equal" neighborhoods during the Jim Crow era. An enduring, eternal theme of the African American middle class has been that self-help and individual responsibility would bring about equality of opportunity, and home ownership was one of the most important goals pushed by race leaders throughout the period.[9] Bishop George Clinton of Charlotte, one of North Carolina's race leaders at the turn of the century, declared that "every Negro that acquires a home of his own, or builds up a substantial business, thereby becomes a more worthy and helpful factor to the community as a whole."[10] Bishop Clinton asserted in a booklet entitled *Colored Charlotte,* published in 1915 to celebrate the "race progress" of Charlotte's "better class" of blacks, that blacks could earn full participation in southern society by property ownership, exemplary citizenship, and the "moral, social, religious and general development of the community."[11] By 1900, only two generations after slavery, complex class distinctions had developed within African American society. As blacks rose into the middle class, they abandoned some cultural traditions and assimilated to middle-class white culture. In a magazine article in 1908, Booker T. Washington noted:

> [W]hite men know almost nothing about the better class of Negro homes . . . many of them handsome modern buildings, with all the evidences of taste and culture that you might expect to find in any other home of the same size and appearance. If you should inquire here, you would learn that

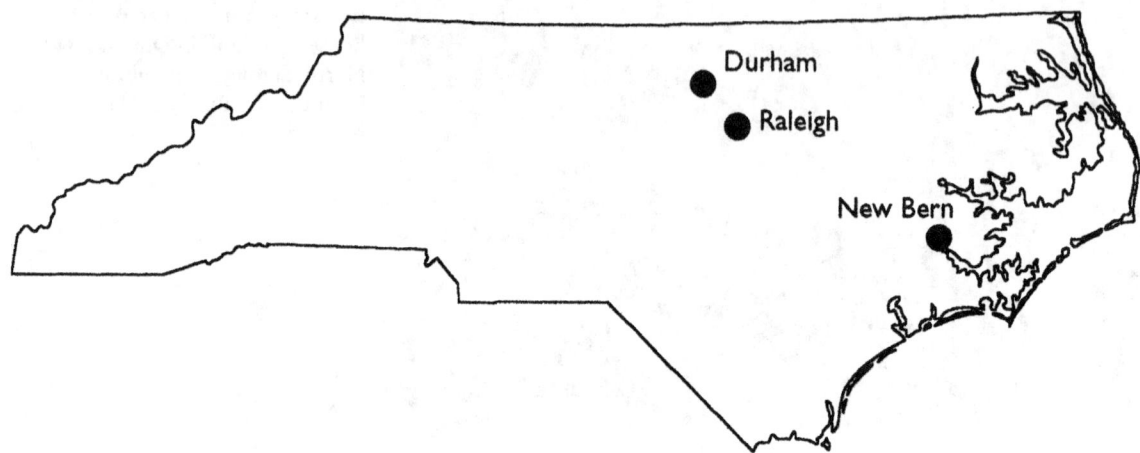

Fig. 16.3. New Bern, Raleigh, and Durham. The three cities are located in eastern and central North Carolina.

the people living in these homes were successful merchants, lawyers, doctors, and teachers. There is nothing picturesque about these dwellings, and nothing to distinguish them from any other houses of the same class near-by; they are not usually recognized as Negro homes."[12]

As did most of white middle-class America, Washington interpreted one's house as an outward sign of one's industry and prosperity.

African Americans certainly made distinctions between home-owned and rental housing. Mary Hamilton, daughter of a black barber in Raleigh in the early 1900s, described the tenant/homeowner mixture in her childhood neighborhood in value-laden terms: "Well, a lot of rental houses were what my mother called railroad houses, one room right behind the other. But all of the houses owned by individuals were different. They had from five to six rooms, or more, large porches, and the lots were good and large."[13] Any house two rooms wide or two stories tall—because it therefore clearly departed from a shotgun—confirmed status within the black community.

Very few African Americans were able to purchase property for many years after freedom, and when they got land they held on tenaciously. For example, a system of inheritance in North Carolina black communities called "heir land" insured that the precious land would never be sold out of the family.[14] By not making a will, either intentionally or unintentionally, each generation left the land to all of the heirs—not just children but the extended family. This "heir land" eventually became the property of hundreds of people and could, practically speaking, never be sold because of the legal difficulties of getting that many people to take action. Even today, "heir land" is a legal nightmare for lawyers.

New Bern

Owner-occupied black communities developed in every sizable town in North Carolina during the early twentieth century, but most of these early black middle-class enclaves perished under urban renewal of the 1960s and 1970s. Black neighborhoods in the eastern North Carolina port town of New Bern were spared this fate. New Bern, which boomed in the early nineteenth century, was predominantly African American, and had by far the largest number of free blacks of any town in North Carolina: almost 13 percent of the population.[15] Like the slaves, who had been scattered throughout town on their masters' property, free blacks often lived among whites. Prosperous tailor John R. Green's two-story house still stands on Johnson Street in the heart of old New Bern. Barber John C. Stanly's large dwelling still fronts on New Street in central New Bern. "Barber Jack," as he was known, owned 127 slaves, more than any other free Negro slave owner in the South.[16]

For some twenty years after the Civil War, African Americans continued to reside among whites in the heart of New Bern.[17] In the 1890s, attorney George White, the first black lawyer in New Bern, bought a house on Johnson Street which had been built for a white family. White's next-door neighbor, Furnifold Simmons, was a white lawyer who led the "White Supremacy" campaign mounted by the Democratic Party. White was elected to the United States Congress in 1897, but Simmons campaigned successfully against so-called "Negro Domination" of elected offices in North Carolina. When the Disfranchisement Amendment passed in the state in 1900, George White abandoned New Bern for Philadelphia, saying in despair: "I cannot live in North Carolina and be a man and be treated as a man." White was the last African American congressman elected from the South until the 1960s. In the next block of Johnson Street, Isaac H. Smith, a wealthy African American real estate developer, built a house for his family. When it burned in 1922 his widow built a large brick Foursquare on the lot. As Booker T. Washington pointed out, there is nothing to distinguish these blacks' houses from the whites' houses of their neighbors: all are amply-sized brick and frame dwellings of similar form and finish.

Apart from this black elite, the rest of New Bern's black community lived on the other side of the tracks, across Queen Street behind the white cemetery and away from the "healthy breezes" blowing off the Neuse and Trent Rivers. This area had been the edge of town prior to the Civil War, where blacks and whites intermingled, and after emancipation large numbers of freedmen from plantations poured into the area.

There, in a section known as Frog Pond, on Bern Street, and along West Street near West Street School, which had been established in 1872 and became the main black high school for the county, African Americans built substantial I-Houses—the very symbol of middle-class values in white neighborhoods. The Great Fire of 1922 destroyed forty blocks of Greater Duffyfield, wiping out these I-Houses as well as buildings labeled as "Negro shacks" and "Negro tenements" on Sanborn maps and large clusters of decent rental housing.

After the fire, Frog Pond arose from the ashes, and the black middle class constructed brick and frame Foursquares, exact counterparts of the housing built by white middle-class families in New Bern. A number of large Craftsman houses built for black middle-class families in the 1920s and 1930s, such as the J. T. Barber House (fig. 16.4), anchor the Frog Pond neighborhood. Near the Barber House is the home of Mr. and Mrs. Harvey who worked at the school. Mr. Sparrow, a brick mason, built a handsome brick Foursquare for himself and his wife, a teacher at West Street School. Another brickmason, Sam Poole, built a Foursquare with stylish patterned brickwork one block over. This community symbolizes New Bern's legacy of black freedom since before the Civil War, when a distinguished population of free blacks already possessed the traditions of self-sufficiency and free enterprise.

Fig. 16.4. J. T. Barber's Foursquare House. Barber, the principal at West Street School, built this comfortable, nationally popular house type across from the school.

Raleigh

In Raleigh, the main impetus for the growth of a strong African American community was the founding of two colleges. In 1866 northern white Baptist missionaries established Shaw Collegiate Institute for freedmen on the "South Side," and in 1867 northern white Episcopalian missionaries established St. Augustine's Normal School to train black teachers on the north side of Raleigh. Now Shaw University and St. Augustine's College, these institutions became centers of African American culture and attracted blacks who came to teach or to be taught, and they called Raleigh "Culture Town" (fig. 16.5).[18] Sociologist E. Franklin Frazier believed that the missionary schools taught thrift and character, which created a group of black leaders with a sense of responsibility for bettering their race. He defined this original black middle class of the 1880s–1910s period as teachers, doctors, dentists, preachers, government employees and businessmen, who made up about 2½ percent of all employed blacks, expanding by 1955 to about 12 percent.[19]

The African American community of Idlewild grew up around St. Augustine's College. The streets were subdivided in 1908, and by the 1920s there were a number of blocks of owner-occupied housing and little rental property. A mixture of cottages and large Victorian and Craftsman dwellings went up in the 1910s and 1920s. Dennis Taylor, a laborer on the Seaboard Railroad, bought a two-story front-gable house at 310 Heck St. in 1910. It was the first house he had ever owned. As his granddaughter says, "Most of the blacks who were coming into the area were buying homes and aspiring to be somebody. . . . We were a self-respecting area. People were home owners and they worked hard to keep their homes looking presentable."[20]

Testimonials to the struggle to buy a house and to the significance of home ownership as a symbol of "being somebody" also sometimes appears in the "ex-slave narratives" collected by WPA interviewers in the 1930s. One Idlewild resident, Hilliard Yellerday, was interviewed when he was in his seventies by a Federal Writers' Project volunteer. Born a slave in 1861 on a Mississippi plantation and sent to North Carolina during the war,

Fig. 16.5. Sunrise Breakfast Gathering in Raleigh's "Culture Town." This meeting was held at the home of Bishop Delany, head of St. Augustine's College, about 1920. From *Culture Town: Life in Raleigh's African American Communities*, 1993.

Fig. 16.6. Hilliard Yellerday House, Raleigh, in 1995.

Yellerday told of growing up in a sharecropping family and farming until he was in his early forties:

> I had not gotten one hundred dollars ahead in all this time so I got a job with the railroad, Seaboard Air Line Shops in Raleigh, North Carolina and that is the only place I ever made any money. I worked from 1903 until 1920 with the Seaboard Air Line Railroad as flunkey. I worked as box packer and machinist's helper. Mother and father died without ever owning a house but I saved my money while working for the Railroad company and bought this lot 157 X 52½ and had this house built on it. The house has five rooms and cost about one thousand dollars. I've been so of late years I could not pay my taxes. I am partially blind and unable to work anymore.[21]

Yellerday's five-room house still stands on Oakwood Avenue in the Idlewild neighborhood, across the street from St. Augustine's College (fig. 16.6). It is a Victorian cottage of the type common to middle-class white neighborhoods in Raleigh. Somehow Yellerday paid his taxes and lived the rest of his life, to 1950, in his beloved house, and passed it on to a descendant.[22]

But some blacks never had a chance to pass on their first home to their children. Dilly Yelladay, born right after the war, moved to the new black neighborhood of South Park, beside Shaw University in Raleigh, in the early twentieth century and told a WPA interviewer in the 1930s that "I have worked most of my life since I come to Raleigh, buyin' a home, but I got ole and couldn't keep up the payments and they come down here and took my home. Twas the wurst thing thats come to me in my whole life. Less you tried it you can't imagine how bad it makes you feel to have to give up yer home."[23] Raleigh's black neighborhoods are full of the modest houses of African Americans who came to "Culture Town" to "be somebody."

Durham

Durham, the famous tobacco factory town, was a New South city that grew up by the railroad tracks after the Civil War and had no legacy of either slavery or free black occupation. Freedmen moved into Durham to work in the tobacco factories, and they rented land from white farmers on the other side of the tracks, across from the factories. The area, centered on Fayetteville Street, became known as Hayti (pronounced "Hay-tie"), and a black commercial district appeared by 1902. A group of race leaders, including businessmen, preachers, and teachers, assisted by white philanthropists, began to create institutions that nurtured a middle class. In 1898 three black businessmen founded the North Carolina Mutual Life Insurance Company, which quickly became the largest Negro insurance company in the world. Lincoln Hospital for blacks was built in the area in 1901. Dr. Charles Shepard, who later had a large brick residence built on Fayetteville Street, founded a training school for blacks (now North Carolina Central University) in 1910.[24] By 1912 the black middle class in Durham had become legendary among American blacks, and leaders and scholars such as Booker T. Washington, W. E. B. Du Bois, and, later, E. Franklin Frazier wrote articles about the success of black capitalists and businessmen in Durham.

Du Bois found in Durham a remarkably diverse new economy. Durham's black world of Hayti had come closer to the goal of self-sufficiency than probably any other black settlement in the South. Durham was Du Bois's definition of progress:

> [T]o-day there is a singular group in Durham where a black man may get up in the morning from a mattress made by black men, in a house which a black man built out of lumber which

black men cut and planed; he may put on a suit which he bought at a colored haberdashery and socks knit at a colored mill; he may cook victuals from a colored grocery on a stove which black men fashioned; he may earn his living working for colored men, be sick in a colored hospital, and buried from a colored church; and the Negro insurance society will pay his widow enough to keep his children in a colored school.[25]

Durham's history illustrates an unintended benefit of Jim Crow segregation, the mushrooming of black businesses. In the harsh climate of the segregated South, blacks who had patronized white businesses and white doctors and other professionals in the presegregation years of the 1880s and 1890s turned to black businesses and professionals after 1900, producing a growing middle class of enterprising African Americans.

This independent class built attractive single-family residences along Fayetteville Street, Hayti's main street, and along side streets from the 1890s to 1910s. Hayti ran along a ridge with a vista across to white Durham to the north and occupied land of equally attractive outlook as that of white neighborhoods in Durham. The Hayti streetscapes include rambling Victorian houses, brick and frame Neoclassical style houses, and neat cottages, including documented Sears and Roebuck–ordered dwellings (fig. 16.7). The Scarborough House on Fayetteville Street illustrates the long tradition of using salvaged materials in the African American community. It was built largely of Colonial Revival materials salvaged from a house demolished near Lincoln Hospital about 1912.[26] In the 1920s a neighborhood of faculty houses, known as College View, developed beside North Carolina Central College. Bungalows, Spanish Colonial Revival houses, Tudor and Craftsman cottages line Formosa Avenue and Pekoe Street, which meander picturesquely around the North Carolina Central College campus (fig. 16.8).

Comparing Intentional Communities

Are these African American communities aesthetically different from white communities? The streets of owner-occupied houses, however modest, in Frog Pond, Idlewild, and Hayti are indistinguishable from white middle-class streets of the same era. It should be no surprise that middle-

Fig. 16.7. African American Residences in Hayti Neighborhood, Durham, in 1995.

Fig. 16.8. African American Residences, College View Neighborhood, Durham, in 1995.

class African American neighborhoods look a lot like white neighborhoods of the same class, which were their prototypes. In the area of architecture, blacks acculturated into mainstream American culture at the same rate as other racial and ethnic groups. When intentional black neighborhoods are compared to intentional white neighborhoods, differences vanish—there is no longer white or black architecture, but simply middle-class architecture.

Yet, when we picture a historic black neighborhood, many of us conjure up a street of shotgun houses. Because rental houses, often shotguns, sheltered the majority of African American families during the era, this is a statistically valid image. Certainly shotguns and other forms of rental housing are not lesser artifacts of the African American experience or cultural tradition. Nevertheless, they no more symbolize African American aspirations than a row of tenant cabins represent white aspirations. Historians have an obligation to judge cultures not only by statistical tables, but by the products of individuals' free agency. As a 1908 African American study, *The Negro American Family,* summarizes, "A race has a right to be judged by its best."[27] Of course, we must document African American architecture with objective fieldwork and research, but the statistics generated from such study should be weighted by the symbolic significance of each agency type. Out of one hundred dwelling units in an African American neighborhood of the Jim Crow era, approximately ten will be owner-built or owner-occupied. Yet, these intentional houses are the only examples of the free agency of African Americans.

The documentation and preservation of historic African American communities is a way to acknowledge and celebrate the achievements of black Americans during the beginnings of apartheid in the early twentieth century. Holding owner-occupied black neighborhoods up as examples of black success in the face of Jim Crow racism illuminates the darkness of this period of African American history. This housing of intention suggests that middle-class values were a powerful shaper of middle-class African American sensibility in this period. Housing in the era of Jim Crow participates in the central debate within the African American community at the time: the accommodation policy of Booker T. Washington versus the confrontation policy of W. E. B. Du Bois. The men apparently agreed on at least one thing: both viewed intentional black communities as one solution to the race problem, Washington because blacks were achieving their goals without threatening the status quo, and Du Bois because these enterprising blacks were achieving success on their own terms. When we distinguish the housing of intention from the housing of domination, we can begin the celebration.

Notes

1. Thematic African American Historic Architecture Surveys have been conducted in New Bern, Wilson, Raleigh, Winston-Salem, and Durham, North Carolina, under the auspices of the State Historic Preservation Office.
2. John Michael Vlach, "The Shotgun House: An African Architectural Legacy," *Pioneer America* 8 (1976): 47–70.
3. For a preliminary discussion of this topic, see John Michael Vlach, *The Afro-American Tradition in Decorative Arts* (Cleveland, Ohio: Cleveland Museum of Art, 1978).
4. All over the antebellum urban South, blacks, enslaved and free, typically resided in all parts of the city. See David R. Goldfield, "Black Life in Old South Cities," *Before Freedom Came: African-American Life in the Antebellum South* (Richmond: Museum of the Confederacy, and Charlottesville: Univ. Press of Virginia, 1991), 138.
5. Jeffrey J. Crow, Paul D. Escott, Flora J. Hatley, *A History of African Americans in North Carolina* (Raleigh: Division of Archives and History, North Carolina Dept. of Cultural Resources, 1992), 122.
6. Langdon E. Oppermann, "Winston-Salem's African-American Neighborhoods," report produced for the Forsyth County Joint Historic Properties Commission, Winston-Salem, N.C. 1993, 15.
7. Crow, Escott, and Hatley, *A History of African Americans in North Carolina,* 130.
8. *Oxford English Dictionary* (Oxford: Oxford Univ. Press, 1989), 16: 583.
9. See general discussions of this in Crow, Escott, and Hatley, *A History of African Americans in North Carolina*; Janette Greenwood, *Bittersweet Legacy: The Black and White "Better Classes" in Charlotte 1850–1910* (Chapel Hill: Univ. of North Carolina Press, 1994); E. Franklin Frazier, "Durham: Capital of the Black Middle Class," in *The New Negro: An Interpretation,* ed. Alain Locke (New York: Albert and Charles Boni, 1925), 333–40.
10. Greenwood, *Bittersweet Legacy,* 143.
11. Ibid., 239.
12. Booker T. Washington, "Negro Homes," *Century Illustrated Monthly Magazine* LXXVI (May–Oct. 1908): 73.
13. Mary Delaney Hamilton interview, May 30, 1989, in "Raleigh's Roots," a collection of oral histories, Raleigh Historic Properties Commission, Raleigh, N.C.
14. This practice occurs primarily in rural areas.
15. Alan D. Watson, *A History of New Bern and Craven County* (New Bern: Tryon Palace Commission, 1987), 307.
16. Loren Schweninger, "John C. Stanly and the Anomaly of Black Slaveholding," *North Carolina Historical Review* (Apr. 1990): 169.
17. Blacksmith Samuel Jackson, storekeeper William Jones, and shoemaker John T. Havens were African Americans who lived in the heart of New Bern. See Thomas W. Hanchett and M. Ruth Little, "The History and Architecture of Long Wharf and Greater Duffyfield" (New Bern, N.C.: Historic Preservation Commission, 1994).
18. The Delany sisters, authors of the recent best-seller, *Having Our Say,* are the daughters of Bishop Delany, head of St. Augustine's College, and the first black Episcopal bishop in the United States in the

early twentieth century. Sarah Louise Delany, Annie Elizabeth Delany, and Amy Hill Hearth, *Having Our Say: The Delany Sisters' First 100 Years* (New York: Kodansha International, 1993).

19. E. Franklin Frazier, *On Race Relations: Selected Writings* (Chicago: Univ. of Chicago Press, 1968), 256.

20. Interview with Mildred Taylor James, 1989, in *Culture Town: Life in Raleigh's African American Communities,* Linda Simmons-Henry and Linda Harris Edmisten (Raleigh: Raleigh Historic Districts Commission, Inc. 1993), 156.

21. Interview with Hilliard Yellerday, quoted in George P. Rawick, ed. *The American Slave: A Composite Autobiography: North Carolina Narratives, Part 2* (Westport, Conn.: Greenwood Publishing Company, 1976) 15: 432–33.

22. *Raleigh City Directories, 1923–55.* From 1951 to at least 1955, Mrs. Evelyn (Emile) Yellowday [sic] lived here.

23. Interview with Dilly Yelladay at 909 Mark Street, Raleigh, in the 1930s. Rawick, *The American Slave: A Composite Autobiography: North Carolina Narratives, Part 2,* 15: 428–30.

24. Claudia P. Roberts, *The Durham Architectural and Historic Inventory* (City of Durham and The Historic Preservation Society of Durham, 1982), 259, 339–42.

25. W. E. Burghardt Du Bois, "The Upbuilding of Black Durham," *The World's Work* (Jan. 1912): 338.

26. Roberts, *The Durham Architectural and Historic Inventory,* 126.

27. *The Negro American Family,* ed. W. E. Burghardt Du Bois, The Atlanta University Publications, No. 13 (Atlanta, Ga.: The Atlanta University Press, 1908), 65.

CHAPTER 17

Pamela H. Simpson

Linoleum and Lincrusta: The Democratic Coverings for Floors and Walls

In the second half of the nineteenth century, new industrial techniques produced a variety of novel architectural materials that were imitative of older, more traditional ones. Expanded production and improved distribution systems meant that the new products could be produced cheaply; thus, decorative effects that previously had been available only to the rich could now be enjoyed by the growing middle class. The focus of this chapter is on two examples of the new materials: linoleum for floors and Lincrusta-Walton, an embossed covering for walls. Both were invented by an Englishman named Frederick Walton.[1]

The legend is that one day the young Walton (fig. 17.1) noticed the top of a paint jar had a skin of oxidized linseed oil. He peeled it off and began playing with the rubberlike piece, thinking of ways to use it. This led to a series of experiments, and eventually, in 1860, the first of a series of patents that would be the basis for linoleum. The name came from *linum*—Latin for flax, from which linseed oil is made, and *oleum,* Latin for oil; thus, literally, "linoleum" means "linseed oil." Essentially, linoleum is oxidized linseed oil mixed with ground cork dust, gums, and pigments, which are then pressed between heavy rollers onto a canvas backing. Walton set up his first linoleum factory in England in 1864. By 1866 the Linoleum Manufacturing Company, as it was called, was reporting steady sales, and by 1869 the company was exporting its product to the European Continent and the United States.[2]

Walton's chief competition was the older oil-cloth trade centered in Scotland and Lancashire. He had tried to interest several of the larger firms in his new product, but to no avail. Oilcloth was made largely by a hand-process of applying successive layers of sizing and paint to a piece of canvas and then covering it with a block-printed design. It had been an economical, practical, and

Fig. 17.1. Frederick Walton. Walton was the inventor of linoleum. From *Industrial and Engineering Chemical News* 12 (7) (Apr. 10, 1934): 119.

popular floor covering since the eighteenth century. Often sold in rug-sized pieces, by the 1870s it was also available in wall-to-wall sizes. Its waterproof qualities made it popular for halls, kitchens, stairways, and washrooms.[3]

Walton's new linoleum was superior to the painted oilcloth because it was thicker, more waterproof, resilient, and much longer-wearing. Its popularity was such that, as soon as Walton's patents expired in 1877, the older oilcloth firms began to try to imitate it. Walton instituted legal proceedings against the large Scottish firm called Nairn for infringement of his trademark when it began to manufacture and sell its own brand of linoleum.

But in 1878, the British Courts ruled against Walton, largely because he had made the mistake of failing to register "linoleum" as his trade name. The interesting part of the ruling was, however, the court's declaration that the word "linoleum" was now public property since it was in such widespread use. It had taken less than fourteen years for linoleum to become such a ubiquitous feature of homes and commercial buildings that it was considered commonplace.[4]

Walton's company was thus in competition with a variety of rival firms by the late 1870s and 1880s. The Scottish town of Kirkcaldy had not only the Nairn Company, but also Barry, Ostelere and Shepherd as well as the Fife Linoleum Company. There were two other firms in Fife, another in Dundee, the large factory of James Williamson and Son in Lancaster, and several other firms near London.

Walton's Linoleum Manufacturing Company continued to expand its markets and sold patent rights to firms in Germany, France, and America. In 1872 Walton sailed to New York to help Joseph Wild establish the American Linoleum Manufacturing Company. Walton spent two years supervising the building of the factory and company town on Staten Island, and he named the place "Linoleumville."[5] In 1879 *The Carpet Trade* journal reported, "The manufacture of sheet oilcloth has been considerably interfered with as of late . . . by the introduction of linoleum" and cited, as one reason, the popularity of the new American company.[6]

The next major technological improvement in linoleum was Walton's introduction of "straight-line inlaid linoleum" in 1882. In early linoleum, pigment was mixed with the ground so the material was a solid color. This was an advantage over the older oilcloth because it could hide wear. When designs were used, they were printed or painted on the surface, just as on oilcloth. The disadvantage to this was, of course, that the pattern wore off with use. What Walton and the other firms wanted was a way to make the patterns just as permanent and long-wearing as the linoleum base.

Walton's original patent had referred to the idea of an inlaid linoleum but gave no mechanism for its production. Various experiments had led to a stencil method where color could be introduced by forcing pigments through a slotted tray. That could produce multicolored "molded" or "granulated" inlay in somewhat fuzzy-looking patterns, but it could not imitate the precision of a tile design. The first experiments with straight-line inlaid linoleum depended on handwork (fig. 17.2). Linoleum was made in various colors; the pieces were cut and then laid by hand into patterns. The roll was heated and rerolled so pressure and heat fused it into one. By 1890 Walton, again in the lead, invented a way to do all this with a machine (fig. 17.3).[7]

Walton was no longer a controlling partner in his original firm and was unhappy with its support for this new product, so he sold out and started the Greenwich Inlaid Linoleum Company in 1895. But again, his new product was so good that other manufacturers either bought his patent rights or came up with their own versions of his inlaid linoleum. The obvious superiority of the new product was reflected in the advertising, which boasted that the colors went "straight through to the back." Inlaid was more expensive, however, and the cheaper printed forms continued to be produced.

By 1910 there were at least six linoleum manufacturers in the United States. Wild continued in business until the 1930s. In Philadelphia there were the firms of George Blabon and Thomas Potter. In New Jersey, there was Cook's, and an American

Fig. 17.2. Linoleum Assembly Line. These workers are making straight-line inlaid linoleum by hand-piecing the design. From *Scientific American* 143 (Oct. 1930): 313.

Fig. 17.3. Walton's Giant Rotary Press. This press was used for creating straight-line inlaid linoleum. From *Scientific American* 143 (Oct. 1930): 312.

Fig. 17.4. Armstrong Advertisement. This c. 1920 advertisement is typical of those addressed to women consumers. Courtesy of the Hagley Museum and Library.

branch of Nairn's, but the one that eventually would dominate them all was the Armstrong Cork and Tile Company of Lancaster, Pennsylvania. This company had started in the 1860s as a cork manufacturer. Ground-up cork dust was the chief binder in linoleum, and by the 1880s Armstrong was selling its cork debris to Wild and other linoleum manufacturers. Charles D. Armstrong decided that with so much of the raw product readily available to his company, he might as well start making linoleum himself; and in 1908 his company did. Armstrong led the way with new advertising techniques in the late 1910s that were the first linoleum ads to be addressed directly to the consumer rather than the retailer. They appeared in magazines like the *Ladies Home Journal* and the *Saturday Evening Post* and helped to increase the market demand (fig. 17.4).[8]

The number of companies producing linoleum continued to expand in the early twentieth century. Britain led in export production, but Germany soon began to rival it. In Canada there was the Dominion Company, and there were also factories in Australia, France, Belgium, Austria, Italy, Sweden, and Russia. Linoleum was a worldwide product, as were its raw materials. The linseed oil came primarily from South America and the United States, the cork came from Portugal and Spain, the jute for the canvas backing came from India and Pakistan and was processed into burlap in Scotland. Linoleum was also used all over the world, especially where the various European colonial powers had established footholds. World War I greatly disrupted this network, but it quickly re-established itself in the postwar period.[9]

In 1910, cheaper felt-based versions of linoleum were developed. Congoleum is the best-known example, and it enjoyed wide popularity as a cheap substitute for linoleum especially in the 1930s. It did not wear as well or as long as linoleum and was not as waterproof, but it was so cheap it could be easily replaced. It was especially popular in ruglike widths and its patterns often imitated carpet.[10]

Linoleum was eventually replaced in the 1950s and 1960s with the introduction of plastic-based products. Today, most of what people call "linoleum" is actually vinyl floor covering. Still, linoleum remained one of the most popular and widely used floor coverings from the 1870s to the 1960s, a period of over ninety years.[11]

As great as had been the success of his linoleum, Walton is also known for another invention: a resin-based wall covering called Lincrusta. Walton patented it in 1877 and at first called it "Linoleum Muralis"—or linoleum for walls. After the court ruling deprived him of the exclusive use of the term "linoleum," Walton changed the name of his new product to Lincrusta-Walton, this time with a registered trademark so no other company could appropriate it. Again, he based the name on Latin: *Linum* for flax or linseed oil, *crusta*, for relief. Lincrusta was essentially the same material as linoleum. Oxidized linseed oil was its chief ingredient, but wood pulp instead of ground cork dust served as a binder. The mixture was pressed between heavy rollers, one of which was engraved to create the embossed relief design. Originally, Lincrusta was pressed onto a canvas backing just as linoleum was, but that proved too stiff and was replaced in 1887 with a waterproof paper backing. Lincrusta could convincingly imitate wood paneling, stamped leather, or decorative plaster in low relief (fig. 17.5). Walton advertised it as "Solid in Color! Solid in Relief! Solid in Value!"[12]

While linoleum appeared everywhere—from battleships to kitchens—Lincrusta was a more "artistic" product that was used in upper middle-class dwellings, lodges, pubs, taverns, and yachts. In the United States, the firm of Frederick Beck began to produce it in 1883, and by 1911 it was being advertised in the Sears, Roebuck catalog. Lincrusta was widely popular well into the 1930s. It is still produced in England today, but its hey-

Fig. 17.5. Walton's Showroom, 1900. Walton displayed Lincrusta and other relief decorations in London. Courtesy of The Whitworth Art Gallery, Manchester University.

day was the 1880–1930 period.[13] Lincrusta was such a success that a host of similar embossed wall coverings were introduced in the late 1880s and 1890s in an attempt to compete with it. Anaglypta, a paper-pulp–based product that could take on high relief, found its share of the market. Other rivals' included Cordelova, Cameoid, Salamander, and Tynecastle Tapestry and Vellum. However, none of them ever challenged Lincrusta-Walton's position as the "King of Wall Hangings."[14]

This brief chronology of the invention, production, and distribution of linoleum and Lincrusta sets the stage for the next step, which is to further explore the reasons for the popularity of these materials. Advertising and trade literature provides a useful resource for understanding something of the cultural values they embodied. A close reading of the rhetoric used to promote the new materials reveals certain qualities that were particularly championed.

Comfort. This was increasingly a value to the late-nineteenth- and early-twentieth-century consumer. The expanding middle class had the money and leisure to expect greater comfort in their homes and businesses. Linoleum was often seen as better than older, more traditional floor coverings such as marble, wood, or tile in part because it was resilient. As one ad claimed, "linoleum is, par excellence, a comfortable floor. Cork and oxidized linseed oil are naturally elastic and combine to make a sort of cushion that absorbs the shock of footsteps."[15] This made it suitable not only for homes, but also for businesses, factories, and stores—anywhere someone would have to stand for long periods. Moreover, "linoleum is always warm as contrasted to the coldness of tile and marble . . . and unlike rubber tile, it does not 'draw' the feet or make them hot and feverish."[16] The reference to "feverish feet" may relate to nineteenth-century medical ideas, but it is also a reminder that advertising claims can not be taken literally. Still, the central message that linoleum is a more comfortable floor covering than its competitors and that comfort is a desirable and expected quality is clearly stated.

Cleanliness. The late Victorian period sometimes seemed to be obsessed with this idea. Modern germ theory had revolutionized many aspects of waste disposal, water distribution, and sanitation. It seemed that any product boasting of sanitary qualities had a ready-made market. Linoleum and Lincrusta both made the claim. Linoleum was waterproof, nonskid, and easy to clean. There were even assertions that it had antiseptic qualities. In 1913 a German scientist reported on experiments that suggested that the oxidizing linseed oil gave off a germicide gas. This claim was often repeated in the advertising literature, making linoleum seem especially suited to kitchens, bathrooms, nurseries, and hospitals (fig. 17.6).[17]

Lincrusta, too, was considered a sanitary material since it could be cleaned with soap and water, unlike other wall coverings. This point was made by an English journal which noted, "Amongst the many contributors to these twin sisters, Hygeia and Art, the name of Mr. Walton is, and will long continue to be recognized as that of a man whose inventive powers have placed within the reach of the great bulk of the middle and upper classes, a material peerless as a sanitary agent and of a beauty that need fear no rival."[18] The sanitary qualities of Lincrusta were further underscored when it won a Gold Medal at the 1884 International Health Exposition in London.

Durability. This was another chief value of the period. At a time of rapid social change, the idea that technology could provide enduring, permanent building materials seemed to promise stability for the future. Both linoleum and Lincrusta made the claim. Unlike the earlier floor cloth, linoleum was thick enough to wear well. There were reports of its lasting sixty years or more. Armstrong eventually said that it would "last as long as the house."[19] Lincrusta was often described as "permanent" and "indestructible." This point was humorously underscored by A. G. Butler in 1943 when he wrote of helping to clean up the rubble of bombed out London houses. He commented on the "triumph of Lincrusta," adding, "I do not mean aesthetically, but quite the opposite, in a military sense. No material, I think, has stood up to blast so stoutly. That bumpy, adhesive skin on walls and ceilings, aping rich plasterwork has counteracted many blows from bombs, even sustaining whole surfaces by itself."[20]

Unlike wood and marble, linoleum was easy to install, though the manufacturers recommended professional layers for the best results. The earliest

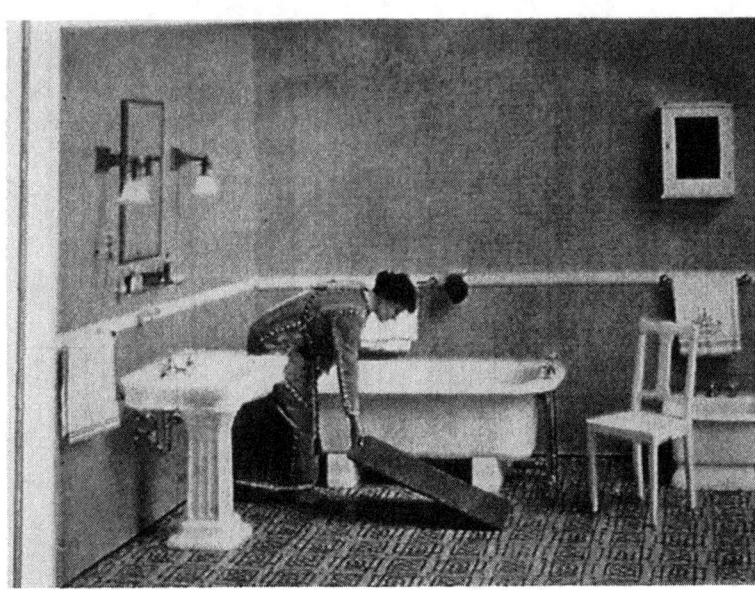

Fig. 17.6. Armstrong Advertisement. Linoleum's sanitary qualities made it suitable for bathrooms. From *Told in the Store* (Lancaster, Pa.: Armstrong Cork Company, Linoleum Department, 1915), 57.

linoleum had been simply tacked down like a carpet. The Armstrong Company again led the way, advocating cementing the linoleum over a felt base to avoid cracking. The Armstrong method made the linoleum a permanent floor, not a temporary floor covering. Lincrusta, likewise, was easy to hang and could be fitted as decorative panels for doors, mantels or furniture, though its chief uses were for walls and ceilings. Like linoleum, it was also considered a "permanent covering."[21]

Because of their waterproof qualities, linoleum and Lincrusta were often promoted for use on ships. Lincrusta was a popular wall covering for yachts and luxury liners, including the *Titanic*. Linoleum was used extensively by the navies of Britain, Germany, and the United States as a nonslip, nonsplintering, waterproof covering for decks. Its special thickness gave it the name "Battleship Linoleum," but its reputation for durability made it also popular for schools, hospitals, and public buildings. Its plain color—Battleship gray or brown—was used everywhere, especially in government buildings, post offices, and schools.[22]

One particularly outrageous claim for the durability of linoleum came in 1900 when an exhibitor at the Paris Exposition installed one-inch-thick linoleum in several driveways and courtyards to test it as a road covering. The thought was that it would muffle the sound of horses hooves and carriage wheels. The developer of this product was so confident of its success that he claimed he was negotiating with the French Government for a contract to pave the entire Champs Élysées with linoleum.[23]

Artistry and Economy. One of the chief claims for the virtues of linoleum and Lincrusta, especially in comparison with other materials, was that they provided "art" at a reasonable price. This argument was made again and again in the advertising.[24]

Linoleum was produced in an amazing variety of patterns. The early solid colors of brown and gray were soon superseded by an annual display of new patterns and forms. By 1918, Armstrong was advertising 380 designs in its pattern book and each year more were introduced. They included mosaics, tiles, parquetries, granites, marble, and "carpet" patterns (fig. 17.7). Some well-known artists contributed designs, including Joseph Hoffman and his Wiener Werkstätte colleagues, who exhibited new linoleum patterns at the San Francisco

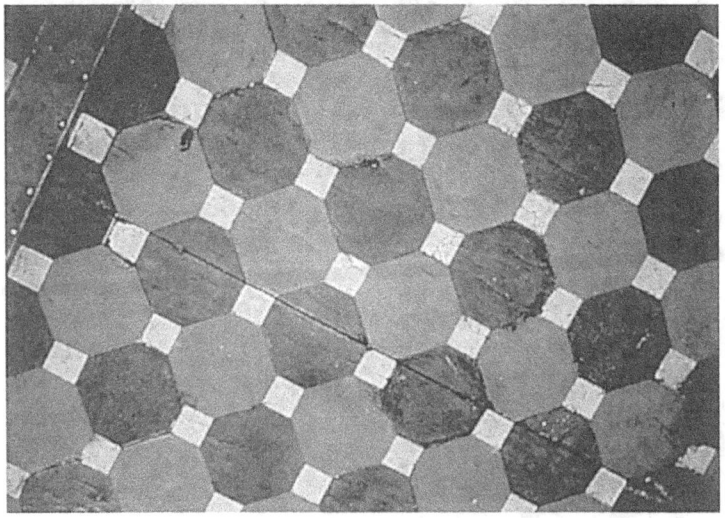

Fig. 17.7. Straight-line Inlaid Linoleum. This Radford, Virginia, kitchen floor, built c. 1910, is in green-blue, dark red, and white.

Panama-Pacific Exposition in 1915.[25] Peter Behrens and Henry Van der Veld produced designs for the German Werkbund between 1913 and 1930. Trade journals frequently commented on the sophistication of the European designs.

Lincrusta, too, was produced in an amazing variety of forms. From the first it could imitate leather and plaster. In 1906 the company brought out a tile imitation for bathrooms, and in 1912 a very convincing and wildly popular imitation of oak dado paneling. Well-known designers such as Christopher Dresser in England and Hector Guimard in France contributed designs for Lincrusta, but Walton also used in-house staff to produce a "cheap" line of dados and friezes. As the *Journal of Decorative Arts* noted in 1881, "even the poorest household can have their walls made beautiful by Lincrusta-Walton, while those of unlimited wealth may indulge their taste and fancy to any extent."[26]

The Question of Imitation. Advertisements repeatedly made the claim that more expensive traditional materials such as tile, marble, wood, or plaster could satisfactorily and economically be replaced by linoleum and Lincrusta. Sometimes the claims seemed a bit outrageous, as in a Cook's ad in which a man holds up a square of linoleum parquet in one hand and wood parquet in the other and asks, "Which is Which?" It seems improbable that anyone could have difficulty telling the difference between wood and linoleum, but that did not stop the claims. There was even the assertion that linoleum parquetry was better than the wood version because it would not splinter and was easier to clean; but most of all, it was cheaper.[27]

In spite of all their practical, durable, decorative, and inexpensive qualities, both linoleum and Lincrusta occasionally came in for criticism, and when they did, it was usually because of their imitative nature. An 1884 booklet promoting Lincrusta-Walton reflected a defensive tone when its author commented, "It is urged by aesthetic writers that no imitative machine stamped ornament can be good. While we admit the theory and agree that no stamped Lincrusta can ever give to an art lover the keen pleasure of a . . . Cellini or a carving by Gibbons. . . , we believe we are doing good work for art by making known that a material exists, within the reach of all, capable . . . of receiving an infinite variety of . . . decoration. . . ."[28]

The reference to "aesthetic writers" who thought that "no imitative machine stamped ornament could be good" was, of course, to John Ruskin, his followers, and his predecessors, who had championed handicraft over machine-made forms. In *The Seven Lamps of Architecture,* Ruskin had argued that all machine-produced decorative products were inherently inferior to handmade ones, both aesthetically and morally, and urged people to do without "all the short, and cheap and easy ways" of making things. "They will only make us shallower in our understanding, colder in our hearts, and feebler in our wits."[29] William Morris also saw imitative decorative materials as threatening to handicraft and complained that "the real thing presently ceases to be made after the makeshift has been once foisted onto the market."[30]

The other side of the debate was voiced by those who championed new materials if they were well designed. They agreed that one material should not imitate another, but argued that new materials would be acceptable if they had an expression of their own. Hence, designers like Christopher Dresser could publish designs for linoleum and provide patterns for Walton's Lincrusta. Even the defenders would never have approved of linoleum parquet, however. It was the sort of thing the designers sought to do away with while they educated the public to a higher taste. The public, however, seemed to have its own ideas and went on willingly embracing both linoleum and Lincrusta in all their imitative forms.

The sheer popularity of linoleum and Lincrusta

was another reason for the scorn that was sometimes heaped on them. This is particularly true of linoleum in the history of preservation. For years, it was considered something to rip out to get down to the "real floor." It is only very recently that it has begun to receive attention as a historic floor covering and as something worthy of preservation and reproduction.

In an 1882 publication, linoleum was referred to as a "makeshift" for "making bad floors tolerable."[31] The idea that linoleum might serve as a temporary floor until one could afford something better was also reflected in the places it was used in the home. The advertisers said it was "suitable for every room in the house," but, in actuality, this was not usually the case. Linoleum was perfectly suitable for kitchens, bathrooms, and entrance halls, but when used for other rooms, such as bedrooms, dining rooms or parlors, it was often a temporary expedient to be eventually replaced or covered with a rug.[32]

Similarly, Lincrusta became so commonplace in the early twentieth century, especially in Britain, that it was sometimes disparaged as well. A. G. Butler in his 1943 comments about Lincrusta standing up to German bombs, reflected upper-class, elitist views when he referred to it as "bad and trashy decoration" and went on to say, "It quite hurts me to think that something we have scoffed at for years has turned out to be an able ally in the fight. A pity it is so unattractive, especially when painted chocolate."[33]

Modern and Democratic. Despite elite rejection, there is clear evidence of middle-class acceptance of new materials like linoleum and Lincrusta. The fact that they were machine-made was not something to apologize for, but something to celebrate. It made them "modern," while handicraft products were viewed as old-fashioned and needlessly expensive. The inexpensiveness of linoleum and Lincrusta also made them "democratic." An 1888 article promoting Lincrusta in *The Painters Magazine and Coach Painter,* for example, noted that "[a]rt in the past ministered to but a few who were lords of the earth. The temple and the palace were alone thought worthy of adornment. In the past it was the few only who were noble—in the future it will be the many and art is rapidly becoming democratic in the consequence. . . ."[34] In other words, machines made ornament affordable to a broader population, just as changes in social structure, wealth distribution, and voting rights laws had broadened political enfranchisement.

The new materials were also considered "modern" because they were better than those they replaced. Linoleum could imitate marble, a traditional, elite material, but it was not "cold" like marble. Lincrusta could look like leather or plaster, but would not crack as they would, was easy to clean, and would last longer. The promoters of linoleum and Lincrusta defended their imitative qualities by calling them modern "re-creations," "artful facsimiles," and "synthetic substitutes."[35] And there is ample evidence that the public agreed. A helpful analogy to explain this might be to think of the contemporary acceptance of nylon hosiery for silk or synthetic rubber for automobile tires. Linoleum and Lincrusta eventually became accepted in their own right.

In conclusion, this analysis of the advertising and promotional rhetoric for linoleum and Lincrusta reveals something of the values they embodied for their public. Practical, durable, economical, and ornamental, they were the products of the new industrial age. It is perhaps not surprising that the newly expanded middle class largely created by the industrial revolution, would embrace the products of industry. Cheap, quick, and easy to install, these materials were also modern, clean, practical substitutes that democratically expanded the availability of ornamental effects.

Notes

The author wishes to thank the many people who gave help and support for this project. Two Glenn Grants from Washington and Lee University enabled summer travel to collections. The staffs at the Library of Congress, The Avery Architectural Library at Columbia University, The Staten Island Historical Society, the Cooper-Hewett Museum and Library, Winterthur Museum and Library, Hagley Museum and Library, The Canadian Centre for Architecture in Montreal, the National Science and Technology Museum Library in Ottawa, the National Archives in Ottawa, the National Art Library at the Victoria and Albert Museum in London, and the Bodleian Library in Oxford were all wonderfully helpful. In addition, I would like to thank Gavin Grant from the Kirkcaldy Museum and Library, Kirkcaldy, Scotland; Joy McKenzie and Terry Griffiths of Crown Decorative Products, Darwen, Lancashire; Neville Thompson at Winterthur, Larry McNally at the National Archives in Canada, and Charlie Sachs of the Staten Island Historical Society for their special assistance. A number of colleagues offered examples, references, review, and other forms of help, including Annmarie Adams, Joanna Banham, Catherine Bishir, Betsy Cromley, Alex and Doreen Cross, Winifred Hadsel, Kim Hoagland, Donna Hole, Delos Hughes, Kate Hutchins, Jan Jennings, Tom Jester, Sally McMurry, Bonnie Parks Snyder, and David Vaisey.

1. Frederick Walton, *The Infancy and Development of Linoleum Floorcloth* (London: Simpkin, Marshall, Hamilton, Kent and Co., Ltd., 1925). See also Bonnie Parks, "Floorcloths to Linoleum: The Development of Resilient Flooring," in *The Interiors Handbook for Historic Buildings,* vol. 2, ed. Michael J. Auer, Charles E. Fisher III, Thomas C. Jester, and Marilyn E. Kaplan (Washington, D.C.: Historic Preservation Education Foundation, 1993).
2. Linoleum Manufacturing Company, Ltd., Record Books 1865–1905, Greater London Record Office.
3. For a history of oil floorcloth, see Parks, "Floorcloths to Linoleum," and Helene Von Rosenstiel and Gail Caskey, *Floor Coverings for Historic Buildings* (Washington, D.C.: Historic Preservation Education Foundation, 1993).
4. Adrian Room, *Directory of Trade Name Origins* (London: Routledge and Kegan Paul, 1982), 110, and *Fife Free Press,* Feb. 2, 1878, clipping file, Kirkcaldy Museum and Library, Kirkcaldy, Scotland.
5. Charles L. Sachs, *Made on Staten Island* (exhibition catalogue), Richmondtown, Staten Island, N. Y., Staten Island Historical Society, 1988. Also, curator's files, Staten Island Historical Society.
6. "Floorcloth," *The Carpet Trade* 10 (Oct. 1879): 17–18.
7. William B. Coleman, "Frederick Walton, Inventor of Machinery for the Manufacture of Linoleum and Founder of the Linoleum Industry," *Mechanical Engineering* (May 1935): 297–302; Coleman, "Frederick Walton, Centenary of the Birth of the Inventor of Linoleum," *Industrial and Engineering Chemical News* 12 (7) (Apr. 10, 1934): 119, 128; Barry, Ostlere and Shepherd, Ltd., "Linoleum, Historical Development," typescript, n.d. after 1929, Kirkcaldy Museum and Library.
8. *Armstrong Linoleum Pattern Book,* 1918, 5–6; *Armstrong Linoleum Pattern Book,* 1926, 4, Avery Architectural Library; Armstrong Cork and Tile Company, *H. W. Prentis, Jr., 1884–1959* (company biography of man responsible for the national advertising campaign) (Lancaster, Pa., 1961). Hagley Museum and Library.
9. "Linoleum Makers Face Shortages," *Dry Goods Economist* 69 (July 31, 1915): 7.
10. Hazel Dell Brown, *The Attractive Home, How to Plan Its Decoration* (Lancaster, Pa.: Armstrong Bureau of Interior Decoration, 1928), 38. Winterthur Museum and Library. Armstrong's version of the felt-based floor covering was called "Quaker Rugs," a named that evoked an image of simple modesty and thrift.
11. Leo Blackman and Deborah Dietsch, "A New

Look at Linoleum, Preservation's Rejected Floor Covering," *The Old House Journal* (Jan. 1982): 9–12., and Blackman and Dietsch, "Linoleum, How to Repair It Install It, and Clean It," *Old House Journal* (Feb. 1982): 36–38.

12. W. G. Sutherland, *Modern Wall Decoration* (London: Simpkin, Marshall, Hamilton and Kent and Co., 1893).

13. Lincrusta is presently produced by Crown Berger, Akzo Nobel Decorative Coatings, P.O. Box 37, Darwen, Lancashire BB3 OBG, England. Also see Bruce Bradbury, "Lincrusta-Walton, Can the Democratic Wallcovering Be Revived?" *Old House Journal* (Oct. 1982): 203–6.

14. Bruce Bradbury, "Anaglypta and Other Embossed Wallcoverings, Their History and Their Use Today," *Old House Journal* (Nov. 1982): 231–34; Alan V. Sugden and John L. Edmondson, *A History of English Wallpaper 1509–1914* (New York: Charles Scribner's Sons, 1925): 245–50; Lesley Hoskins, ed., *The Papered Wall, History, Pattern, Technique* (New York: Harry N. Abrams, 1994): 160–63.

15. *Business Floors of Armstrong Linoleum* (Lancaster, Pa.: Armstrong Cork and Tile Co., Jan. 1924): 4. Avery Architectural Library.

16. *Linotile Floors* (Pittsburgh, Pa.: Armstrong Cork and Tile Co., 1920): 8. Avery Architectural Library.

17. "Germs vs. Linoleum," *Dry Goods Economist* 68 (Nov. 29, 1913): 23 and *Helpful Hints for Linoleum Salesmen* (Lancaster, Pa.: Armstrong Cork and Tile Co., 1918): 11. Avery Architectural Library.

18. "Lincrusta-Walton," *Journal of Decorative Arts* 4 (Mar. 1884): 472.

19. Brown, *The Attractive Home*, 13.

20. E. A. Entwisle, *A Literary History of Wallpaper* (London: B. T. Batsford, Ltd., 1960), 139.

21. Brown, *The Attractive Home*, 18.

22. *Sweets Architectural Catalogue* 1927–28, B1576-77, B1576-772, and *Carpet and Upholstery Trade Review* 26 (13) (July 1, 1895): 42.

23. *Carpet and Upholstery Trade Review* 31 (17) (Sept. 1, 1900): 58.

24. *Helpful Hints for Linoleum Salesmen.*

25. *Dry Goods Economist* 68 (June 20, 1914): 267.

26. "Lincrusta-Walton," *Journal of Decorative Arts* 4 (Mar. 1881): 29.

27. *Carpet and Upholstery Trade Review* 42 (7) (Apr. 1, 1911): 1, 7.

28. Mme. Le Prince, *Lincrusta-Walton Decoration* (New York: Fr. Beck & Co., 1884), 12.

29. *Complete Works of John Ruskin*, ed. E. T. Cook and Alexander Wedderburn (London: George Allen, 1903–8) 8: 219.

30. Morris, "The Arts and Crafts Today," address delivered in Edinburgh in 1889 in *The Collected Works,* ed. May Morris (London, New York: Longmans, Green, 1910–15), 23: 366. These ideas are also discussed in Julie Wosk, *Breaking Frame, Technology and the Visual Arts in the Nineteenth Century* (New Brunswick, N.J.: Rutgers Univ. Press, 1992).

31. *Floors, Utile and Beautiful* (London: Jas. F. Ebner, 1882), 1. Canadian Centre for Architecture.

32. Interviews with Doreen Cross, Ottawa, 1993; Myrle E. Hemenway, Boulder, Colorado, 1993; Ted Seder, Hot Springs Village, Arkansas, 1993; Winifred Hadsel, Lexington, Virginia, 1994; and David Blair, Canterbury, Kent, 1995 all revealed memories of a hierarchy in room-use appropriateness for linoleum.

33. Entwisle, *A Literary History of Wallpaper,* 139.

34. Quoted in *Wallpaper Trade Department* (Mar. 1888): 109. Canadian Centre for Architecture, Montreal.

35. *Journal of Decorative Arts* 41 (Jan. 1921): 25.

Select Bibliography

Allen, James B. *The Company Town in the American West.* Norman: University of Oklahoma Press, 1966.

Anderson, Benedict. *Imagined Communities: Reflections on the Origin and Spread of Nationalism.* London: Verso, 1983.

Badger, R. Reid. *The Great American Fair: The World's Columbian Exposition and American Culture.* Chicago, Ill.: Nelson Hall, 1979.

Bishir, Catherine W., et al. *Architects and Builders in North Carolina: A History of the Practice of Building.* Chapel Hill: Univ. of North Carolina Press, 1990.

Blake, Peter. *God's Own Junkyard: The Planned Deterioration of America's Landscape.* New York: Holt, Rhinehart and Winston, 1964.

Bluestone, Daniel. "A City Under One Roof: Skyscrapers, 1880–1895." In *Constructing Chicago,* 104–51. New Haven and London: Yale Univ. Press, 1991.

Blumin, Stuart M. *The Emergence of the Middle Class: Social Experience in the American City, 1760–1900.* Cambridge: Cambridge Univ. Press, 1989.

Bodnar, John. *The Transplanted: A History of Immigrants in Urban America.* Bloomington: Indiana Univ. Press, 1985.

Bradbury, Bettina. "Women's Workplaces: The Impact of Technological Change on Working-class Women in the Home and in the Workplace in Nineteenth-Century Montreal." In *Women, Work, and Place,* ed. Audrey Kobayashi. Montreal: McGill-Queen's Univ. Press, 1994.

Braude, Ann. *Radical Spirits: Spiritualism and Women's Rights in Nineteenth-Century America.* Boston: Beacon Press, 1989.

Brown, Kenneth O. *Holy Ground: A Study of the American Camp Meeting.* New York: Garland, 1992.

Buder, Stanley. *Pullman: An Experiment in Indus-*

trial Order and Community Planning, 1880–1930. New York: Oxford Univ. Press, 1967.

Bushman, Richard L. *The Refinement of America: Persons, Houses, Cities.* New York: Alfred A. Knopf, 1992.

Candee, Richard M. *Atlantic Heights: A World War I Shipbuilder's Community.* Portsmouth, N.H.: Portsmouth Marine Society, 1985.

Carson, Cary, Ronald Hoffman, and Peter J. Albert, eds. *The Style of Life in the Eighteenth Century.* Charlottesville and London: Univ. Press of Virginia for the United States Capital Historical Society, 1994.

Çelik, Zeynep, Diane Favro, and Richard Ingersoll, eds. *Streets: Critical Perspectives on Public Space.* Berkeley: Univ. of California Press, 1994.

Coolidge, John. *Mill and Mansion: A Study of Architecture and Society in Lowell, Massachusetts 1820–1865.* New York: Columbia Univ. Press, 1942.

Crawford, Margaret. *Building the Worker's Paradise: The Design of American Company Towns.* New York: Verso, 1995.

Cromley, Elizabeth. *Alone Together: A History of New York's Early Apartments.* Ithaca and London: Cornell Univ. Press, 1990.

Doyle, Don H. *New Men, New Cities, New South: Atlanta, Nashville, Charleston, Mobile, 1860–1910.* Chapel Hill: Univ. of North Carolina Press, 1990.

Foner, Eric. *Reconstruction: America's Unfinished Revolution 1863–1877.* New York: Harper and Row, 1988.

Forty, Adrian. "The Modern Hospital in England and France: The Social and Medical Uses of Architecture." In *Buildings and Society: Essays on the Social Development of the Built Environment,* ed. Anthony King, 61–93. London: Routledge and Kegan Paul, 1980.

Garner, John S. *The Model Company Town: Urban Design through Private Enterprise in Nineteenth-Century New England.* Amherst, Mass.: Univ. of Massachusetts Press, 1984.

Garreau, Joel. *Edge City: Life on the New Frontier.* New York: Doubleday, 1991.

Garrison, J. Richie, Bernard L. Herman, and Barbara McLean Ward, eds. *After Ratification: Material Life in Delaware, 1789–1820.* Newark, Del.: Museum Studies Program, Univ. of Delaware, 1988.

Glassie, Henry. "Architects, Vernacular Traditions, and Society." *Traditional Dwellings and Settlements Review* 1 (6) (1990): 9–21.

——. *Folk Housing in Middle Virginia: A Structural Analysis of Historic Artifacts.* Knoxville: University of Tennessee Press, 1975.

Greene, Jack P. "Colonial South Carolina and the Caribbean Connection." In *Imperatives, Behaviors, and Identities: Essays in Early American Cultural History.* Charlottesville: Univ. Press of Virginia, 1992, 68–86.

——. *Pursuits of Happiness: The Social Development of Early Modern British Colonies and the Formation of American Culture.* Chapel Hill: Univ. of North Carolina Press, 1988.

Harris, Richard. *Unplanned Suburbs, Toronto's American Tragedy, 1900–1950.* Baltimore: Johns Hopkins Univ. Press, 1996.

Hayden, Dolores. *The Grand Domestic Revolution: A History of Feminist Designs for American Homes, Neighborhoods, and Cities.* Cambridge, Mass.: MIT Press, 1981.

Herman, Bernard L. *Architecture and Rural Life in Central Delaware, 1700–1900.* Knoxville: Univ. of Tennessee Press, 1987.

——. *The Stolen House.* Charlottesville: Univ. Press of Virginia, 1992.

Herman, Bernard L., and Michael Steinitz, eds. *A Singular List of Buildings: American Architecture and Landscape at the End of the Eighteenth Century.* Knoxville: Univ. of Tennessee Press, forthcoming.

Hobsbawm, Eric, and Terence Ranger, eds. "Introduction: Inventing Traditions." In *The Invention of Tradition*. New York: Cambridge Univ. Press, 1983.

Hodder, Ian. *Reading the Past: Current Approaches to Interpretation in Archaeology*. Cambridge and New York: Cambridge Univ. Press, 1986.

Hutchins, Catherine E., ed. *Everyday Life in the Early Republic*. Winterthur, Del.: Winterthur Museum, 1994.

Hyde, Ann Farrar. *An American Vision: Far Western Landscape and National Culture, 1820–1910*. New York: New York Univ. Press, 1990.

Innes, Stephen, ed. *Work and Labor in Early America*. Chapel Hill and London: Univ. of North Carolina Press for the Institute of Early American History and Culture, 1988.

Isaac, Rhys. *The Transformation of Virginia 1740–1790*. Chapel Hill: Univ. of North Carolina Press for the Institute of Early American History and Culture, 1982.

Jakle, John, and Keith Sculle. *The Gas Station in America*. Baltimore: Johns Hopkins Univ. Press, 1994.

Keister, Kim. "Charts of Change." *Historic Preservation* 45 (3) (May/June 1993): 12–19, 91–92.

Keller, William B. "Collecting and Using Fire Insurance and Real Estate Atlasses: An Individual Perspective." *Arts Reference Services Quarterly* 1 (3) (1993): 31–48.

Kenny, Judith. "Polish Routes to Americanization: House Form and Landscape on Milwaukee's Polish South Side." In *Wisconsin Land and Life*, ed. R. Ostergren and T. Vale Madison, Wisc.: Univ. of Wisconsin Press, forthcoming.

Kuropas, Myron B. *The Ukrainian Americans: Roots and Aspirations 1884–1954*. Toronto: Univ. of Toronto Press, 1991.

Kwolek-Folland, Angel. *Engendering Business: Men and Women in the Corporate Office, 1870–1930*. Baltimore and London: Johns Hopkins Univ. Press, 1994.

Landes, Joan. *Women and the Public Sphere in the Age of the French Revolution*. Ithaca: Cornell Univ. Press, 1988.

Landscape Research. *Built in Milwaukee. An Architectural View of the City*. Milwaukee: City of Milwaukee, 1980.

Leiding, Harriet Kershaw. *Historic Houses of South Carolina*. Philadelphia: J. B. Lippincott, 1921.

Lieb, Chester. *Main Street to Miracle Mile: American Roadside Architecture*. Boston: Little, Brown, and Company, 1985.

Linden-Ward, Blanche. *Silent City on a Hill: Landscapes of Memory and Boston's Mount Auburn Cemetery*. Columbus: Ohio State Univ. Press, 1989.

Lounsbury, Carl R. *An Illustrated Glossary of Early Southern Architecture and Landscape*. New York: Oxford Univ. Press, 1994.

Lowenthal, David. *The Past Is A Foreign Country*. New York: Cambridge Univ. Press, 1985.

Margolies, John. *The End of the Road: Vanishing Highway Architecture in America*. New York: Penguin/Hudson River Museum, 1981.

McCombs, W. Douglas. "Therapeutic Rusticity: Antimodernism, Health, and the Wilderness Vacation, 1870–1915." *New York History* 76 (4) (Oct. 1995): 409–28.

McGahan, Elizabeth. "Inside the Hallowed Walls: Convent Life through Material History." *Material History Bulletin* (now known as *Material History Review*) 25 (Spring 1987): 1–9.

Meyer, Richard E., ed. *Cemeteries and Gravemarkers: Voices of American Culture*. Logan: Utah State Univ. Press, 1989.

Mosher, Anne E., and Deryck W. Holdsworth. "The Meaning of Alley Housing in Industrial Towns: Examples from Late Nineteenth and

Early-Twentieth Century Pennsylvania." *Journal of Historical Geography* 18 (2) (1992): 174–89.

Moulder, Cathy. "Fire Insurance Plans as a Data Source in Urban Research: An Annotated Bibliography of Examples." *Arts Reference Services Quarterly* 1 (3) (1993): 49–62.

Olson, Sherry. "Occupations and Residential Spaces in 19th Century Montréal." *Historical Methods* 22 (3) (Summer 1989): 82.

Pierson, William. *American Buildings and Their Architects: Technology and the Picturesque, the Corporate and Early Gothic Styles.* Garden City, N.Y.: Doubleday, 1978.

Reisser, Craig Thomas. "Immigrants and House Form in Northeast Milwaukee." M.A. thesis, Univ. of Wisconsin-Milwaukee, 1977.

Rotoff, Basil, Roman Yereniuk, and Stella Hryniuk. *Monuments to Faith: Ukrainian Churches in Manitoba.* Winnipeg, Canada: Univ. of Manitoba Press, 1990.

St. George, Robert Blair, ed. *Material Life in America 1600–1860.* Boston: Northeastern Univ. Press, 1988.

Schmitt, Peter J. *Back to Nature: The Arcadian Myth in Urban America.* New York: Oxford Univ. Press, 1969.

Sculle, Keith A. "Oral History: A Key to Writing the History of American Roadside Architecture." *Journal of American Culture* 13 (3) (Fall 1990): 79–88.

Siders, Rebecca, and Pamela Edwards. *The Changing Landscape of the St. Jones Neck Under the Influence of the Dickinson Family, 1680–1850: An Exhibit Script.* Newark, Del.: Center for Historic Architecture and Engineering, 1994.

Siders, Rebecca, et al. *Agricultural Tenancy in Central Delaware, 1770–1900: An Historic Context.* Newark, Del.: Center for Historic Architecture and Engineering, 1991.

Simmons-Henry, Linda, and Linda Harris Edmisten. Interview with Mildred Taylor James, 1989. In *Culture Town: Life in Raleigh's African American Communities,* 156. Raleigh: Raleigh Historic Districts Commission, Inc., 1993.

Simon, Roger. "Housing and Services in an Immigrant Neighborhood." *Journal of Urban History* 2 (4) (1976): 435–58.

Simon, Roger. "City-Building Process: Housing and Services in New Milwaukee Neighborhoods 1880–1910." *Transactions of the American Philosophical Society* 68 (5) (1978): 1–64.

Simons, Albert, and Samuel Lapham Jr. *The Octagon Library of Early American Architecture, Volume I: Charleston, South Carolina.* New York: American Institute of Architects Press, 1927.

Simons, Albert, and Harriet P. Simons. "The William Burrows House of Charleston." *Winterthur Portfolio, III.* Winterthur, Del.: Winterthur Museum, 1967, 172–203.

Sloane, David Charles. *The Last Great Necessity: Cemeteries in American History.* Baltimore: Johns Hopkins Univ. Press, 1991.

Smith, Alice, and Daniel Huger Smith. *The Dwelling Houses of Charleston.* Philadelphia: J. B. Lippincott Company, 1917.

Stilgoe, John R. *Common Landscape of America, 1580–1845.* New Haven and London: Yale Univ. Press, 1982.

Stoney, Samuel Gaillard, Albert Simons, and Samuel Lapham Jr. *Plantations of the Carolina Low Country.* Charleston: Carolina Art Association, 1938.

Upton, Dell. *Holy Things and Profane: Anglican Parish Churches in Colonial Virginia.* Cambridge, Mass.: MIT Press for the Architectural History Foundation, 1986.

———. *Madaline: Love and Survival in Antebellum New Orleans.* Athens: Univ. of Georgia Press, 1996.

van Ginkel, Blanche Lemco. "Slowly and Surely (and Somewhat Painfully): More or Less the History of Women in Architecture in Canada." *Society for the Study of Architecture in Canada Bulletin* (Mar. 1991): 5–11.

Venturi, Robert, Denise Scott Brown, and Steven Izenour. *Learning from Las Vegas.* Cambridge, Mass.: MIT Press, 1972.

Vlach, John Michael. "The Shotgun House: An African Architectural Legacy." *Pioneer America* 8 (1976): 47–70.

Von Rosenstiel, Helene, and Gail Caskey. *Floor Coverings for Historic Buildings.* Washington, D.C.: Historic Preservation Education Foundation, 1993.

Waddell, Gene. "The Charleston Single House: An Architectural Survey." *Preservation Progress* 22 (2) (Mar. 1977): 4–8.

Wall, Diana diZerega. *The Archaeology of Gender: Separating the Spheres in Urban America.* New York: Plenum Press, 1994.

Wallace, Anthony F. C. *Rockdale: The Growth of an American Village in the Early Industrial Revolution.* New York: Knopf, 1972.

Wallman, Sandra. "Introduction." In *Social Anthropology of Work,* ed. Sandra Wallman. London and New York: Academic Press, 1979.

Waters, Mary C. *Ethnic Options: Choosing Identities in America.* Berkeley: Univ. of California Press, 1990.

Weiss, Ellen. *City in the Woods: The Life and Design of an American Camp Meeting on Martha's Vineyard.* New York: Oxford Univ. Press, 1987.

Wells, Camille. "The Planter's Prospect: House, Outbuildings, and Rural Landscapes in Eighteenth-Century Virginia." *Winterthur Portfolio* 28 (1) (Spring 1993): 1–31.

Williams, Michael. *Americans and Their Forests: A Historical Geography.* Cambridge: Cambridge University Press, 1989.

Williams, Michael Ann. *Homeplace.* Athens: Univ. of Georgia Press, 1991.

Wright, Gwendolyn. *Building the Dream: A Social History of Housing in America.* Cambridge, Mass.: MIT Press, 1981.

Wrigley, Robert L. "The Sanborn Map as a Source of Land Use Information for City Planning." *Land Economics* 25 (2) (1949): 216–19.

Contributors

ANNMARIE ADAMS is associate professor at the School of Architecture, McGill University, Montreal, Quebec, where she teaches courses in architectural history, material culture, and housing research. She is the author of *Architecture in the Family Way: Doctors, Houses, and Women, 1870–1900*.

ANNA V. ANDRZEJEWSKI is a Ph.D. candidate in art history at the University of Delaware, where she is writing a dissertation entitled "Architecture and the Ideology of Surveillance in Modern America, 1870–1945." She studied modern art at Washington University in St. Louis, where she received her B.A. and M.A. degrees. She has worked as a research assistant for the Center for Historic Architecture and Engineering (CHAE) at the University of Delaware, and she is currently employed as an architectural historian and project manager for Cultural Heritage Research Services (CHRS) in North Wales, Pennsylvania.

JAMES MICHAEL BUCKLEY is a doctoral candidate in the Architecture Department at the University of California at Berkeley, where he is writing a dissertation on the architecture and urban form of the redwood lumber industry in California. He received a B.A. from Yale University in American studies and art history and a master's degree in city and regional planning from the University of California, Berkeley. He is also a practicing city planner, with fifteen years of experience in housing and community development in the public and nonprofit sectors.

EDWARD A. CHAPPELL directs the Department of Architectural Research, which has the responsibility for the care and interpretation of historic buildings and landscapes at Colonial Williamsburg. Since coming to Colonial Williamsburg in 1980, Chappell has made fieldwork a central element of the foundation's research efforts. He studied history at William and Mary and architectural history at the University of Virginia.

TIMOTHY DAVIS received an A.B. in visual and environmental studies from Harvard College and a Ph.D. in American civilization from the University of Texas at Austin. He is interested in combining photography and cultural geography to explore the evolution of the American landscape. He has written on cultural landscape photography, American parkway development, and contemporary landscape issues while exhibiting and publishing photographs on related topics. The photographs in this essay are part of an ongoing series documenting recycled roadside architecture.

CLIFTON ELLIS is in his first year of the Ph.D. program in architectural history at the University of Virginia. His specialty is domestic architecture in eighteenth-century Virginia.

SUSAN W. FAIR is a self-employed folklorist and writer who earned her doctorate in folklore and folklife from the University of Pennsylvania. A specialist in Alaska Native material culture, she is the author of a number of essays on the subject and has two books in press, one on the concept of tradition among contemporary Alaska Native artists and the other an ethnohistory of Inupiaq life on the Tapqaq coast of the northern Seward Peninsula. She is presently working on a place-name project in the same area while teaching anthropology and folklore at the University of Alaska Anchorage. Fair lives with her son Michael in Eagle River, Alaska.

GEOFFREY M. GYRISCO earned a B.A. in history and archaeology from Cornell University and a Ph.D. in American civilization from George Washington University, specializing in American material culture and American urban archaeology. He served as an archaeologist for the National Park Service, then as the archaeologist for the District of Columbia. While working for the Pennsylvania Historical and Museum Commission and KCI Technologies, Inc., in Harrisburg, Pennsylvania, he began studying the traditions and architecture of the Orthodox and Eastern churches. This study was furthered by the Vernacular Architecture Forum trip to Ukraine in 1991. Gyrisco has been discovering his own family's lost roots in Carpathians of the former Austro-Hungarian Empire. Currently, Gyrisco is chief of the Survey and Registration Section of the State Historical Society of Wisconsin and a co-editor of the *Buildings of the U.S.* series. He is the author of several papers on ethnicity in archaeology and architecture, as well as numerous reports, papers, and publications in archaeology and historic preservation.

RICHARD HARRIS is professor of geography at McMaster University in Hamilton, Ontario. He is editor of *Urban History Review* and author of *Unplanned Suburbs: Toronto's American Tragedy, 1900–1950* (Baltimore: Johns Hopkins Univ. Press, 1996).

BRUCE HARVEY is currently a historian with Brockington and Associates, Inc., in Mt. Pleasant, South Carolina. He is also a Ph.D. candidate in the history department at Vanderbilt University in Nashville, Tennessee. He received a B.A. in history from Allegheny College in 1985, and an M.A. in applied history from the University of South Carolina in 1988. This chapter draws from his dissertation in progress, which examines three World's Fairs in the South in the late nineteenth and early twentieth centuries.

BERNARD L. HERMAN teaches at the University of

Delaware where he is an associate professor of art history. He is also associate director of the Center for Historic Architecture and Design and a member of the faculty of the Winterthur Program in Early American Culture. A past editor of *Perspectives in Vernacular Architecture,* Herman is also author of *Architecture and Rural Life in Central Delaware, 1700–1900,* and *The Stolen House,* both winners of the Abbott Lowell Cummings Award. His current book project is *Town House,* a study of architecture and material life in the early American city.

M. RUTH LITTLE, a native North Carolinian, has been studying the vernacular material culture of North Carolina and the South since the 1970s, first for the North Carolina State Historic Preservation Office and presently as an independent consultant. Her firm, Longleaf Historic Resources, operates out of Raleigh. She received her M.A. in art history at Brown University and her Ph.D. in art history, with a specialty in material culture, from the University of North Carolina at Chapel Hill. She has authored numerous articles and books on North Carolina architecture and is currently completing *Sticks and Stones: Three Centuries of North Carolina Gravemarkers.*

CARL LOUNSBURY is an architectural historian in the Architectural Research Department at the Colonial Williamsburg Foundation. He received his undergraduate degree in English and American history from the University of North Carolina and earned an M.A. and Ph.D. in American studies from George Washington University. Dr. Lounsbury is a past president of the Vernacular Architecture Forum. He is also a lecturer in historic preservation at Mary Washington College and in the art history department at Virginia Commonwealth University. In recent years, he has undertaken studies of early American churches, markethouses, courthouses, and seventeenth-century rows in Jamestown and southeastern England. His publications include *Architects and Builders in North Carolina: A History of the Practice of Building* (with three others), *An Illustrated Glossary of Early Southern Architecture and Landscape,* and *An Architectural History of South Carolina's First Statehouse and Charleston's County Courthouse.*

TANIA MARTIN earned her M.Arch at McGill University and B.Arch at the University of Toronto. She is currently pursuing doctoral work in the history of architecture at University of California, Berkeley. Her dissertation will expand her ongoing investigation of convents in nineteenth-century Montréal.

SALLY MCMURRY holds a Ph.D. in history from Cornell University. Currently she is professor of history at the Pennsylvania State University, where she teaches a variety of courses in U.S. history. Her research interests include nineteenth-century rural history, women's history, and cultural history. Her publications include *Families and Farmhouses in Nineteenth-Century America: Vernacular Design and Social Change* and *Transforming Rural Life: Dairying Families and Agricultural Change.* She has served as a VAF board member.

WILLIAM D. MOORE is a doctoral candidate in the American and New England studies program at Boston University where he is writing his dissertation on the architecture and material culture of Masonic temples in New York State between 1870 and 1930. He is currently director of the Chancellor Robert R. Livingston Masonic Library and Museum in New York City.

JULIE RICHTER is a historian in the Department of Historical Research at the Colonial Williamsburg Foundation. She earned her Ph.D. in history at the College of William and Mary. Currently

Richter is working on a study of the origins and the development of the slave community in eighteenth-century Williamsburg.

REBECCA J. SIDERS received her B.A. in American studies from the University of Delaware in 1985. Since then she has been employed as a research associate at the Center for Historic Architecture and Engineering at the University of Delaware, where her work centers on preservation planning and the reconstruction of historic landscapes. She is presently a Ph.D. candidate in American civilization at the University of Delaware. Her dissertation will focus on the material world of nineteenth-century agricultural tenants in central Delaware.

PAMELA H. SIMPSON holds a Ph.D. in art history from the University of Delaware. She is the Ernest Williams II Professor of Art History and head of the art department at Washington and Lee University in Lexington, Virginia. She has worked as a consultant and surveyor for the Virginia Department of Historic Resources and is co-author of *The Architecture of Historic Lexington*. She has also served as a board member and second vice-president of the Vernacular Architecture Forum.

With the move from architectural survey work to managing the education program for the American Planning Association, CAROLYN TORMA's field work shifted focus to the near-at-hand, her office environment. Her previous study of work examined the housing of rural workers in South Dakota. Other publications include a film and presentations looked at the architecture of various immigrant groups, women, and even mining sites in the Great Plains. Her years of work in Kentucky led to her first publication on county seat plans.

DELL UPTON is professor of architectural history in the department of architecture at the University of California, Berkeley. His books include *Holy Things and Profane: Anglican Parish Churches in Colonial Virginia*; *America's Architectural Roots: Ethnic Groups That Built America*; *Common Places: Readings in American Vernacular Architecture* (with John Michael Vlach); *Madaline: Love and Survival in Antebellum New Orleans*; and *Architecture of the United States*. He is completing a study of the urban cultural landscape in the early republic.

Index

Illustrations are indicated in **boldface**

Accomac County, Va., 6
African-American slavery, xix
African Americans, 150; and architecture, xxiv, 268–79; free, 150, 159, 161; material culture, 268–79; of the middle class, xxiv, 268–79; as wage laborers, xxvi
Aiken-Rhett House, Charleston, S.C., **53**
Alaska, xxiii, xxiv, xxvi, 167–77, **168**
Alexanderson, A. P., 83
Alston, Israel, 152
Alston, John, 149, 154, 160, 162
Alston, Jonathan, 152
Alston, Mary, 152, 153
American Association for Municipal Improvements, 184
American City Diner, Chevy Chase, Md., 105
American Federation of Labor (AFL), 87, 91n22
American Legislators Association, 185
American Linoleum Manufaturing Company, 282
American Planning Association, 184, 186–94
American Public Works Association, 184
American Society of Planning Officials, 184
Anchorage, Alaska, **176**
Anderson, Benedict, 199
Anderson, Smart, 45
Andrews, William, 6
Andrews, William, House, Accomac County, Va., **6**
Andrzejewski, Anna, xxi
Anglican gentry in eighteenth-century Virginia, 25–36
Anglicization of American architecture, xix–xxi; and social replication, 62
Ansonborough, Charleston, S.C., 42, **42**, 43
Anthony, Susan B., 243
Antrim Parish Va., 26, 33
Appalachia, xxii
Applebaum, Herbert, 183
Arcata, Calif., 77
Architectural Style: Art Deco, 185; Colonial Revival,

Architectural Style, *continued*
127, 277; Craftsman, 273; Georgian, xx; Romanesque, 120, 123; Spanish Renaissance, 127; Victorian, 273
Architecture, and civic boosterism, 115–30; commercial, 93–110; of company towns, 75–88; of convents, 212; of cultural accommodation, xxiv, 268–79; of dissenting religions, 23–35; and eighteenth-century evangelicalism, 30–35; and ethnicity, xxiii–xxiv, 167–79, 199–205, 268–75; of farm tenant house, 149–62; of food storage in Alaska, 167–77; of forest industry, 75–88; of labor relations, 149–62; native American, 167–77; of office work, 183–94; and racial identity, xxvi, 268–79; and religious culture, xxvi, 23–35, 199–205, 212–24, 230–41; and social hierarchy, xix, 3–17, 46–49, 66–69, 189–91; of social subordination, xviii; of urban slavery, 41–54
Arlington, Va., 102, **102**, **103**
Armstrong, Charles D., 285
Armstrong Cork and Tile Company, 285, 288
Art Deco Society, 107
Ashley River, S.C., 67, 119, 122
Asmus, Christian A., 129n16
Atlanta, Ga., 99, 118, 120, **120**
Auer, Louis, and Son, 258
Augusta County, Va., 38n10
Austin, Tex., **94**, 100, 104, 105, **105**, 106, **110**
Automobile suburbs, 259–64
Averill, John, 120

Baker's Landing Tenant House, Del., 157–58, **158**
Balloon frame construction, 151
Ballston, Va., 98, **98**
Baltimore, Md., 118
Banister River, Va., 26
Bank of Richmond, Va., 15
Banner of Light, 232, 239
Baptist, New Light Separate, 31; in Virginia, 23–35
Barber, J. T., 273
Barber, J. T., House, Durham, N.C., 274
Barnhard, H. L., 235

Bates, James, 24–25, 32, 34
Bay, Elijah Hall, House, **44**
Beck, Frederick, 285
Behrens, Peter, 289
Belle Isle, Lancaster County, Va., 26, 27, **28**
Ben and Jerry's Ice Cream, 99, **100**
Bennett, Samuel, 152
Benson, Susan Porter, 183, 185, 186, 188, 189, 189, 194
Berail, Phil, 174
Berkeley County, S.C., **61**, 67, **67**, 68, **68**, 69
Bermuda, 7
Bernstein, Rebecca Sample, xxiv
Bethune, Angus, 49
Birdsall, Byron, 175
Blabatsky, Helena Petrovna, 243, 244
Blabon, George, 283
Blaydes House, Hull, England, 48–49, **49**
Blockinger, E. A., 86
Blodgett's Landing, N.H., 241
Bluestone, Daniel, 183
Blumin, Stewart, 17
Bocquet, Peter, 54
Bocquet, Peter, House, Charleston, S.C., 48, **48**
Bordley, John Beale, 154, 155, 165n20
Boston, Mass., 63, 101
Bourgeau, Victor, 213
Braced frame construction, 151
Bradbury, Charles W., 131, 132, 139, 142, 143
Braude, Ann, 241
Brewton, Miles, House, Charleston, S.C., 59, 66
Brown, Andrew, 157
Brown, Denise Scott, 175
Brown, E. Gerry, 235, 238, 243
Brown, H. H., 237
Brown, Kenneth, 231
Brownlow, Louis, 184, 186, 187, 188
Buckley, James, xxii
Budington, H. A., 233
Bunkhouses, 78, 79, 83
Burlington, Vt., **100**
Burnham, Daniel, 122, 194
Bushman, Richard, 17

Butler, A. G., 287, 290
Byrd, William, II, 25, 29

Cabell, Flora B., 239
Caches, 167–77, **168**, **170**, 178n3, 179n6, 181n32
Cairns, William J., 243
California, 75–88, **77**; lumber camps, 75–92
Cambridge, Mass., **242**
Canada, xviii, xxiii; Houses of Parliament, xviii
Carey, Francis, 119
Carney, Eunice, 172
Carson, Cary, 6
Carson, William, 76, 82
Carter, Robert "King," 30
Carter Croxton House, Essex County, Va., 8, **9**, 14, 15
Catholicism, xxvi
Cemeteries, 131–43; Cypress Grove (Fireman's Cemetery), New Orleans, 138, 139, **140**, **142**; Lafayette, New Orleans, 131, **132**, 139, 142; Laurel Hill, 142; Mt. Auburn, Cambridge, Mass., 142, 241, **242**; New Burying Ground, New Haven, Conn., 139; Oak Dale, Urbanna, Ohio, 241; St. Louis Cemetery #1, New Orleans, 133–35, **137**, **138**, 139; St. Louis Cemetery #2, New Orleans, 135, **136**, 139
Center for the Study of Urban Inequality, 184
Chandalar River, Alaska, 168
Channell, Martha, 10, 12, 113, 17, 21n30
Channell, Martha, House, Southampton County, Va., 10, **11**, 12
Chappell, Edward, xix, xx
Charles City County, Va., 6–7, **7**
Charleston, S.C., xvii, xviii, xix, xx, xxiii, xxvi, xxvii, xxix, 41–54, **42**, **43**, **44**, **46**, **47**, **48**, **53**, 58–69, **59**, **65**, **68**, 115–28, **123**, **124**, **125**, Chamber of Commerce, 119; the Exchange, 63; Interstate and West Indian Exposition of 1901, 115–28, **123**, **124**, **125**
Charleston County Council, 59
Charleston County Courthouse, 58–69, **59**, **69**
Charlotte, N.C., 271
Chastellus, Marquis de, 29
Chesapeake, xviii, 4–5, 16

Chesapeake Bay, 107
Chesterfield County, Va., 15
Chicago, Ill., 183–94, **185**, **186**, **189**, **192**, **193**
Christian, Daniel, 174
Christie, Alexander, House, Charleston, S.C., 46
Churches: Holy Assumption Church, Lublin, Wisc., 202; Holy Trinity Church, Thorp, Wisc., 202; Pompion Hill Chapel, Berkeley County, S.C., 67, **67**, 68, **68**, 69; St. Constantine's Church, Minneapolis, 206–7, **206**, **208**; Saints Cyril and Methodius Ukranian Catholic Church, Olyphant, Pa., 207; St. James Church (Goose Creek), Berkeley County, S.C., 60, **61**; St. John the Baptist, Huron, Wis., 202; St. John the Baptist Greek Catholic Church, Minneapolis, 206, 207, 208; St. John the Baptist Ukranian Catholic Church, Pittsburgh, 207; St. Mary's Church, Minneapolis, xxiv, 201, **201**, 202, 203, 204, 205, **205**, 207, 208; St. Mary's Church, Two Rivers, Minn., 202; St. Michael's Church, Charleston, S.C., 60, 63; St. Michael's Greek Catholic Carpatian Orthodox Church, Minneapolis, 208; St. Michael's Ukranian Orthodox Church, Minneapolis, 207; St. Panteleimon Russian Orthodox Church, 208; St. Philip's Church, Charleston, S.C., 65
Clapp, Theodore, 139
Clar, C. Raymond, 88
Clarendon, Va., 100
Cleveland Park, Md., "Park and Shop," 95
Clinton, Bishop George, 271
Coke, Reverend Thomas, 39n22
Collins, Mary Parish, 50
Collins, Stephen, 50
Collins, Timothy, 159
Colonial Revival Movement, 127
Colonial Williamsburg Foundation, 3
Commercial Architecture, 93–110
Commercial strip malls, xxiii, 93–110
company towns, xxii
Condit, Kenneth, 168
Condit, Kenneth, Cache, Moose Pass, Alaska, **169**
Condit, Margaret, 168

Congoleum, 285
Conley, Sara Ward, 129n16
Coolman, Henry, 122
Cooper Bee House, Charleston, S.C., 46, 47
Cooper River, S.C., 68
Cope, Thomas P., 134
Corbit, Daniel, 159, 162
Cordella, Victor, 204, 206, 207
Cormier, Ernest, xviii
Cornford, Daniel, 86
Corotoman Plantation, Lancaster County, Va., 30
Council, Amos, 12
Council, Amos, House, Southampton County, Va., 12, **12**
Courthouses: Charleston County, S.C., 58–69, 59, 69; Warwick, Great Britain, **64**
Cowgill's Corner, Dela., 155–56
Cox, Elisha, 32
Crane, Leon, 173
Croxton, Carter, 8, 17, 20n21
Cruikshank, Moses, 168, 169
Crystal Palace, London, 1851, 116
Cuthfert, Percy, 174

dairies, 8
Dallas, Tex., 101
Danylewycz, Marta, 216
Davis, Tim, xxiii
Deetz, James, xx
Del Norte County, Calif., 76
Delaware, xxi, xxii, xxvi, 149–62, **150, 151**
Delaware Valley, Pa., xxi
Delwood Plaza, Austin, Tex., **94**, 106
Denny, Thomas, 152–53
Dickinson, John, 152
Dowler, Bennett, 134
Downey, Calif., 106
Dozier, Richard, 31
Dresser, Christopher, 289
Dubofsky, Melvin, 78
Du Bois, W. E. B., 276
Durham, N.C., 270–71, **271**, 274, 276, 277, **277**, 278
Dutch roofs, 65

Dyrud, Keith, 202
Dzubay, Peter, 201–2

Eagle Fire Company, 139
Eagle's Nest, Charles City County, Va., 6, 7
East Los Angeles, Calif., 102
Eastern Shore, Va., 5, 16
Eden Shopping Center, Arlington, Va., 102, **102**
Edge Cities, 93, 97
Edwards, Jonathan, 31
Edwards, Madaline, 131–35, 139, 141–43
Eel River, Calif., 79, **80**, 83
Eiffel Tower, 116
Eklunta, Alaska, 176
Ellis, Clifton, xx
Essex County, Va., 8, **9**, 14, 15, 16
Eureka, Calif., 76, 79, 85
Evanston, Wyo., 99
Evelyn, John, 241
Evening Post (Charleston, S.C.), 120
Exhibition of the Arts and Industries of all Nations, London, 1851, 116
The Exposition, 126
Expositions: Atlanta, 1881, 117; Atlanta, 1887, 117; Cotton States and International Exposition, Atlanta, 1895, 120, **120**, 121–23; Jamestown Tercentenary Exposition, 1907, 117; Louisville Exposition, 1886, 117; Panama-Pacific Exposition of 1915, 289; Paris Exposition of 1900, 288; Philadelphia Centennial Exposition of 1876, 116; South Carolina Interstate and West Indian Exposition of 1901, 115–28; Tennessee Centennial and International Exposition, Nashville, 1897, 120–22, **121**; World's Industrial and Cotton Centennial Exposition, New Orleans, 1885, 117; World's Columbian Exhibition of 1893, Chicago, 116, 117, 122, 185

Facts magazine, 237
Fair, Susan, xix, xxiii
Falardeau, Marie-Anne (Soeur Saint Jean de la Croix), 212–24, 225n6
Farm labor, xxi; lease labor, 159–61, 164n18
Farm tenant houses, 149–62

Federal Census, 15
Federal Writers' Project, 274
Ferguson, Dixon, 9, 17
Ferguson, Dixon, House, Southampton County, Va., 9–10, **11**, 12
Ferguson, James, 200
Fife Linoleum Company, 282
Findlay, A. C., 259
Firemen's Benevolent Association, 138
Fitchburg, Mass., 236
Fitchburg Railroad Company, 232, 235
Flats, Polish, 254–59, **257**, **258**, 264
Flint, Mich., 251–52, 259–64, **260**, **261**, **263**, 265
Flooring material, 281–90
Forest industry, 75–88; and band saws, 77; circular saws, 77; laborers, 78, 86; migrant labor, 78; and narrow gauge railroad, 77, 79; and oxen, 77; and up-and-down frame saw, 77
Forkner, Andrew Jackson, 154
Forkner House, Del., 159
Fort Penn, Dela., 161
Fort Yukon, Alaska, 169
Fourierists, xxvi
Fox, Nettie Pease, 238, 239
Franklin County Times (Mass.), 233
Fraser, Charles, 60
Frazier, E. Franklin, 274, 276
French, A. B., 238
Fruit Dispatch Company, 127

Gardner, H. F., 233
Gell, Monday, 45
Gender, and office work, 183
Georgeson, F. T., 85
German Werkbund, 289
Gilbert, Bradford, 120, 122–23, 126
Gilbert, Cass, xviii, 204
Glassie, Henry, xix, xx, 3, 169
Glen, Governor James, 58
Goad, Charles, 254
Golden Gate Bridge, Calif., 76
Goochland County, Va., 15
Goodpaster Village, Alaska, **170**

Goodwill Thrift Stores, **96**, 98
Gowans, Alan, 252
Grain production in Virginia, 6
Grassy Creek Meeting House, 33
Great Awakening, 31
Greek Catholic and Orthodox Churches, 200–202
Greek Catholic Immigration, 200–201
Green, John R., 273
Greene, Jack P., 62
Greenwich Inlaid Linoleum Company, 283
Grey Nuns (Les Soeurs Grises), xxvi, 212–24
grist mills, 8
Groth, Paul, 100
Guimard, Hector, 289
Gupta, Akhil, 200
Gyrisco, Geoffrey, xix, xxiv

Halifax County, Va., xx, 23–27, **25**, **27**, **29**, 30–35, **35**, 37n5, 38n10, 39n22
Hamerski, John, 258
Hamilton, Mary, 272
Hammett, Benjamin, 45
Harris, Richard, xix, xxiii, xxvi
Harvey, Bruce, xxix
Hayden, Dolores, xxvi
Herman, Bernard L., xix, xxi, 66
Hines, C. C., 41
hipped roof, 66
Historic American Buildings Survey, 12
Historic district zoning, Charleston, S.C., 128
Historic preservation, 95–96, 109; and adaptive use, 98
H. J. Heinz Company, 83
Hobsbawn, Eric, 199, 200
Hodder, Ian, 43
Hodge, Baxter J., 129n16
Hoffman, Joseph, 288
Holbrook, Stewart, 78
Holdsworth, Derwyck, xxv
Home Owners Loan Corp., 260, 262, 263
House type: central passage plan in Virginia, 4, 7, 23; foursquare, 273; hall-parlor, 27, 154; house and garden, 152, 154, 158–59, 161, 165n27;

House type, *continued*
    I-house, 273; shotgun, 268, 269; single house, xix, 41–54, **42, 43, 44, 53**
Howells, William Dean, 232
Hull, Canada, xviii, 212;
Humboldt Bay, Calif., 79
Humboldt County, Calif., 76, 79
Hunt, Gilbert, 23, 25, 30
Hunt, Gilbert, House, Halifax County, Va., 23–24, **24**, 25–26, 34
Hunt, James, 23, 25, 26, 30, 34
Hurlock, James, 153, 154
Hurricane Hugo, 58, **59**
Hutcheson, Francis, 241
Hutchison, Janet, xxv

Immigrants: Barbadian, 60, 71n11; East Slav, xxiv, 200; Lapp, 170; Norwegian, 170
Industrial paternalism, 82
Industrial Workers of the World (IWW), 79, 86–87, 91n22
Ingraham, Joseph Holt, 134, 135, 137
Interior finish and social hierarchy, 3–17, 46–49, 66–69
Invention of tradition, 199
Ireland, Archbishop John, 202–3, 206
Isaac, Rhys, 45
Isle of Wight County, Va., 4, 13, **14**
Izenour, Steven, 175

Jackson, J. B., 103
Jackson, John, 153–54, 159
Jackson, Reverend Sheldon, 170
Jackson Hole, Wyo., 99
Jacobs, Alfred Henry, 84
Jacobs, Jane, 96–97
James River and Kanawha Canal, 15
Jarratt, Reverend Devereux, 30
Jensen, Vernon, 87
Jim Crow Era of Segregation, 268–79
Jolly Giant Mill, 77
Jordan, Sally, 13, 17, 22n31
Jordan, Sally, House, Isle of Wight County, Va., 13, **14**

Kenai Peninsula, Alaska, 169
Kenny, Judith, 255
Kent County, Dela., 150, **150**, 153, **156, 157, 158**, 161
King George II, 58
Kirkcaldy, Scotland, 282
Kitchen, 45
Klinkenborg, Verlyn, 264
Kreider, Frank W., 129n16
Kullman Industries, 105
Kwolek-Folland, Angel, xxv, 182, 185, 189, 192

Labor radicalism, 78
Ladies Home Journal, xxv, 285
Lafayette Cemetery, New Orleans, 131, **132, 139**, 142
Lake Pleasant, Mass., **233, 234, 235**
Lancaster County, Va., 26, **28**, 30
Langley, Batty, 69
Larned, Sylvester, 139
Las Vegas, Nev., 104
Latrobe, Benjamin, 133–35, 137
Latrobe, John H. B., 134, 137
Laurence, Sydney, 175
Leger, Peter, House, Charleston, S.C., 46, **47**, 56n14
Leland, John, 31
Lexington Park, Md., 96, **96**, 108, **109**
Lincoln Hospital, Durham, N.C., 276
Lincrusta, xxiii, 285–90
Linoleum, xxiii, 281–90
Linoleum Manufaturing Company, 281–82
Little, Ruth, xxiv
Livermore, Mary A., 243
Log construction, 24, 25, 34, 153, 167, 170, 180n15
London, England, 61, 63
London, Jack, 173, 174
Loring, Elvira S., 236
Lounsbury, Carl, xvii, xix
Lublin, Wis., 202
Lucas, Eliza, 63
Lumber town, cookhouses, 78–79; barracks, 78
Lumberjacks, 78, 86
Lyman, Harvey, 233

MacDonald, Donald, 86
Magnolia, Dela.,157–58
Mail order houses, 252, 277
Majestic Diner, Austin, Tex., 105
Manhattan, 96–97
Manning, Margaret, 50
Manning, Thomas, 50
Manning, Thomas, House, Portsmouth, Va., 50
Manufacturer's Record, 126
Margolies, John, 95
Marshall, Daniel, 31
Martin, Janice, xxvi
Martin, Tania, xix, xxv
Mauss, Marcel, 177
Maxwell, Edward, 223
Maxwell, William Sutherland, 223
McCarty, Daniel, 26
McCarty, Jarrod, 34–35
McCarty, Jarrod, House, Halifax County, Va., 34–35, 35
McDonald's, 95, 105, 106, 114n26
McPhee, John, 173
Mendocino County, Calif., 76
Merriam, Charles, 184, 187
Middletown, Dela.,149
Milwaukee, Wis., 251, **253**, 254–59, **256, 257, 258, 259**, 264–65
Minneapolis, Minn., xxiv, 199–208, **201, 203, 204, 205, 206, 208**
"Miracle Mile," 93, 95, 102, 112n10
Mississippi River, 133–34
Monmouth County, N.J., **240**
Montréal, Canada, xxv, 187, 212–24, **213, 214, 215, 217, 220, 221, 222**
Moody-Clayton House, New Castle County, Del., **151**
Moore, William, xxv, xxvi
Moose Pass, Alaska, 168, **169**
Morris, William, 289
Motels, and transients, 113n15, 113n16
Mother House of the Grey Nuns, 212–14, **213, 215, 217, 220**, 221–22

Mott House, R.I., xx
Mount Airy, Richmond County, Va., 27, 28
Mowatoc Hotel, Eureka, Calif., 85
M-roof, 65
Mt. Auburn Cemetery, Cambridge, Mass., 241, **242**
Murie, Margaret, 174
Myers, Elizabeth, 50
Myers, Moses, 50
Myers, Moses, House, Norfolk, Va., 50

Nairn Company, 282
Nashville, Tenn., 118, **121**
National Association of Housing Rehabilitation Officials, 185
National Cash Register, 83
National Park Service, 95
National Register of Historic Places, 95
Native American: architecture, 167–77; landscape, xxiv; legend, xxiv
Native Americans: Alaskan, Alutiiq, 169; Athabaskans, 167, 169, 171; Dena'ina Athabaskans, 176; Gwich'in Athabaskans, 168; Koyukon Athabaskans, 171; Eskimos, 167, 169; Holikachuk, 170, 171; Ingalik, 170–71; Inupiat, 168, 169, 172, **172**; Yup'ik, 168, 169, 171, 172
Naylor, William Rigby, 63
Negro Building, Charleston West Indian Exposition, 122
Nelson, Edward W., 171
New Bern, N.C., 270, **270**, 271, 273, **274**
New Burying Ground, New Haven, Conn., 139
New Castle, Dela.,151
New England Magazine, 239
New England Spiritualist Camp Meeting Association, 233, 235, 243
New Haven, Conn., 139
New Kent County, Va., 12
New Orleans, xxvi, 131–43, **132, 136, 137, 138, 139, 140, 142**
New York, N.Y., xviii, xxii, 101, 118; World's Fair of 1939, 116
New York Times, 234, 235

Newport News, Va., 119
News and Courier, Charleston, S.C., 126
Niantic, Conn., 237, 238, 243
Nicolie, Talkeetna, 173
Ningeulook, Hattie, 171
Nob Hill, Dawson City, Alaska, 173
Norfolk, Va., 50, 117, 119
North American Free Trade Agreement (NAFTA), xviii
North Carolina, 268–79
North Carolina Central University, 276, 277
North Carolina Mutual Life Insurance, 270, 276
North Coast, Calif., 75–88
Northampton County, Va., 5, 5, 15, 16
Northern Neck, Va., 5, 6, **6**
Northumberland County, Va., 26, 37n5
Nottingham, Robert, 5

Oak Dale Cemetery, Urbana, Ohio, 241
Ocean Grove Camp, N.J., 239, **240**, 241
Olcott, Henry Steel, 243–44
Oliver, William, 32
Olmstead, Frederick Law, 122
Olson, Sherry, 187–88
Onset, Mass., **237**, **243**
Onset Bay Grove, Mass., 236, **236**
Onset Bay Grove Association, 235, 238, 239
Orlin, Lena, 43
Orthodox and Eastern Church Architecture, 199–208

Pacific Lumber Company, 76, 79, 82–86, 88, 92n30
Pacific Lumber Mill, 83, 85
Page, Mann, 37n5
Panama-Pacific Exposition of 1915, 289
Parade Magazine, 95
Parker, Charles A., 231
Paxton, Joseph, 116
Pear Valley, Northampton County, Va., 5, 5, 8, 13
Pennoyer, C. W., 83
Peoria, Ill., 253
Père Lachaise Cemetery, Paris, 137
Perseverance Fire Company, 139
Petty, Francis, 32

Philadelphia, Pa., xviii, 63, 116, 283; almshouse, 136; cemetery, 141–42
Philadelphia Centennial Exposition of 1876, 116
Philadelphia Fire Engine Company, 139
Philadelphia Hospital, 133
Philadelphia Insurance Company of North American, 41
Philadelphia Society for the Improvment of Agriculture, 150
Phosphate mining, in S.C., 119
piazza, 53, 60, 66
Piedmont, Va., xx, xxi, 3, 25–35
Pinckney, Charles, 63
Pintard, John, 134–35
Pittman Grove (Methodist) Camp, N.J., 239
Pittsylvania, Va., 33
Plantation landscape, Virginia, 43
Poe, Edgar Allan, 134
Pompion Hill Chapel, Berkeley County, S.C., 67, **67**, 68, **68**, 69
Poole, Sam, 273
Pope, Alexander, 241
Popoff, Constantine, 205
Portsmouth, Va., 50
Potter, Thomas, 283
de Pouilly, J. N. B., 137, 138, **140**
Price, Bruce, 223
Pringle House, Charleston, S.C., 42
privy, 8
Procter & Gamble, 83
Pullman, Ill., xxii

Quaker migration, 166n33
Quebec, Canada, xxv, xviii
Queen Victoria, xviii
Quincy, Josiah, 62, 66

Radburn, N.J., 184
Radford, Va., **288**
Rainbow Row, Charleston, S.C., 60
Raleigh, N.C., 271–72, 274, **274**, 275
Ranger, Terence, 199
Reck, Geno, 253

Index 311

Redwood Highway, Calif., **81**, 83
Redwood Industry of California, 75–88
Reisser, Craig, 255
Reshetar, Stephen, 201–2
Revere, Paul, House, Boston, Mass., 102
Richardson, A. H., 232, 233
Richmond, Va., 26, 269
Richmond County, Va., 30
Richter, Julie, xix, xx
Rideau Canal, Ottawa, Canada, xviii
Ridgely, Dr. Henry, 156
Ridgely Tenant House, Del., **150**, 155–56, 158
"River gods" of Connecticut, xxi
Road View Farm, New Kent County, Va., 12
Roanoke Baptist Associaiton, 31, 33, 39n22
Robert Grose House, 161
Roberts, Bishop, 61, 65, **65**
Roberts, Francis, House, Halifax County, Va., 24, 25, **25**
Robinson, Billy, 45, 54
Rochester, John, 5
Rochester House, Westmoreland County, Va., 5, 8
Rockefeller, John D., 185
Ronaldson, James, 141–42
Room use, 153; in Charleston, S.C., 45–54; dining, 23; parlor, 8
Roosevelt, Theodore, 127
Roth, Leland, xxv
Royal Victoria College, McGill University, 223
Royal Victoria Hospital, 223
Ruskin, John, xviii, 289
Russell, Nathaniel, House, Charleston, S.C., 59
Ryan, James, 149, 154, 160

Safdie, Moshe, xviii
Salvation Army Store, 96
San Francisco, Calif., 76, 87
San Jose, Calif., 102
Sanborn Company, 251–64
Saturday Evening Post, 285
Savannah, Ga., 119
Scarborough House, 277
Schuyler, Montgomery, 127

Schwab, LaVern, 253
Scotia, Calif., xxii, 76, 79, **80**, **81**, **82**, 83–88, **84**, **86**, **87**; Hotel, 79, 83; Men's Social Club, 83, 84, 87; Savings Bank, **86**
Seaboard Railroad, 274
Sears, John, 175
Sears, Roebuck Co., 252, 277, 285
Seward Peninsula, Alaska, 69
Shakers, xxvi
Shaw, Alexander, 26, 30
Shaw, Alexander, House, Halifax County, Va., **29**, 34
Shaw Collegiate Institute, now Shaw University, Raleigh, N.C., 274, 276
Shismaref, Alaska, 171
Shopping malls, xxiii
Shotgun house, 268, 269
Sidders, Rebecca, xxi
Sierra Club, 107
Silver Spring, Md., 106–7, **107**, 109
Simmons, Francis, 49
Simmons, Furnifold, 273
Simon, Roger, 255
Simpson, Pamela, xxiii
Single family residences, construction of, 251–64
Single House, xix, 65–66
Smokehouse, 8
Smith, William L., 129n16
Social Science Research Council, 186
Society for Commercial Archaeology, 94
Society for the Preservation of New England Antiquities, 102
Society of Architectural Historians, 94
Society of Friends, 150
Sons of Joshua, 232
South Carolina Interstate and West Indian Exposition of 1901, 117, 121–23, **123**, **124**, **125**, 135
Southampton County, Va., 9–13, **11**, **12**, 14, 15, 16
Spanish-American War, 126
Spears, Joseph, 50
Spelman fund, 184, 186
Spiritual Offering, 238
Spiritual Scientist, 235, 236, 238, 239, 243
Spiritualist Camp Meetings, 230–44

Spiritualist Camps: Aetna, Carmel, Maine, 237; Island Grove, Abingdon, Mass., 232–33; Lake Pleasant, Montague, Mass., 231–35, **233**, **234**, **235**, 239, 241, 243; Nickerson's Grove, Harwich, Mass., 232; Onset Bay Grove, Wareham, Mass., 231–32, 236, **236**, **237**, 239, 241, 243, **243**; Pierpont Grove, Melrose, Mass., 232, 235; Verona Park, Bucksport, Maine, 237
Spradley, James, 188
Springfield Republican (Mass.), 234
St. Augustine's Normal School, now St. Augustine College, Raleigh, N.C., 274, 276
St. Louis Cemetery #1, New Orleans, 133–35, **137**, **138**, 139
St. Louis Cemetery #2, New Orleans, 135, **136**, 139
St. Mary's Church, Avington, Hampshire, Great Britain, 67, **68**, 69
St. Paul, Minn., 204
Stanly, John C., 273
Starbucks, 99
Stearns, Elder Shubal, 31
Stephanski, John, 257
Sterczinski, Stanislaus, 255
Stinchombe, Arthur, 184, 188, 194
Storer, Dr. H. B., 235
Story, Justice Joseph, 241
Stowe Retreat, Buckinghamshire, 241
Streetcar suburbs, 254–59
Strip malls, 103–5
Suburban development, 251–64
Sweeney, Kevin, xxi

Talkeetna, Alaska, 177
Tayloe, John, 28
Taylor, Dennis, 274
Tea tables, 51–52
Teague, Walter Dorwin, 94–95
Television comedies: "Bewitched," 95; "The Brady Bunch," 95; "Dennis the Menace," 95; "Leave It to Beaver," 95
Temple, Sir Richard, 241
Terry, Moses, 26, 30
Terry, Moses, House, Halifax County, Va., **27**, 34

Theosophical Society, 243–44
Thompson, George W., 129n16
Thoreau, Henry David, 230
Thorp, Wis., 202
Tidewater, Va., xix, xx, 3
Timber frame construction: balloon frame, 151; braced frame, 151
Tompkins, Daniel, 126
Torma, Carolyn, xxiv, xxvii
Toronto, Ontario, Canada, 252, **253**, 254, 259, 263
Toth, Father Alexis, 202–4
Towles, William, 26
Tulagi Place, Lexington Park, Md., 108, **109**
Turner, Nat, 14
Tyree, Francis, 6

The Undiscovered Country, 232
University of Chicago, 184, 186, 194
Upper Appomattox Company, 15
Upton, Dell, xxvi, 4, 42, 49, 66
urban architecture, 41–54; landscapes, 45–54
Urban boosterism in the South, 115–28

Vanderhorst Row, Charleston, S.C., 54
van der Veld, Henry, 289
Venturi, Robert, 94, 175
Vernacular Architecture Forum, xvii, xviii
Vernacular Architecture Studies, vii–xix; and the analysis of social context, xviii; Anglicization of American architecture, xix, xx, xxi, 62; building forms and power structure, xxiii; and domesticity, xxxiii; and ethnicity, xiv; and gender, xxiv–xxv; and labor relations, xxi; and landscape studies, xxvii–xxix; and political culture, xxi; and social hierarchy, xxiii
Vesey, Denmark, 45, 54
Virginia, xviii, xix, xx, xxi, 3–17, 25–35; grain production, 6; suburbs, 102; New Light Separate Baptists, 23–35
Vlach, John, 268

Wadell, Gene, 42
Wagener, Frederick, 119

Index

Wahlfeld Manufacturing Co., Peoria, Ill., 252–53, 264
Waite, Ezra, 66
Walden Pond, Concord, Mass., 232–33
Wallman, Sandra, 183, 187–88
Wal-Mart, 95
Walton, Frederick, 281, **282**, 283, 285
Wareham, Mass., **236**
Washington, Booker T., 271–72, 273, 276
Washington, D.C., 99, 102, 186, 187, 190
Washington State, **78**
Waters, Mary C., 200
Weaver, William Woys, xxi
Weiss, Ellen, 231, 234
Welch, W. H., 120
Welfare capitalism, xxii, 83
Wells, Camille, xviii
Western Union Telegraph Expedition, 169
Westmoreland County, Va., 5, 15, 16, 26
Westover, Charles City County, Va., 27, 29
Wharton Tenant House, 156, **156**, 157
White, George, 273
White, John, 161
White City, 116–17
Whitefield, George, 31
Whitehead, Catherine, 14–15, 17, 18n7, 21n30
Whitehead, John, 14–15
White-Warren Tenant House, 161

Whitewash, 151, 154
Widgeon, Maria, 13, 21n30
Wierner Werkstatte, 288
Wild, Joseph, 282, 283
Wildwood (Rio Dell), Calif., **80**, 83
Williams, H. S., 235
Williams, John Shoebridge, 241
Williams, Reverend John, 33
Williamsburg, Va., 5, 63
Williamson, James and Son, Lancaster, England, 282
Wilson, Hattie, 232, 243
Winema Theater, Scotia, Calif., **84**, 84–85, 87
Winston-Salem, N.C., 269
Wister, Owen, 127
Wooden chimneys, 12, 21n26
Woodford House, Richmond County, Va., 26, 27, **30**
Worlds' Columbian Exhibition of 1893, Chicago, 116, 117, 122, 185
Works Progress Administration (WPA), 274
Wyoming, Evanston, 99; Jackson Hole, 99

Yellerday, Hilliard, 274, 276
Yorktown, Va., 5
Young Men's Business League, 119, 120
Yukon, Alaska, 168, 172, 173

Zwicker, Julius G., 129n16

Exploring Everyday Landscapes: Perspectives in Vernacular Architecture, VII was designed and typeset on a Macintosh computer system using PageMaker software and set in Sabon. This book was designed by Kay Jursik, composed by Kim Scarbrough, and printed and bound by Thomson-Shore, Inc. The recycled paper used in this book is designed for an effective life of at least three hundred years.

www.ingramcontent.com/pod-product-compliance
Lightning Source LLC
Chambersburg PA
CBHW051207290426
44109CB00021B/2371